# Letters & Liars

Joanna Mendelssohn is the award-winning art critic for the *Australian*, and a senior lecturer at the College of Fine Arts, University of New South Wales. Her previous books include *Lionel Lindsay: an artist and his family*.

# Letters & Liars

## Norman Lindsay and the Lindsay family

### Joanna Mendelssohn

Angus&Robertson
An imprint of HarperCollins*Publishers*

**Angus&Robertson**
An imprint of HarperCollins *Publishers*, Australia
First published in Australia in 1996
by HarperCollins *Publishers* Pty Limited
ACN 009 913 517
A member of the HarperCollins *Publishers* (Australia) Pty Limited Group

Copyright © Joanna Mendelssohn 1996

This book is copyright.
Apart from any fair dealing for the purposes of private study, research, criticism or review, as permitted under the Copyright Act, no part may be reproduced by any process without written permission.
Inquiries should be addressed to the publishers.

**HarperCollins***Publishers*
25 Ryde Road, Pymble, Sydney NSW 2073, Australia
31 View Road, Glenfield, Auckland 10, New Zealand
77—85 Fulham Palace Road, London W6 8JB, United Kingdom
Hazelton Lanes, 55 Avenue Road, Suite 2900, Toronto, Ontario, M5R 3L2
*and* 1995 Markham Road, Scarborough, Ontario, M1B 5M8, Canada
10 East 53rd Street, New York NY 10032, United States of America

National Library of Australia Cataloguing-in-Publication data:

Mendelssohn, Joanna, 1949–.
   Letters & liars: Norman Lindsay and the Lindsay family
   ISBN 0207 182728.
   1. Lindsay, Norman, 1879–1969 — Family. 2. Lindsay family.
   3. Artists — Australia — Family relationships. I. Title.
759.994

*Front cover photograph:* Norman Lindsay at Springwood c.1930s, by Harold Cazneaux.
Courtesy of Image Library, State Library of New South Wales.
*Back cover photograph:* Norman and Lionel Lindsay, Sydney 1902.
Photograph taken the day Lionel left for Spain. Courtesy of Peter Lindsay.

Printed in Australia by Griffin Paperbacks, Adelaide

9 8 7 6 5 4 3 2 1
99 98 97 96

For
*Peter Lindsay*

Note: As far as possible I have kept to the spelling and the idiosyncratic grammar of the original documents.

# Contents

Acknowledgments *ix*
1 Legend *1*
2 Peeling an onion *6*
3 Lionel's story *15*
4 Daryl Lindsay and *The Leafy Tree* *26*
5 Norman according to Norman *41*
6 Memoirs of a muse *54*
7 Rose's manuscript secrets *61*
8 Mistress and wife *77*
9 Mary *91*
10 The ghosts of Creswick *124*
11 The other Jane Lindsay *158*
12 Interlude 1994 *166*
13 John and Mary *168*
14 What John knew *192*
15 *Redheap* and the justifiable act of censorship *211*
16 Trust *225*
17 Last secrets? *240*
18 A conclusion of loyalties *259*
Family tree *262*
Chronology *264*
Bibliography *269*
Endnotes *273*

# Acknowledgments

My research into the Lindsay family began in 1980 when I was commissioned to write a limited edition book on Lionel Lindsay's woodcuts. I discovered Lionel's letters to various friends in the Mitchell Library, and so found myself absorbed in another person's life, and from them, the lives of other members of the Lindsay family. Throughout this period I have had the help, encouragement and support of Peter Lindsay, Lionel Lindsay's son. He has read and commented on letters as I transcribed them and also read many draft manuscripts. His constant urging for me to produce more for him to read has acted as a greater incentive than any deadline.

Peter's sister, Jean Charley, has also been of great assistance, as has her daughter, the actor Helen Lindsay. Norman Lindsay's daughter, Jane Glad, and her daughter, Helen Glad, have been wonderfully patient with their time, knowledge and insights and opened many doors for me in my research. Lin Bloomfield has been generous with her time and knowledge of Norman's things.

Many members of the Lindsay family have been extraordinarily kind in giving access to personal papers, as have some other private collectors. Of the people who knew the Lindsays, Veronica Rowan and Dr Earle Williams were most helpful in their comments on the unknown Isabel.

Peter Lindsay, Jane Glad, Lin Bloomfield and the Ballarat Fine Art Gallery have granted copyright permission to quote from the words of members of the Lindsay family and to reproduce images of their work. Meg Stewart kindly gave permission to quote from letters by her parents, Douglas Stewart and Margaret Coen. Jack Lindsay's estate gave permission to quote from Jack Lindsay's letters.

The manuscript librarians of the Mitchell Library, La Trobe Library and National Library of Australia have been ever helpful in giving me ease of access to documents and making copies when necessary. This book is very much a product of their guardianship of our cultural heritage.

I was assisted in part by a College of Fine Arts Faculty Research Grant which enabled me to use a laptop computer in libraries, and, at the beginning of my research, a Currie Fellowship awarded by the State Library of New South Wales bought me the time to bury myself in work. For the time this project was a Ph.D. thesis at the University of Sydney, Elizabeth Webby was an encouraging and enlightening supervisor. Ian Hicks suggested the title for the book.

As always, my children Lucy, Sylvia, Nicholas and Rebecca gave me constant insights into the complexities of sibling relationships — a prerequisite for any Lindsay research.

But the book could never have happened if it were not for the continuing encouragement and practical assistance of Barbara Mobbs.

Joanna Mendelssohn<br>Sydney 1996

# 1

# *Legend*

There once was an artist who lived in the Blue Mountains above the city by the sea.

Norman Lindsay's house was different from the Scottish hunting lodges, English cottages and Indian bungalows that shared the hills. It spoke of Greece and Rome and classical beauty. There were colonnades and courtyards of stone, the sun was welcome as a friend and the cold accepted when it came. His garden was filled with statues of fantastic beauties, of nymphs and satyrs and fauns. At night they seemed to come alive and join with the spirits of the nearby bush.

The city below was run by people who wanted more than anything else to be respectable, partly because they knew they were not. There were still people alive who remembered when the city had been a convict colony, and some of the civic fathers were the children, grandchildren or great grandchildren of convicts. In 1899 a new governor had come to the colony and, thinking he was flattering these people for the remarkable progress they had made, quoted them a verse adapted from Kipling: 'Greeting! Your birthstain have you turned to good'. He was never forgiven and there was some less than polite sniggering many years later when he was discovered to have had an affair with his (male) secretary.

By the early twentieth century the respectable people of the city went to church on Sunday in their best clothes and aspired to live in neat brick houses with red tiled roofs. Because they were scared of their own past they pretended they had no history, but revered instead the history of a place ten thousand miles away that they called 'home'. And because they were scared of the warmth of their own flesh they condemned wayward hedonists who surfed in the warm ocean and who lazed in the sun and made love on the sandy beaches, even on Sundays.

The city fathers encouraged the working men to have beer (which was taxed), but turned hotels into gigantic lavatories where booze was swilled for fear of the civilising conversation of gregarious drinking. At 6.00 p.m. sharp all the pubs were closed and the men went home to their neat houses with neat gardens and neat wives and neat children. For this place was seen as a paradise where people could own their own dwellings and acquire an everyday affluence that their ancestors could only dream of in that distant 'home' ruled by kings and queens.

The artist changed all that. He drew human bodies in hedonistic pleasure, happily admiring themselves and others. His paintings were works of abundance: of food and wine and music in excess. He painted women, large and generous, laughing with pleasure at the joy of their sexual powers. He once told his respectable brother that he painted women *with* pubic hair 'so that more beautiful babies would be born'. There was the magic of procreation in his art. He painted small men, and he himself was small, adoring these gracious women who joined with large muscular men to become gods and goddesses of Olympus. In his paintings and drawings an imaginary classical Greece came south, and sirens called sailors to a fate they ought to welcome. A poet once described his art as having 'a grace and naturalness that the ancients themselves had not been able to achieve', and this was the opinion of many.[1]

His art was condemned by the respectable people he called 'wowsers' (a name which instantly evokes mean-minded fundamentalists who even today campaign against the city's Mardi Gras and want to confine sex to the marriage bed). But he kept on painting and drawing and making etchings and selling them. For despite widespread condemnation, Norman Lindsay was the most popular artist in Australia. Every week the *Bulletin* magazine (which was then widely read throughout the Commonwealth) published his cartoons. These would attack the evil Chinese, the dastardly Hun, the corrupt politician and the evils of capital punishment. And such was the power of his magical line that a Lindsay cartoon helped sway the argument. One of his early cartoons, *Waiting*, showed the Victorian premier planning the hanging of a woman, the woman's newly born infant at her side. After it was published the sentence was commuted to life imprisonment. It was not really surprising that people who opposed the mean-mindedness of the town called his liberation 'genius'.[2]

Norman Lindsay also wrote. He wrote polemical articles on the nature of art and the life of the artist which appeared in the prestigious magazine *Art in Australia*. He wrote a book, *Creative Effort*, about why an artist has to be supreme and free to liberate himself and his art. It was a grand polemic on the eternal values of art and why art was of greater importance than life itself. Many people read about *Creative Effort*, and some even read its confusion of theories on life, existence and spiritual courage.

And he wrote novels. His first novel, *A Curate in Bohemia*, was a comic piece on the bohemian life of artists in what was already called 'the naughty nineties', living in Melbourne in the last years of last century. The only people offended by that were the originals of his artist subjects who had since become respectable and famous. He wrote *The Magic Pudding*, a wonderful comedy of serendipity and food, featuring a koala with the unlikely name of Bunyip Bluegum and a pudding called Albert. It became an instant favourite of the children in the neat houses, and even their parents agreed that Norman Lindsay was a fine comic writer when he turned his back on sex.

But then he wrote *Redheap*, a story of the life of young people in a country town, a novel so scandalous that when it was first published in London in 1930, it was instantly banned in Australia and remained banned for twenty-eight years. Other Lindsay novels were published, with favourable reviews. Most of them celebrated the life of the same small town in Victoria where a boy might grow up and be rewarded with a girl, where uncles and mothers were the only curse of life and where curates were condemned to outer darkness. Because he showed them that there was a life away from red tiled roofs and Anglophile respectability, and because he dared to write a book that could be banned, Norman Lindsay became a hero to the young writers and poets of Sydney. He was a Real Artist.

A Real Artist must have a muse, and Norman's muse was Rose. By the time she was the subject of frequent photographs in the Sydney society papers she was well into her thirties, beautiful and imperious, a large, full-breasted woman. That was in the 1920s, but it was well known that she had come to Norman when she was only a girl, and had lived with him for many years without the respectable stamp of marriage. Friends had visited them in the mountain retreat, but such was the nature of those years that she was never noticed in public until they were married.

That only happened in 1920, just before they had children, two little girls, Jane and Honey. Norman had other children, adult sons from his first marriage — Jack, Ray and Phil, born early in the century — who joined the poets and artists who were nurtured by his genius. Their mother, Katie, had married Norman after a brief passionate affair at the turn of the century, and other than the children their marriage had been a hollow one.

Later on, after Rose's body aged too much to model for his fantastic figures, Norman moved away from the mountains, leaving his family behind. But Rose was always there as his inspiration and as his manager, for an artist cannot be worried about crude money matters. When World War II broke out he returned to the mountains, to Springwood, and they lived together until the 1950s when Rose became so ill that she moved to the city to be nursed by her eldest daughter, Jane.

Norman Lindsay spent the last years of his life alone, visited by his friends, the poets, and was the subject of constant tributes by many of the people whose lives he had liberated. Well before he died he had arranged for the well-known author, John Hetherington, to write his official biography.[3] After Lindsay's death on 21 November 1969, the local Katoomba radio station broadcast his funeral and many mourned the man who drew and painted and wrote so passionately for freedom from the tyranny of wowsers. He had arranged to leave his house as a museum, which is why tourist coaches will always drive up the narrow road in Springwood to see where the authentic, home-grown genius had lived and worked.

One of the glories of Norman Lindsay was that his genius had not flourished in isolation. Three of his brothers were artists. A sister was also an artist — but Ruby died young in London in the influenza pandemic of 1919. A family of artists, including one creative genius, is what every country needs when it is trying to establish a separate cultural identity.

The Lindsay parents weren't artists. Robert Charles Lindsay was the town doctor of the little Victorian gold-mining town of Creswick. An Irishman from Derry, he had come to find his fortune in the 1860s and had found a wife and family instead. His wife, Jane Elizabeth Lindsay, became the mother of ten children, five of whom were artists. Percy, born in 1870, painted exquisite oils; Lionel ( 1874), was the leading print-maker of his generation and also the country's most influential art critic with a private collection of great European prints; then there was Norman ( 1879); followed by Ruby ( 1887) ; and last of all, Daryl ( 1889), who was both an artist and the Director of the National Gallery of Victoria. Daryl married Joan, who was known as both a painter and a writer. Lionel and Daryl were very much figures of the establishment. They were both knighted by Sir Robert Menzies, leaving Norman to be both artist and rebel. (The non-artists in the family are not the subject of this discussion.)

# LEGEND

The only unusual aspect of the Lindsay family's life was their maternal grandfather, Thomas Williams. He was a fierce Victorian intellectual, an Englishman who emigrated to become a missionary to the Fijians, a preacher of sermons, a writer of letters and author of an influential anthropological tome, *Fiji and the Fijians*. He died in 1891, so he could have been an influence only on the older children. But he loved art and took Norman to the new Ballarat Fine Art Gallery, where he would admire Solomon J. Solomon's *Ajax and Cassandra* , one of the great Victorian set- pieces in the collection. He would comment on the hard brown muscle of the man and the smooth white flesh of the woman. At home he roped off a section of the verandah of his Victorian cottage where some white paint had splashed in the shape of a stork and reminded the children of the beauties of accident. When he was a child Norman was pale and sickly, so he was forbidden to go outside and play with his brothers. Instead he drew, and his drawings were observed by his grandfather who seized on them and commented on them with all the solemnity of Mr Ruskin discussing Turner.

But Thomas Williams was a fierce old man and he knew his grandchildren were sinners who must be washed in the blood of the Lamb, and he told them so on many occasions, which is why Norman hated wowsers with all the passion of a child refused pleasure on a Sunday. Norman's mother, Jane Lindsay, was as devout as her father but she combined his moral rectitude with the powerful snobbery of the social elite in a small town and he grew up despising her hypocrisy.

In the last years of his life Norman Lindsay fell out of artistic fashion. Daniel Thomas, then curator of the Art Gallery of New South Wales, called his art a 'voyeuristic fantasy', and the eminent art critic Robert Hughes wrote that his eroticism was 'the very embodiment of adolescent sexual fantasy as it was in the days before teenagers were allowed to go to bed together'.[4] But these people belonged to a cultural elite. They did not speak for the ordinary people who liked the bawdy and the vulgar, who admired painted nudes and pirate ships.

Even now, twenty-six years after his death, the ghost of Norman Lindsay seems to haunt the gardens of his old house, coaxing nymphs out of concrete fountains, turning smooth-skinned gum trees into naked girls frolicking with fauns in the bush, making magic out of air.

The story of Norman Lindsay is one of the great myths of our culture, yet so much of it is untrue.

# 2

# *Peeling an onion*

*I* was in the Mitchell Library at the State Library of New South Wales. Now the Mitchell is amazingly large, but then it was a small room at the end of a dark corridor, lined with polished wood shelving. High on the walls were some of the great masterpieces of colonial painting, all from David Scott Mitchell's original gift to the people of Sydney. Space was scarce, and the casual reader might find herself sharing a table with the eminent historians Manning Clark or Bernard Smith, or maybe with a postgraduate student rushing to finish a thesis. There is a democracy in the seating of research libraries.

I was there because I was researching a biography of Lionel Lindsay and was going to indulge my passion for Lionel's letters. Through the letters of his later years, especially those written to his friend Harold Wright in London, I had come to like this intemperate man. I knew how he loved Albrecht Dürer and had, in the 1940s, purchased some of his finest engravings and woodcuts, and how he loved his asthmatic wife, Jean Dyson, and had nursed her until her death. I knew how he hated the Surrealists, liked Margaret Preston's art (even though he complained she couldn't spell), loathed Sidney Nolan and admired Russell Drysdale. Now it was time to read of his early years through his correspondence with his brother, the most famous of all Australian artists, Norman Lindsay.

But the manuscript wasn't there for me to collect.

'I'm sorry, you can't have that one,' the librarian said brightly. 'The Norman Lindsay papers in Manuscript 742 are on an embargo until 2003.'

'What!'

'Norman's wife, Rose, sold them on condition they not be accessed for twenty-five years after her death. She only died in 1978.'

But these were the letters that would fill the gaps in Lionel's life, that might even explain why this man was so loved and hated, and now I couldn't have them.

I was not interested in that cliché of Australian art and literature, Norman Lindsay. Like most art historians of my generation I found Norman Lindsay to be of decidedly limited interest. He was a sexist, racist reactionary who was responsible for some of the most virulently jingoistic propaganda posters of World War I. Lionel's bigotry was complex and contradictory and relieved by surprising gestures of humanity on a grand scale. To my mind, Norman was consistently one-dimensional and boring.

I didn't care what terrible secrets his widow was hiding in the Mitchell Library papers. All I wanted was Lionel.

Lionel Lindsay was the author of most of the interesting art criticism published in Australia until the late 1930s and the etcher who nurtured the Australian print-making revival in the early twentieth century. His etchings, drypoints and wood engravings (so fine and so precise) made his international reputation in the 1920s and 1930s. And unlike many artists who like only their own work, Lionel spent some of the profits from his etching on buying Old Masters: Dürer, Rembrandt, Turner, Constable and that often unacknowledged master of etching, Charles Meryon. He was knighted by Robert Menzies and wrote *Addled Art*, possibly the most hated attack on modern art ever. Lionel was much more fun than Norman, but Norman was the artist everybody knew. And now Rose, famous only as Norman's wife and muse, was stopping me from telling Lionel's story.

'I'm sorry,' the librarian said. 'Here's the card. You can see it's marked and I can't let anyone have it.'

The card was labelled in red ink: 'Embargoed — Restricted access'.

'I don't want anything except the Lionel letters,' I pleaded. 'I'm not interested in Norman. I don't care what he did. It's Lionel I want.'

A more senior manuscripts librarian had come over on hearing that someone wanted the Norman Lindsay papers. The answer was still a firm 'No'.

'But it's a restriction, not an embargo,' I argued. 'Who can see them?'

'Jane Glad, the artist's daughter,' was the reply. 'Rose thought she might need them to write about Norman.'

This was luck. I knew Jane's daughter, Helen Glad. For many years she had worked at the Bloomfield Gallery, the largest dealer in Norman Lindsay material. I often called into the gallery to see their exhibitions and speak to Lin Bloomfield, and we had become friends. I phoned her as soon as I could.

'I'll write,' Helen said. 'Jane doesn't really like being bothered with all the paper work these days. They should let you have them if I say so.'

The response to Helen's letter was negative. Helen Glad was not mentioned in Rose's conditions when the papers were sold, therefore she had no right to even see them. Only Jane could be considered an interested party.

'I was a child when Rose sold them,' Helen said. 'Of course she wouldn't have mentioned me. Jane was the writer. I'll speak to her and see if she can do anything.'

'It's no good,' I sobbed to Peter, Lionel Lindsay's son. 'I'll never get them. It's not as if they were even written to Rose. And some of the letters in the index were written to your father. I just don't know what to do!'

Peter lives in a flat in Kirribilli. At seventy-seven he was the oldest small boy in Sydney, spending his days watching the ferries wander around the harbour, admiring the aircraft carriers and sailing boats, remembering old friends, old campaigns and his life with his father. In the sixteen years I have spent reading the Lindsay family's private mail, Peter has become my closest friend. In January 1985 he had already written to libraries asking them to give me access to any restricted records.

'I'll write again,' he told me. 'They're not Rose's letters and she had no business to do that. Whatever she's trying to hide has nothing to do with Dad.'

I didn't hold out much hope. Somebody, I forget who, had told me how Jack Lindsay, Norman's eldest son, was denied access to his own diary once it was put in the Mitchell. If they would stop someone reading their own words, what hope would I have?

In April I went to the La Trobe Library in Melbourne where restrictions once placed by members of the Lindsay family had been lifted with the passing of time and the death of some of the correspondents. The La Trobe had trolleys full of Lindsay family papers. Peter had lodged many of his father's papers there, and later Daryl had given them his collection of family memorabilia. From the 1920s until Lionel's death in 1961, Daryl and Lionel Lindsay wrote to each other at least once a fortnight. Their letters covered art, books, politics and especially family issues.

Sir Daryl Lindsay, the youngest Lindsay son, was one of the great operators of the Australian art scene. His paintings are in public collections, his wife Joan had a successful independent career as a writer, but his long-term importance in Australian cultural history lies in the way he turned the National Gallery of Victoria into a major museum and pushed for the creation of the National Gallery of Australia. Like any good tactician he combined broad knowledge with rat cunning. This meant that he was able to mix as a social equal with politicians and newspaper proprietors as well as artists and scholars. He spoke their language.

The La Trobe papers were the start of the Lionel Lindsay story and I spent three weeks in Melbourne taking notes and arranging for photocopies. The La Trobe letters were filed in boxes, each sheet numbered, and I was allowed to photocopy the material, something the Mitchell would never allow. There were the letters Lionel wrote to his father on his trip to Spain in 1902, travelling on a cargo boat to Marseilles. And much later, letters to his wife, Jean Dyson, written from Spain (which may explain why this conservative man became such a vocal opponent of Franco and all fascists).

But it was the letters between Lionel and Daryl Lindsay that showed me my canvas was too small, and that the published accounts of the famous Lindsay family of Creswick, Victoria were nowhere near the truth. So I read further into the La Trobe papers — letters by other children, letters by their parents.

The clamouring voices of the Lindsays now became too much for me and I realised that more questions needed to be answered if I wanted to write a balanced story. Lionel was the third of ten children and it became only too clear that his sense of responsibility for his family, and his anger at some of their actions, coloured his life. I had always thought of the Lindsays as an affluent middle-class family, but so many of the letters were about money and the obligation to care for indigent relatives. By the 1940s, when Lionel was in his seventies, his anger towards 'these Creswick Lindsays' virtually spits off the page.

There were so many different family members named, damned, and loved in the letters that I started to think there must be at least twenty Lindsay children, not ten. There was also a mystery person. Some letters had belittling asides on someone called 'Goo', apparently female, apparently a close relative. In Daryl's letters, I read that Goo stayed with their sister Pearl and her children in Ballarat when another sister, Mary, collapsed under the strain of nursing their mother in the family home. Goo was befriended by Joan Lindsay, and treated badly by Mary.

'Who is Goo?' I wrote in my notebook.

# LETTERS & LIARS

I repeated the question to Mrs Felicity Shaw, one of Pearl Lindsay's daughters. I had driven up to her house at Mt Macedon because Peter had told me she knew more Lindsay family history than anyone else. I had been told Felicity had spent a lot of time visiting Mary in her last years, caring for her when she was bedridden in a nursing home. Felicity Shaw was very conscious of her Lindsay family heritage. Her house, newly rebuilt after the Ash Wednesday bushfires, was called 'Lisnacrieve' to honour the original Lindsay family home at Creswick.

Mrs Shaw was in her seventies, wearing a neat tailored wool suit and sensible shoes. Because I had an introduction from her cousins she greeted me kindly. And then I asked the wrong question.

'Who is Goo?'

Her mild hazel eyes looked suddenly hard and her initial friendliness vanished. 'I really don't know,' she said. But her eyes said she did, and that she was afraid.

I cast around for a safe question, to put her mind at rest.

'I wonder, could you tell me about your memories of Mary? What was she like when she was looking after you and your brother and sister when you were small?'

'She would say, "We're going to Town and we think we're a lady",' Mrs Shaw said. And that was all. Mrs Shaw did tell me about the awful man from the university who said bad things about the Lindsays one day in Creswick, and the horribleness of Rose who was not a lady, whom she had never met nor would have wished to know because she was 'common'. But there was to be no more information. Instead, afterwards, letters were written by Mrs Shaw warning relatives not to give me any information as I 'wanted to destroy Lionel Lindsay'.

When I came back to Sydney with boxes of notes and photocopies of letters loaded into the boot of the car, I drove north to Turramurra and asked Lionel's daughter, Jean Charley, the same question.

'Who was Goo?'

'It was Isabel, dear,' she replied. 'She was the youngest. Mary didn't like her. I think she was supposed to be not quite all there, but she wrote to me. Do you want to see the letters?'

As I sipped my sherry I looked at the small bundle of letters, all on pale blue paper, each no more than two pages long. Isabel Lindsay's handwriting was curiously unformed, all pot-hooks in copperplate, but she was literate. She wrote of birthdays and babies, memories of Jean's own babyhood, wondering how the pretty child she had known in the years before World War I could be a grandmother.

In search of Isabel I phoned Sir Joseph Burke, retired Professor of Fine Arts at the University of Melbourne, who had visited Mary, Robert and Isabel Lindsay in the years after World War II. Until his retirement he had been one of the three guardians of the Lindsay papers now in the La Trobe. The other two were Peter and Daryl Lindsay.

'Isabel seemed slow,' he said. 'But probably because Mary and Robert were so fast. They really were brilliant — living in total isolation in Creswick, writing letters to their famous brothers. You would think they would be dull living that life, but their minds were so sharp.'

A mildly retarded relative didn't explain much. The letters by Lionel and Daryl contained real anger at some undefined act of cruelty. And then there was Mrs Shaw's hostility when her name was raised. By now I wanted the Mitchell's papers for what they might reveal about Isabel and Mary, as much as for the book I was writing. I wanted to find out why Daryl refused to speak to Norman after about 1930, and what terrible thing Norman had done to cause Lionel to refuse to communicate with him for the last forty years of his life when they had been so close earlier. I desperately wanted to read the letters to find out the loves, the hates, the friendships and the enmities of this family. Letters from Norman had been published in a huge volume in 1979, but it was all his story, the artist as genius let down by his inadequate family.

A book was taking shape in my mind. It was to start with images from an imaginary family photograph album. All the Lindsays now were starting to flesh themselves out for me. It would focus on Lionel, but now I knew the context I needed for him was not political or artistic. Lionel could only be understood as a member of his own family, coming from its peculiar cultural mix in a country which still saw itself at the end of the world. But the Mitchell held the letters I needed.

As predicted, Jane's request to let me see Lionel's letters was rejected. She could read the papers but was not allowed to nominate anyone else to have the same access, even though she herself was no longer interested in using them as source material for a book. Rose's conditions on the letters had been 'deliberate and unequivocal' and were therefore not to be changed.

I was spending a fair amount of time in the Mitchell working on other Lionel Lindsay correspondence, going through the papers of the artist

Sydney Ure Smith and the wool magnate Sir James McGregor.

'I hope you realise some of those Manuscript 742 papers are stolen,' I said one day to a librarian. 'Rose wasn't exactly getting on well with Norman, and some of them are to Lionel anyhow.'

'Are you sure?' was the response.

'Well, that's according to the guide,' I said. 'Volumes 6 and 7 are all Lionel to Norman, and volume 26 has letters to Lionel from Adam McCay. I don't see how they could belong to Rose.'

'Did you know Jane wrote back to the Mitchell?' Helen asked me soon afterwards. 'She can be quite determined.'

Jane's letter of 6 August 1985 was addressed to Baiba Berzins, then manager of the Australian Research collections.

'Whilst my mother's wording does appear deliberate and unequivocal,' she wrote, 'I feel she would not have stood in the way of proper research. At the time of the bequest she could not have foreseen the interest in recent years of "Lindsayana" — a situation I believe both she and my father would have thoroughly approved of — and the restrictions were placed more to protect anyone who may have been slandered than anyone else. I believe, given the passing of time, this is no longer a problem.'

It was a plea for access for scholars, a plea to open the covers and let people read about the complex relationships which surrounded the Lindsay family. It was also a plea on behalf of her children who were denied the details of their own family history. Jane did ask to retain some control over the material. 'I feel written permission, from myself or my nominated agent, must be sought,' she wrote.

Some weeks later I was at home when the phone rang. It was the Mitchell Library. 'You can see the Lindsay papers,' I was told.

※

In the following years the process of exploring this material became like reading a multi-layered novel, but the act of physically transcribing notes from the letters and trying to place them in context meant that I entered this world of grand quests, art, and sibling rivalry. The lives of these dead Lindsays became more real to me than the commonplace things of everyday life. Each time I opened a blue-bound folder a different part of the same complex story would start to unfold.

I knew now that Lionel Lindsay once passionately admired Rudyard Kipling, a writer he later criticised, and that he and Norman had been the closest of brothers and that their quarrel of the 1920s was simply the culmination of a long bitter division. It had all started with *Redheap*, the novel which was banned, or rather with Norman's very early version of the same novel which he called *The Skyline* when he wrote it in about 1916. The quarrel between the brothers was there in all its searing intensity. Quarrel followed by reconciliation, followed by final hopeless separation.

Then there were the unposted letters. Some of these are drafts of letters later sent (which I subsequently found in other collections), but others were fiery insults written by Norman in the heat of the moment, which Rose wisely failed to send off.

Increasingly it was the letters that told stories which had little to do with Lionel that entranced me. They lured me back to the Lindsay papers long after my legitimate research was done. They were a major revelation of the broader context of Australian material culture. There were all Jack Lindsay's letters to his father from the 1920s when Jack and his friends (with Norman's support) had started *Vision*, a literary magazine promoting Norman's philosophy, pure and unexpurgated from *Creative Effort*. Jack's friends were Norman's disciples, and they too wrote.

I had studied Kenneth Slessor's long poem, *Five Visions of Captain Cook* at school, and now I read the letter Slessor wrote to Norman, enclosing the first draft, humbly submitting it for his hero's approval. 'I'm enclosing some verses which may interest you,' he wrote. 'It would make a splendid field for Ray's historical paintings, if I could interest him in it.'

Ray was Norman's second son from his first marriage. There were also letters from Phil, the youngest son, and one from Norman to Katie, their mother. Their story had nothing to do with Lionel, and precious little to do with the nature of Australian literary culture. But my interest in it became obsessive.

Partly to organise my thoughts about the Lindsays, and partly to stake my claim as the first person to study these papers properly, I wrote an article for the *Age Monthly Review*. It appeared in February 1986 with the title, 'More Leaves from the Lindsay Tree'.

There was a bit of drama just before the article appeared. Mrs Shaw phoned the editor of *The Age* and claimed he was about to publish an article which would destroy her family. Sensing the possibility of a genuine news story in the literary supplement he checked it out, but was disappointed to find it was nothing of the sort, just a piece on old manuscripts.

I finished the biography of Lionel and it appeared in 1988 with the title *Lionel Lindsay: An Artist and his Family*. By then I had had two more children and had started to write art criticism for the *Bulletin*. I had left the Lindsays behind me, except for continuing private friendships, and those letters, snatches of which continued to colour my understanding. I had moved house, but kept the boxes of Lindsay files, and sometimes when my twins were asleep and the older girls were out, I would find myself reading them, trying to sort out the puzzles of their tangled lives.

I found a copy of John Hetherington's authorised biography, *The Embattled Olympian*, in a second-hand bookshop, which was also my source for Norman's novels as well as his autobiography, *My Mask*. I read accounts of Norman Lindsay written by his old friend Douglas Stewart, and essays praising him by A. D. Hope and others. I came to notice that these books and articles were often contradicted by the letters I had read, and the memories of those still alive.

Reading the letters for pleasure, collecting copies of other letters from members of the family as I pieced together the larger picture, I started to understand why all previous biographies of Norman Lindsay were less than frank, and I would now argue they had to be in order to protect an old and ill lady who is now dead. 'Lady' is a deliberate choice of word. None other will do.

My problem now is how to tell this story. A simple narrative won't work — there are too many inconsistencies, too many liars. I suppose I could play it like a computer game, or perhaps it could be told like one of those children's adventure books where the reader can follow half a dozen interlocking narratives, with different endings, flipping madly back and forth through the book. There is no single common thread to this story, except the family itself with all its contradictions and its emotions. Much that is important in this account of the lies and the cover-ups in the Lindsay family has been lost to common knowledge.

So I will have to lay out all the pieces, one by one. Most of the time when I have tried to tell this story I have felt as though I were peeling an onion. Each skin, each narrative, each writer of letters, reveals a new one underneath. If I peel them all back, and lay out my pieces of onion skin for all to view, there may be a story.

# 3

# Lionel's story

In 1980, shortly after I started researching a book on Lionel's woodcuts, Peter gave me a copy of his father's autobiography, *Comedy of Life*. It had been published in 1966, some five years after Lionel's death.

'I kept on at him to finish it,' Peter said. 'But towards the end he just wasn't interested. So whenever he told me a story I told him to put it down and sometimes he did. After he died I put it all together and gave the manuscript to Doug Stewart.'

Douglas Stewart, eminent poet and at that time senior editor for Angus & Robertson, was one of the most constant advocates of Norman Lindsay's work. Peter paused, and looked at me with a smile. 'In the end I even wrote some of it myself. Dad had told me the story lots of times, so it really was him — only I wrote it down.'

*Comedy of Life*, with Peter's foreword, shows the nature of its origins. The first part is a confidently written narrative of Lionel's childhood and youth, but after a certain point it fades into short, disconnected anecdotes and memories of people and places. But the story fleshed out what I already knew of the Lindsay family. Creswick stopped being the sleepy country town I had once visited and became a goldfields town above a creek, with red mud and dust dominating.

> *From the station to the railway bridge stretched the half-filled-in shafts of the derelict diggings. Between the dumps the Cape-broom bloomed in spring and goats strayed peacefully cropping the thistles, until surprised by some band of small boys on their way to the Deep Paddock, a perennially filled swimming-pool.*

The artists' father, Dr Robert Charles Lindsay, is described by Lionel as a robust Victorian with a robust Victorian father's drinking habits. 'In the good old nineteenth century it was considered nothing unusual for Pa to come home "loaded",' he wrote. 'Keene's "drunk" jokes in *Punch* were perhaps the most enjoyed of his wonderful drawings.'[1]

There is also a bawdy anti-Catholic sense of humour in the story that Lionel has his father telling of how he drove out to visit the sick wife of a country publican.

*Knocking at the door he entered the bedroom to find the priest busily engaged with the invalid in the Venerean rite. 'I'm afraid Father,' said the doctor, 'that I have arrived too late, as I see you are administering extreme unction.'*[2]

Lionel's story has several reminders of the divisions of class and religion which governed Australia in the late nineteenth century.

One of the notables of Creswick was the snobbish neighbour Captain Dowling who seduced a helpless orphan girl, leaving her pregnant and destitute. Dowling kept a collection of exotic birds in his large mansion, 'The Ferns'.

*. . . splendid parrots, great blue and military macaws, and cages full of coloured birds, while peacocks strutted about as familiarly as barndoor fowls. The familiar magic of Arabian nights could do no better.*[3]

Lionel made several prints of *The Ferns*, based on drawings from the final years of its dereliction, and in his writing it was clear that this garden was an early source of wonder for the Lindsay children and an introduction to exotic beauty.

Another source for their imaginings came through books. The Lindsay children were well read in the popular fiction of their generation: Walter Scott and Alexander Dumas. They enjoyed Scott's medieval world in *Ivanhoe* and the absurd heroics of *The Three Musketeers*. But there was also real meat: the classical bawdy tales of Rabelais and Villon which were read to them by their grandfather, Thomas Williams. This gave them access to Renaissance French literature, and showed that jokes about bodily functions were all a part of the great tradition of western culture.

Both parents insisted the children attend the Methodist church on Sunday, but Percy, the eldest, usually managed to avoid the boredom. Lionel would smuggle novels into church, and later discovered the more salacious parts of the Bible, which he read during the never-ending sermons. Jane

# LIONEL'S STORY

Lindsay, the missionary's daughter, is seen as a kindly figure, although devout in her faith and as determined as her husband that all the children should attend church. In this the parents were aided and abetted by two aunts, Jane's sisters, who had settled in Creswick.

*One aunt lived in the street next to our home, and the priest, who was nearly always drunk, mistook her cottage for his own and, as no houses were locked in those days, walked in and my Aunt Selina found him asleep in her own bed. I never ceased ragging her about her intimacy with him until I drove her nearly distracted. It was glorious revenge.*[4]

Lionel's self image from the *Comedy of Life* is that of family rebel. He is the boy who tries to run away from church down to the old gold diggings and has to be dragged back by the family groom. But when he could, Lionel would lead his siblings to the old Chinese quarter where they had an entrée into a world away from middle-class life. Here he learnt of prostitution and opium.

*The Chinese camp was our Paradise. Here were two joss-houses, from which the burning joss-sticks could be looted, and here lived a wizened old Chow called Sinkum who would match his inimitable fi-shang toffee against our pennies. At the entry of the Chinese camp stood the dwelling of Ginger Mary Ann, a bedraggled representative of the oldest profession on earth, and as we passed we cast curious glances at the opened door or window and would sometimes see the old ginger-beer maker, who had been replaced in the affections of his wife by another, taking his ease in his drum.*[5]

Lionel's childhood was dominated by that stern patriarch, the Reverend Thomas Williams. But in introducing him, Lionel wrote a disclaimer.

*Anything my brother Norman has written about our grandfather in his novels is quite fictional. He was greatly admired by the Ballarat people for his integrity and interest in the intellectual life. He was devoted to good literature and annotated his Shakespeare and other books. In his missionary days he was scolded by his brother parsons for reading the Lusiads! and grew more tolerant in his old age — a true indication of mental progress.*[6]

But what had Norman written? I had a half memory of comic, senile old men and whining hypocritical clergy. Would anyone connect the great Methodist scholar missionary with those figures of low comedy?

According to Lionel, Thomas Williams took a lively interest in all his grandchildren. He encouraged Lionel's first choice of career as astronomer by sending him to work in the Melbourne Observatory. And when he realised that this grandson was an empirical atheist he spoke to him:

> . . . *wearing that expression of preternatural gravity I have seen only on the faces of God's saints, took me aside before Sunday morning prayers, and said, 'Cecil tells me that you don't believe God made the world in six days', to which I replied in suitable geological language, 'I see it is quite hopeless,' he said in a pained voice, 'I can only pray for you.' Which is about all he could do, for he couldn't argue. We were separated by the stars, and there was no place in my heavens for his old Jew God with a white beard.*[7]

After Lionel's brief career as an astronomer ended, he returned to Creswick to study for matriculation. This is recalled as a less than pleasant time for the fifteen-year-old boy. He was caught drunk in church, and relieved his boredom by keeping an illustrated diary which was greatly admired by Norman.[8]

Lionel's habit of drawing was his salvation. In 1893 some visiting actors admired his skill and within months he was working in Melbourne as a cartoonist for the *Hawk*, a police gazette. This was the start of the career of the Lindsay family, the artist illustrators who were to dominate the graphic arts in Australia for the next half century.

In 1896 Lionel brought Norman to Melbourne to act as his ghost on the *Hawk*, while Lionel was working on the *Free Lance*, a new illustrated weekly magazine which was a cooperative effort by Lionel and his friends.

> *If Norman did not come, the prospect of helping the family later, should the* Free Lance *prove a success, would be jeopardised through the impossibility of one artist doing the work of two papers at the same weekend.*
>
> *. . . His frantic appeal telling me to demand his services was not needed, for it is difficult to refute the claims of the only member of a family earning a living.*
>
> *He was just sixteen years of age, and had already under my direction been making illustrations to Dumas and Shakespeare in the style of Edwin Abbey — his own choice. At sixteen a boy generally plays hell, unless denatured by religion or morality, and I was assured that Master Norman's conduct during the past year had been nearly insupportable.*[9]

The 1890s depression had greatly reduced Dr Lindsay's income, as the once thriving town shrank with the closure of the banks and people could no longer pay their bills. It is clear from Lionel's story that from very early in his career he saw himself as the one obliged to support his family, and that this perception coloured his relations with his siblings. Percy is easily dismissed as an artist who preferred his social life to actual work, but Lionel was weighed down with the realities of supporting a large family on a small income.

There was little money in the Melbourne years, especially as Norman was more inclined to spend money on girls than food. 'The budgeting for two on a salary of thirty-five shillings necessitated a "skeely" hand,' Lionel wrote. 'And rent, meal-tickets, tobacco, and working materials, and the placing of five shillings in the savings bank against the spites of destiny, left little over for beer on a Saturday night.'[10]

Most of the anecdotes in Norman Lindsay's first novel, A Curate in Bohemia, are based on these years in Melbourne. On one occasion Norman used the Thomas Williams connection to persuade Methodist printers to employ the two Lindsay boys as illustrators for Sunday school texts, and Lionel wrote:

*For those texts we received half-a-crown a drawing, and though we deplored the time taken from etching and woodcutting, we made up for it by many humorous inventions. If you examined the sacrifice of Isaac you would see that Abraham was wearing check trousers and elastic sided boots; that the eminent prophet Isaiah sported a bell-topper, and that the helmets of the Roman soldiers were suspiciously like bowler hats. On these being questioned, the latest archaeological discoveries and the authority of the British Museum were solemnly proffered in support, and so enormous is la bêtise humaine — which Renan said alone gave him the idea of eternity — that they were solemnly accepted.*[11]

But there was also art. These years were filled with discussions on painting, lessons at the National Gallery School, drawing from the model, exhibiting in student exhibitions and planning careers as great illustrators and artists. With their fellow bohemians, including Hugh McCrae, Will Dyson and Randolph Bedford, they formed the Ishmael Club, a dining club with its resident god, a Maori-inspired statue carved by Norman.

Then there was Charterisville, a haven for artists at an old dairy farm on the outskirts of Melbourne. Here they shared a cottage with fellow artist Ernest Moffitt who spoke to them of the Pre-Raphaelites and the English woodcut tradition as well as Beardsley and Whistler.[12] 'Young Norman was a mighty observant child,' Lionel wrote. 'He talked very little, but he absorbed everything, and the foundations of his art were surely laid, as we smoked far into the night, upon the art talk of two elder students steeped in their subject.'[13]

This is the older brother writing, protective and encouraging, but also irritated at the way the younger learnt from this encouragement and then failed to acknowledge it. Young Norman turned from artistic journalism to work on his first series of *Decameron* drawings, his first memorable works.

*Norman was lucky in possessing a sedentary temperament and a fixed purpose in life. Though he joined in any fun of the moment with gusto, he went back to his work-table with relief. No theories or metaphysical misgivings then troubled his existence. An occasional wench, a Saturday night singsong with our crowd, and a prize-fight at Nathan's were pleasures enow. The present never occupied his mind, though he was keenly alive to passing humours, and he found in the costume and comedy of the Decameron a world to his taste. He worked slowly, and often late into the night.*[14]

Charterisville is remembered in terms of classical idylls, romantic music and making myths of the past. I have seen a photograph of that time, presumably taken by Lionel. Norman is posing as a spirit of the woods, his slight body and muted colouring belong to such mythology, and the intense blue of his eyes is not seen here. The photograph is faded and yellowed, a bit like a memory of times past, of a youth lost in fantasies of long ago.

Lionel's expeditions to Western Australia and Spain, which he undertook without members of his family, do not enter this story of simple pleasures. In 1902, on his way to his first Spanish adventure, Lionel stayed with Norman in Sydney where his younger brother had become cartoonist for the *Bulletin*. And it is at this point that the coherent narrative of Lionel Lindsay's memoirs suddenly breaks. First there is a description of Norman's voyeurism:

*When I was staying with him at Blues Point he would crawl every night along a stone wall fronting a terrace, remaining* perdu *for a couple of hours, to record with delight on his return the antics of some fat cit [businessman], engaged with a lady in the exercise of her ancient profession, or the exquisite pantomime of a domestic row. He passed many an afternoon lying on a hillside to watch, through a fine Rose Deerstalker I had given him, the antics of children at play, the happenings in backyards and verandas, piecing together the 'things seen' into a lively character sketch.*[15]

Then the narrative collapses as Lionel's thoughts suddenly move forward in time to the writing of *Redheap*.

*The first version was clumsier but funnier, for he was influenced by Freud when he came to revise it thirty years later. (He fell for anything about sex, like a woman for fashion.)*

*The texture of the book is coarse, and though, as we know, the respectabilities are ever the breeding ground for hypocrisy, none of the average decencies or aspirations of life finds a voice in it, with the exception of Mr Bandparts. A perpetual row seems ever in progress and little sordid egotisms clash and fester. The one saving grace is humour, but humour always at the expense of a victim. Apart from presenting a picture of township manners in its period, more interesting to the psychologist is the view it affords of the author's mind, of his incurable Peter Pan-ism. The sickly child, mothered a lot and kept indoors, so that he saw life mostly through a windowpane until he went to school, seems never to have forgotten a necessary limitation of liberty, and revenged himself upon his family and friends (and particularly his mother) when he came to write* Redheap. *In stirring and reviving the past, all the old rancours blossomed again. He made repeated trips to Creswick to pump his mother and gather any shreds of gossip that might be woven into the web of the book . . . There is exact minor portraiture, composite portraiture, in which the traits of three families are amalgamated by little realistic touches, which to anyone acquainted with the original would appear to be inspired by fact . . . What is so base in these relations is the attachment of sex incident to actual people, the stigmatising of the innocent. Madame Bovary was actual and historical — the case of Ethel a calumny.*[16]

The link is clear. Lionel saw Norman as a voyeur, using his own family and others as models in *Redheap*. Other than the defence of their mother, the only reference to the defamation of a particular character was Ethel. But the identity of the person on whom this character is based is not given.

What were the facts about *Redheap*? Australia was a wowser society. Norman wrote about sex in an Australian country town. The book was banned. That was the kind of country Australia was before the 1970s. I have dim childhood memories of a Victorian politician called Arthur Rylah talking of the potential of literature to corrupt his teenage daughter, and using this as an excuse to ban books. Surely there was nothing particularly remarkable about this act of censorship?

I found a copy of *Redheap* in my trusty second-hand bookshop and read it for the first time in years. It is the story of a family and its friends and connections. A nineteen-year-old boy, Robert Piper, is bored with life and keeps a diary. He has a girlfriend, Millie, whose father is a hypocritical clergyman. Millie becomes pregnant and Robert's tutor, Bandparts, gives worldly-wise wisdom. Millie has an abortion with the help of her alcoholic mother and lives happily ever after. The Piper family are drapers in a town like Creswick. Robert's mother is a rich portrait of Victorian hypocrisy, his grandfather a comedy of senile dementia. Robert has two sisters. The elder, Hetty, is nearing a 'certain age' when she will be an old maid and is determinedly wooing the new doctor. Ethel, the younger, is having a clandestine affair with Arnold, a married bicycle shop proprietor. When the affair gets out of hand and he wants to leave his wife for her, Ethel marries Hetty's beau and Hetty loses her temper.

After reading *Comedy of Life*, it was easy to see how this novel could give offence to Lionel. The character of Robert is clearly modelled on him, just as the observant little, Peter Piper is Norman's self-image. With Lionel identifying his mother as Mrs Piper, it was clear that other family members were also involved. In particular, the Lindsay sister on whom the character Ethel was based would have had reason to be distressed.

*Comedy of Life* led me from writing catalogues of Lionel Lindsay's art into researching his life for a possible biography. Old photographs and descriptions by his relatives gave the impression of a dark, handsome man, bursting with energy, overwhelming everyone around him with his enthusiasms.

His comments on *Redheap* became one of the leads for my research into the Lindsay papers. I knew I needed to identify Ethel, Hetty and the other characters. The importance of *Redheap* to the Lindsay family and the consequences of its banning were reinforced when I read the letter that Lionel wrote to Peter in 1940, when he first started to write what became *Comedy of Life*:

*I am writing the facts about Redheap, the famous quarrel, and the Spiritualist outbreak . . . and all the rest. This will come to you or the Mitchell Library. I'm not proud of the Lindsay name that little N. L. was always so busily wiping his vain tail on. And for the sake of you Dan and Bingo* [family name for Lionel's daughter, Jean] *(and the kiddies) I'm starting with documents I found the missing letters that are superb evidence, and his stinking letter to me, and I am now going to buy a typewriter for £2 as I cant trust the documents out of my hands.*[17]

When Lionel wrote this, *Redheap* was still banned, a notorious case in the history of Australian censorship, a tribute to local prudery. But what was the quarrel and the 'Spiritualist outbreak'? There is no account of a quarrel in *Comedy of Life*, just a series of remarks to make it clear the brothers were no longer close.

I asked Peter about the letter and what his father had hoped to include in his memoirs, and what had actually been published. He looked a bit sheepish.

'I wouldn't do it now, not after what I know Norman wrote about Dad,' he said. 'But at the time Norman was an old man, and he was respected by everybody. So I cut it out. I've got it here somewhere. Do you want to read it?'

The pages were yellowed and the paper cracked with dryness.

'I typed it out for him. I typed everything for him so that it would be ready for the book.'

The typescript was headed 'The Facts About Norman Lindsay's Spiritualism'. It was about three thousand words long, signed by Lionel and dated 1939–40. On the last page Peter had written: 'I removed these pages from my father's Autobiography "Comedy of Life" as I did not want to cause unnecessary pain to NL in his last years. I believe every word to be true.'

The manuscript is a narrative rambling in different directions, but it reveals what Lionel had to say about Norman's faith in spiritualism during World War I, and it gives one reason why Lionel's friendship with his brother ended.

*He had never expressed the faintest interest in religion, except in a natural animus against priests and all puritans as enemies of life: and he was possessed by the same contempt for Christianity as myself. Yet a trifling cause, innocent and casual, led later to astonishing results. This was the illustrating of a story in* The Lone Hand *magazine by James Edmond, in which some mining engineers bore so deep that they strike Hell, and the devils come up through the bore hole. No one, not even Dürer, conceived a better devil than this powerful beast from the pit, half out of the ground and roaring like a madman. The insensate rage, and consuming hate that emanated from the beast was a triumph of imaginative realism. Came the Great War and this devil was employed to epitomise the remorseless brutality of the Hun, and so grew later into his pet symbol of the powers of Evil, to be used in many etchings and drawings like the Tom of Bedlam series. What is curious is that this hybrid horrific gorilla was created in cold blood, a shape to adumbrate abnormal ferocity and strength, and that later the artist grew to believe in the existence of his creation, just as Blake insisted on the validity of his vision: 'It must be right because I saw it so.'*

*. . . the 'Abyss', a story that Norman read to me after dinner at Springwood sometime in 1915. This story in the vein of* [Ambrose] *Bierce*

and [H.G.] Wells, centres on the ability of an evil artist, who is studying in Paris, and interested in a primeval world, to summon and draw at will the monstrous hybrids of his imagination. He comes to Australia, and finds near his home in the Blue Mountains the ideal background in the grey mass of a hill that rises sheer from a ravine at his feet. Here he places a seat, and in the light of afternoon when the hill loses colour, and becomes a mysterious grey wall, he plays with his fancy and summons his hallucinations from the depths of the valley. They climb the rocks at the edge and crawl towards him. In the end they get him.

. . . It was [David] Low who introduced the ouija board to Norman, having thoroughly frightened himself by the revelation of his own thoughts on the alphabetical toy. Our fine brother Reg had been killed in France and our father not long dead, when I went up to Springwood to spend a couple of weeks — my year's scanty holiday. These had been the pleasantest interludes of the year for both of us. Working all day and talking half the night, we could never exhaust our various interests . . . Now I was confronted with a performance by Norman and Rose on the ouija board.

It is not enough to say that I was dismayed. I was literally overcome with nausea and pity: for with that extraordinary mimetism and memory for the characteristic phrase, which usage had made a second nature, my brother asked and answered questions with additions of remembered tones and voices, suiting the answer to the character addressed, whether Reg or our father . . . I was also not slow in noticing that Rose, quite cynically, was urging the stick unnoticed by her rapt accomplice, whose gaze was fixed upon the board and seemed animated by a magnetic change.

. . . At the end of the performance, when Norman had left the room, told Rose that I had seen her manipulating the stick, and that this was a dangerous game to play with one so highly strung. She very cynically replied: 'Oh: it keeps him quiet, and you don't know what a lot I have to put up with here.' 'Well, your blood on your own head' I said, 'you can never say where this will lead to.'[18]

*Comedy of Life*, as published, ends in about 1903, after Lionel's travels in Spain and England and his departure for Italy where he fell in love with Jean, the sister of fellow bohemians Will, Ted and Ambrose Dyson. In the later stages of the book, Norman is mentioned only as Lionel's host when he moves to Sydney to find work in advance of his marriage. Then, after Norman travels to London, Lionel writes of having to look after his brother's business affairs. The brother who was a companion is now simply another obligation. Rose, Norman's second wife, is mentioned only once, and their married state is implied, rather than stated. Instead it is Lionel's brother-in-law, Will Dyson, who comes to the fore as his close friend when he makes suggestions on how Lionel could draw his first political cartoon for the *Evening News*.

Siblings, other than Norman and a few passing references to Percy's idleness, do not intrude into these memoirs. It is as though the author was either totally estranged from his family or had made the conscious decision that their lives were not to become public property. From my conversations with Lionel's children, as well as what I had gleaned from the La Trobe Library and the index to the Mitchell letters, I knew that Lionel remained in contact with Daryl and his sisters. Therefore it had to be the latter choice. Was this purely a generational thing, this notion that public and private worlds should never meet? Or were there secrets which this public figure did not want to see discussed, at least in his own lifetime?

Other than Norman's own comments, which were not published until after his death, there was another inside account, in book form, of the Lindsay family. This was *The Leafy Tree*, the family history as written by Daryl, the youngest Lindsay brother.

# 4
# *Daryl Lindsay and The Leafy Tree*

When I was researching Lionel Lindsay I found Daryl's memoirs both intriguing and frustrating.[1] Intriguing because they always seemed to promise so much, and frustrating because they gave so little away. This man was the ultimate diplomat, apparently frank, giving picturesque details but revealing nothing unsavoury.

*The Leafy Tree: My Family* was a book that demanded repeated and close reading to check possible internal contradictions and double meanings. Unfortunately, it has been out of print since the late 1960s and I searched second-hand bookshops in vain. In the end I took slabs of photocopies of the sections which concerned Lionel from a library copy, and had to be content with them while I struggled to understand his life and the place of his family in it.

It wasn't until after I had finished my biography of Lionel, at a time I had consigned my interest in the Lindsays to a mental backburner, that a copy of the book came to me. I had become the art critic for the *Bulletin*, writing about art in the curious transition of boom to bust that was the late 1980s. One day I was talking to the photographer, Paul Wright.

'You like the Lindsays, don't you?' he asked me.

'Well, I've written on Lionel,' I replied. ' I like Jack, but I'm a bit iffy on Norman. Why?'

'I've got this book by Daryl. Actually it was given to my parents years ago, and I don't know what to do with it. It's called *The Leafy Tree* or something. Do you want it?'

Paul's present of *The Leafy Tree* was one of the factors that led me back to the unfinished business of the Lindsay family papers.

~

Unlike *Comedy of Life*, *The Leafy Tree* covers the whole family, or most of it. Its central argument is advanced not by Daryl, but by Robert Gordon Menzies, then Prime Minister of Australia, who contributed the foreword. Menzies wrote that the Lindsay family, as an entire family, had been central to the development of an Australian culture: a notion which was accepted then, but which would be controversial today. 'Between them, the Lindsays have written a remarkable chapter in the artistic history of Australia — unsurpassed in any family history — and have given to Creswick a share of immortality.' [2]

Daryl's story starts with a historic source, James Lindsay's *The Lindsay Memoirs*, a privately published family history of the descendants of James Lindsay, a Presbyterian farmer from Ayrshire who settled in Derry in 1678.[3] His sons distinguished themselves in the siege of Derry and were subsequently rewarded by William of Orange. One branch of the family became prosperous linen merchants, others entered civic life, and in the mid–nineteenth century some emigrated to the Australian goldfields. One of these, Eleanor Johnson, encouraged her nephew, a recently graduated medical doctor, Robert Charles Lindsay, to come to Australia.

Clearly Norman Lindsay and his family did not spring unheralded from the red mud of the goldfields. The whole family belonged to an older culture: the art and literature of the western tradition were part of their personal heritage.

Daryl introduces parents, siblings and friends in turn, commenting generously on each, and so what appears at first to be the whole Lindsay family is laid out for the reader's attention. All is seen from the personal perspective of this second youngest Lindsay child. The skill in Daryl's writing is the way he combines the personal with the historical, so that most readers never once question the veracity of his narrative.

Daryl Lindsay was born in 1890, two years before the death of his grandfather. Accordingly, he acknowledges anecdotes provided by others, rather than claiming them as his own. That most dogmatic ancestor, Thomas Williams, is praised for his endurance and his contribution to scholarship in his anthropological study, *Fiji and the Fijians*.[4] In writing about Williams' lack of sexual prudery, Daryl introduces for the first time one of the mainstays of his story, Mary Lindsay, and her role as a keeper of family history.

> *My sister Mary who has a clear and vivid memory of the old man tells me that, when the Ballarat Fine Art Gallery acquired its first important picture,* Ajax and Cassandra *by Solomon J. Solomon, he was overjoyed and dragged everyone he could lay his hands on to see what was, in his opinion, a great masterpiece. She adds it was Grandpa who was really responsible for making the family conscious that art was something that mattered.*[5]

Mary is honoured by Daryl as the grown-up sister who cared for the small children, 'who seemed to gather together the threads of our individual lives'.[6] She was scholarly and serious, the focal point of their young lives, and the person who instilled in young Daryl an appreciation of literature, especially Turgenev and Austen.

Daryl makes it clear to the reader that he is drawing on Mary's memories as well as his own, and includes some of her writing describing the chaos of life with a large family.[7] He acknowledges the strain of her care for the family with the comment that:

> *Had she not been tied down to this life of household drudgery I believe, with her knowledge and feeling for literature, she could have made a name for herself as a writer. She had an observant eye and an individual and amusing mode of expression. She was very popular with literary friends of Lionel and Norman who were always urging her to write, but apart from becoming a racy and indefatigable letter writer, she let her talent slip by.*[8]

He describes his father, Robert Charles Lindsay, as a figure of warmth, affection and style. He dressed as a dandy but had a medical smell of chloroform about him, and was a remarkable and daring horseman. As with Lionel's story, there is an early reference to financial problems:

> *My father had a good practice but he invested what money he had in gold mines — always the wrong ones. He had many stories to tell of the mining field — the Midas, the Great Berry lead mines — and of the Australasia disaster, when they struck old workings and the mine was flooded and twenty-two miners lost their lives.*[9]

He is seen as a man of culture, a good doctor, a teller of bawdy tales 'so full of red meat that they cannot be printed'.[10]

Their mother was :

*. . . deeply religious in the best sense of the word. She had a strong sense of character and an amazing fund of sheer common sense. She could cope with anything from an absconding bank manager who wanted to blow his brains out to harnessing up a pair of horses in the middle of the night to go to a mining disaster. She was a wonderful cook and a great gardener.*[11]

The harridan of the myth has vanished. Instead, the married life of the Lindsay parents is seen as the consequence of a horseback romance between the dashing young Irish doctor and the Fijian-born minister's daughter fresh out of school, a romance marked by blushes and fair hair tumbling down. Instead of domestic misery caused by a preaching mother, the Lindsay parents are presented as being of different temperaments, balancing each other with love in a large and busy family.

*The humdrum affairs of everyday life were left to Janie (Daryl's mother) to deal with as best she could. Janie, with her father's implicit faith in the Almighty, would say philosophically: 'Well the Lord will provide.' The Lord usually did through the medium of her sons' pockets.*[12]

In the account of his own life, Daryl starts with his early memories and the birth of his younger sister Isabel. She features as a babe in arms, and then is dropped entirely from the family history until her death, when she is described as having been 'an invalid for many years'.[13] The first time I read *The Leafy Tree* I didn't notice her absence, now I started to wonder why she was given no personality by the brother who was closest to her in age. Did he feel there was nothing to be commented on because she was mentally deficient, as I had been told? Or was there something else? Was Daryl simply hiding the shame of a family member who could never be described as brilliant? I probably would have decided that Daryl was simply the kind of man who regarded feebleminded female relatives as irrelevant to any kind of public family history, if I had not remembered the start of my Lionel Lindsay research and the way Felicity Shaw froze with rage when I asked her about 'Goo'.

As with Lionel's account of himself, Daryl is keen to be seen as a difficult child, his problems accentuated by deafness caused by continual ear infections. The book reproduces Percy's painting of his pugnacious infancy. From what I was told by his former colleagues, Daryl maintained his determination throughout his working life. The state school, which Lionel praised for its teaching, is seen by Daryl as 'a hideous building with classrooms painted a dingy yellow with a chocolate coloured dado'.[14] Daryl ran away from school on his first day after kicking the headmaster on the shins, but was forcibly returned by his eldest brother Percy: 'In later years, over a drink, he admitted that it was a dirty thing to do'.[15] Percy Lindsay always seems to appear in his brothers' writing with drinks and good cheer without paying, gracefully avoiding boring household tasks, managing to escape from his girlfriends' beds just before their fathers or brothers come home. His return of young Daryl to school is about the only instance I've come across of him acting responsibly.

The dreariness of school was countered by a real education from the world of books, to which Daryl was led both by parents and siblings.

*Books were everywhere at 'Lisnacrieve'. Mostly good strong classical meat, much of it tough and indigestible for infant stomachs. Large illustrated volumes of Shakespeare, Milton, Dante with illustrations by Gustave Doré (a hot favourite with Norman), volumes on domestic furniture and European architecture and historical costumes. The French novelists Balzac, Flaubert, and Maupassant who led Lionel to the passionate study of European languages. I leaned to the English sporting works of White-Melville and Surtees.*[16]

In Daryl's memory of his family, references to these literary sources are mingled with portraits of real people whose lives were as fantastic as any fiction, and whose practical jokes were both bawdy and bigoted. He gives more of a context to Creswick than Lionel does. There is a stronger sense of a network of friends, of the social elite and the working class who serviced their needs. Other citizens of Creswick are remembered with affection, including Mr Peacock, the modest shopkeeper whose son was to be Premier of Victoria. Entertainment included musical evenings with sit-down suppers. In his memory of a small-boy raid on the adult supper served to guests, Daryl directly refutes the part of the Norman Lindsay legend that claims Jane Lindsay was a wowser who banned alcohol from the house.

*Reg and I slept in a room across the passage and, when the guests had retired to the drawing room, we would get out of bed and sneak into the dining room and gorge ourselves on what was left, including the remains of the wine, which tasted rather sour to me. In a stupor I staggered to bed but once, Reg, his courage fortified with liquor said, 'I'm going to the party.' This he did;*

*but he could not quite stay the distance and fell flat on his face on entering the drawing room.*[17]

Lionel dominates Daryl's account of his siblings, partly because he was the first to leave home and then later because he was the brother closest to him. But he is also featured because he best embodies *The Leafy Tree*'s other agenda of reclaiming the entire family from the glorification of Norman. Lionel is given precedence so that Daryl can argue against Norman's claim that Lionel was not really interested in art and only became an illustrator by accident.[18] Lionel is at first the passionate self-dramatising adolescent who has a thirst for knowledge larger than Creswick or its modest lending library. He is beloved by the family, and especially old Ellen, the domestic servant who came out from Ireland to be Robert Charles' housekeeper when he emigrated. And above all Lionel is the family scholar, and an indefatigable artist:

*During these busy formative years, young Lionel was constantly drawing — if he was not drawing he was reading or talking (if he could get an audience). With almost superhuman energy for a boy of his age he sought to satisfy his thirst for knowledge which was unquenchable . . . Even at that age, he had the judgment and taste to discriminate between the genius of Charles Keene as a draughtsman and the ephemeral fashionable drawings of Du Maurier.*[19]

Most of Daryl's account of Lionel's Melbourne years and Spanish adventures is based on Lionel's recollections, and some incidents are taken directly from *Comedy of Life*. There is, however, the thirteen-year-old Daryl's memory of his brother, newly returned from Spain in 1903, re-enacting a bull-fight, his eyes flashing with enthusiasm.

*Pushing back the dining room table after dinner, an old rug in his hands, he acted the bull, fight from beginning to end with dramatic gestures. The entrance of the bull, the work of the picadors, the banderillos, to the final killing of the bull by the matador. My mother sat wide-eyed, not really knowing what it was all about, and the rest of us were entranced by the performance of our handsome elder brother.*[20]

And then there was Norman. He was the famous, the most talented, the sickly, the brilliant one. And, in Daryl's account, not especially physically attractive. He was teased as a child because he looked like a Jew.

*Norman Alfred was undoubtedly the most of talented member of the family. A delicate boy, he was forced to spend most of his time indoors and, according to my sister Mary, from a very early age was scribbling and covering sheets of paper with drawings. My first recollection of him is when he would have been about thirteen. I can see him now — a thin, hawk-faced boy with a mobile mouth, darting blue eyes and sensitive hands — sitting in front of the dining room fire on a bleak winter's morning, being fed with hot buttered toast by old Ellen while he swatted up his homework. His beaky nose earned him the name of Ikey Bentwick after the local pawnbroker.*[21]

Was this the source of his famous anti-Semitism, I wondered? Lionel's anti-Semitism arose because he blamed Jews for the Old Testament, and he hated Christianity. The prejudice was compounded by English conservatives who complained to him about the market for modern art. Times have changed so much that it is hard to remember anti-Semitism only ceased being 'respectable' during World War II. But nothing Lionel ever said or wrote about Jews was as personal as Norman's cartoons. Perhaps children teasing his beaky nose, combined with mocking suggestions as to his paternity, could lead to a real hatred of this particular group. On the other hand Norman was also vicious about Chinese people and no one ever made jokes about him having an Asian appearance.

*The Leafy Tree* gives intriguing hints of other family stories. Norman is mentioned as marrying young. According to Daryl he married his first wife, Katie Parkinson, in 1899. Her family is thanked for taking Norman's work to Sydney and hence securing his job at the *Bulletin*, which made him famous.

Daryl praised Norman's cartooning work and his black and white tonal drawings which made his name among Australian artists, a rare honour. In a considered judgment, Sir Daryl Lindsay — the retired Director of the National Gallery of Victoria, one of the great connoisseurs of his generation and of his culture — likened his brother's best early drawings to those of Rubens. Both the quality and quantity of his work is admired for its energy and finesse, but Daryl is careful to tell the reader that Norman's etching skills were derived from Lionel, and his visual sources were from the classical culture of their boyhood home. Norman is therefore seen as a product of the Lindsay family values, rather than a denial of them. Daryl argues that the notoriety of Norman Lindsay's sensual vision in Australian society was caused largely by the limitations of the provincial milieu in which he operated:

*Pollice Verso was sent to Melbourne on exhibition and purchased for the National Gallery of Victoria on the advice of the Director, Bernard Hall,*

> *strongly supported by Sir Baldwin Spencer . . . Its purchase brought forth a barrage of abuse from an unenlightened, unsophisticated press and public. Howls of agony went up that £150 of public money should be spent on this unbridled slap in the face to Christianity. A similar outburst came when the superb collection of William Blake's illustrations to the* Paradiso *and* Inferno *was acquired some fifteen years later for the Gallery.*[22]

Less controversially, *The Magic Pudding* is praised for its contribution to children's literature.

Daryl glosses over the circumstances of the dissolution of Norman's first marriage. Katie and the children are simply not mentioned when he writes of Norman seeking fame in London in 1910. The end of his marriage is blamed by implication on the collapse of his health after the European excursion.

> *He was also domestically unhappy and in the following year his marriage was dissolved. He had three sons, John, Philip and Raymond. John had taken his B.A. when he was eighteen and was a brilliant classical scholar; later he made a name for himself in London as a writer and translator of Greek plays. Philip followed him to London and distinguished himself as a writer of historical novels which earned him a wide public. He died in 1958. Raymond was an artist who made no particular mark and did not live long enough to develop what talent he had.*[23]

The only hint of another, concealed, story between Daryl Lindsay and his brother is at the end of the chapter introducing Norman, when Daryl notes:

> *. . . that owing to a difference of opinion on family matters, we have not seen each other for over thirty years. That has been my loss but it does not detract from my affection for him as a person and for the many kindnesses he showed me as a young man.*[24]

Daryl's other siblings are treated in less detail than Lionel and Norman, and some of the dismissals are harsh. The eldest Lindsay child, Percy, was 'completely devoid of any sense of responsibility about anything or anybody and never changed throughout his long life', but became a talented painter of landscape on a small scale, while living a life devoted to pleasure.[25] The second son, Robert Elliot Alexander Lindsay, is described as 'a strange complex character partly due, I think, to the fact that he was delicate from a child and all his life suffered from some form of dyspepsia . . . [with] all the social graces to which the other boys never gave a thought.'[26]

As I read this I started to wonder how Norman could have been a solitary ill child if Daryl's adult deafness was caused by constant childhood ear infections and Robert was 'delicate'? From reading Lionel's letters I knew this very long-lived family was obsessive about its health to the point of hypochondria. Most large families have a running saga of childhood illnesses: runny noses, febrile babies, strange rashes and vomiting. The Lindsays were just the same, and if Norman had really been so fragile he would hardly have lived to be ninety.

Robert was a new Lindsay, not mentioned by Lionel, of no account in the legend of Norman. Daryl wrote of him as the bank clerk who went to London after designing a dress for Nellie Melba. There he became a clerk with the Fisheries Department and made hats for duchesses.

His inhibited life was balanced by the robust friendliness of Pearl, 'a cheerful, happy-go-lucky girl who in looks and temperament took after my father'.[27] The story of her life — flirtations, marriage and early widowhood with three young children — is given without detail or emotion, although a brief description indicates that the dour Colin McPhee, her husband, was not to Daryl's liking. He notes that after she was widowed, Pearl lived first with her mother and later separately in Ballarat, 'where she resides to this day'.[28] By contrast, the next Lindsay daughter, Ruby, is treated in earnest detail as the beautiful girl who wanted always to be an artist and was encouraged in her ambition by her elder brothers and by Mary. Her romance with the dashing young cartoonist, Will Dyson, is recorded, as is the wedding when the bride was embarrassed by the crowd waiting to see her.

> *She got stage fright, bolted through the house into the backyard and picking up her skirts, scaled the adjoining fence into the churchyard. Pink in the face, she made her entry through the vestry. And what is more, the ceremony over, she took to her heels at the church door and was chased back to the house by an hilarious bridegroom, to be greeted by cheers and laughter over the champagne in the old drawing room.*[29]

After their marriage Ruby and Will left for London where Dyson's cartoons led to him being appointed war artist for the AIF. There, Daryl, who served as Dyson's batman on the western front, came to know Ruby well. At the end of the war he took her with him to meet their Irish relatives.

> *It was her first holiday for some years and she was as light-hearted as a schoolgirl and captivated all the Irish Lindsays. The plague of pneumonic influenza was sweeping through Europe . . . In Dublin Ruby picked up a*

*germ and arrived back in London with a temperature and died four days later.*[30]

Did Daryl lavish so much detail on Ruby because she figured large in his life, as he travelled on that last journey with her? Or was it that, for Daryl Lindsay, any sibling who was an artist deserved attention? Reg, two years older than Daryl, was never an artist, but he is described in some detail as handsome and athletic — admired by all the girls in the town. He became a forester before enlisting in the AIF in 1915.

*I followed him some months later but, although I was in France in 1915 and 1916, we never had the luck to run across each other. He was killed by shell-fire on the Somme in 1917 while, as I was told by one of his battery, dashing out of a dugout to rescue a bottle of rum. It was all thoroughly in character.*[31]

Reg and Ruby both died young and make romantic figures in the family story. It could well be that Daryl was simply honouring the dead of his family in this very personal memoir.

By the time Daryl Lindsay retired he was a major figure in the cultural life of the Australia. He had been the most successful director of the National Gallery of Victoria, he had fostered cultural relations between Australia and Europe, he was a close friend and confidant of Keith Murdoch, the newspaper magnate. Just before his retirement he was knighted by the Queen, shortly after he had put his arm around her mother and told her confidentially: 'You know Ma'am, you're the only one of your family who knows a damned thing about art.' There was sufficient reason for him to think that an account of his own life, as well as that of his brothers, would be of some public interest.

Daryl wrote of himself as a stubborn but unmotivated young man, rescued from a life of idle uncertainty by jackarooing near Collarenebri, hundreds of miles from what some people would call civilisation. Later he became an overseer in the Riverina, a region closer to home but still hot, dry and distant. These pre-war experiences, more than any other factor, gave Daryl Lindsay his close links with the squattocracy and led to his later career as a painter of horses. When war broke out he enlisted and was sent to France. He makes light of his experiences at Armentières, but recognised that the 1916 decision by his brother-in-law, Will Dyson, to have him seconded as his batman almost certainly saved his life. It also drew him towards a life of art.

*All this time Dyson had been urging me to draw, and under the stimulus of working with him, I filled sketch books with drawings of Diggers, standing about or sitting by the roadside, in their billets and ambulances, stretcher bearers and disabled tanks on the Somme. Little did I think at the time that they might have any future interest or value.*[32]

Later he was seconded to become a medical artist for the AIF at Sidcup in England, and there met Sir Henry Tonks of the Slade School, London. He became a student and a protégé of Tonks who helped foster his later Australian career. On his return to Australia in mid–1919, Daryl found family acceptance and encouragement for his new career as an artist, and repaid this by taking examples of Norman's and Lionel's etchings back to England to show Bond Street art dealers. Colnaghi, the premiere English dealers, were interested only in Lionel Lindsay's etchings and talked of contacting him for a possible exhibition. While in England, Daryl was offered the directorship of the Leeds Art Gallery, but on Tonks' advice rejected it to return home where his unique blend of administrative skills and artistic knowledge would have a greater impact.

In London he met again with his brother Robert, who was living in two small rooms above a flower shop in Chester Square and working as a milliner. Daryl obliquely implies Robert Lindsay's sexuality without stating it. After all, he did write the book from the perspective of an older generation, at a time when homosexuality was illegal.

*Robert was still the sedate well-dressed Londoner; still at the same good address. But he had cultivated a mode of speech that was very English — almost more English than the English. It was most amusing. He had left the Fisheries and somewhere in Belgravia had got himself a small millinery establishment with a clientele of the right people; but he did not discuss it nor did he give me the address. Wishing to see him on a matter of some urgency, I ran him to earth, I think to his annoyance, to find him with pins in his mouth and ribbons in his hands fitting a toque on a plump old dowager. It was all so much in character.*[33]

Robert was best man at Daryl's wedding to Joan a'Beckett Weigall, and at the wedding fussed over the clothes of the bridal couple. Daryl and Joan kept in close contact with him during these London years, admiring the way he kept his West End appearance on a small income. Daryl records that, after a bad accident when he was knocked down by a bus, Robert returned home to live with Mary, where he entertained new friends 'with amusing stories of English life'.[34]

# DARYL LINDSAY AND *THE LEAFY TREE*

Daryl and Joan returned to Australia to family reunions and eventually a home in the country at Mulberry Hill. Lionel reappears in Daryl's history as the internationally successful artist brother who could find Dürer engravings and Rembrandt etchings in London junk shops. There are friendships with Keith and Elisabeth Murdoch and Robert Menzies. The artist George Lambert made a drawing of Jane Lindsay, by then very old, when he was staying with Daryl in 1929. That was shortly before the Great Depression caused Daryl and Joan to leave their house to live more cheaply elsewhere.

In 1940, Keith Murdoch invited Daryl to become curator at the National Gallery of Victoria, and later he was appointed director. He used his position of influence with Murdoch to acquire the young Joseph Burke as founding professor of Fine Arts at Melbourne University. Daryl writes briefly on these years, perhaps he was so secure of his place in this country's history that he felt it would be crude to praise himself.[35]

*The Leafy Tree* concludes with a cool assessment of those members of the Lindsay family who became artists. Ruby is remembered for sensitive line drawings which did not fully develop until after her marriage. Lionel and Norman are both assessed as essentially black and white artists. But Lionel is also seen as the thinker of the family, the connoisseur, scholar and writer. It is Percy, a mediocre hack in black and white, the careless bohemian who was not interested in material success, who was understood by Daryl to be the true colourist.

*It was left to Percy, the non-intellectual of the family — the outwardly simple soul who went gaily through life without a care in the world — to be in oils, the best painter and colourist of us all.* [36]

There is a final piece of artistry to this most carefully constructed family history. When commenting on the long friendship between Norman and Lionel Lindsay, Daryl wrote:

*During these years they corresponded almost weekly at great length and with the gloves off. Where these letters are today I don't know but, if in existence, they should make lively reading for some future historian interested in the Lindsay family.*[37]

By the time I reread *The Leafy Tree*, I realised that Daryl Lindsay not only knew precisely where those letters were, but that he had been involved in having some of them stored in a safe place. He also knew that many letters were not to be made available until long after his death.

It was this comment that led me to question every description, every event in *The Leafy Tree*, and in the end to judge it as a beautifully written illusion. It was almost the opposite of Joan Lindsay's book, *Picnic at Hanging Rock*. At the end of that you know there are questions without answers to leave you puzzling through the night. But with *The Leafy Tree* there was just a sense that secrets the author knew had been kept well hidden. When I read it through again, as well as noting the absence of Isabel, I realised Daryl had simply left out any reference to Rose.

There is no index to the text, so it takes close reading to see that the only mention of her name is on the family tree on the inside cover where she is called 'Rose Saudy', and given no date of birth. But this was the muse, praised by poet and journalist, who appears in so many guises in Norman's art. She was Rose the flamboyant, who stands cheekily beside Norman, wearing nothing but frilly underwear and black stockings in the photograph which appears on the back of the collected letters of Norman Lindsay.[38] Rose, who as the stately matron wowed them all at the Artists Balls in the 1920s. Rose, who is acknowledged in story, magazine article and movie as the one who was always there to inspire genius.

Just as Rose is not mentioned, neither are her daughters Jane and Honey. Perhaps Daryl decided that this branch of his family tree should be lopped off, that it was somehow illegitimate because it came from a second marriage. Or was the hostility to Norman's later life somehow bound up with Rose and that second family of girls? It was the kind of question where there could only be one source for an intelligent answer. I went to see Peter Lindsay in Kirribilli.

≈

'I suppose you don't want a drink if you're driving?' asked Peter. He had made me lunch, a chilled soup followed by whitebait cooked in a white sauce. 'You really need a little one with this.' I agreed, and he poured me a generous tumbler of riesling.

'Daryl could be quite ruthless you know,' he said. 'He only wanted his view of anything to come out, and he wanted to decide what was good and what wasn't. I remember when Dad died he wanted to burn all his Spanish watercolours because he didn't like his use of colour. "You're not doing that," I said and I stopped him. They were good paintings, but Daryl just didn't see Spain like Dad did.'

'Why wouldn't he have liked Rose?' I asked.

'All sorts of reasons, but they wouldn't have been why she wasn't in the book. It's like Dad's paintings. If he didn't think it was good enough, it wasn't there. He did that with his mistress too. You don't find any mention of her anywhere, but she lived with him and Joan at Mulberry Hill for years.'

'Mistress? What mistress?' I asked. Peter had a way of dropping information bombshells without warning.

'I don't think Joan minded,' he said. 'She was there for years. She didn't like me though. I think she thought I was going to get some money from Daryl's estate when he died. But he provided for her with a block of flats, so she wasn't even in the will.'

It all seemed very much in Daryl's character. Public life and private pleasure were to be strictly separated. Only the official version was to be revealed.

---

I was still wondering about Daryl and *The Leafy Tree* when I drove up to Wahroonga to see Bingo (Jean), Lionel's daughter. She had left her cottage in Turramurra and had moved into a hostel.

Bingo had a small flat there, where she managed to keep a surprising amount of art, photographs and old papers.

I asked her about Daryl and *The Leafy Tree*, and she looked at me shrewdly.

'I thought you might ask that,' she said. From a drawer she produced some letters. 'He wrote quite a lot to both me and Pete after Dad died. Pete gave his letters to the La Trobe Library, but mine are here. You might find them interesting, so get them copied.'

That night I read in Daryl's neat hand:
*You may know that my reason for writing the 'Leafy Tree' was purely to stop Jack Hetherington writing a history of the Lindsay family — Jack Hetherington a decent pedestrian journalist with a religious admiration for N.L. who he had never met . . .* [39]

As I read this I started to think that even though he had not stopped Hetherington from writing about Norman, Daryl had succeeded admirably in his objective. Long before I read *The Leafy Tree* I had read John Hetherington's *Norman Lindsay: The Embattled Olympian*, which had become the standard biography and had been surprised that such an apparently full-blooded life as Norman's had produced such a tame book.

LETTERS & LIARS

Because I kept on feeling that I still only had a few parts of a most tantalising jigsaw puzzle, I turned again to read Hetherington's book.

# 5
# Norman according to Norman

*Norman Lindsay: The Embattled Olympian* was first published in 1973, four years after Norman's death, so I knew the author had read *My Mask*, Norman's autobiography, published posthumously in 1970, but apparently written in 1957.[1]

John Hetherington, who wrote *The Embattled Olympian*, was a feature writer for *The Age*, and, at the time Norman commissioned him to write the book, was well known as the author of biographies of Field Marshal Blamey and Sir John Monash. In the years he spent researching Norman, Hetherington also wrote a fairly bland biography of Nellie Melba. He was therefore a reasonable choice for an eminent person seeking a favourable verdict from history. From the late 1950s until Norman's death in 1969 there was close contact between biographer and subject.

It is a curious act of egoism to appoint an official biographer in one's own lifetime, an act by someone so sure of their own destiny that they will open themselves up to another person's scrutiny. Of course it is not uncommon — politicians do it all the time. But there are inherent dangers for both biographer and the living subject. The biographer's sense of privilege and the mutual need for approval can lead even the most critically minded writer to become a Blanche d'Alpuget to another's Bob Hawke. Even when the publication of the authorised biography must wait for the death of the subject, the best of writers can become so involved with their material that in the end they speak for their subjects, becoming little more than post mortem press agents.

*The Embattled Olympian* is a most reverential book. Despite the many years spent researching it, or perhaps even because of them, the author openly retreats from parts of his subject's life. There are small sections which a journalist could describe as 'colour', but no real sense of context. Because of the nature of the writer, it is almost inevitable that this would be so.

As Daryl had noted, John Hetherington was in essence a newspaper feature writer. The stylistic constraints of journalism, the need to summarise a complex issue in as few words as possible and to concentrate on one issue alone, shaped his entire approach to writing. It was an approach that came from his early years in reporting local government, before his one-time patron, Keith Murdoch, took him away from routine work and gave him the promise of promotion.[2]

As with many male journalists of his generation, John Hetherington had the 'luck' to be appointed an official war correspondent in World War II. The War gave him the chance to meet with men who were deciding the fate of the country, and his first books came out of his wartime experiences. He began by writing profiles of eminent soldiers, and later there were full scale, but nevertheless glossed-over, biographies. After the war he moved to the arts, writing brief lives of artists and writers for the more leisurely Saturday papers.

In newspaper terms Hetherington was one of the new breed of writers who would add colour to a story without abandoning facts. There were physical descriptions of faces and mannerisms, and sometimes of methods of work. These were usually mixed with anecdotes so that any real analysis of what the subject achieved was neatly avoided. Hetherington's technique made him a popular feature writer with his own by-line at a time when this was not common in the daily press, and he was given regular time off for his other prestigious job of writing books.[3]

There were little details about *The Embattled Olympian* which niggled as I read. It was dedicated 'To JEAN for all the things you are'. Who was Jean? Hetherington's first wife, Olive, was dead. His second wife (who is not named) typed the manuscript, but her name was Mollie. There were no children, and even when I went through the Hetherington papers years later, there was not one Jean. Had he put it there as a mystery like Orson Welles' Rosebud in the movie *Citizen Kane*? Would I find she wasn't a person after all? The Lindsay family had so many Jeans and Janes it could have been one of them, except that I was to find they were either dead or had never met Hetherington. So

'Jean' remains a mystery, a reminder that perhaps John Hetherington was the kind of man who could use his wife as a workhorse and dedicate the book to another woman.

Other than Norman, the two Lindsay family members acknowledged for their special assistance were Daryl and Peter. When I first read the book I had simply noted their presence. But on this rereading there were other absences. Where were Mary and Rose? From Daryl's account, which was obviously a major source of Hetherington's book, Mary was a key figure in the family and presumably had given some assistance. And unlike Lionel and Daryl's narratives, the legendary Rose Lindsay was here in all her insouciant glory, but not thanked for the information only she could have provided. The lack of such basic courtesy to these two women became another puzzle which I had to solve.

Hetherington's book returns to the story of the sickly child in a large healthy family; but a child who watched and who drew. 'His were never the infant scratchings of an untutored hand,' he wrote.[4] Instead, Norman amazed his family with his skill. He was closest to his older sister Mary, whom he always called 'Mame'. She encouraged his learning, but the boy genius did not need her guidance long, as he was reading *The Coral Island* at the age of five. *The Coral Island* had been one of my favourite bloodthirsty books from primary school years, all cannibals and castaways written in lush colours. But Norman must have been a most precocious five-year-old to have read the prose with ease.

This book was starting to read like the legend of the artist as super-brain, one of the golden oldie myths of art history. From Giotto to Picasso, artists have supposedly emerged as total geniuses in their infancy. It is a modern version of the Greek goddess Athena springing fully formed out of the head of Zeus. And just as believable.

There are brief descriptions of other siblings and of Norman's parents. But, in marked contrast to Lionel's and Daryl's stories, Dr Robert Charles Lindsay reads as a bit of a prude. His 'sensibilities were shocked by the wild drinking sprees' of the Victorian goldfields of the 1860s.[5] He is the hardworking country doctor, and his relationship to his wife is written as a piece of masculine pragmatism: 'He was not a man to go long unwed — he needed a wife beside him and a family around him.'[6]

Jane Lindsay is no longer the doctor's loyal assistant or the subject of a romantic dalliance on horseback, but instead is praised for her ability to make jam. Thomas Williams is very much to the fore in this story, taking the young

Norman to see Solomon J. Solomon's Victorian masterpiece, *Ajax and Cassandra*, and praising his early efforts. Hetherington ignored Peter's account of Jane painting watercolours and teaching her children to draw, and Daryl's stories of his father's taste for fine furniture. Instead it was Thomas Williams alone who gave the Lindsay children their facility with pen and paint, and gave Norman his genius.

The girls are 'beautiful' (Ruby), or 'loyal' (Mary), and Isabel is 'delicate'. Pearl is ignored in order to respect her privacy. Hetherington does concede that Ruby was passionate about her art, but this is not linked by him to any desire to be financially independent. In the index Ruby is listed under her husband's name, not her professional name, and her career is seen as less important than her marriage. Her position in Hetherington's story is reflected in a wrongly captioned illustration labelled 'Will and Ruby Dyson', when it is in fact a 1920s photograph of the older Dyson with their daughter Betty. [7]

*The Embattled Olympian* is a tale of a young man so passionate about Albrecht Dürer that he steals a print from the local lending library. This is excusable as Norman experienced 'a feeling of kinship with Dürer'. So close was this kinship that even 'the faces were almost identical'.[8] He was, however, a bit of a larrikin; he played truant for six months by successfully forging his mother's signature on a letter to the principal of the local state school.

Norman left Creswick with all its restrictions by following in the footsteps of his big brother Lionel. According to Hetherington, Lionel 'had inherited some of Grandpa Williams' skill as a draughtsman and now and then played about with drawing'.[9] This had led to him being offered the job of illustrator for a sleazy Melbourne weekly magazine, *The Hawklet*. Norman heard of Lionel's exciting life and when Lionel needed an assistant to 'ghost' for him while he worked on another magazine, Norman was the obvious candidate.

John Hetherington's account of Norman's student years is reminiscent of both Norman's *A Curate in Bohemia* and Lionel's *Comedy of Life*. The difference is that Hetherington writes of Lionel as being mean with money, cheating his little brother out of his just earnings. It is a story of poverty, girls, pipes, and drawing classes with art students but no teacher. Self-taught geniuses dispense with teachers, even in art school. But they had the encouragement of friends, especially the young black and white artists, Ernest Moffitt and the handsome Will Dyson. When Moffitt died of peritonitis in 1899, Norman illustrated the book Lionel wrote in his memory.[10]

The turning point for Norman's career was some drawings admired by Will Dyson. They were experimental illustrations to Boccaccio's *Decameron*, started as one of a series of plans by the brothers to establish their careers as artists. Earlier they had agreed to write and illustrate a great pirate novel in the tradition of Robert Louis Stevenson and with a journalist friend, Ray Parkinson, had signed their names in blood to the venture.[11] (When I was in the La Trobe Library I saw the letter, written in mock archaic script, the blood fading with the years.) This time around, Boccaccio's classic tales of sex and adventure in fourteenth-century Italy captured their fancy. Ray Parkinson came into it in a way, because it was his sister, Katie, who was Norman's inspiration.

Here was the first detailed account I'd read of Katie Parkinson who became Katie Lindsay. At the beginning, this was an illicit relationship, to be concealed from family and friends because Norman broke the moral code of his class and seduced the sister of a social equal.

'Not that it could be counted as a seduction — Katie had met him half way,' wrote Hetherington.[12] That sentence has to rate as one of the more outrageous expressions of the old male–female double standard. Katie came from a self-consciously middle-class family. Her mother was a widow. How could a girl who knew little of the realities of sexual relations be in an equal relationship with a young artist about town, a man who drew dead bodies in the morgue for a living?

Katie fell pregnant and she and Norman married before telling their shocked families. Her sister's husband, Jack Elkington, took Norman's Boccaccio drawings to Sydney where they were shown to the *Bulletin* and the artist Julian Ashton, the most powerful figure on the Sydney art scene. From this, Norman was offered the choice of a travelling scholarship to Europe and work as the *Bulletin*'s cartoonist. He became the cartoonist and moved to Sydney. 'Katie pouted' at the thought of moving so far from her family, and this is the first evidence of disagreement between the young couple.[13]

In Sydney, Norman soon became established as one of the country's leading cartoonists. In a world without television, where photographs in newspapers were expensive and poor in quality, the cartoonist was king. His cartoons influenced the decisions of government, and he was rewarded with fame and money.

Then I started to read of Rose Soady, the young model, described as 'a girl of unswerving resolution', who was desired by Norman's friend Will Dyson.[14] But in this story she does not become Norman's lover until the marriage with Katie is well and truly over. Hetherington's account of the decline of Norman and Katie's marriage, which covered the birth of their three sons, is that of a professional man disengaging himself from an unfortunate entanglement. But here was a surprise. John Hetherington, the staid biographer who happily sanitised Dr Lindsay's robust life by making him prudish about strong drink and prostitutes, has Katie in a sexual relationship with Will Dyson. From his perspective I suppose it stands to reason — the kind of girl who would fall pregnant outside of marriage was likely to have extramarital affairs.

Who was the source of this information? All I could find before I read the manuscripts was *Rooms and Houses*, Norman's semi-autobiographical novel. Here, characters based on Dyson and Katie have an affair which consequently frees the characters based on Norman and Rose to ride off into the sunset. *Rooms and Houses* was first published in 1968, well after the death of both Katie Lindsay and Will Dyson. Norman must have told Hetherington the story, but surely a cautious biographer would have to rely on more than one source, especially as manners and middle-class morality in the first decade of this century were rather more conservative than they are today. This account was placed in a biography to be published after the subject was dead. What kind of person would posthumously justify his life in this way? This was more than simply giving colourful information to a journalist for a newspaper article. The stories Norman must have told Hetherington about his first marriage were told for posterity. This man obviously cared about what history thought of him.

Norman travelled to London in 1909, ostensibly to take his illustrations of the legendary lover, Casanova, to an overseas publisher, but in reality to escape his marriage with Katie. And this is where I started to find Hetherington's story absurd, for Norman travelled with his good friend Will Dyson and his bride, Ruby Lindsay. They were friends. There was no hint of hostility between Norman and Will. Did Hetherington actually believe Will had an affair with Katie and then remained close friends with Norman? And if Ruby and Will were married in 1909, then when did their romance begin and Dyson's affair with Katie end? Nothing seemed to add up.

The next year, when Rose was reunited with Norman in London, the unmarried couple was snubbed by the respectably married Dyson. This was the start of Rose's role as Norman's official consort as they openly lived together. They were welcomed by Robert Lindsay, in his new incarnation as a milliner in London, and also by Dr Lindsay who visited London as part of his work as ship's doctor. But Norman was not a success in England. According to Hetherington, the prudery of the English art critics and media meant that they failed to recognise his brilliance.

On his return to Australia, Norman discovered that Katie had moved to Brisbane to be with her sister Mary and Mary's husband Jack. Brisbane became the home of the young Jack Lindsay and his brothers Ray and Phil as they grew up with only a faint memory of their father.

In Sydney, Norman became ill with pleurisy, a development from the unhealthy life of London. Katie came down to see him in hospital to formalise their separation, and Rose nursed him back to health. They moved to the mountains for his convalescence, and, one day while riding alone, Norman discovered an old cottage near Faulconbridge. This he bought, and it became the basis for the famous Lindsay home at Springwood with its columns and fountains and statues.

Was his health the only reason for the Lindsay retreat from the wider world stage of London? Hetherington writes with some bitterness of the way 'he had been jarred by an English critic writing on the *Satyricon* who had dismissed him as merely an accomplished illustrator'.[15] But this was only a small hiccup in the glorious career.

By the outbreak of World War I, Norman was experimenting with literature — he had already written reminiscences of the Melbourne years which were published as *A Curate in Bohemia* —and now he began the novel which became *The Cautious Amorist*. He saw fiction as a relief from the physical effort of drawing and the novel especially as 'a useful form of intellectual exercise'.[16]

The war years saw the death of both Dr Robert Charles Lindsay and Norman's younger brother Reg, events noted by Hetherington as tragic, but not surprising. The continuing war, however, was depressing, and dominating all life. Partly as a distraction from the war, Norman wrote his children's story, *The Magic Pudding*, which 'carried him over a particularly black patch early in 1917 when Reg was killed'.[17] This was an instant success, and it soon entered the pantheon of classic children's literature.

Norman Lindsay's major artistic achievement of the war years was to turn to etching. In this he was aided by Lionel, who was already well known as a print-maker. But Norman's lines were more intensely black, his compositions more extravagant, than the conventional work of his brother. In a curious analysis Hetherington wrote that etching 'placed the final seal on his relationship with Rose'. While Norman made the beautiful polished plates incised by acid, she printed them in crisp editions, 'her splendid body' straining at the wheel on the press.[18] The muse was now a true handmaiden to the arts, always assisting, never creating. I wondered what the patient Mollie, Hetherington's wife, thought of this comment on marriage as she typed yet another draft of the manuscript.

By the end of the war Norman had another passion, one that inevitably led to a rift with the sceptical Lionel. Norman, with Rose's assistance, was using a Ouija board to summon the dead, including his father and Reg. It all tied in with the unpublished manuscript Peter had lent me, the one about Lionel's denunciation of Norman's faith in the world of spirits. Hetherington summarised Lionel's response by writing that Lionel announced his scepticism by sending a letter signed 'Mahomet's uncle'.

After he divorced Katie, in order to marry the pregnant Rose, Norman renewed contact with his son Jack, now a brilliant student at Queensland University. Jack came to Sydney to join his father who had by now written a book expounding his faith in the artist as god, *Creative Effort*.

I have always found *Creative Effort* the most impossible book to read, a combination of turgid prose and hectoring nonsense. It owes much to Nietzsche and more to Plato, one of the most curious philosophical mixes imaginable. But I can see that in the years following World War I, it was important for the survivors of a changed world to try to make sense of it all. And a philosophy which proclaimed the existence of a greater reality than the material world of pain, and argued that artists were of supreme importance, could be very seductive to a middle-aged man.

---

Hetherington wrote of the 1920s as a jaded time for Norman, when all went stale and he felt his art to be at a standstill. His account of Norman's depression during this period is hard to reconcile with his public persona as the mentor to a new generation of writers and a continuing friend to poets like Hugh McCrae. The most lasting impression Hetherington offers of Norman Lindsay in the early 1920s involves relationship with his son Jack, that enthusiastic scholar of all things classical.

Jack had moved to Sydney to be close to his father after he graduated from Queensland University. The other Lindsay boys, Ray and Phil, also came down from Brisbane to join Jack and meet their father, and helped create a bohemian ambience in Sydney. Writers and musicians clamoured at the feet of Norman Lindsay: Leon Gellert who became a life-long friend; Kenneth Slessor who matured as a poet under Norman's influence; Brian Penton the journalist and writer, and the musicians Arthur Benjamin and Adolf Beutler. And there was *Vision*, the magazine edited by Jack with Slessor as poetry editor, which promoted Norman's philosophy and enjoyed Norman's Svengali-like patronage. His main way of helping young writers was to illustrate their works, knowing that the chance to buy reproductions of his drawings guaranteed sales. And as often as he and Rose were prepared to cope with the disruption, a steady stream of young writers, artists and composers would travel up the mountains to Springwood to sit at the feet of the master. But from the perspective of the artist, the young took more than they gave.

Norman's sense of staleness was part of the background to the final quarrel with his brother Lionel. This was caused by Lionel's dislike of *Creative Effort*, followed by an accusation that he gossiped about Norman to their mutual friends. Then there was the 1923 exhibition of Australian art in London where Norman's work was damned as pornographic by the famous English artist, William Orpen. The worst of this was that Norman admired Orpen's art and was shocked at his response. About the same time, some of Norman's art was banned in Adelaide, and a major London exhibition was notorious rather than successful.

According to Hetherington, Rose encouraged Norman to take up dancing, which he approached with a sense of unease. She brought car loads of fashionable people to Springwood for parties, which he did not especially enjoy. Instead he turned to writing, and produced *Redheap*, a novel about the sexual adventures of boys and girls in a country town which bore a remarkable resemblance to Creswick, Victoria. Even with this he could do no good; *Redheap* was banned and described as a disgrace to Australian literature. By way of compensation, it was published to some acclaim in both England and America. Even the special Norman Lindsay issue of *Art in Australia* was impounded by police, although their heavy-handed censorship was overturned on appeal.

John Hetherington's explanation for the banning of *Redheap* was the prudery of small town Victoria and the way people of influence, especially Norman's mother, brought pressure to bear on the authorities. Was this the reason that Daryl ceased to speak to Norman? From the evidence of *The Leafy Tree*, Daryl Lindsay did have a strong sense of family loyalty, and from my conversations with Peter I knew him to be quite ruthless as far as his own interests were concerned.

By the early 1930s the strains of the *Redheap* scandal, and what Hetherington called 'the psychological discords of middle age', led Norman to leave Rose and move to a small studio in Bridge Street, Sydney.[19] Hetherington implies Norman had an affair at this time. But who was the lady? Was she very young, fresh flesh to warm his aging bones? Hetherington's reference to the value of a young mistress to Charles Dickens indicates that she may well have been.

If she was young in 1934, Norman's mistress could still have been alive as I researched. The need to protect her identity may well have been the reason for placing a restriction on the Mitchell Library papers. But why? The restriction was placed by Rose Lindsay who surely, as the wronged wife, had no reason to protect her husband's girlfriend.

Norman's rift with Rose occurred at about the time of his mother's death in 1932, but John Hetherington that Norman and Jane had never been close, and in her last years had little contact: 'Why they fell out is not clear,' he claimed.[20] Presumably it had little to do with *Redheap* because that was published only two years before Jane Lindsay died. In any case, many mature sons have little to do with their mothers and, from Hetherington's account, Creswick was hardly to the fore in Norman's life.

More important to Hetherington's story was the way Rose fled to America at the outbreak of World War II, taking Norman's most important drawings and paintings with her. She must have had great faith in Norman's work to undertake this mission. But the artworks were all destroyed when the train that was taking them across the United States caught on fire. Rose was devastated. When she returned to Sydney, shamefaced and grief stricken, Norman played the hero, telling her that he would paint her some more which would be just as good, but they were gone forever.

Rose returned to live with Norman at Springwood for some years after the American episode. Eventually, poor health drove her to live with their daughter Jane and her family at Hunters Hill. Norman moved between living a hermit's life at Springwood and staying with his friends Douglas and Margaret Stewart in Sydney. Stewart had been one of Norman's great admirers since he first came to Australia from New Zealand in the late 1930s and Norman had encouraged publication of his early poetry. By the 1950s Douglas Stewart was one of the most influential literary figures in the country. His wife, Margaret Coen, was a painter of watercolour still lifes. They seemed appropriate friends for an aging artist.

Norman continued to write and to paint, and always people visited him at Springwood: writers, journalists, scholars and even historians recording him for national archives. Best of all, a local publisher, Ure Smith, finally published his novel *Redheap*. Censorship had been lifted, and the wowsers were in retreat.[21]

In the late 1950s Norman experienced some disappointments. The *Bulletin* changed management and sacked him — their longest-serving cartoonist — because he was no longer of use. His son Jack, who lived in England, and with whom he had quarrelled and then been reconciled, wrote his memoirs *The Roaring Twenties*. Norman took offence at Jack's comments on beliefs Norman had held in distant past, so they quarrelled again.

After Mary's death in 1968, Norman was increasingly isolated, living a frugal existence in his Springwood retreat, planning his funeral and the way the house would be a museum after his death. (The house was owned by Rose, not Norman. After his death, Rose sold it to the National Trust, which now operates it as a museum.)

Hetherington's conclusion is of a sometimes difficult hero, but a hero nonetheless: an artist and writer who transformed the world around him by the power of his genius.

By the early 1990s when I read *The Embattled Olympian* for the second time, I realised that John Hetherington had known far more than he included in his account.

'Why?' I asked Peter. 'Why didn't he put in at least what Norman wrote in *My Mask*? He must have read it. Even if Norman didn't tell him in his lifetime, *My Mask* came out well before Hetherington's book. I just don't understand it.'

*My Mask* appears to have been written in its final form about the same time as *The Leafy Tree*. Bearing in mind that Mary also worked on her reminiscences there must have been a time in the 1950s when a whole swag of Lindsays were writing accounts of their childhood.

'That's a horrible book,' Peter said. 'Look what Norman wrote about his grandmother, laughing at her death. And look what he wrote about his mother!'

Norman had written of Jane as a tyrant and a wowser, but her prudery was not entirely her own fault. 'My mother had a satanically strong will, but she was the creature of a deplorable tradition in conduct and morals.' The villain was Christianity, and in particular the Methodism of Thomas Williams, as well as the social mores of the middle class. The result was a bitter conflict between the parents, with the children as onlookers. 'I should like to exhibit my mother in more gracious terms,' Norman wrote. 'But I search my memory in vain for any lighter or happier view of her.'[22]

'The thing is,' Peter said, 'she had ten children, and you can imagine what that was like. You have to be able to keep them under control. But she was kind.'

'At least he thanked Mary,' I said.

'Mary was a hypocrite,' said Peter. 'She didn't disagree with him like Dad did when he was wrong, just always told him how good he was to her even when she knew he was wrong.'

'But I still don't understand why Hetherington wrote such a tame version of Dr Lindsay, your grandfather. I know Norman told a lot of journalists that he was an old drunk, but in *My Mask* he's much kinder about the drinking. And I love that story about the postmaster.'

It is a classic Lindsay family tale, based on visual humour and bodily functions:

*There was a morose postmaster in Creswick, the town of my youth, who kept trotting horses. His name was Hayes and he had a face like a ginger-whiskered bull-dog, and one day he asked my old man to have a look at a trotter which was off its feed. My old man prescribed a drench in a warm bran-mash and a brisk trot afterwards. The drench he made up himself and then went forth to line up the town for the spectacle. Trotters of course are raced in a two wheeled vehicle which seats the driver directly under the animal's rump. There you see how aptly the word 'practical' applies to a joke which attaches its subject to the fundament of an animal whose sphincter muscles have been accelerated by a laxative drench. Hayes took the main street at racing speed before he could turn the horse and sprint back home in a frenzy, breathing between the squalls.* [23]

'John Hetherington was a gentleman,' Peter replied. 'He was probably shocked at the things Norman had told the journalists. He really was a decent chap, not like Norman. He wouldn't know how to be decent about anyone. Norman was especially horrible about Dad. He said he cheated him of money, and that was when Dad was looking after him in Melbourne. Norman was hopeless with money, absolutely hopeless. When he went to London, Dad had to look out for Katie and make sure she didn't cheat Norman, and look what he did to Dad in his novels! Almost every one of them has a character based on Dad, and they're all made to look ridiculous.'

Peter was right. Norman even admitted it in *My Mask*.

> In respect to those literary exercises [his novels] *I am forced to face an accusation of duplicity which I was quite unaware of practising at the time when we were living the experiences I afterwards wrote about. There is no escaping the fact that, under the genuine admiration of the young brother for the elder I harboured treachery, else how could Lionel as a youth have presented himself to my later meditations as an enchanting figure of comedy? And that complexity taints all my relations with him through life, and endures at this present moment, though we have had no personal contact for years: genuine affection corrupted by the satanic ingredient of humour.* [24]

'It was because Hetherington was a gentleman,' Peter continued. 'He had to think of the feelings of other people. That's why the book doesn't have much on them. But he was too kind to Rose. She was no lady. Look what she said about me to the newspapers! And that was just to upset Dad.'

'What did she say?' I asked.

'When she came back from England in the 1930s she told the newspapers that I'd written to Al Capone about wanting to become a gangster. I had written, but not like that. Dad was furious.'

Peter, when he was young and naive and living in London had written to the notorious Mr Capone, inquiring about his way of life. Rose simply exaggerated the story to the waiting press and claimed he had asked to become an apprentice gangster. It was sufficiently close to the truth not to be a direct lie, and sufficiently far from it to cause Lionel a great deal of grief. But causing grief to Lionel had been the reason for telling the story in the first place.

---

In 1967 Rose had published her memoirs with the catchy title *Model Wife*. Perhaps with her status of 'non-lady', Rose's book might be open about the questions I was starting to ask myself about the life of Norman Lindsay and the quarrel which split the family. Perhaps too she knew why *Redheap* was banned. In any case the memoirs of a muse should make good reading.

# 6

## *Memoirs of a muse*

'Why didn't Daryl ever mention Rose in *The Leafy Tree*?' I asked Bingo, Lionel's daughter, one day. I had come to talk to her about her memories of Lionel and his friend, Robert Menzies.

'She wasn't a lady, dear,' Bingo said as we sipped our sherry. 'I never met her, but I heard she was quite awful. The sad thing was that one of her sisters did laundry for friends of ours, and she was very sweet. But Rose was different. Daryl wrote to me when her book came out. Do you want to read his letter?'

Bingo had a habit of asking obvious questions. Time and time again she would pull out letters that added shape to my story, or would confirm something I had found out. She rarely volunteered fresh information, but often produced the evidence that showed my instinct had been right.

'I have not read her last book and I don't think I shall as I'm quite sure I'd be disgusted with it,' Daryl wrote. 'She was just a common harlot. And glories in it.'[1]

'Daryl always did have definite views,' Bingo said. 'It's quite odd really, because Joan liked the book. But then Joan was fey, very eccentric. That's probably why she liked Isabel. This is *her* opinion.'

Bingo handed me another letter. It seemed odd to me that the perceptive but other-worldly (and I suppose 'fey' is the right word) Joan Lindsay, author of *Picnic at Hanging Rock*, should have been married to the shrewd Daryl.

'One can't help admiring her [Rose] for becoming a professional writer,' she wrote.[2] Joan had enjoyed *Ma and Pa* (the first volume of Rose's autobiography) and was looking forward to reading the new work.

I returned to Rose's book, which I had first read years before when I was researching Sydney Long. Rose's very first nude modelling job had been for

Long's 1902 painting, *Flamingos* (now in the collection of the Art Gallery of New South Wales), where she posed for both nymphs. Here was evidence of the subjective nature of perception. Long painted her as a delicate, almost androgynous figure gazing at the dark red birds. Then, when she had established a reputation as a good artists' model, Norman painted her with opulent curves, oozing sexuality.

As a case for the importance of Rose to Norman's career, *Model Wife* is an impressive piece of writing. It is an expanded and surprisingly frank version of some articles Rose had first written with the title 'Rose Lindsay's Memoirs' in the *Bulletin* of 1953.[3] The style is direct and deliberately uninhibited — this is Rose thumbing her nose at all those people who professed to admire her husband while sneering at her. But she is also writing to modify both Norman's vision of himself and the views of those family members who wanted to eliminate her presence. Rose knew as early as 1931, when she and Norman were in London, that he was working on his autobiography and that it was in her interests to have her own version available.[4]

What she describes is at first a decidedly odd relationship. Rose started her diary just after she and Norman became lovers. (I wish I could read that one!) She had started keeping it at his suggestion, but then she discovered Norman had a duplicate key to the box where it was kept so that he could read it in her absence. She changed the locks and kept on writing.[5] What kind of man was Norman Lindsay? I could accept him reading his brother's diary when he was a child, but to get his mistress to keep a diary so he could read it behind her back seemed bizarre. Was he vain or just prurient?

*Model Wife* is a book which would have been hard to publish in the mainstream press in Australia before the sexual revolution of the late 1960s. In the earlier version Rose fudged the details of their relationship, but by 1967 the social environment was such that Rose Lindsay could admit that as a teenager she had left home to be with a married man, who ostensibly remained with his wife for the first seven years of their liaison.

But there was still some bravado in the aged Rose Lindsay setting the record straight about her long-term romance with the country's most famous artist. The punning title was a direct contradiction of the way Rose was seen by the conservative side of the family, and although it was the publisher's choice and not hers, it sets the tone for the rest of the book.[6] Rose saw no reason to be ashamed of her origins as a member of the cockney under-class which provided a great number of Australia's nineteenth-century European immigrants. But in her writing she is always aware of how the middle classes, from the neighbours at Lane Cove to the wives of the respectable men of Sydney, continued to regard her. She became an artists' model because her father had left the family destitute and the money was better than slaving as a waitress, but as she wrote:

*The women of Lane Cove where I now lived, did not approve of artists' models — which apparently gave them the right to stare at me without seeing me.*

*The men smiled when their wives were not with them; the women would say good morning to my sister Alice, and ignore me.*[7]

She records meeting Norman when she was working as an art school model for Julian Ashton. Their romance started when she was seconded to meet his friend Will Dyson.

*He had already told Bill, who had just come from Melbourne, that he would get a girl for him. I was the pick. Well, he was hoist on his own petard within a couple of weeks.*

*He was living at Northwood then . . . and Bill was staying with him. His wife had gone to Melbourne for the birth of Ray. After a couple of meetings in town I was invited to Northwood to pose.*[8]

The men's game was seduction — Rose was seen as a sexually available girl who could easily be dumped when Will returned to Melbourne, and one who was also an experienced model to work with when they felt like making art instead of love. Rose, however, turned the tables on both. Photographs of her in some of the poses that recur in Norman's later work are included in Model Wife, and in all of them there is an air of sizzling sexual tension.

There are points in Rose's story that contradict Hetherington's and Norman's accounts, and as they are not necessarily to Rose's advantage they must be noted and probably believed. Katie had not gone to Melbourne in a huff, she had gone back to her family to have her second baby in a supportive environment, presumably because she was socially isolated in Sydney. Ray Lindsay was born on 26 August 1903, which gives a fairly precise starting date to the affair. Other accounts don't have Norman and Katie's marriage breaking down so early.

Norman, Rose and Will were not alone in the house. Rose notes that Lionel, who was preparing to marry Will's sister, Jean Dyson, had 'an air of disapproval' at the irregularity of introducing another woman in Katie's absence.[9] While glossing over the details, Rose makes it clear that before Katie's return she was working as Norman's exclusive model in a room in Rowe

Street. After Will Dyson went back to Melbourne, 'the trio had broken up', and Lionel, newly married, refused to come to the new studio.[10]

Rose contradicts Norman's stories that Katie was not interested in his studios by giving a graphic account of her trying to find both the studio and her husband, while Rose and Norman hid inside. The newly established couple shared many studios and alternative living arrangements over the next years, while Norman kept up the pretence of being with his family.

Although Lionel eventually accepted her as a fixture, he did not see Rose as fit to enter the same social circles as his wife. Likewise, Will Dyson did not encourage his sister to befriend his former girlfriend.

*It was in Bill's room that I met Lionel's wife, Jean. They came in unexpectedly to see Bill, so I had to be introduced. I noticed that the introducing was left to Norman, while Lionel stood back looking as though he had never seen me before, and Bill sat on his camp bed in a gloomy manner.*[11]

Rose's recollection of incidents shows her as a girl having fun, discovering details of dressmaking and fashion with the friendly assistance of young men, and the unwelcome lascivious attentions of older ones. The one older man she welcomed was Dr Robert Charles Lindsay, for many years the only member of the family to accept unquestioningly her status as Norman's lover. She treated him as a father.

It is clear from her account that Norman Lindsay did at times feel some conflict in obliging both his wife and his mistress. It is also clear that quite early in their relationship he was aware that the young, naive Rose needed to be protected in order to escape social ostracism. She was incapable of understanding that some of their fellow tenants were prostitutes until warned by Norman to avoid 'those tarts', and when he came to draw an illustration (*Three Women*) for a poem on the inevitable degradation of prostitution, she was not allowed to be the model.[12] She resented the way she was 'neglected' for this commission.

After Norman left for London in 1909, travelling with Will Dyson and Will's new bride Ruby Lindsay, Rose was left behind for some months to avoid the embarrassment of Norman openly deserting his wife and children. In this period Lionel became her moral guardian, as well as looking after Norman's financial interests, and in the end he despatched her to London when Norman asked for her. She wrote with droll humour at the way she angered Lionel when she asked for a good cabin on the ship. 'The demand for the porthole was about the last straw, but an easier way of getting rid of me than dragging me to the Gap and hurling me over,' she writes. 'Personally, if I had been in his shoes, I would have chosen the latter, gleefully.'[13]

There are brief mentions of shipboard flirtations, and men who followed her to Melbourne for romantic interludes, but in Rose's story there is only one man and his name is Norman Lindsay. He, however, is revealed as increasingly prudish as she becomes his public possession rather than his private prize. In London she is greeted with a demand to 'wipe that paint off your face', as he endeavours to pass her off as a suitable companion for an ambitious young artist.[14] On her return to Australia with Norman she is suitably modest on board the ship. When the purser from her outward voyage asks why there are no more parties and moonlit dances, her reply is brief: '"Had my wings clipped", I told him'.[15]

From the time they returned to Australia in 1911, Rose was effectively administering Norman's career.[16] During World War I, when Lionel came to Springwood to teach Norman etching, it was Rose who learnt 'the dirty jobs: cleaning copper, filing the edges, grounding and smoking the plates and printing progress proofs'.[17] And it was Rose who kept the records of each edition.

In this story, Lionel is the loyal brother, helping find a house at Artarmon for the couple on their return from England, as they were openly living together. It is clear from Rose's account, as it is in no other, that Katie Lindsay (whom she always called 'Kate') did not permanently leave Lavender Bay for Brisbane until she learnt that Rose had returned to Sydney with Norman.[18]

Throughout most of *Model Wife* Rose writes of men, not their wives. She is constantly aware that 'respectable' women will not meet her. On the voyage home from England she sat with fellow passengers, lounging on the deck chairs, writing letters and diaries:

*Sitting well back and pretending to read a book, I was able to glance at their writing. Mrs Heddle wrote, 'Norman Lindsay is aboard; a girl (not his wife) is constantly with him.' Alex wrote, 'I'm sitting here with Norman Lindsay and his tart — both bore me.'*[19]

According to Rose, Lionel hid his visits to the illicit couple from Jean. However, he fades away from the narrative for reasons which are never explained. The eldest Lindsay son, Percy, and Norman's father Robert Charles were the only other two regular family visitors to Springwood, although in London Rose and Norman did meet regularly with Robert Lindsay who was leading a life of bijou elegance. But when Robert was out walking in the street with his man friend, he 'passed us with an unknowing glance, either he did not want his friend to meet us, or us to meet his friend'.[20] Robert, through his homosexuality, and Norman, through his choice of heterosexual partner, were both social exiles in a world of conformity.

Rose's life was increasingly constrained by her social invisibility. In London she was snubbed by Ruby and Will Dyson, because she was a mistress and not a wife. In Sydney the writer Louis Stone brought his wife to meet Rose, but spoke sternly to Norman on the need to marry her.[21]

Rose showed her diplomatic and managerial skills when she neglected to post Norman's scathing letter to Stone,[22] just as she did not post Norman's letter withdrawing his works from a London exhibition after they were criticised as sexually depraved.[23] Rose did not see the change in status from mistress to wife as a milestone in her career. She was more concerned that the children, who precipitated the event, would not turn out to be part of a saccharine family circle, but rather would end up as two young mischief makers.

*Usually when they got pally it meant something treacherous was at hand. Such as selling my wedding ring and their father's discarded gold dental plate at the old-gold shop — this at the tender age of fourteen. Their defence was airtight. I had never worn the ring before I was married and seldom did after.*[24]

Marriage did change Rose's status in the eyes of some people. She was invited to functions as 'the artist's wife', while before marriage she was expected to remain modestly invisible. But some never forgot. Even after Rose's marriage, 'Miss [Thea] Proctor graciously did not notice me', which seems odd, as Thea Proctor was very well known both as an artist and as the extremely close personal friend of the artist George Lambert.[25] But the change in status meant that Rose and Norman were now asked to invite visiting celebrities, including Nellie Melba and a Siamese Prince, to Springwood.[26] And, in a final sign of acceptance, 'Frank Fox (long since Sir Frank) asked us to lunch at the Café Royale with Madame, his wife, who was very gentle and sweet; both of us forgetting that Madame did not care to know me in the early days'.[27]

Reading Rose's barbed accounts of social snubs was to be confronted yet again with the shock of how much attitudes have changed in less than one lifetime. Rose and Norman's scandalous relationship of the early twentieth century is banal and suburban today. Was it that they were living the life of the future, or was it that their non-marital status helped create that future for us? Would Robert Lindsay have remained a social exile if he had been alive today? I had a sudden mad vision of Robert as the toast of Sydney, designing amazing costumes for the Gay and Lesbian Mardi Gras, and the young Rose rising to stardom in the social set, by virtue of her affair with the famous artist.

After the birth of her daughters, Rose befriended Norman's adult sons from his first marriage, finding she now had the intellectual strength to tease them about their passion for Freud and their admiration for their father.[28] It is as though, with her own newly established status as mother of Norman's daughters, Rose could be magnanimous to the sons.

*Model Wife* ends in the 1930s, just after an extended trip to Europe and America. This is the time at which, according to Hetherington, Norman left Rose. Did this very open woman really keep the secrets of the bad years of her marriage?

'There was more,' said Helen Glad, as we talked over coffee. 'She sent a final section off to Ure Smith, but it got lost after they decided not to publish it.'

If the last section of *Model Wife* was as frank as the first part I could imagine a publisher 'losing' an account which at the very least would be socially embarrassing and was most likely defamatory. But Rose Lindsay had already made arrangements in case the wowsers suppressed her story. It was such a brilliant idea that I found myself chortling with glee as I sat in the Mitchell Library and realised the full impact of the model wife's strategy.

# 7
# Rose's manuscript secrets

In order to protect her posthumous reputation and to verify the account of her life in *Model Wife*, Rose placed the supporting papers for her story in the Mitchell Library. This was one of the secrets of Manuscript 742. It was the complete documentation to prove that she was the hard-working, hard-done-by wife of a famous artist.

In addition, this woman, with little or no formal education, had found a truly creative use for library manuscript collections. She had found how to turn history into a time-bomb. As if anticipating the way in which the later part of her autobiography would be 'lost' by the publisher, she had placed in the library letters which justified her conduct and damned her enemies, and the restriction on access meant that anyone who could dispute her version would be safely dead when it was lifted. When it came to marital wars, and thwarting a man who passionately wanted to be one of the immortals, Rose Lindsay took no prisoners.

But Rose was more than a vengeful wife smiting her enemies with ancient letter bombs. She was the complete family archivist, keeping letters which linked Norman to the leading literary figures of his day, preserving letters, poems and plays by Jack; keeping letters from her mother-in-law Jane — and, what I had originally yearned for, letters from Lionel. I started to ask myself about the strong sense of family obligation she so obviously felt, her sense of duty to those who were connected to her through kinship or friendship, and her singleness of purpose in executing long-term revenge through the public library system. In *Ma and Pa*, the first volume of her autobiography, she had written of childhood poverty when her father deserted his family and left them homeless.[1] Rose knew that needy families only survived if they stayed together.

In the end I found myself seeing these thousands of letters as a complex, if disjointed, account, a story with no heroes (although the twenty-year-old Jack Lindsay is rather splendid) and one heroine — Rose herself.

~

The epic tale which she constructed in these pieces of private correspondence is of a family which is intimately entwined with the creation of art and literature, while at the same time obsessed with the more basic passions of sibling rivalry and sexual jealousy. It is a story of people who were, on the surface charming, and apparently frank, who wrote hostile damaging letters about their closest friends and relatives, and were distraught when called duplicitous. Rose's story is there in the Mitchell manuscripts in her own words, in expressions of hypocrisy from her enemies, and in expressions of sympathy from those who, in other contexts, were less than kind. There is also the gradually changing relationship between Rose and Norman — from passionate love, to the social order of marriage, to the distance of separation.

Rose occupies an interesting position in the Lindsay story. Both of Norman's parents came from families where there was a history of young men falling in love with inappropriate (working-class, usually Catholic) women, and, as a consequence, leaving home for overseas or interstate. Less than a hundred years before Rose cheekily posed for Norman, John Lindsay, the elder brother of Robert Charles Lindsay, had to leave Ireland for California, and about fifty years after that, Tom Williams, the brother of Jane Lindsay, had to leave Victoria for Western Australia. In both cases these moves were seen as the only way of expiating the shame of loving a girl from the 'wrong' background. Like his uncle and his great-uncle before him, Norman chose someone 'from the gutter', but stayed with her; leaving his wife and children for her. Someone judging the Norman–Rose relationship from the narrow perspective of Norman's family would see his conduct towards her as extraordinarily generous. But Rose never accepted their constraints, nor did she regard herself as a lesser being simply because her family was poor. In her eyes there was no inequality.

Her world was shaped by pragmatic concerns. She saw both men and women in terms of sexuality, power and money. Her interests were remarkably similar to those of her sister-in-law Pearl Lindsay, and it is hardly surprising to see that a friendship developed between these two women.

When reading the letters, and seeing how neatly they linked with Rose's published story in *Model Wife*, I had to remind myself that this was no accident. Rose had selected only 'appropriate' letters for the Mitchell collection. Despite the initial appearance of abundance, this is heavily edited mail. Some letters have no apparent connection to the rest of the correspondence, but their placement ensures a particular story could be given some kind of credence. And others have been cut with scissors, with potentially embarrassing revelations ending mid-sentence. Mostly those are letters by Will Dyson and Robert Lindsay.

I thought of the collections of letters which had been sold by Norman to collectors like Keith Wingrove and Harry Chaplin, and the large collection of Lindsay family papers deposited in the La Trobe Library by Lionel, Daryl and Peter. In those collections Rose was not always so favourably portrayed.[2] But this is her story, told at her pace.

The early volumes contain Rose's letters to Norman. They start with love letters written about 1909–10 when he was in Europe. Her writing style is informal, relaxed, although the spelling is eccentric. But all the Lindsays appear to have adopted their own idiosyncratic spellings of many words, and their punctuation is best described as original.

The letters show both Rose's personal insecurity at the position Norman had left her in, and a protective, almost maternal, love for him. 'Kiddie are you very very fond of me?' she wrote. She always called him 'Kiddie' in the early years. 'I want badly to be with you and Oh I do hope we wont have to be apart again.'[3]

It was an empty life with her true love so far away. All she could find to do was dressmaking. 'O Kiddie this is an awful damn life,' claims another letter. 'The days never end. If it wasn't for the reeding of books and the washing of bumble I don't know what I'd do.'[4]

But after some time the tone changes to a coy defensiveness. 'I have not seen any of the studio friends. at all. And so far there has been no more trouble with any men. I have not met any. I tell you this in case you think I'm not writing all I do.'[5]

But then I turned to volume six of the letters and found Lionel's version of the same story. From these letters, and others collected by Harry Chaplin, it is clear that Norman and Lionel Lindsay were extraordinarily close from the 1890s until shortly before the end of World War I. Lionel was so obviously proud of Norman's talents and uncertain of his own, and for many years deferred to Norman as the superior artist.[6] Lionel had looked for work in Sydney largely because his brother was there. Lionel had also served Norman's interests with Rose. It is clear from his letters that he owed no loyalty to Katie, whom he did not see as a fit wife for the great man who was his brother.

In order to conceal Rose's existence from Katie, Rose had been given the pseudonym 'George' by Norman, Lionel and their friends. The very expensive social life of 'George' is one subject Lionel discussed with Norman.

*. . . This since you left would swear she's been spending £3.10 a week. I don't cite these instances for mean economy's sake but just to show you how much consideration you can expect from any but a devoted woman. — And I thought that George had some of your interests at heart . . .* [7]

One of the myths that Rose and Norman wove about Lionel was that he was mean with money. There is a letter from Lionel to Norman which gives his opinion on Rose's travel arrangements. It also shows the zeal with which Lionel executed his mission of acting in his brother's interests, and indicates why Rose was suddenly delivered to Norman in London some months earlier than originally planned.

*. . . I've been a good deal worried about this business of George. I had heard nothing (though I had written about six weeks ago) from her. She was much perturbed after your departure, looked thin and not well. I advised her to forget her pains and that moping was a fools game for her health — to go, all this summer, in for surf bathing as a cheerful, healthy occupying business. I told her that if she did the six months would go quickly and she'd be all the better for the exercise. After that seeing her a couple of times at the L. H. [Lone Hand], the last was a letter saying she had just dined with [probably Bernhard] Wise, Julian Ashton and Count somebody or other. There was a note of vanity in the letter, and I felt inclined to write to her in a cave canem view, but I thought that possibly Ashton had asked her and though I knew that Wise to be a perfect <u>cureur de dames</u> never suspected his interest . . . this last week came as a letter recounting your cable, and another with your second. I met George, took her to lunch and had an uncle's talk to her. It strikes me that have been having a good time at Chesters she seems a bit apathetic about going which gave me the sense of a bad omen.* [8]

'This looks like a good one,' Helen Glad said. We were going through stacks of old family photographs, trying to sort out possible illustrations for this book.

The photograph showed Rose on a Sydney beach, wearing a stylish black swimming costume. She is turning to face the camera with a smile, her slim, pale beauty offset by the bronzed hero hauling in a fishing net. Rose had written in pencil on the back: 'Dave Smith the Boxer hauls in the fish net. photo Taken by Monty Grover. at this Time Norman was in London.'

'Who was Grover?' Helen asked.

'One of the all time greats of local journalism,' I replied. 'In 1910 he became the editor of a rundown newspaper, the *Star*, and turned it into the Sydney *Sun*, which was really the first modern tabloid in the country. He wanted Lionel to be the cartoonist, but he didn't go.' I looked again at the photo. 'Rose seems to be having fun there,' I said. 'The spunky boxer seems to be quite taken by her.'

'No wonder Norman sent for her,' Helen commented. 'I've just been cataloguing photographs for Josef Lebovic's big Sydney beach exhibition, and in 1910 respectable men wore tops on their swimmers. He really is quite risque.'

Had Grover sent the photograph to Norman to show that Rose was acting up while he was away? Or had Rose sent it herself, to arouse her lover's jealousy so that she could join him?

⁂

From Rose's perspective Lionel's letters may have been useful in showing her grief over Norman's absence and also Norman's irrational jealousy which led him to cable Lionel, asking him to spy on Rose. And they could be used as evidence of Lionel's parsimony.

But there are other readings. In addition to looking after Norman's interests in Sydney, Lionel was sending money from both himself and Norman to the Lindsay family back in Creswick. It was only when I read Lionel's letters from the early years of this century that I started to understand the full extent of the financial crisis that damaged the family. I had always assumed the Lindsay family was affluent, and that the accounts of hard times in Lionel's and Daryl's autobiographies had been exaggerated to show off their subsequent success. Now I started to read evidence which suggested that they understated the amount of assistance the Creswick home had needed.

Lionel met Rose at the *Lone Hand* office because he had taken the job of proofreading galleys in order to help support his parents and siblings. There had been some kind of financial disaster caused by Dr Robert Charles Lindsay's financial incompetence tinged with a hint of medical scandal. Lionel's own salary could support his immediate family, but the extended family needed a second income. He had not sought out rumours of Rose's active social life; the complex fiscal affairs of Katie Lindsay and her children took up enough of his time. But, acting on his brother's behalf, Lionel did confirm the stories and then sent Rose to Norman in London where Norman claimed he needed her.

A letter by Rose balances Lionel's letter to Norman and indicates the way rumours were spread in an ever-gossiping Sydney art scene:

*. . . having lunched with Lionel and talked over my going away. He was very upset over my little trouble and asked me ever so seriously if I had ever been unfaithful to you and heaps of things of a private nature he wished I'd know such as did I want it. When first we met he was inclined to be stern and alarm me bitterly for causing you not to work and being like all other women.*

*I got angry and said. Well if you're going to start like this you can go to the devil. At which he smiled and told me to be sensible. I'd made up my mind to leave in two weeks time but he has his own opinion and wanted to book me off the day after tomorrow which is quite impossible. So he's fixed me up to leave Saturday week.*[9]

It took me some time to work out the identity of the author of some letters written in strong black ink, comically misspelt, and distinctively flamboyant. They were very cut about, with sensitive sections obviously deleted. Reading further, I found one illustrated with a stylised penis, signed 'Sygned Bill Guelph Res'. 'Bill' was Will Dyson, and the subject was the very start of the romance between Norman and Rose and his place in it.

*I know I ought to write and I want to write but it seems to me that all the words and all the ideas in the world have been used up and thinking has gone stale. I want to write something that will be worth the reading but the blank sheets of paper stare at me in their spotless purity — accusative . . .*

*. . . But dear good kind Joe you might have done me for my girl but I love you and if you and me wasn't born to be pals well then I am not the handsomest honest honourable young fellow I know I am not. Well the unblessed Trinity was a happy and gay little trinity while it lasted and it had every reason so for seeing that it comprised three of the most invaluable fellers that could ever blew and they are the three over whom most of my available*

*tenderness has been shed and my dear old John, there aint much that I wouldn't sacrifice for any one of the three.*

*. . . For I am a handsome bon-viveur famous for my sining who is very fond indeed of both of you and her and he feels this parting keenly and objects to it with great shrieks in the middle of the night waking the family up.*

*. . . I reminds you that letters should not live long after being read when your child wives are within city walls!* [10]

This suggests more than a slight variation on Rose's story of how she and Norman became a couple. An 'unblessed Trinity', to be mourned in such extravagant terms, implies a ménage à trois which became a duo, rather than a series of couplings. At first this story seemed vaguely familiar to me, then I remembered why. *The Cautious Amorist*, probably Norman's first novel although it wasn't published until 1934, is based on the way a young beauty shipwrecked on a desert island convinces three men that she cares for each one alone while having simultaneous affairs with all of them. Was Norman drawing on his memories of those first few weeks with Rose when he wrote the novel? Then I read another letter:

*. . . Well how goes the gay little party — has God yet withdrawn from you those powers of vital manhood (ado) which were tottering to their fall ere I had left. Pray God he has not for the sake of two I love, ole Rose and ole Joe my spirit is ever with you — he hovers round you, delighting in your joy with great delight for though you can shut ole Bill out of some of it you can't deprive him of the gratification of knowing that some fun is coming the way of the two people round whom his affections most intimately twine and absence from the field of action has freed his mind from any discreditable emotions that were evoked by the feeling that he was the naked stranger in whose face Jove was to shut the door.*

*. . . There was a time when I seldom went to bed without a certain somebody coming up, sitting on my bed while we talked with bated breath of very tender language of another certain somebody who shall be nameless.* [11]

In Norman's own accounts of his relationship with Rose, and those written under his patronage, there is a curious skirting of the class issues surrounding the introduction of Rose Soady to his intimate life. A respectable girl, like Katie Parkinson or Jean Dyson, would not be introduced to a male friend as 'a girl to cheer his [Dyson's] Sydney stay'.[12] In the early years of this century, even in a big city, a respectable girl would not visit the home of a bachelor, nor that of a married man in the absence of his wife. These fragments are an indication that later family descriptions of Rose as practically a prostitute were based on relayed accounts of her actual behaviour. Rose may have kept the letters to show how Dyson once cared for her, and also to compare his obvious passion for her with his first written account of Ruby Lindsay, the woman he later married. The first reference to Ruby is in a letter from Bill to Norman.

*. . . forth a torrent when she tells me of it. She pretends that she was angry because I seemed to think she was considering his offer. But she was angry because she saw the interfering hand of male protectorship. She a silly little buggar in a lot of ways. She thinks she is so able to take care of herself which I suppose she is but I am dam certain she doesn't know enough to save herself from the nasty compromise of herself. The foolish child resents me advising her. She has had so many of these young pricks taking on themselves the airs of guardianship that she resents my attempts to direct her faltering footsteps — I, who am a truly great man.*

*. . . But sir I bore you. She had done quids worth of work for nothing so far. She keeps every appointment Wheeler makes with a punctuality full of trepidation. He keeps them when he wants to. He insisted on her finishing work in rush thats still waiting for him. (He has got her frightened of him).*

*But I bore you.* Perce [Lindsay, for whom Ruby was ostensibly keeping house until his wedding] *says he wont allow her to have a room of her own in town, which is more or less right. I will be getting one myself she can use. Did Perce say anything to you regarding his marriage? you might tactfully remind Sanders that the 'B' [Bulletin] is our only source of income except for a bob or two from Punch so that as little delay as is convenient in . . .* [end of fragment][13]

After the death of both Ruby and Will Dyson, Norman claimed that the two had no reason to disapprove of Rose as 'they had been lovers' before their marriage.[14] This letter, probably written in 1907, with its reference to sharing a studio, may have been used by Rose to substantiate that claim. She may have thought it showed Ruby's stubbornness, or even the comparative coolness of Dyson's feelings towards his future wife. Despite its truncated nature the letter does show Dyson's admiration for Ruby Lindsay's integrity and persistence in making her way in a difficult male world. And it shows that Ruby had the kind of qualities that a man like Dyson might look for in the woman he would marry.

Some of the letters which show Rose in a neutral light appear to have been placed by her in the collection to show consistent patterns in Norman's behaviour. One of the themes is the way he always deceived those closest to him. In 1903, within weeks of Norman and Rose becoming lovers in the Northwood home, the home which was supposed to be for Katie and the enlarged family, someone, presumably Will Dyson, told Katie that her husband was involved with another woman. Norman wrote to her denying the rumours.[15] This letter verifies Rose's account in *Model Wife* that Katie was in Melbourne to be with her family when her second child was born. When Katie wrote to Norman, accusing him of being unfaithful, he replied:

*I spent all today running round this damned place trying to get some money for you which I couldn't get owing to MacLeod [publisher of the Bulletin] being away — when I came back I got your last letter. As to your anonamous correspondent weather he or she exists outside your brain I don't care a hang about. You don't imagine you're going to infect me with vagaries of the Mr Millar order. But what does affect me, and what I see behind every line you write, is the one unconscious discontented cry against me, and why — if I had merely been an acquaintance of yours, and never anything more to you than a chance lover, you would probably now think of me with kindness. Instead of which I've been a pretty good man to you, and yours, when they wanted help, and, stuck to you and never been unfaithful to you, and so I have apparently earned your complete hatred. Have I been such a bad husband to you, Katie —*

*You see, you can't persist in denying that I've been of service to you. The mere fact of having clothed fed and kept you is at least a slight service — and what else. You cry against my friends, am I to have no friends. — You speak of Mrs Elkington's return as being sent by God to give you advice.*

*Well I may be an altogether unpleasant person to you, and you may hate me as much as you please — but if my concerns are to be made the subject of conversation for your little family fireside — I think I'll have a word to say. You are reckoning without my pride and my individuality if you think I'll swallow that sort of pill.*

*Now there are only two lines of conduct open to you. If you prefer to believe me the iniquitous bad hearted cruel heartless thoughtless person that your letters make me out, well. There's nothing more to be said. We'll live apart, and you shall have a fair allowance to live on. You see, your attitude to me is not gratitude for what I've done — but indignation that I haven't done more.*

*The other line of conduct — well, you can have me still for what I'm worth — and I'm not a bad sort, Katie, and I'm willing to love you and look after you and give you all I can. I love you now, but its uphill work loving a girl who says she hates you every time she writes — Now be a sensible girl, Katie dearest, give up cursing and damning me at every turn, and give me a little affection in return for all I will give you . . .*

*Ever your pal, Norman.*[16]

I wish I knew how Rose found the letter. Perhaps Katie sent it back with other mementos of Norman after their separation was formalised, or she could have left it behind with other household goods when she finally fled to Brisbane with the children. For Rose, it must have shown a further twist of Norman's dishonesty in his dealings with women. The conventional story of Norman's life, the one told to biographers and friends, and almost certainly the one told to Rose herself, was that this marriage was, from the start, an empty shell and meaningless to both parties. Yet at the same time as Norman was in the first flush of passion for Rose, he denied her existence and tried to sooth his wife.

It appears unlikely that Norman knew Dyson was Katie's source. In a fragment of a letter to Bill, which can be dated as late 1903, Norman gives a humorous account of the preparations for Lionel's wedding but also refers to the separate household and studio established with his new lover.

*. . . But to come back to business. Her and me are doing very nicely in the room, though clouds is brewing on the horizon and storms is eminent.*

*Katie came up and knocked firmly on the door today, but we laid very low and not saying a word so she went away again. So out I goes silently round the block and meets her comin down by accident.*

*. . . We [Rose and Norman] are settled in a house at Waverly — at which I sleep and eat Breakfast, but of the rest of the day am seldom seen by mortal eyes — save perhaps a casual observer might note at meal times a lank but thin figure wearing an extra size in boots slinking down back streets about five yards of the rear of a singularly beautiful female in a large hat.*

*. . . By the way, the trip is only postponed by a little, but if I cannot fix it for about a fortnight from now, I will have you over by the neck. For it seems to me that we are only wasting time in living thus asunder.*[17]

This is both confirmation of Rose's comment in *Model Wife*, and proof that Norman's first wife did not passively accept her new status as a subordinate to her husband's mistress.[18] The reference to a trip is presumably the journey to Melbourne in 1904 when Ruby Lindsay first met and disliked her future sister-in-law.

There is no other direct correspondence with Katie, even when she and Norman were finally divorced. From other letters, and their son Jack's memoirs, I knew that Katie had first moved to Brisbane near the Elkingtons when Norman was in England. Her movements and her financial irresponsibilities are recorded in letters from Lionel to Norman.

After Norman and Rose began openly living together in Sydney, Katie settled in Brisbane where she lived as 'Mrs Norman Lindsay', but without a husband. The best description I have read of the fugitive persona of Katie Lindsay comes from Jack in his autobiography, *Life Rarely Tells* :

*She had a knack of making friends with anyone on sight and could never pass an empty house without trying to get inside and see what was there . . . (Always I see her in a parasol-nimbus, a glistening underwater fluorescence of shadow, listening.)*[19]

Jack also records the way his mother gradually lost any sense of her own self as she moved from boarding house to rented house, always searching for a centre of existence that somehow evaded her with the end of her marriage. When Lionel arranged for a formal deed of separation, Katie 'was extremely miserable and gave all Norman's pictures and drawings to Mary [Elkington]. From this moment she went steadily down into a distractedness that ended in a settled melancholia'.[20]

Rose's papers show that in 1918 Katie was presented with a *fait accompli*, a divorce settlement organised on her behalf without her knowledge, which finally gained her grudging consent. The key letter in this is written to Norman by William MacLeod, the managing director of the *Bulletin*, who was acting as Norman's agent to ensure that the divorce occurred before Rose gave birth to Norman's child.

Norman appears to have made a lifelong practice of arranging for others to manage the financial side of his life. In his early years it was Lionel, and late in his life it was the solicitor Alan Renshaw. From the time he was first involved with Rose she was both his studio assistant and secretary. In the period just after World War I when the final quarrel with Lionel was in its early stages, either Bertram Stevens of *Art in Australia* or William MacLeod tended to his more complex affairs.

MacLeod wrote:

*My dear Lindsay,*

*As promised I visited Brisbane last Monday and interviewed Dr Elkington and opened up the question of your divorce. Provided adequate provision was made for the support of the mother and children he was favourable to the scheme, and made an appointment for me to meet Mrs Lindsay at his home in the afternoon. In the interval he prompted his wife to break the matter to Mrs Lindsay and to advise that it would be to her interest to apply for a divorce.*

*When we met at Elkington's house your wife consented to the proposal provided that alimony was granted equal to her present allowance and that you would secure to her one half of your Bulletin dividends in the event of your death. Also you are to make her a gift in cash and pay all legal and other expenses entailed by the action.*

*With regard to the cash gift. She at first wanted a £1000 to buy a house, this sum I said would be fatal to the whole matter, but I gather from Dr Elkington that he can persuade her to accept a couple of hundred pounds.*[21]

Letters in other collections show how close Norman was to Jack Elkington, a friendship which endured after Norman left Katie and the children.[22] In her divorce settlement, Katie was placed in an unwinnable position, with no one to act as her advocate, and the world of reasonable men was opposed to her.

One of the other underlying themes of the letters is the friendship and then the feud between Norman and Lionel Lindsay's. This sprang, in part from the older brother's feeling that he was exploited by the younger, both as a secretary and as a researcher of source material. Lionel emerges as the major source for both Norman's art and his fiction: he was a library of a man just waiting to be opened and plundered. In about 1915, when Norman started his series of pen and ink drawings based on the life of François Villon, Lionel provided more than the original idea and the literary source.

He wrote:

*I take it you will illuminate the text by any suggestion in it that illustrates the life and character of François. The thing will be to cram the book with dissolute pranks, lawlessness, the fear and attraction of black death, the pangs of hunger and love, Gothic architecture; I have some great photographs to help you there!*[23]

The events that changed the balance between the brothers and led to their final quarrels are recorded in great detail. The death of their father in late 1915 and the attempt by both of them to write some fiction about the Creswick of their boyhood (which Lionel soon abandoned), the borrowing of Lionel's boyhood diaries for Norman's fiction, and Lionel's responses are all there. The key event which finally tore the brothers apart is skimmed over.

There are a few letters from the young soldier Reg Lindsay on conditions in the Ballarat training camp, then Mary's curt note about the official telegram to say that he was killed in action. In letters in the La Trobe Library, Norman refers briefly to conversations with him from beyond the grave. But why did Norman feel he could speak to his dead brother?

Some years ago I came across Reg Lindsay's last letter. It is pasted in the inside cover of one of the books Harry Chaplin sold to the Fisher Library. Reg, who was nine years younger than Norman, was not concerned with art. He was a man's man who loved beer, girls and an outdoor life. In 1915 he joined the AIF and went to war. He missed out on Gallipoli, but was in the trenches at Ypres by the next year. On 29 December 1916 a friend was going on leave, so he wrote an uncensored letter to Norman. Reg's letter is laced with deadpan wit as he wrote of lice and death, rats, rotting corpses and mud in winter on the western front:

*If we have to hang out here till the going gets hard enough to spring off — well! Our spring wont have as much bight in it as it had before — Its the survival of the hardest. Chaps crack up everyday — cannot weather it — the continual mud is a heart breaker. If its not mud and drizzle — its frost and bitter cold — that thaws and the goings worse than ever — snow and sleet vary the discomfort — Yes its a great show.*

*. . . Wandering over the ridge the other day in search of firewood — which is hellish scarce — hunting through old Hun trenches and dugouts — I couldn't help going back to look at a dead Hun I had passed — Laying on the broad of his back — head and shoulders twisted slightly sideways, rifle on the ground that had fallen off his left shoulder — the right withered hand tightly holding a bomb, which he had evidently been on the point of throwing before he was knocked.*[24]

Reg Lindsay died on 31 December 1916, two days after this letter was written. By the time Norman read it he knew of his death, so it must have seemed like a message from beyond the grave. Reg had told his famous cartoonist brother that the men at the front admired his propaganda cartoons and that he wanted Norman to keep on attacking the anti-conscription movement: 'they are too despicable to live'. And so Norman made propaganda posters throughout the war, with the German army as a giant monster, and heroic Australian soldiers whose firm-jawed features bore an uncanny resemblance to those of the dead Reg.

Reg's death was probably one of the triggers for Norman's belief in spiritualism, which his mother interpreted as a return to her fundamentalist Christianity. When Lionel was ill Norman wrote to him that 'Reg told us you had it, but that there was nothing to fear'. Mary was prepared to believe in order to keep Norman's friendship, but Lionel could not although he did feel that spiritualism had added depth to his brother's art.[25] He had a point. Several of Norman's early etchings show a dramatic contrast between a world of shadows and the glory of an imagined immortality.

Ongoing grief at Reg's death, and the way Norman denied it through his experiments with spiritualism, contributed to the dissolution of the friendship of the brothers. But Lionel was also depressed by Reg's death —his subsequent feelings of worthlessness were expressed in constant letters to Norman. At the very end of the war, almost two years after Reg's death, Lionel wrote of his life, 'And nothing well enough done to be looked back with honest pride. It makes me think that the man who should have died in France was not poor Reg but one easier spared.'[26]

Grief alone was not enough to end such a close working relationship. Ultimately the friendship between the two foundered because Lionel felt that Norman was both exploiting his goodwill and failing to take his artistic career seriously. Norman, in his turn, saw Lionel as a constantly complaining, self-obsessed, mediocre artist.

Lionel wrote:

*I write to you with some inquietude and not a little bitterness of spirit, for I can see with that 'werry fine edge' of Sam Weller's that you and I are upon some road of divergence.*

*With the clear sight of 43 —* de sans nassis *as Master Francis [Villon] says, I see that the long and devoted interest to you and your work which like a succubus has weakened my initiative — is today repaid — and I speak only of a spiritual repayment — by an apathy to me and my work which I believe unworthy of the man I have ever loved in you. Wrongly or rightly, I have come to the conclusion, that friendship with you is as base an affair of artistic utility . . . I have come reluctantly to the conclusion that your preferences in friendship are due to the vampirism of your talent demanding fresh chorus of stimulus, or to some other motive, I can only just surmise.* [27]

And Norman was less than frank in his dealings with his passionate brother. In one letter he wrote:

*Your heroes always were demigods, but it is you who supply the emblem of demigodliness, not they. But do you think, if I laugh at [Christopher] Brennan [the well-known poet] a little, I also laugh at you? What is most lovable in you only shows me what is least lovable in Brennan.*

*. . . Do you think I claim to be a better man than you because I claim to see through liars and emotionalists more easily than you can?*

*. . . Dear Joe I love you for your love of these impostors. When I see you lavishing respect on a disgruntled little weevil like [Walter] Jeffrey [editor of the* Evening News*], a spectral lecher like [John] Le Gay Brereton [poet, later Professor of English Literature at Sydney University], a black Calvinist like [George] Robertson [founder of Angus & Robertson], and base belly-hound whats-his-name, I can only see a fine heart letting its generosity be trampled on by pigs.*[28]

But shortly afterwards Norman was writing to Rose in rather less temperate tones:

*It seems that he [Lionel] now goes round saying that I have admitted that he understands my point of view, but that he completely rejects it. This is the use he makes of my pleasant note to him, and it is the last straw. I shall never have anything to do with the animal, who is beneath further consideration. I thoroughly dislike him and am not going to pretend anything else, and now I shall kick him at every opportunity.*[29]

It was a strange privilege, reading the ebb and flow of this fight between brothers in the bound pages of books in the Mitchell Library. My first knowledge of the quarrel had come from reading Norman's letters, both in the La Trobe Library and in Howarth and Barker's edited *Letters of Norman Lindsay*. I already knew of Norman's denial of death and faith in a world of spirits.

*Death is not a thing to shudder at, but to look forward to. If it were not for one thing I must do before I die, if I have the luck, I would be glad to start on this adventure tomorrow.*[30]

Both brothers had the advice and sympathy of their partners as they moved apart. There are no letters by Jean Lindsay, but both Peter and Bingo told me they remember her urging Lionel to stop putting Norman's interests ahead of his own. After reading *Model Wife* I expected to find that Rose had always disliked Lionel. In the early 1920s she perfected the art of the sardonic comment at Lionel's expense, claiming 'the Brute' was always trying to sell his pictures ahead of Norman's, and that his 'bitter Dyson home' was 'all bunkum pose'.[31] She also reported with glee the joke a Melbourne dealer apparently made about 'L.L.' standing for ££. Then I found that in December 1915 Rose had written to Lionel asking him to be the executor of her will: ' You would be the only one I could trust to look after Norman's interests. He would be so hopeless on his own'.[32] I'd found that one in the La Trobe Library. Was it simply family loyalty that made Rose echo Norman's opinion of his brother? Or was it that Lionel only ever supported Rose's presence as a studio model and mistress? He certainly facilitated Norman's continuing connection with Rose, but there is no record of him supporting either a divorce or remarriage. The only letter by Lionel that I could find on the matter was one cautioning Norman against divorce because of the consequences for his relationship with his sons. It was therefore in Rose's interests as she moved towards motherhood and marriage to encourage the inevitable rift between her lover and his brother.

# 8

# *Mistress and wife*

In 1919 Norman wrote a long and confused letter to Bertram Stevens, the editor of *Art in Australia*. While much of the letter concerned Stevens' failure to admire *Creative Effort* and attacked Lionel for being 'too fond of the smell of witchburning for my fancy', the letter has two references to another concern. Norman wrote that 'since Rose and I set about trying to produce life itself', he had avoided the air of Sydney which was likely to cause illness.[1] His attitude was in part coloured by the 1919 Spanish influenza pandemic which was to kill Ruby, and in any case, Norman was constantly anxious about illnesses. But it also showed a sense of preciousness about any child he and Rose may have. In another passage in the same letter Norman writes of his fear that any illness suffered by him 'would put me beyond the possibility of doing something I had set out to do, which was the bringing to life of a child by Rose'.[2]

This is in marked contrast with Norman's attitude towards Katie's pregnancies, which had either been dreaded or accepted as part of the normal lot of women. Rose and Norman lived together for over fifteen years before starting a family. So why the change? For Norman, World War I, with the death of his father and brother, made him realise that even he might be mortal. He had lost contact with his sons, who were now well into their teens, and he felt the need to somehow continue himself. For Rose's part, she may have wished to marry, as the conventions of middle class morality made her *persona non grata* without a wedding ring. A child could be an excuse for precipitating the event, or it could simply be that once she reached her thirties Rose realised that the time for safe childbirth would soon be over.

The decision to have a child preceded the divorce from Katie, but also precipitated it. By the time of Rose's first pregnancy, fear of the influenza pandemic meant that she stayed in the mountains where a local doctor was unable to manipulate a transverse presentation when she was in labour. The child was still-born, and Rose almost died.

Rose spent her next two pregnancies in a nursing home in Strathfield where Jane Lindsay was born on 16 January 1920, two days after her parents were married. Because Norman worked in Springwood, the family was separated at this time for weeks on end. Later they were apart when baby Jane was ill and Rose stayed with her at the nursing home. Rose would also take the children on seaside holidays while their father worked at home. Their letters show that at a time when Norman was apparently soaring on Olympian heights, he was totally emotionally dependent on Rose. When Jane was ill in hospital he wrote:

*Dearest, if you want my love, I want yours. The only thing I fear is pain for you. You know that I would hang onto life to the last gasp to be with you.*

*. . . No two people ever came closer to each other. Let us make that knowledge our happiness. I love you now as never before, my dear girl.*[3]

By contrast, Rose's letters of this period are more matter of fact, concerned with money and with snippets of gossip, usually about Lionel. When their second child, Helen (nicknamed Honey) was born Rose wrote pragmatically of their possible finances in the event of Norman's death.

*. . . the promises made to Creswick people would cut 3 quarters into everything you leave and I have still to start and save for their lump sums. And I do think that you must think of Creswick before you do of anyone else.*

*This is a dismal sort of Lionel Lindsay letter and I do hate to write it but I do want you to think over it. Well I notice that your passion for responsibility is developing with your age.*[4]

The enmity that Norman and Rose now felt towards Lionel led them to demonise him as a constantly whingeing, money grubbing tyrant, who only made art in order to sell it. This was in marked contrast with their perception of Norman's art which sold extremely well, on its own merits.

There were other deaths in the Lindsay family in the years following the death of Dr Lindsay and Reg, and these appear to have been one of the factors in reconciling the conservative Creswick Lindsays to Rose. There are references in both the La Trobe and Mitchell papers to the way that Pearl's husband, Colin McPhee, committed suicide, leaving her with three young children and no means of support. Norman and Lionel both came to the rescue, increasing the already considerable financial burden of supporting the Creswick household. Then in March 1919, just after Rose had lost her first child, word came from London that Ruby Lindsay had died.

The links between Creswick and Rose grew slowly, and although the letters on both sides were written with remarkable intimacy, Rose never visited her husband's boyhood home, nor did old Jane Lindsay ever come to Springwood. Initially the ice was broken with a visit by Mary, brought to Springwood by Norman in 1918. After this visit, Jane wrote to Norman, thanking him for the presents chosen by Rose for her and her daughters: 'I couldn't understand how Rose could have chosen what was wanted and what was most acceptable to each of us'.[5] A year later Rose received a clearer expression of acceptance when Norman reported she was away on a holiday after losing the baby: 'It was wise of you to give your girl a holiday,' Jane wrote. 'She must be a splendid girl and one so faithful is hard to meet with these days.'[6]

It is fairly clear why Rose kept these letters. In their generosity and old-fashioned loving kindness, they totally contradict the tyrant mother of the Lindsay myth. They also show that at least until the mid–1920s when the correspondence ends, Norman had a close and loving relationship with his mother. The bullying matriarch who was fictionalised in his novels *Redheap*, *Saturdee*, and *The Cousin from Fiji*, has vanished, and in their place is a pious woman, caring so much for her unconventional son that she will accept his relationship with Rose, simply because she is part of his world.

After his mother's death, at Norman's request, his brother Robert burned many family papers, including some of Norman's letters. By then Norman was embarrassed by his spiritualist phase which he had left behind him, and he also wished to perpetuate the story of the hostile mother.[7] But Rose kept the letters addressed to her and some of those sent to Norman, as well as some of Mary's. From these it is clear that after Reg's death Jane was so determined to embrace her wayward son that when she heard he had been talking to the dead Reg, she incorporated Norman's spiritualism into her fundamentalist Protestant faith.

*The whole of your letters is a wonderful delight to me & fills me with love & praise. I have always felt that there was a great work going on in your minds, or as you say conscious, & that it was through your arts you would speak, & show the world the beauty of your mind through the beauty of your work.*

> . . . I know all the beautiful thoughts which you give me in your letters they fill me with such happiness & open out such a new life, new & lovely thoughts and this beyond to writing . . .
> . . . Now about our Reg. How wonderfully plain & reassuring all Reggy's answers are; the perfect happiness that is waiting for us, the joy of our dear ones who have gone before & how true; that it is living that is so painful, ever living misunderstood causes such pain.
> . . . I love reading my children's letters & usually I read one of yours when I get into bed so my last thoughts are full of lovely remembrances of you my very precious son.

Jane had a spiritual experience of her own on the night of Reg's death, which sustained her belief in ghostly visitations. While she was praying at his bed, she had heard her son call her name and knew that he was dead. 'I do not think it strange my Reg called to me,' she wrote to Lionel at the time. 'For he knew I was sleeping in his room and he also knew that it was there I prayed for him and many a night when he was at home with me I have stood beside his bedside, looking at his young face and countless prayers went up to God for him.'[9]

Lionel did not take his mother's vision as anything other than the folly of a religious mind. December 31 was also Daryl's birthday, and there were two Lindsay boys fighting in France. It was only natural that his mother would think of both sons that night. There is a sense of a rift with Lionel in many of Jane's letters to Norman, a rift she believed was caused by his failure to share her faith. She hoped that like Norman he too would come to believe in the goodness of God. From this, even in the absence of Norman's letters, it is easy to guess that Norman probably implied a belief in traditional Christianity to comfort his mother in her grief.

By the time of Rose's second successful pregnancy (after her marriage to Norman), Jane had completely welcomed her into the family circle and wrote letters of comfort to her new daughter-in-law.

> . . . I always felt when my hour of trouble came that God was very near to me & I want you to feel the same, just ask his help & he will help you dear Rose.
> . . . I want you to know that I love you not only for all you have been to Norman, but for your own self. The great courage you have always shown in very distressing circumstances have shown me this true & loving woman that I feel you are.
> God Bless you dear.[10]

## MISTRESS AND WIFE

In the following years Rose became Jane's confidante, the recipient of information about Mary and Pearl, that Jane could not discuss at Creswick. Sometimes she marvelled at the insights of Rose's wisdom and understanding, not knowing that Rose and Norman were corresponding with Mary (and probably also Pearl, although few such letters have surfaced). Because she administered Norman's affairs, Rose became the dispenser of largesse to her husband's extended family, accepting obligations that he would not have undertaken on his own.

As Norman Lindsay's wife and the mother of his daughters, Rose became a force in Sydney's artistic circles — she was described in contemporary accounts as 'magnificent' and 'forceful', but also 'domineering'. This confident woman of the 1920s who was photographed by Harold Cazneaux, all draped in respectable white, is hardly recognisable as the saucy wench photographed by Norman in her underwear. There are a few hints in the letters that her husband was not happy with the change from artist's model to gracious muse. And then there was the problem of the changing nature of their sexual relationship. For most of their time together Norman and Rose had used contraceptives. Robert Charles Lindsay ensured that all his sons knew how to avoid both the hazards of unwanted pregnancies and venereal disease. After the accidental birth of Jack, Norman took no chances. Then, for about five years while Norman and Rose were trying to have children, there were no inhibitions, no artificial barriers to pleasure. But by the early 1920s matters had changed. The tantalising mistress who had become the available wife insisted that her husband use the unpoetic barriers of mechanical contraception. Norman in Springwood wrote to his son Jack in Sydney:

*At the last moment it occurs to me that I am out of French letters. (I perceive a fine spectacle of the ingenious inventor of those speeding through space pursued by the insensate millions who have suffered a temporary period of strangulation in their abortive effort to escape back to earth in a rubber bag) but feminine terror of those lurking embryos demands the employment of his artistry, so will you get me a pounds worth.[11]*

Rose had good reason to fear pregnancy. A letter from her gynaecologist written after Helen's birth indicates that another pregnancy could be fatal.
 . . . *I am very glad to know you are better that you have reached a state of 'harmony with your environment'. that's a good phrase. Keep there.*
 . . . *Keep good. Keep happy. Count your blessings they are all more than some people possess. You have two babies. Lots of people would give*

*their health for one. And you have Norman. Bless him and keep him and yes you have me as a little friend so there you are —* [12]

And then there was the problem of Jack. It had not been Norman's idea to initiate contact with the sons of his first marriage. The Mitchell letters show that it was Bert Stevens, the editor of *Art in Australia* (who met Jack when he accompanied his mother to Sydney for the divorce), who then urged Norman to at least show some interest in his brilliant offspring. I knew about Jack's childhood and youth from his own account in *Life Rarely Tells* and *The Roaring Twenties*. His uncle, Jack Elkington, after whom he had been named, had arranged for him to attend Brisbane Grammar where he flourished, won scholarships, and ultimately became a classical scholar at the University of Queensland. Because his mother always refused to criticise his father, Jack retained an idealised vision of Norman, even though his father never once wrote.

The two volumes of letters and manuscripts from Jack start passionately and lovingly with a note written after Norman, his neglectful parent, sent him some prints and an affectionate if somewhat pompous letter claiming: 'I have long wished and intended to write to you, but have waited until it might be easier for us to communicate without the stress that time and circumstance have forced on our relations.'[13]

*Dear Daddy* [the nineteen-year-old scholar wrote],

*How can I express the absolute joy with which I found your letter awaiting me in the Men's Common Room at the University — the moth that found the Star within its reach: Tantalus in his arid centuries getting a draught of desired water — no simile can express the heart-leap I had when I saw your writing and opened that package. There can be no mis-understanding between us — there never could have been: my vision of Beauty coincides too entirely with yours ever to admit of that. Though I cannot draw — yet my silence is full of the same unapparent passions as your full music. I believe flamingly in Life, naked and unashamed, before the divinity in it was shamed into clothes and prudery by convention — and in Love, the crown of Life, and all its lusts.*[14]

Jack settled in Sydney after graduating, and formed a close adoring relationship with Norman. The stimulus of the brilliant Jack can be observed in both sides of the correspondence, as Jack left his father's letters at Springwood when he went to Europe. It was when I was reading Jack's later letters, and the responses Norman made to them in letters to other people, that I started to sense how

Norman was so easily able to imagine his son an enemy. Despite having the appearance of a wide social circle, Norman Lindsay conducted most of his communications by mail.

As a freelance artist, Norman Lindsay drew his *Bulletin* cartoons at home and sent them down to Sydney by mail. Norman had some dealings with his editor, but rarely ventured out of Springwood. Because he was so isolated, it was easy for him to see plots where none existed, to have both fantasies and suspicions concerning of the world outside; to brood over letters and to imagine offences where none were intended.

When visitors came, they came by appointment, usually for the weekend. Later, there were parties, organised by Rose, featuring the conspicuous consumption of Norman's wealth. The successful artist had servants and luxury cars, but all was not well. In his old age Norman claimed that 'the major cause of disruption in all marriage is sexual discontent, no matter what febrile excuses that discontent may snatch at to relieve its oppression'.[15] He sounds as though he were writing from personal experience.

―

Even though I had first read the letters of Margaret Coen in 1985, I could not write about them until after her death in 1993. People have the right to live their lives in some kind of privacy, but the dead belong to history. Rose filed Margaret's letters so that her story should be told, took them out of Norman's reach so that he could not prevent the telling, and placed them in the library to expose the identity of Norman Lindsay's secret mistress, who, as the wife of Norman Lindsay's friend, Douglas Stewart, appeared to be a woman without an adventurous past.

Douglas and Margaret's daughter, Meg Stewart, wrote in her mother's biography that Margaret was originally brought to Springwood by Dick Hore, a fellow commercial artist.[16] Years before, Norman had taught her cousin, Jack Flanagan, and she had long dreamed of the great artist on the mountain who could, perhaps, give her enlightenment. By the end of the weekend he was advising her on watercolour technique and had invited her to come again.

The first extant letter from Margaret to Norman is a 'fan letter', written in praise of *Redheap*, which had just been banned. He had given her a copy after the second visit.

*Redheap's absolutely spiffing. I abandoned all work etc to read it and retired to bed on Saturday night after having read and reread it, worn to a frazzle with laughing. I think that the part where Millie retires to the parsonage full of gin and other things and 'Poohs' the Rev Kneebone, is priceless.*

*. . . I tried Mum out well though, reading the book in front of her, and laughing etc in on inordinate manner, also remarking that it was gorgeous, but she really must prepare herself for Mr Lindsay's frankness, and then saying that Grandma Coen would not like the book, (Grandma Coen is 86 and still runs M Coen General Importers). Anyway Mother at length cried out. 'Oh tell us some of the hot bits Peg' which I did sparing her nothing.*

*. . . I've had a lovely time with the paint box, indulging in nudes and cats, I suppose I'll really have to control myself where the cats are concerned, I think the nudes are improving a bit . . .*

*Regards to all — best wishes, Margaret.x*[17]

The seventeen-year-old Coen was a large young woman, embarrassed by her size, and entranced by the slightly built middle-aged man with piercing blue eyes. Norman had always admired large women, 'the dominant feminine', as he called them. But the subordinate relationship of the young artist to the old master is clear.

Shortly after this letter was received, Rose Lindsay decided that she and Norman should flee Australia because of the censorship of *Redheap*. But according to the descendants of Rose Lindsay the travel plans had less to do with the banned book, and rather more to do with Norman's interest in the beautiful young artist who was appearing as a model in some of his paintings.[18]

Although Rose placed letters in the Mitchell from Mary and Daryl commenting on Norman's affair with Margaret, she kept her own reactions hidden from future public scrutiny. There are none of the cartoons drawn by Rose, scornfully labelled 'Romeo and Juliet', showing a skinny, diminutive Norman walking with a mountainous Margaret.[19]

This then is the love interest only implied in Hetherington's book. Margaret is the reason why Norman took a studio at No 12 Bridge Street Sydney. Howarth and Barker, the joint editors of Norman's collected letters, describe this period: 'His marriage was undergoing a middle-aged strain, and the partial separation brought about by living in town with only occasional visits to Springwood relieved the tension.'[20]

There are no letters extant between Norman and Margaret for the period from 1934 to 1939 when he lived at 12 Bridge Street, two doors from her studio.

## MISTRESS AND WIFE

Most of the correspondence in the Mitchell papers dates from the early years of World War II when Norman had returned to Springwood and Margaret was ensconced in his studio. Her early awe of Norman was transformed by time into an almost maternal love. A note by Rose on one of these letters from Margaret to Norman reads: 'Feb 1942. Very amusing example of the "Puss Puss period" ', an indication that the wife found the cloying language of the mistress rather pitiful. There is a marked similarity between the tone of these letters and Rose's early letters to Norman, when she too mothered him, and managed his life.

*Dearest Puss,*

*. . . Fourteen shillings and sixpence arrived from England from 'Redheap' so I promptly put it into the bank every penny counts for Puss. that will mean a couple of models. Hilda* [Townsend] *has been painting here today with me, very glad to escape from Pop. One of your bugbiters came up and Hilda fiercely sent him about his business. I told Frith* [Art Editor of the *Bulletin*] *to be sure and send you a joke block. and told Mr Prior about your tobacco I will bring it Saturday morning. A letter came from Perth asking for an exhibition, I will bring it up to you. How is my dear Puss and Figaro his cat, I think he is a very privileged puss. I think he knows it, give my love to all the cats. I will write and let puss know when I am arriving and anxious to get a letter to puss. look after yourself and don't be too saving about meals. I really think that you should have something a bit more substantial for lunch than a sandwitch you can afford dear cat to have a nice little meal in the middle of the day I think that the country air is more stimulating than here and puss could eat a little more.*

*. . .*

*Love to dearest Puss.*
*Puss.*[21]

Well into the 1940s Margaret arranged for models for Norman, did his banking and fretted over his eating habits, all in a way that, after Rose's brittle independence, must have been comforting for a man who always demanded the services of others. Margaret continued to care for him after he returned to Springwood, and became friendly with his daughter Jane who was also living at the house. Later she continued to nurture Norman even after Rose returned from America, even to the point of directing what food his wife should cook for him.

[Drawing of a cat at the top of paper]

*Dear Puss,*

*I arrived in town safely , last night. I felt very blue leaving puss and had a weep in the train but I had no idea how beautiful and convenient everything is up there. I am getting busy on the studio so that when puss comes down he will be surprised to see how clean it is; it really is terribly fusty, it makes me think I have neglected poor puss, But you really can't get at it to clean it puss unless you can turn the whole place upside down and I could not do that with poor puss eating and sleeping here, you won't know it puss when it is nicely done out . . .*

*. . . Make sure puss that they give you a green veg every day and pears or apples. and keep up your food . . .* [22]

From references to the war to in the undated letters, it is clear that as Norman was gradually easing out of his sexual relationship with Margaret and both were turning towards a lasting friendship, she had already become involved with Douglas Stewart. Meg Stewart's *Autobiography of My Mother* dates the introduction of Stewart to Coen's circle as late 1938.[23]

Rose was not content to let Margaret speak for herself. The poet Hugh McCrae was a friend of both Rose and Norman. The following letter by McCrae to Rose was artlessly placed in the Mitchell collection.

*. . . Margaret had an affair with me lasting nearly four years. Norman probably knew about it earlier than I imagined. At any rate, I told him frankly, later — believing I was running the risk of losing his friendship, perhaps even earning his enmity. He said it was no affair of his, and hasn't changed towards me since, at all.*

*I was working extremely hard and irregularly at money-making jobs for about a year, and for the last six months of that saw little of M. One night Doug brought her over here . . . and there was a very foolish business, beginning with me smacking her face (as promised twice in advance IF) because she kept taking and drinking the drinks of rum I poured for Doug. He left the dinner table where this all happened, put on his overcoat, stumped out calling Margaret to follow, which she did.*

*He came back, advised me that he and Margaret had been 'having an affair, surely you knew that', for a couple of months . . .*

*. . . God save us! how could I have had such a happy and successful marriage without always having had a mistress? Or don't one's women friends understand these things any more than one's wife would?*[24]

The general intimacy of the letters from McCrae does lend credence to the belief of those in the Lindsay circle that Rose and McCrae were lovers.

McCrae's own letters in the Mitchell and Fisher Libraries are internally contradictory and do not lead to any great confidence in his unsupported assertions on any matter. The personality of Margaret Coen revealed in this letter is rather different from that of both the authorised accounts of her life and the memories of those who knew her well. But as Rose Lindsay would have relished reading of Margaret's humiliation, it was a satisfying letter for its recipient.[25]

Mary, who had continued her friendship with Rose, wrote to her when she heard of Norman's defection to Margaret, and offered sympathy:

*Tragic: I think — simply tragic the whole thing, of course he'd leave out the wench when it comes to writing. — Anything else would be unsafe. Lord! the last thing he wants is to give anything to help a definite separation. I see all thro these letters the feeling that you two in spite of everything, really belong — that when he's fighting you, he's fighting himself. That wench or any other wench in the universe couldn't be anything but incidental . . . Rotten about his work going absolutely fut, isn't it? Those lines about the sterility of his work made me feel like Hell, because I've felt that he's felt that for years — that its been getting less and less interesting. I tried my hardest to stop Bill Dyson & any of them who have gone for him about his work, trying to make them understand that they couldn't help — that a man had to make or mar his own salvation . . .*

*. . . Next to yourself, Norm has meant more than anyone except my mother, & I feel, next to you that I know him more than the others.*[26]

'I don't know if you have heard the news about Norman,' Daryl wrote to Mary in a letter that was sent on to Rose. 'I believe there has been a definite split with Rose — that Norman has a flat in Sydney at the Wentworth Hotel and a studio nearby. I believe its over a girl that N. is interested in and according to Sydney gossip, is living with — its all rather silly at his age —'[27] Thanks to Mary's support, Rose was able to feel less isolated, although she later realised that Mary almost certainly sent equally sympathetic letters to Norman.

The retention of undated fragments, combined with the wholesale destruction of letters from certain periods from some correspondents, makes parts of Rose's papers frustrating reading. Others who asked for their letters to be destroyed had them kept for posterity. On what basis did Rose make the decision to place letters in the library? She almost certainly kept letters by Norman's brother Robert to show the extreme repugnance she felt for him and to illustrate how Norman plundered him as a source.

If I write here that Rose probably kept letters by Mary which indicate her ignorance of childbirth so that she could mock her as a frustrated old maid, it will spoil their impact later on. But this is the point where I must ask why some letters were kept and others destroyed. I am sure Rose did destroy some of Mary's letters because her worst ones have never surfaced, although several people connected with the family have referred to their contents. I'm even aware that she and Norman wrote letters 'to history', with the obvious intention of informing a future historian. Some of these went to those assiduous collectors, Harry Chaplin and Keith Wingrove, but Rose did not trust them to reveal the dirty family linen. This too is a possible motivation for Rose depositing the papers in the Mitchell — so that family history would not become items of trade among collectors.

My favourite among the 'posterity' letters was written by Rose to Wingrove, not to Norman, but she placed a copy of it with the other papers.

June 14 53

> ... I noted that you in your last but one letter said something to the effect that I must feel some pride in my association with N.L. I certainly do not swell on that score. Any Lindsay is poison to handle. And when I look back on the years of sickness that I had to deal with, I wonder at my stupidity, and now I seem to be in for it again. No sir I do not like it. It's all very fine for admirers like you to stand off at a distance full of admiration. Which reminds me by the way that your wife must be heartily sick of the name of Lindsay — also reminds me that a friend of your Air Force days — a Frenchman was in charge of David Jones Art Gallery. Can't remember his name. On meeting me at the gallery, at once said how often he had spent nights with you going through NL's bits. He seems to be a nice bloke and should do much to put the DJ Gallery on the right track.
>
> Norman is better again after a bad few days. I despair of getting anything done that I want to do with these constant tray carrying periods — He is scribbling at something — and writing long letters particularly to Mary, letters written with an eye to Mary passing them on to Professor Burke [Joseph Burke, Professor of Fine Arts, Melbourne University] who is a keen collector. And Mary writes just as false, fulsome ones. It appears that she is now happier that Bert [Robert Lindsay] has gone. (I'd be too) She had no rest or peace with him. Now it appears that she is the one calm isolated Lady of the Manor. Surrounded by Loons ... She was furious when she found that Pearl had visited here last year. In fact she Forbade Pearl to come. She was well aware that Pearl would tell too much. I enjoyed it all.

*Apparently Mary has had drunken bouts for years. And at that I don't wonder. Bert hid it; and her doctor friend was a help all the time. Pearl said that when she took her girl to the Creswick home to be married from the old ancestral 'alls Mary enlivened the night by getting to the festive sherry. Good soul insisted on remaining home from the church service to get the food ready despite the fact that Pearl had all the food catered for in Ballarat and merely needed to be laid out. So when they got home Mary was merry and as the night wore on more so. Till she was discovered walking down the passage way completely nude. And was hustled back to her room and locked in for fear of the new groom getting a far too soon and far too intimate glimpse of his aunt by marriage . . . Pearl said that she met Mary in a lane in Ballarat once. And after a few words that didn't agree with Mary she threw herself down in the path and started screaming — to people hastening to the scene Pearl said 'Its nothing she always does this when she is crossed.'*

*I always considered Bert a tight lipped frustrated old queen. And a snob. He sent me a letter that he said he had received from his friend Lady So and So of London, full of gossip about a lady companions antics <u>(But in his own handwriting)</u> . . . Also another stunt was to send over an occasional book that we might like to read. On the leaf always in it was a book inscribed to Bert from some overseas famous author or a Duke or Duchess. Also in Bert's disguised handwriting. He played a game of makebelieve . . .* [28]

Speaking of tricks of handwriting, by the time this letter was written, Rose's handwriting had changed so that it was similar to that of Norman.

The second-hand retailing of gossip from Pearl, Mary's most hostile sibling, shows that Rose had a ribald, if malicious, sense of humour and an eye for comedy. The act of placing this letter in her own papers and addressing it to the conservative Keith Wingrove was a way of ensuring that incidents such as Mary becoming drunk at the wedding, and Robert writing his fictional histories would survive. She even manages an oblique attack on Wingrove and his obsessive courtier-like relationship with Norman Lindsay. But in telling the story, enough of Rose's essential self comes through to show why the more conservative members of the Lindsay and Dyson families continued their hostility towards her.

The letters deposited by Rose only imply the reasons she eventually left Norman to live with her daughter Jane at Hunters Hill. There are mentions of Rose's arthritis in letters from Mary, along with expressions of sympathy linked to complaints about Isabel. But was arthritis enough to cause the separation?

There are also early letters from John Hetherington about the biography, and the start of a story about why he ignored Mary in his acknowledgments. By the time Hetherington was writing to Rose she was living permanently with Jane and only occasionally visiting Springwood, driven there by Jane or Jane's husband, Bruce Glad.

I kept asking myself why the correspondence with Hetherington had stopped, and why Rose sold the papers in 1962 at the time when Hetherington was writing *The Embattled Olympian*. For some reason, Rose had decided John Hetherington was not to see the bulk of this correspondence.

As the years went past it became a nagging question, but one which had stopped being central to my interest in the Lindsays. Instead I started to mine the letters gathered by Rose and others as I tried to puzzle out the position of the complex and difficult Mary Lindsay in the family.

# 9
# *Mary*

By reading through the letters and linking them with the published books on the Lindsay family, I started to form confusing but intriguing images of Mary Lindsay, the fourth child and eldest daughter. She was the daughter at home, dutifully caring for her mother and sisters. She was the manipulative old witch despised by John Hetherington and mocked in her old age by Rose and others for her spinsterish ignorance. She featured among Norman's and Daryl's earliest memories, but was hardly mentioned by Lionel. Reading Mary's letters it was clear that this was a person of considerable literary talent. Why hadn't she taken up a career? Ruby was allowed to be an artist; surely Mary with all her family connections in journalism could have been a writer?

'Dad always said that the trouble with Mary was that she was a coward,' said Peter. 'It's not as though she didn't have the chance to achieve anything. Did you know he once arranged for her to have a journalist's job in Sydney? But she didn't take it, because she was too scared! It was easier for her to stay in Creswick and complain about her hard lot.'

'How hard was her lot?' I asked.

'She'd nursed her mother when she was old, and there was Isabel who was a bit odd, but it was hardly a difficult life. She seemed to spend most of her time writing letters about various family members, complaining about them behind their backs. She was really surprised when nobody believed her in the end.'

'She had some sense of family responsibility though,' I ventured. 'Whenever I go to the Ballarat Art Gallery there's something else they've bought with the Mary Lindsay Fund, so she must have left them money.'

'That was probably because of Daryl,' came the reply. 'Mary hated Daryl, and Joan too for that matter, but when she was sick and in the nursing home Daryl looked after her and came to see her all the time. He was the president of the Ballarat gallery, and he was always very good at getting people to give money. She didn't have any children, so she probably felt she could leave it to charity. And she was very proud of what the family had done. There was also guilt, I suppose.'

'Guilt?'

'When my grandmother died, Mary got the lot. It didn't worry Dad, but it was unfair on some of the others and there was a lot of resentment.'

'Did you ever meet her?' I asked. These Lindsays were great travellers. They spent years combing the world but, strangely, visits interstate were far less common.

'I know I saw her when I was a child, but I don't remember that,' he said. 'Then, a few years before she died, I visited Creswick with Bill Ritchie who was one of the trustees of the Ballarat gallery. Well, when we came into the room she looked at Bill and said: "Peter! I'd know that face anywhere!" And gave him a great big kiss. The joke was that she'd been talking to Bill only the week before!' He sat back in his seat and gave a big grin.' I really like that: "Peter, I'd know that face anywhere". She was the kind of person who *had* to know things, or think she did.'

In his memoirs Norman seemed to feel that Mary was owed some special tribute.

> ... she is the dominant figure of my infant days ... She seems to have taken a sort of proprietorial charge of me; all small girls have something of the school mistress in them. It wasn't at all the embryonic maternal in her, for she never had a spark of that, even loathing dolls in her small girl days. Books were her passion and they have lasted her through life ... Mary was not permitted to read fiction of any sort, for which reason she was forced to hide behind her bedroom door and read it by the small streak of light that filtered through the hinged aperture, so that she practically ruined her eyesight, and early in girlhood had to be fitted with glasses ... [1]

Norman was often less than generous to members of his family in his writing, but here he thanked Mary, who was two years his senior, for the way she had nurtured him and he damned his parents for the way she had to fight for her intellectual growth.

In maturity, the nurturing older sister became a financial dependent as the successful Norman joined with his brothers in supporting the family at

Creswick. Because Mary needed her brothers' money she could not afford to alienate any of them. Through all the family quarrels she was the one member of the family to whom they all wrote. But Mary would take Norman's part, even after the publication of *Redheap*, *The Cousin from Fiji* and *Half-way to Anywhere* when she realised how he had plundered her life to make his art.

How true then were Lionel's comments, passed on by Peter, about her 'cowardice'? Had she ever tried to escape from the straitjacket of small town life to the freedom of the metropolis? Didn't Lionel, who was always allowed adventures, notice the different treatment meted out to his sisters?

In 1893, when Mary was fifteen, Lionel had left home in search of artistic adventure. In their childhood he was the leader of the gang of Lindsay children, the one who led all rebellions against parental authority. Mary saw herself as one of three rebels in the middle of the family, along with Lionel and Norman. The eldest, Percy, was always adept at charming his way out of social obligations, while Robert remained the dutiful son. In her old age Mary complained to Daryl about the restrictions their mother had placed on them.

*Mother concentrated on Lionel, Norman and me. She was out to save our souls, and you younger ones have no idea how the poor woman took it out of herself in the process: I think Lionel, the most conspicuous member of the family, got the worst of it but, as I told Norman (and he agreed with me) that their early success was mainly due to the fact that they couldn't breathe at home, and couldn't get away quickly enough from their Mother.*[2]

The Mitchell papers hold one desperate plea by Mary, dated 1898. It was written at the time that Norman, Lionel and Percy were living precariously, making freelance illustrations and undertaking odd jobs in journalism. But they had the freedom of the city.

Mary wrote:

*This afternoon we got your letter which made us all weep. Also Perce's note he made some vile but truthful hints about your uncleanliness. Now what an advantage it would be to have me down with you. I'm a business beggar on the clean tack. You ought to see the way I keep my room — spotless: —*

*I've got Perce's sketch of the studio hung over my place of rest. I never say my evening prayers without wondering if it is as clean as it looks. Some of the Pics which are discretely slurred over look very promising — to say the least. I wonder if you regard your models like Browning's artist — 'as types of purest womanhood'.*[3]

The boys were having fun and Mary wanted to join them. But she could not imagine a world in which she was an active participant and not a handmaid. Even when she eventually travelled, it was to be as Robert's housekeeper in New Orleans. Bearing in mind that her position in the Creswick household was that of eldest daughter and unpaid housekeeper, this is hardly surprising.

Their mother was a product of Evangelical Methodism who believed that everyone was called by God to do their duty, according to their station in life. The children's grandfather taught a Bible-based theology of Old Testament patriarchy. Jane was the eldest daughter, her father's favourite, the one who nursed him in his final illness, despite her large and busy family. The relative position of women in the Lindsay family is further revealed by the story of Ruby Lindsay, six years her junior, who nevertheless escaped to a public career. Mary aided the younger Ruby's departure to Melbourne, officially under the protection of Percy for whom she was supposed to keep house.[4] Later, when Percy married and the pretext of Ruby's domestic duties could not be sustained, she had to resist a determined effort by her eldest brother to send her home.[5]

Percy's careless lifestyle was countered by a personal fastidiousness. This was just as well as Ruby was not famous for her domestic expertise. In 1910, when Norman stayed in London with Ruby and Will Dyson, he complained that 'Rube's idea of a full meal is half a small fish and bread and jam'.[6] Ruby was fortunate in being the seventh child. There were three more babies born after her, but it was Mary, not Ruby, who cared for them.

Mary Lindsay's life was largely shaped by events in the family which both nurtured and confined her. Although her brothers were taught at both the state primary and Creswick Grammar schools, and Pearl attended Creswick Grammar, Mary's formal education came from a series of governesses.

One of the writers Mary most admired was Jane Austen. Many of Mary's later letters read as though they may be working drafts for novels or short stories written on a small scale, stories that owed something to Austen, Turgenev and Flaubert — all writers of detail and domestic drama. But just as most of her reading was confined to the nineteenth century and earlier, so the social observations of Mary and her circle of sheltered small-town women also operated according to archaic social rules.

As the town moved out of its crude goldfields phase into a more settled existence, the Creswick middle class adopted the values of an older England. In their isolation, it seemed to the parents of this limited circle that they were upholding the standards of a distant Europe. The phenomenon of immigrant cultures preserving archaic versions of the mother culture is a well-known consequence of colonisation. It is not surprising that the respectable English immigrants of the Victorian goldfields preserved unrealistic images of 'home'. However, they had another motivation. Very few of the Creswick families came from the social elites of Great Britain. In Australia, social position was defined by success as much as by birth, and the sharp British divisions between Established and non-Established Church, yeoman farmers and the 'county', and soon were blurred. The marriage of Jane Williams to Robert Charles Lindsay would have been highly unlikely in Britain, as he was from a traditional land-owning family which could trace its wealth to a Royal gift, while she was merely the daughter of a Methodist minister whose father had been a tradesman. But in the new world, the daughter of a prominent Methodist was entitled to the best boarding school education, and the status of 'Doctor's Wife' made Jane part of a very small social elite.

The principal victims of this mind-set of snobbery were the daughters of the middle class. They lacked the freedom to mix with the children of shopkeepers or miners and therefore retired to the 'refinement' of the local tennis club. The only men these women were permitted to meet were from within their own class boundaries, but the men had the freedom to socialise with working-class girls. In any case the men often left the small towns for university or jobs in the more fluid environment of Melbourne. But if they returned they were expected to conform to the rigid society based on parental fantasies of 'home'. There is a hint of these values in comments on Percy Lindsay's socially dubious behaviour when he chose to marry an 'old flame', Jessie Hammond, the daughter of a shopkeeper.

Lionel's departure to Melbourne was precipitated by the economic depression of the 1890s and the subsequent decline in Doctor Lindsay's medical practice. Under the circumstances, university education for their most academically inclined son would have involved extreme sacrifice for the family, so the invitation for him to work as an illustrator, even on a disreputable tabloid such as the *Hawk*, must have seemed fortuitous.

Shortly after Lionel left home, Jane Lindsay, then aged forty-five, conceived her tenth child. Jane Isabel Lindsay was born in February 1894 and Mary, who nursed her as a baby and lived with her until frail old age sent her to a nursing home, always resented 'this unfortunate failure of our mother'.[7] On one level Isabel's existence was a continuing reminder of the arrival of the years of poverty, when their mother became more extreme in her Protestant faith and, as an economy measure, stopped having dinner parties and other entertainments with wine, while Robert Charles took refuge in the bar of the

American Hotel. But for the adolescent Mary, there was also the realisation that there was some sort of physical intimacy between her parents.

At the same time as she was trying to come to terms with her own body, with girlish romantic dreams and disturbing fantasies, Mary Lindsay was already facing the drudgery of crying babies, snivelling children and a constant round of household duties which included juggling a budget on a seemingly imaginary income. Daryl later wrote 'it was always Mary who seemed to gather together the threads of our individual lives.'[8]

Excitement for Mary came in the form of the return to Creswick of Lionel, Norman and Percy with their intellectual friends and city sophistication. Mary features as a figure in the complex photographic tableaux staged at Creswick by brothers and friends. Some of these photographs record Ruby clad in nothing more than a fur rug and Norman wearing only a loincloth. Mostly Mary appears slightly inhibited, as though these fleshly entertainments were beneath her. But in one extremely complex tableaux of Lindsays and Dysons dressed in sheets to approximate Grecian dress, Mary appears so relaxed and happy that she becomes almost as beautiful as Ruby. These excursions by young bohemian men to Creswick remained a high point of her life. Mary also had holidays in Melbourne, where she would stay with sober Williams relatives but was free to spend time with her artist brothers and be taken around town by Lionel.

As her brothers became first independent and then financially secure, Mary took more of the burden of household management on herself. In the early years of this century, some time after 1903 when Lionel was married, there was a major financial crisis at Creswick. It may well have been the result of a failed investment in gold mines, cited by Daryl as his father's chief financial folly, or a shrinking medical practice in a dying mining town. In any case it needed the intervention of those brothers who were earning an income. There are letters in both the Mitchell and the La Trobe collections in which Mary snipes at Lionel and his supposed miserly attitude, then mitigates her attack. In one letter to Daryl she wrote:

*Carefulness started at first in an honest endeavour to do what he could for his family. I have not forgotten that he was the one, when things collapsed here, to make Father hand over to Mother what was left of his life insurance. He was just on the point of selling it for £300 —*

*By the time I paid the debts there was £700 out of the £900 left. Then Lionel was the one who suggested himself that he would help by sending a regular allowance, to Mother and Dad.* [9]

But while Lionel organised and sent money for the upkeep of the home, he would write to Norman complaining of the way the dependent family expected his support as a matter of right.

[They've] . . . *had £12 a month regularly from me and if they've been whining they can go hang themselves as far as I'm concerned. I'm done with the expectation of any kind of gratitude, with fate showing at* [indecipherable] *late . . . I'm feeling as* [here the letter is torn] *and sick that I could curse all things and everybody — my forbearance is exhausted.*[10]

Norman and Daryl also resented the burden of Creswick. But Mary, as the recipient who had to await fraternal bounty and forever manipulate to get more, was hardly in an enviable position. In contrast to the confined and conspiring world of women at Creswick, Mary appears to have spent most of her life dreaming romantic dreams of the liberated world of men, and writing in their praise to Norman:

*Men I find whether young or old, mentally sympathetic or not, allow me to be myself. While most women mistake my incurable politeness for a certain softness of the brain, and get in all the missionary work they can to improve or alter a personality.*[11]

Peter Lindsay was right about Mary declining the job offer. In the Chaplin papers there are some of Lionel's letters to Norman, written when Norman was in London in about 1910. They show that Lionel arranged for Mary to have one of the few positions then available for a woman in journalism. Montague Grover, the man who had photographed Rose in her black swimming costume and whose afternoon newspaper the *Star* was about to transform into the Sydney *Sun*, offered her a job as editor of the women's page in the new publication. If she had accepted the offer it would have enabled her to leave Creswick with honour. Lionel, who had been approached by Grover to leave the *Evening News* to become the official cartoonist on the new paper, urged her to take the job.

*I wrote advising her to take it saying I'd advance necessary funds for coming over but have had no reply so far — the sooner the Creswick menage is broken up the better for everyone as the old man with the famous chateau of Lisnacrieve (may it crive a burst) for a refuge will haunt the scene of his misdeeds till removed by force (which heaven forefend).*[2]

The 'misdeeds' are never actually detailed in the letters which have been kept. Perhaps there was no malpractice and the colourful old doctor was simply a reminder of the town's disreputable past — an unwelcome reminder to those who wished to forget how they had made their fortunes. There may have been problems involving drinking, but there is also the family story that Robert Charles Lindsay's quiet task of performing abortions was starting to be noticed. There is another account, which I have been unable to verify, that Dr Lindsay accidentally used too much ether on a woman in labour. She survived, but another doctor had to be called in. Lionel issued an ultimatum to his father that there would only be continuing support for the family if Robert Charles stopped practising. Then Lionel wrote to Norman a letter which implies that their father was no longer a competent medical practitioner:

*I had a dismal letter from Mary saying the old man is behaving like a lunatic and was only saved by Dr Sleeman — cases again and worse than ever. I won't worry you with the details but am writing to say that if he'll go straight you and I will allow him £1 a week until you come back and perhaps more then on condition that he takes on no more. Cash to stop immediately if he does. I'm writing him as stiff a letter as I can and if I can't flick him in the raw there'll be no grace in the language. They'd best get him from Creswick as a change of place will leave him fewer opportunities...*[13]

What a change from the convivial doctor of their childhood, respected by the community, singing in his Irish tenor at town concerts, riding out to tend to his patients in the middle of the night. Now the successful sons took on the role of stern parent, forbidding the wayward child to play with his toys.

In 1910 Robert Charles left home, working his way first to England and Ireland and then back to Australia as a ship's doctor. He had hopes that his Irish relatives would help rescue the family's fortunes, but this did not happen. Instead he continued to be a short-term guest and a long-term embarrassment to his disapproving adult children. When he came to London, Norman wrote to Lionel:

*Your news that the old man is close at hand is an evil omen. I'm tired of McCawber Bob. And expect he'll quarter himself on me until he gets another ship — the £300 he hoped to borrow from his relatives I see was a vain hope; I suppose he'll drift about now, or see the inside of a gaol if he stays long ashore.*[14]

The Lindsays always did like their Dickens, and the reference to Micawber from *David Copperfield* indicates that the main trouble with their father was most likely financial: an optimistic disposition on a modest income.

# MARY

Mary also left Creswick, but not for the career Lionel had planned for her. Instead, she accepted her brother Robert's invitation to travel to London, and later to live with him as his housekeeper when he was working with a friend at the British Consulate in New Orleans. To modern eyes her decision seems absurd — to pass up the chance of a career for a holiday of housework. But very few middle-class women were in paid employment in the years preceding World War I. It was easier to dream of entering the world of men than actually to do it.

The Mitchell library letters also raise questions about Mary's emotional life. Was there a romance? The men she wrote of were all friends of her brothers, but there was no hint of dalliance there. Did she have a local admirer? And how did she see the relations between men and women?

One thing was clear. Mary felt her intellectual interests were a definite barrier to forming any romantic attachment with a man. In her old age she wrote to Norman:

*I heartily distrust the stories of passionate attachment between past ladies of the Salon and their admirers. The men friends and the intelligentsia of the period no doubt liked to match their wits with these brilliant girls, and many enjoyed for a life time friendships based chiefly on a strong mental sympathy: but you can't get me to believe that a strong feminine intelligence is a necessary lure to the poet, or for that matter any man.*[15]

'She did have at least one proposal that I know of,' said Bingo one day. 'Dad told me this, oh, a long time ago. And of course many of his friends did find her attractive, but she was too scared to get involved with them.'

'Who was the proposal from?' I asked, intrigued. We had been looking at photographs of Mary, and even as a young woman she looked quite formidable, a complete contrast to the luscious curves of Ruby and the placid domesticity of Pearl.

'It was Montague Grover, the editor of the *Sun*,' she said. 'Dad could never understand why Mary didn't marry him, but he wasn't a very attractive man, if you know what I mean. Not the kind of man you could fall in love with. And then there were the children. He had four children and she would have had to look after them. I wouldn't have married him.'

Was this why she hadn't taken the job? I looked up Montague Grover in the *Australian Dictionary of Biography*. According to the entry, he had two sons and five daughters by his first wife, Ada Goldberg, whom he divorced in 1914.

The following year he married a 24-year-old, Regina Roseville Varley. If Bingo's story is true, then the offer must have been made just after Mary came back to Australia.

When Mary finally returned to Creswick, she found the household in disarray. She hadn't wanted to come home but, as she later told Norman, she had received 'a raging letter from Daryl in New Orleans, saying that Dad was very ill, & mother worn out, with the additional worry of the 2 elder McPhee children ( the 3rd baby in the offing)'.[16] Daryl had just enlisted in the AIF and was not able to help at home, and Reg was in a similar position. When they joined the army, both Reg and Daryl nominated their mother as their dependent in order to give Jane some financial assistance. Lionel and Norman were supporting the family with their work in Sydney, Ruby was with her husband and child in London, and Percy was, as always, not fiscally responsible. It was therefore appropriate from Daryl's perspective to ask Robert to pay for Mary's return fare to nurse her dying father and help the family.

When Pearl was left destitute after her husband's death, Norman wrote to Lionel about the financial burden of Creswick:

*There is a curse on these old decaying townships. You and I must make some arrangement to help this new development financially, for poor old Pearl will be quite helpless. It is a cowardly business, this succumbing in the face of difficulties.*[17]

In marked contrast to the death by suicide of Pearl's husband, his son-in-law, Robert Charles' final illness was precipitated by an act of heroism. When the outbreak of war sent him back to Australia, Dr Lindsay found a new mining frontier. He was working at White Cliffs in far western New South Wales when he heard the opal mine was flooded. As a young man, Robert Charles Lindsay had been a hero of the Creswick mining disaster of 1882, when he had walked into the flooded mine to rescue the living and retrieve the bodies of the dead. And so in his old age he tried to emulate his youth and waded underground to rescue the endangered men. In view of his age, seventy-two, it was hardly surprising that he caught a chill which became pneumonia and was sent home to die. Norman did not arrive until the funeral and Mary only arrived in the months after his death, but Lionel saw the sight that led to her recall and wrote to Norman.

*It was a most pitiful sight. The last of the old man. His body wasted to the bone and difficulty in getting his breath audible day and night through the house. He didn't recognise me until just before I left when he asked me where I was going and how long I had been in Creswick. I told him five days and that I was going to Sydney to see you: I then kissed him goodbye and the ghost of his old smile lit up his face for a moment.*[18]

A year later, Reg died. Mary was the one who had to break the news to her brothers. The telegram came on 19 January 1917 and she immediately wrote to Norman:

*Just a line to give you some bad news. Poor old Reg was killed on Dec 31st. We have no particulars — just 'killed in action'. If any further word comes later I'll send it on. The poor old Mater is terribly broken up, of course, but is taking it with her usual courage. Bad as it is, I would rather this than have him come back maimed.*[19]

The Mitchell letters show that in the following years Mary admired the courage of her mother as she bore her grief, first as the young soldiers returned home at the end of the war and then when she heard of the death of Ruby in 1919. But for herself, especially in letters to Norman, Mary denied any sorrow for the dead.

*. . . Mother has given you a wrong impression if you think I am grieving badly over Ruby's death. The tragedy of it all is, of course for Bill and for Mother. One feels ashamed in face of the wrench for them, to have one's feelings even noticed. Indeed: I have suffered such a nausea from violent overstatements with regard to my natural feelings of regret over Ruby's death, that I am more than thankful for the understanding that does not offer the usual conventional expressions of sympathy . . . (I too, have never found it in my heart to wish anyone I really cared for back in the struggle, even poor Reg who went away in the pride of his youth, & whose going affected me more than any other. I never wished him back. In one's dull moods one has at times I'm afraid a little envy of the dead, but my sorrow is & always has been for the living.*

*. . . I have, myself, long since, given the thought of death, change, call it what you will, a foremost place in my thought partly because at times in the long distance life drawn here, it has brought some relief, but chiefly because I know by experience that the more deliberately facing of anything one recoils from, will lessen the sense of fear & in the end bring with it a certain quietude of mind.*[20]

Mary's assessment of her response to Ruby's death is partly an acknowledgment of Norman's spiritualist beliefs, but may also have been influenced by Mary's knowledge of Norman's longstanding quarrel with Ruby. Norman could not posthumously forgive his younger sister and in a letter to Daryl he wrote: 'Well, there's nothing to be said about it. Death is all right for those who go, but a blasted misery for those who remain.'[21]

Daryl had been close to Ruby. It was Will Dyson who had rescued Daryl from the trenches during the war, by making him his batman, and Daryl was with Ruby when she died. Such a response would not have endeared Norman to his brother.

What is evident in the letters of this period is the unambiguous praise of Jane Lindsay by her sons and daughter. They saw the woman who, despite the brave front, placed her mementos of her dead children on her old work table so that she could daily read Ruby's last letter written from Ireland, and be comforted by the photograph of Reg.[22] And Mary wrote to Norman of her love for brave, sad Jane Lindsay:

*[Mother] . . . has a love far less passing than that of most mothers. Its been a great pleasure personally to me to feel your full understanding and appreciation of her really big character. I fully endorse everything you say. Living alongside has never blinded me to her real nobility. To come through the life she's had, not only unhurt, but with every generous impulse strengthened is a tremendous achievement. A woman like that is an inspiration all round. — But what I wanted to say was that some of your thoughts gave her a tranquillity of mind that apparently her religion could not in her two most crushing blows. She has the feeling now that Reg and Ruby are really waiting for her, and that is bringing with it a sense of security & peace about the future.* [23]

Mary's life at this time was not all drudgery and grief. When Norman visited Creswick, he brought her home with him to stay at Springwood, and on this journey she befriended Leon Gellert who appears to have been quite charmed by her wit.[24] He wrote a mock play on how the various Springwood personalities responded to the manuscript of his poems, *The Isle of San*. Mary, who apparently had a bawdy sense of humour, is described as: 'Mary Lindsay — another skite. A wrecker of novelists, a leg-puller of models, a scrambler in gullies, a snarer of crayfish, and a dangerous spitfire (Dressed in a pair of spectacles).'[25]

Thereafter, about once a year, she came to Sydney to stay with Lionel and then with Norman and Rose in Springwood. Through Mary's mediation, Rose was gradually seen by the rest of the family as a suitable wife for Norman, especially as Katie's alcoholic deterioration was becoming public knowledge, and Norman and Rose were planning to have children.

The friendship by correspondence between Rose and Jane Lindsay was rather different from Rose's written communications with Mary. After Rose lost her first child, Mary wrote a letter of sympathy.

*I can't tell you how sorry we were to hear of your break down. Norm did not say what was wrong & I'm wondering just what it is — Funnily enough I've had an odd unpleasant sort of feeling for some weeks past that there was trouble of some sort out at Springwood. Which all my commonsense & cool calm reasoning would not allow me to shake off.*

*I now know it turns out you have been horribly ill, & one has a feeling of being an unconscionable brute of some sort at being unable to help or do something . . .*

*. . . Are you going away for a change or is there still too much influenza about to make that safe? We have 3 or 4 cases in hospital here & you can imagine what a panic Pearl is in. When she gets up in the morning in a mood of special energy, the children know they are in for a Hell of a day. They are dragged off shrieking, & held over the bath, while a stupendous dousing & drenching and gargling and disinfecting is carried on, & when the poor beggars have barely recovered from the suddenness of the attack, they are seized again & the whole performance starts again. They all wear bags of herbs & camphor & God knows what around their necks & are not allowed to forget for a minute in the day that an overload of germs is waiting to devour them if they put their noses out the front gate.*[26]

Mary's response to Rose's second confirmed pregnancy was pleasure, but her letter showed that her knowledge of childbirth and the use of obstetric forceps in difficult labours was, to say the least, theoretical.

*I was very glad to get all the news I've wanted about the event ahead. Lord! I will be glad too when it's all over, & the cat on hot bricks feeling we are all suffering from, in spite of our most tremendous efforts after a philosophic calm gives me some idea how you two must be feeling.*

*If I were you I'd take all that torture chamber paraphernalia & chuck it out the window. Let the unimaginative beasts fix it up again when its wanted. Such a piece of cold blooded barbarianism belongs to the stone age! It will be great if you get a surprise & have a much better time than you expect. Its up to the Fates to give the plucky ones a reward like that once in a while.*

> *. . . I've got a sense of the most absolute security that you'll come through it all right. You'll probably grin at this. I wouldn't attach any importance to it myself, if it were not for the fact that every time a calamity has fallen on the family I've always known months & months beforehand that something beastly was going to happen, & I can't see why the strong feeling of optimism I have this time should not mean something too.[27]*

Despite the constant letters flowing between Creswick and Springwood, there were no visits by Norman to the family home after one memorable stay in late 1920. Rose did not join him, presumably because she was reluctant to travel with baby Jane. In any case, a visit to the very proper Creswick family by the bohemian Rose may have destroyed the budding friendship with her mother-in-law.

From the early 1920s, letters from Mary to Rose and Norman mention the impossibility of living in the same house as Pearl and her children. Rose, pretending clairvoyance, then wrote to Jane Lindsay asking if all was well at Creswick. And Jane's reply showed how she felt she could discuss the 44-year-old Mary's gynaecological problems with another married woman:

> *What a wonderful woman you must be and what a strange power, which could tell you that all was not quite well with Mary. When your wire came she was all right again. What I am telling you is in confidence and only for you and Norman. Mary would be so angry if she knew I would tell anyone. It is just this. I am afraid the change of life is starting early with Mary & she has been suffering dreadfully with her head & her nerves at times are in a bad state & that week she had missed her times, & she did suffer & had so little control over herself. You know this is so unlike Mary, & when she is better she is so wild with herself for giving away. However this month things were all right & she is better, but if I can manage it I want to make her see a Dr when we are in town so that this worried feeling in her head can be relieved. She will not see the Dr in Creswick. I expect I shall have my work cut out to make her see one in Town. So now dear you will understand my anxiety about her. She will not take things quietly & work she will, & have the house clean she will & when strangers come she over does it. However I keep a good look out & around & try to keep worries down. I will write again as soon as we return from Melbourne, but never mention anything I may tell you.*
>
> *. . . I am posting a pair of booties for our little pet & we are all so glad she is getting on all right.*

# MARY

> *With fondest love,*
> *Your Mother.*[28]

The 'little pet' is most likely Helen, born on the fourth of June 1922, so presumably this undated letter was written in the months following the birth. As Jane Lindsay grew older, it seems that she started to think of her daughters as being younger than their years, and they are all seen as 'girls'. When Mary had first started to show the strain of being the mainstay of the household, Jane wrote to Norman, sympathising with her plight.

> ... I have been worried about Mary. She has too much work & worry with Pearl & children & it just gives me to the fears [?] to see a girl like Mary placed in such a harsh condition & the petty troubles of our daily living is crushing all this nobility & kindly sensitivity out of her life. You understand all I mean. Poor Pearl she does not know how she upsets us. I am very sorry for her. She is so unfit for the task she has before her ...[29]

Happy, cheerful, gossiping Pearl had never imagined that she would be a widow with three small children, living in poverty in her childhood home.

Many of Jane's letters to Norman are filled with references to Mary's health, at the same time as Mary was expressing concern at her mother's increasing frailty. In part, the family was indulging its hobby of hypochondria, but there were also power shifts at play.[30] Jane Lindsay still encouraged holidays — in 1922 Mary went to Tasmania — and the annual visits to Sydney continued until about 1925.[31] But by the mid–1920s the language her mother was using in letters to Norman implied that Mary was still a child.

> ... if she only takes care of herself she should keep well. I can never thank you enough dear boy for all your goodness to her, it is only what you say & do that carried weight with a girl like Mary. How she loves & misses you as does the old mother that is writing this letter.
>
> ... How I wish you could have seen the faces & heard the exclamations on Saturday morning when Mary unpacked. The lovely beautiful presents you sent my household. You are indeed kind & generous & I don't think I know anyone with such excellent taste as Norman's wife has. Mary's & Pearl's evening dresses are exquisite & so dainty & fit perfectly. Poor dears they have had to do without these beautiful things for too long, that you can understand how they are appreciated & I feel quite proud of my girls look to feel dressed.[32]

Mary was never shy about expressing her anger in the confines of the house, and Dr James Strachan, who was treating her, wrote to Norman expressing concern at her hysteria and subsequent 'breakdown'. But in her mother's eyes the reasons why this mature woman was unable to cope with life in a small country town, were quite simple.

> . . . she is better now, if she will only take care & do as I wish. I have been expecting this break down for months, & it is a good thing it has happened for her sake she will think a little. The butt of the matter, Norman is: Far too many cigarettes, late hours & excitement. Mrs Strachan gives two or three tea parties a week & then perhaps two nights a week down at our house, never leaving till near 1 o'clock, & then parties up till 2 o'clock in the morning & Mary is always . . . to help entertain & keep them all alive &to her this is most exhausting . . .
>
> Last year when she went to Tasmania she could not smoke & kept good hours took three good meals a day & came back quite plump & well fit to anything. Mary should know better than to wreck her life as she has been doing. I am hoping this will be a warning to her for at times I have wondered where my Mary had gone.[33]

If her mother spoke to her as she wrote about her, it is hardly surprising that Mary came to see Jane as an unreasonable tyrant.

Mary was not the only one writing about the deteriorating situation at Creswick. Daryl, based in Melbourne and at Mulberry Hill, was a frequent, dutiful visitor to his home and passed on his observations to Lionel.

> On Friday I heard by accident that everything was upside down at Creswick so I went and stayed up that night, to find a wretched state of affairs.— Mary on the verge of a nervous breakdown and Mother worrying herself sick about her, and the whole family getting on each others nerves.— The whole thing's a long story . . . Matters have been brought to a head by Sam Fiddian who has got himself mixed up with some sharp business men who are running the local tile works and who are mixed up in some rather shady actions.— Sam who is trying to clear his character is going to sue Dr Strachan for slander and has put Mary down as his first witness . . . I have seen Drs Sleeman and Strachan who say she must be got away at once and at any cost . . . Mary being thoroughly pig-headed did not want to go . . . [34]

It must have been an extremely awkward situation for Mary. Dr Strachan's wife was her closest friend at the time; she had known Sam Fiddian all her life and

# MARY

his mother, Sophie, was her mother's oldest friend. Daryl's wish that Mary hide from the conflict by going abroad, or at least interstate, may well have been prudent and in the end he prevailed. But Mary felt a great deal of resentment towards her interfering little brother.[35] The mysterious feud between Fiddian and Strachan faded from knowledge, but within the house at Creswick there was no peace. The Strachan children, Veronica and David, saw little of the conflict. Their house was only a block away from the Lindsays' and because there was no telephone at the Lindsay house they were the constant carriers of messages between Mary and her friend. To Veronica, Mary appeared much younger than her chronological age, with 'sprightly mind and marvellous stories of her youth. However I realise she was very Irish and said things sometimes, for the sake of the story.'[36]

By 1929 the hostility between Mary and Pearl had become intense. Daryl wrote to Lionel who was then in Europe preparing to visit Bingo, who had settled in India with her husband, Bob Charley, and was awaiting the birth of her first baby.

> . . . things at Creswick have got to such a pass that I simply couldn't go much longer with practically all the responsibility — For the past ten years no one but myself (outside of Creswick) has realised the true state of affairs. It has always been purposely kept from you and Norman who thinks they are getting along nicely — as a matter of fact the position has reached a stage when I can't continue any longer and something has to be done at once if mother is to have her last few years in peace — Pearl, the true daughter of her father, is the crux of the matter and has for years made life unbearable for Mother and Mary . . . (She is unconsciously selfish to a degree and gets into violent passions because every penny is not spent on Her children). . . I have had it from all sides for ten years when I came back from the war.
>
> . . . The only thing it as to do get together a sufficient sum of money to keep Pearl in a small cottage in Ballarat for 3 years — This will save railway fares and Flis is going into an office as soon as she can — I also have assurances that Alex will get a good job when he gets through his exams in two years time . . . I have written to Norman my first letter for five years and have had a delightful self satisfied letter in return — callous to a degree and written with the physcology of a school boy of sixteen — However, he is going to enlarge his allowance to Creswick by 20/- a week . . . [37]

Daryl's concern was always his mother, who was increasingly confused at the way her children waged war through the house.

*Frankly I was completely broken up when I last saw her — she is, as you know, the last to ask for anything and knows nothing of my scheme to get Pearl out of the house — should you be writing please don't on any account mention that I have written this to you — It will only upset her and frankly she should be saved every possible worry just now —* [38]

Daryl arranged for Jane to stay with him at Mulberry Hill for an extended holiday. This was the visit when George Lambert drew her as 'the mother of the Lindsays'. His sensitive drawing of this frail but benign woman, softened by time and lace, is now in the Ballarat Fine Art Gallery. Joan wrote about Lambert's meeting with Jane in her memoir, *Time Without Clocks*, but there is no mention of any family crisis, just the pleasure of having an aged relative come to stay and meet with a famous artist.

In Jane's absence, Daryl returned to Creswick and, without notice, removed Pearl and the children to Ballarat, an action which was always resented by them. On Jane's return to Creswick at the end of the year, Daryl was able to report to Lionel that 'Mother was with us for a month and went back to Creswick looking splendid — she is overwhelmed at the idea of having the house to herself again.'[39]

Norman refused to help with the tangled emotions of Creswick. He would neither take Mary as a guest nor advise his siblings on how to behave. Daryl kept his letter of refusal and lodged it in the La Trobe Library as evidence of the attitude of his famous brother:

*I'm afraid we can't come at your proposal. Apart from the fact that I've been sick for the last two years and have done no work, which makes any added drain on our resources out of the question at present, Rose and I have long considered eventualities which you are suddenly disturbed over and have made what provision for them seems to us a just and safe one and more than that we can't do, in view of this foolishness of thinking you can calculate against the unknown problems of the future. If things are in the state you say they are in Creswick, (financially) I'll increase the weekly cheque, but its quite impossible that I should interfere in rearranging the disposition of the people in the Creswick house. Nerves are the common curse of life and no one is immune from them no matter what age they may be or what conditions they live under. If you can screw any money out of that doddering old good man of a Lionel, do so by all means, but you wont get it. He has such a magnificent sense of his moral responsibilities that he is able to fob them off in talk which is the common trick of all people who indulge in generous emotion.*[40]

# MARY

Norman must have really wanted to get this message to Daryl as there is an earlier version of this in Rose's file of unposted letters in the Mitchell. This means that either she intercepted the letter and he rewrote it, or that he made a first draft which she appropriated.[41]

In 1930, after the publication of *Redheap* caused permanent divisions in the family, Robert Lindsay returned to Creswick from London after an absence of twenty years. From letters written by Robert to Lionel and Norman, it is clear that Mary now had an ally in the house, but one who reinforced all her negative feelings about her situation and who constantly made unfavourable comparisons between rural Australia and the elegancies of London where he felt they both belonged. Robert did not improve the finances of Creswick, but rather increased the burden. Under his regime financial control was effectively removed from Jane and transferred to Mary and himself, with the formal beneficiary being Mary.

. . . *Mother has been utterly impossible, and last week she sent for me at 1.30 am — and upbraided me for trying to get everything into my hands, and that Mary has taken her money (Reg's pension), and that between us we had had it transferred so that she couldn't touch it! pretty flattering when we are both on edge trying to keep the peace with Isabel. All this was caused by Mary —after trying all one day to get her to sign the pension papers she lay back almost in a comatose state and I feed her at intervals all day with sips of brandy and ice. In the end Mary got the P [Post Office] to fix it up — we both signing it and got the money . . . as Mary was passing at the moment, Mother called her in and went for her as if she was a pick pocket — saying she had stolen her money, and that she and I had transferred it over to our own use, making out that she was incapable of signing it — and that perhaps we would be satisfied now we had everything in our own hands (some months ago I made her write a new will, giving the home to Mary to save death duties). . . She has goaded Mary to such a state of nerves that she utterly crumpled up — in a fearful state of hysteria and began screaming. I had to get Strachan to give her a hypodermic syringe to quieten her — which had no effect for some hours — I had to hold her down all the time while she struggled — she was in bed for a week, and no sooner was she able to crawl about again than Mother started her nagging . . .*[42]

Robert's letter provides a disturbing picture of a confused elderly woman in the care of feuding children, two of whom were not prepared to await the formality of death before dividing the estate. It also shows a middle-aged woman under stress being forcibly sedated for the sake of propriety. With Mary given title to the family home, Isabel and Pearl were deprived of any inheritance. They were therefore dependent on their successful brothers for the rest of their lives. As a sop, various siblings were given mementos of their mother on a grace and favour basis. Perhaps it was in the aftermath of the events described in the above letter that Jane asked Daryl Lindsay to continue to provide for his youngest sister, an obligation that Daryl accepted.

Her mother had nursed both Thomas Williams and Robert Charles Lindsay in their senility. Now it was Mary's turn and, as the eldest unmarried daughter, supported financially by her brothers, her duty. But she lacked the inclination and the patience to constantly clean an incontinent old woman and to listen patiently to her senile ramblings. As a way of controlling her reactions to an impossible situation, Mary's doctors prescribed morphia.

In July 1932 Robert wrote to Norman:

. . . *four days ago Mary collapsed in a fit of hysteria and in her ravings I had to almost sit at her all night despite the fact that Strachan had given her the maximum dose of morphia to quieten her — she raved at Pearl and Mother and Isabel — saying how brutally they had treated her and she loathed the lot of them — and kept shrieking — don't let me see them again. All a bit ghastly and for three days afterwards she was a bit of a wreck. Mother thought the faint quite mad, and Isabel, who is the most loathesome moron, making her madder by filling her up with all sorts of fabrications — to enlist her sympathy. I wired Pearl and made her take her away for a week —. She* [Isabel] *went storming and raging — saying I was turning her out of the house, and more hysterical outbursts. — It gave me a pause, the emotional calm after her departure, gave me the first rest I've had for months and quietened Mary, who is the only one to consider.*[43]

Sedation is a traditional treatment for difficult women and morphia gave Mary a kind of peace. From reading Robert's account it seems clear that the drug was administered more for the benefit of those living with her, than for Mary herself. However, long-term use of such a powerful narcotic must have affected Mary's personality, and criticism of her later actions must take her medical condition and its treatment into account.

# MARY

For Mary, her mother's death on 14 November 1932 was a relief, slightly coloured by a perception that others knew she had done her duty and had suffered for it. To Lionel, who contributed to the cost of the funeral, she wrote a restrained account:

*Mother died quietly last night, unconscious, under an opiate for the last 24 hours. Before that it was horrible — nearly a week of almost incessant screaming which did not indicate pain the Doctor said — just delirium.*[44]

With Rose she adopted the jocular tone she shared with Norman when addressing emotional issues and avoided discussing any complex or even contradictory feelings she may have had about the death:

*... My doctor man has put me on some dope that I'll swear is compounded of all the bromides known to science the pleasing effect of which is that you could set fire to the house, or hang my eldest son under my very nose, & I wouldn't care two hoots. These doctors are really very useful members of society.*

*... Just now [Robert] is busy calcimining the walls of Mother's bedroom. His idea is that the family nerves will benefit if that room is altered a bit, & indeed I wont be sorry to see those dirty white walls disappearing under something more cheerful.*

*The funeral passed off nicely—. Dan [Daryl] came up & he & the two Doctors attended. There is always something amusing to me in the sight of Doctors & funerals together. Afterwards Dan offered Bert £1 to go away & have a nice trip. Bert said "no thanks" politely. When he offered me the same or perhaps £2, I said "no thanks" politely. He's a generous fellow is my brother Dan.*

*... Lord! Rose: the best thing that ever happened to me is the death of poor old Mother. Kindly sentimental ladies say behind ones back "poor dear! She couldn't have stood another month of it." I say "rot" loudly. One can if necessary go on and on standing almost anything. The chief trouble with human beings is that they are all able to stand a jolly sight too much — However! Enough of melancholy — its all over now.*[45]

If Mary was hoping that Norman and Rose would invite her to stay at Springwood to recover from the rigours of the deathbed, she waited in vain. By late 1932 Norman was thinking more of the kind of studio he could find in Sydney, and Rose did not want visitors to see the growing crisis in their marriage. Rose also had a strong sense of family loyalty, a belief that family must be supported at all costs. She had seen her mother nurse her father in his last illness, even though years before he had deserted her and the children, leaving them without anywhere to live. Expressions of hostility towards dying mothers, even under extreme provocation, were against her particular ethical code.[46]

After Jane's death Mary made pleas in mitigation for her behaviour during those last years and tried to rewrite history in her own favour.

*One tries to get through by some process of indifference but can't keep the bitterness out. Those last Hellish two years before Mother died, did something to me that I'm afraid will stay till I die —She died I think almost hating me, just because I'd given up everything for her. — cared for her too much. Of course I know she could not help it. Her indominatable pride could not endure the thought of being beholden to any human being — but I don't want to talk about this: keep it to yourself —That's all over — you've got your Hell with you all day & night.*[47]

The reference to Rose's 'Hell' is an indication that Rose had told Mary of some of her problems with Norman. Rose does appear to have understood that Mary's tirades against Jane were written under great stress so when she later regretted what she had written and asked for letters to be destroyed, she assured Mary that this had been done, and Mary wrote in gratitude:

*Thanks for burning those letters of Bert's & mine written in violent moods of depression. Bert at any time was shockingly unsafe, but when I'm in my right mind, I try to see both sides of the question.*[48]

But Rose had kept Robert's letters and later deposited them in the Mitchell.

After Jane Lindsay's death, there was an additional financial crisis for Creswick. As the dependent mother of a soldier killed in action, Mrs Lindsay had been paid a war pension, and with her death that money ceased. From the 1930s until her old age, Mary continued to call in the debts she felt she was owed by her successful brothers. This placed her in a curious position of both power and dependency, as Mary was in a real sense the keeper of family secrets. After 1930 she was the only means of Daryl and Lionel passing information to Norman, and vice versa. But she remained dependent on both their sense of duty and their goodwill. Daryl, Lionel and Norman had long accepted the need to support their mother and now came the realisation that the burden would continue indefinitely.

Mary wrote to Norman about her negotiations for continued support:

# MARY

*. . . One more item of interest. I've screwed £1 a week out of Dan [Daryl] simply demanded it as his contribution to the Isabel problym. Otherwise I told him he could take her for half the year. I explained at length that my little capital was going bit by bit & that I was damned if I'd draw another £1 from what was left — I explained clearly that Isabel wasn't my responsibility any more than the rest of the family — that it was impossible to expect anything more from N. as he, through Rose had practically run everything here all these years. Lionel I said was donating or rather had donated £1 a week so far, explaining when he left Melbourne that he'd keep it up as long as he could — leaving me in the usual pleasing uncertainty as to whether it would come along at the end of each six months.*[49]

There is no indication as to where Mary Lindsay's 'little capital' may have come from, except that in 1961 Pearl Lindsay commented that 'I wouldn't mind owning a quarter of her shares'.[50] Other than the small amount of money from her mother's estate, the most likely source is from the sale of Norman Lindsay etchings which Rose sent her. What this letter does reveal is the way Mary became adept at playing the affluent siblings off against each other in order to achieve some measure of financial security. The simple and devout Isabel would hardly have fitted in with the cultured surroundings of Daryl Lindsay's Mulberry Hill, so Mary's threat had a tinge of blackmail. Lionel, for all Mary's complaints, continued to support her, even though his income from etchings all but vanished in the Depression. Percy was not in a position to help and so avoided the Creswick levy.

Mary's letters to each of her benefactors are written in similarly confiding tones, suggesting that the recipient is the only trustworthy member of the family and condemning the others or claiming ignorance of their motives. For the last thirty years of her life Mary's principal means of communication with her relatives was through writing. Her strategy for self-preservation became only too transparent, with consequences that eventually rebounded upon her.

To Norman she was quite critical of Lionel:

*I'm sure I see in those defiant folded arms and direct gaze, the 'I am the master of my soul' attitude. He wasn't always quite so noble, when up against Bert's infuriating gentility & sneers at those who stank of stables, & were insufficiently washed. What a magnificently contrasting pair — but without a doubt Lionel is & was unique among all the males young & old who ever came our way.— so beautifully unaware of his own absurdities — a gorgeous character!*[51]

# LETTERS & LIARS

Mary then wrote to Lionel and after initially describing Norman as 'l'enfant terrible of the family' she attempted to endear herself to him with the good news:

*(Of course in absolute confidence) that N. is now an extremely unhappy, lonely man, long estranged from Rose, who spends nearly all her time with the eldest married daughter and her children. N. who narrowly escaped being burnt to death last year, & wont leave that wretched dreary place [Springwood].*[52]

In a letter to Bingo, returned from India, Mary wrote that both Bingo and Pearl's daughter, Felicity Shaw, were her 'genuine friends'.[53] However, at the same time she wrote to Norman in rather less flattering terms:

*Felicity McPhee Shaw, on her only very occasional visits, usually has an armful of discarded garments which she is glad to get rid of, being married to a man who is quite well off.*[54]

On reading this I started to wonder about Mrs Shaw and her hostility to me. She must have been a teenager when Daryl moved the family to Ballarat with all the humiliation that involved. Then she became the family visitor to the preceding generation as it endured difficult old age. After Mary's death, Daryl wrote to Bingo that Felicity had visited Mary every week, 'with eggs butter and cream and scarcely a thank you for it'.[55]

Many of Mary's later letters are double-edged with less than subtle reminders of her dependency. Her convoluted response to the fate of heirlooms left by Jane Lindsay is fairly typical of her approach to family members. In 1934 Daryl wrote to Mary and in concluding requested a memento from their mother's estate:

*. . . I have been meaning to ask you about a thing that occurred to me when I was last up. Did Mother mention leaving me anything out of the house in her will. She always said she wanted me to have the dining room side board — of course I don't want it — I would however like to have something out of the house and I wondered if you would care to let me have the Sheffield plate coasters in exchange for that?*[56]

Mary was so angry that she sent the letter to Rose with a covering note:

*I may as well enclose Dan's last letter. Isn't it like the generous lad to try to lift the very best & most valuable bit of old silver. We haven't anything really good & old left but the coasters which are rather lovely & a few good initialled family spoons.*[57]

# MARY

The dispute over the coasters and other furnishings went on for some years with Mary and Robert claiming most of the assets for themselves. In the end Daryl was able to acquire the coasters but received this note, which shows that in Mary's mind at least, he only 'won' because of his superior financial power.

*Thanks for the cheque just arrived*

*I'm sending on Robert's coasters addressed to you at the Gallery.*

*As you say you don't want the bowl, would you mind leaving it at Drummonds the first convenient day? There's just a chance that I might get a good price for it. I wouldn't dream, otherwise of selling it (would rather keep it in the family for the girls) — but looking ahead to the time when R. no longer has his £2 a week job I feel I'm not justified in sticking to any of my possessions that might bring in a good round sum.*

*. . . No! I didn't show your letter to Robert as my desire is to keep peace at any costs in the family. I'm quite sure that he would not appreciate my dear Dan! & talk about prior claims & so on as he knows his £2 a week screw & £1 from the annuity makes it possible for us to live & have quite sufficient food & even a holiday each year.*

*. . . Please don't think I am belittling your help. Your cheques are a great assistance, owing to my one big difficulty in life & that is Isabel — R & I can if necessary, cut down living expenses to the finest point — but with Isabel we never know where we are & what she may do behind my back.*[58]

The half-truth, the emphasis on her own (and Robert's) rights, the attack on Isabel, and the reminder of dependency: all carefully combined. It was after the quarrel over the fine points of their mother's estate that Mary created the mean persona of Daryl Lindsay (even though she continued to take his money). In one letter to Rose she recalled an incident of childhood, which she claimed showed the pattern of the future man:

*. . . he is what he was at the beginning & will be till the end. — the little boy who got up early one Xmas morning & (sleeping in the same room) went thro Reg's stocking & his own, putting the better Xmas gifts into his own stocking, & the lesser toys into Reg's, feeling secure in the knowledge that only Father Xmas had filled those stockings & could know of the dastardly thieving act. He was astounded when Mother, very annoyed, sorted out the toys & saw that Reg got his fair share —*

*Then the little boy again who when given a toy gun & target put up his*

> target on one of the big pine trees, brought in a collection of small school boy friends, & charged them a half penny for 6 shots.
> Only one member of the family like that. [59]

After Jane Lindsay's death, Mary, Robert and Isabel settled into a pattern of life at Creswick, blaming Mary's years of domestic duty for her failure to become a professional writer. Robert, at least as dependent on Mary as she was on him, continued the justification in letters to Norman.

> ... I would not be writing this if Mary had not to put up with the women of this beastly family all her life. What she should have done was to have left this sinister home. When Dum McKay, Monty Grover and Ted Dyson wanted to get her on paper, I can't understand why, with a good eye on the situation she did not say 'to hell with you all' and left them. Even when she started a second time to come over to me she had such a gruelling time from them before she started —that she had to get off at Fremantle, too ill the Dr said to go further . . . and all the time she was convalescing she got indignant letters from Mama upbraiding her for staying away, when she was needed at home! For sheer brutality give me a Christian woman . . . [60]

Daryl's wife, Joan, however, found the time to write, despite the demands of a socially active husband. Mary's dislike of Joan was based in part on her social position as a member of Melbourne's establishment. Then, in later years she realised that this woman, whom she regarded as less talented than herself, had become a well-regarded writer. So she wrote to Bingo:

> This week she [Joan] sent me her second book 'Hard facts and soft'. It's quite brightly written with something of the feel of the places & people. The book is the result of the trip the Carnegie Trust shouted them both, years ago.
> Of course going as they did from one Art Gallery to another, & meeting mostly people mixed up or interested in art, a great many people are mentioned who the common herd, like me, would not know anything about or be interested in. Still, a bright book & will, I guess, sell well. [61]

Daryl, who could be as unkind about Mary as she was about himself and his wife, told Bingo that:

> Mary would make a wonderful study for a Henry James novel — she writes in one 'you know little of these things. I'm a woman of the world etc' the poor dear living in the atmosphere of a dying small country town, laying down the law to Everybody — Being a bit hot headed I have always

*found it difficult to control my temper and listen to a barrage of talk and abuse of myself and all the other members of the Family except N.L. and Robert.*[62]

But he continued to fund this most difficult sister. Lionel, who did not visit Creswick and limited his letters to the occasions on which he sent money, was able to be more harsh:

*It is really astounding to witness where vanity and insolence can carry such a creature as Mary. To think that she could pull our legs for half a second, reflects only her ridiculous assumption of a knowledge of the world. She lives in a world of illusion and simple mendacity.*[63]

Mary was always pointed in her insults. When Daryl retired as Director of the National Gallery of Victoria she wrote 'praising' him for his self interest.

*I think you are very wise & sane to now just spend what you've got on yourself. You've worked hard with nothing but that lift from Mrs May for your success, & without any incumbrances & a wife with money, should after the rest you no doubt need, have a pleasant retiring life.* [64]

When Daryl reported this to Lionel he received a soothing response from his elder brother:

*As to Mary its clear as Villon wrote, her 'spleen bursts on her heart'. She is poisoned with acrimony, and naturally resents your success in life which insults her monstrous vanity. That a perfectly unimportant person should assume such consequence would be amusing if it were not so irritating. I wonder at your patience. I have long given up thinking of Creswick, spoiled for me as a memory by N.L. Robert and Mary — you should never discuss anything with her — she is impervious to reason.*[65]

One of the curious aspects of Mary's behaviour was her penchant for revealing the otherwise unknown last words of the dead. In a way it resembled Norman's passion for the Ouija board, except that Mary pretended the communications had occurred in this world, not the next. After Percy's death she claimed that his last words to her were 'I've had a good innings old girl! And am glad to get out before I become a nuisance.' Likewise Reg, in a letter supposedly written half an hour before he died, and later accidentally destroyed by her, was supposed to have written:

*If I get out of this mess, I'm going to get the best job I can get paid properly for, and then you and I will see things thro together at home. You will never have to go on alone . . .*[66]

In another version of the same story she told Norman that Reg had:

*. . . written half an hour before he was blown up by a German bomb. It was brought to me in a battered leather case by his best war friend Cobber. I burnt that letter as it sounded rather like an indictment of the family here — poor old Reg!*[67]

This is a family of collectors. They knew the value of old documents and photos. If such a letter were written, it is inconceivable that it would be destroyed.

There was still conflict at Creswick, despite Pearl's absence. Robert was a precise perfectionist who demanded that all food, all furnishings, be just to his liking. And there was Isabel. After her mother's death she became not just eccentric, but sometimes wilfully destructive, and Mary wrote that 'the corroding jealousy of this unfortunate failure of our mother is my worst difficulty'.[68]

More trouble was to follow when, in late 1951, Robert died after prostrate problems. Mary became acutely ill with grief at the death of a sibling for whom she cared so much. She was heavily sedated for months. Daryl temporarily placed Isabel in a local boarding house and wrote to Lionel describing the situation. But he did not enjoy the experience of caring for either of his sisters.

*I have just returned from a rushed visit to Creswick — a most painful affair. Mary still very sick and utterly pathetic . . . It's a highly strange thing that a family hard as ours should produce so much hysteria — Isabelle, Mary at the slightest thing going at tantrums — Not just bad temper — but proper yelling hysterics . . . Doctor down to give her morphia and sedatives and when leaving gave Isabelle a serious talk — I sat up the night keeping Mary quiet.*

*[Creswick is] the worst howling mess of two people living on past memories of self-centredness and self pity . . . One can't help feeling sorry for this pathetic figure clinging in the spasms of hysterics intermingled with stray lucid comments of amazing insight into the characters of Robert and Norman and Isabell.*[69]

When Mary recovered, Daryl suggested the best solution for two family problems was for Mary and Isabel to share their home with Kathleen Howitt, a Williams cousin who had been deserted by her husband after their son was born with Down's syndrome. The house was easily big enough to share and the new residents moved in.

After Robert's death, the formal English garden on which he had lavished so much attention became overrun with weeds and ivy. Mary sold the block of land which had been the paddock for the family horses, and wrote letters defending her dead brother. The painter Margaret Olley, who visited Creswick in the 1960s, remembers the house as 'a wreck'. And Mary's depression continued.

In her loneliness Mary turned to writing constant chatty letters to Norman on books and memoirs. She endorsed his opinions on literature and passed misinterpretations of family events on to other relatives. When Rose's arthritis confined her to a wheelchair and she went to live with Jane in Hunters Hill, Mary sympathised with Norman and wrote sagely of Mrs Pepys, endorsing Norman's claim that the only reason Samuel Pepys' wife had objected to his infidelities was that she too was unfaithful.

> ... *How delighted you or I would be to know that certain female ancestors had dallied & brought some passing pleasure into the life of our Pepys. Exactly the same thing is going on at this moment, & ever since cocktail parties came into vogue. The atmosphere becomes amorous, & affairs speedily follow, — & the fact that Mrs P. gave poor Sam Hell over the wild affair doesn't mean a thing. Except one more self defence act. Of course there is no absolute proof. All the same I'm certain she diddled him wherever the opportunity occurred.*[70]

Many of Mary's letters of the 1950s read like de facto family histories, as they create myths out of memories and imaginings. As well as glorifying Norman and damning other siblings, Mary was determined to change Robert's reputation as a family failure who hated his mother. She told Rose:

> *Bert, with his acute Mother complex had always adored his mother. As a boy, & during all those years abroad, he'd save up out of his hard earned small moneys, to send her a good frock, or some nice present. He'd even (when I hadn't a bean) send me too what he could to buy say an Xmas present for his much loved mother. Then, altho I tried to stop it, he came back to Creswick with just sufficient cash to buy a £1 a week life pension with a couple of hundred over to mend the fences & stop this old place from collapsing.*
>
> *The poor chap got the shock of his life to find the appalling change in his once handsome & proud mother. He was horrified of her treatment of me as*

*she had turned violently against me, as proud, dominant women often do at the end of their life, when they become completely dependent on another woman. I was content and there was nothing else for it but to go on & endure it till the end. Quite often poor Mother was for periods senile — but you know how a great love can turn to hatred, Bert simply hated his mother & to ease his outraged feelings let loose on Norman a lot of rubbish, quite ridiculous when applied to a woman of great character & probity.*[71]

Rose drew her own conclusions as to her sister-in-law's veracity. But Mary persisted in trying to redeem the reputation of the brother who had supported her. When she remembered the past, she cast herself always as the sole heroine struggling to care for Pearl and her children as well as nursing her mother. It was hardly surprising that neither Pearl nor the grown children wished to be reminded of the years of quarrelsome poverty in Creswick and Ballarat. In 1953 Daryl told Lionel:

*Fliss [Felicity] has been in Creswick and between you and me has had an eye full of the whole thing as Pearl has never been allowed to forget by Mary that the family kept the children — and she has rubbed it in with rock salt —* [72]

The old hostilities resurfaced in a less crude, but equally destructive form. When Mary started researching family history for John Hetherington, Pearl panicked, misinterpreting the nature of the story which was to emerge. She wrote to Lionel that Mary was 'a horrible old woman', for spreading stories about the past.[73] Mary retaliated with tart comments on Pearl, which indicated the feud was not to be forgotten and that Mary's observant eye was not directed towards introspection.

Mary's hostility to Isabel did not lessen with age. When Jean, Lionel's wife, died in December 1956, Mary wrote to Daryl, asking about Lionel's welfare (Mary's dislike of Jean was too well known to Lionel for her to offer him sympathy). In a quite disingenuous piece of arithmetical logic she argued that it would be to Isabel's advantage if Daryl's support of £50 per year for Isabel were translated into a direct payment of 10 shillings per week with a £5 Christmas bonus.[74]

There may well be a missing letter from Daryl Lindsay querying Mary's management of Isabel's finances. Isabel had spent her life under the impression that she was totally dependent on Mary. She had only ever been given five shillings of the weekly £1 allowance Daryl had sent towards her upkeep, and he had been unaware of this discrepancy.[75] Then, when Isabel was admitted to hospital in 1961, she was miraculously transformed from someone regarded as the village idiot to a normal, amiable old lady who simply needed nursing. She was given some degree of personal privacy when Daryl paid extra to upgrade her room. She discovered, much to her surprise, that she was on an old age pension. Mary had never told her, but simply claimed the money on her sister's behalf on the grounds of her diminished capabilities.

Mary's objections to funding Isabel were also expressed to Lionel when he sent her one of his regular Christmas presents of £1:

*That was very kind of you to send £1 to Isabel — 10/- would have been quite enough . . . I'm grateful to anyone who shows her any kindness . . . There is a curious cunning about the mentally deficient that makes them fully cognisant of the nearest human whose nerves can be best attacked.*[76]

It is clear that Norman was Mary's most continuous correspondent. Her later letters to him are elegantly written, without the directed sting which often characterises her correspondence with Daryl and Lionel. However, there is a sense that both were writing for other readers, as both continually make their cases for their own particular position within the Lindsay family myth that both were so carefully creating. This impression is reinforced on reading one letter from about 1958, shortly after John Hetherington started to research Norman's biography. It is almost certainly a letter that Mary hoped Hetherington would one day read. She was especially interested in reading literary biographies and wrote comparing Boswell's approach to that of recent biographers. In one letter she noted that Mrs Gaskell's biography of Charlotte Bronte had deliberately censored truth because of 'the genteel constraint of public opinion':

*The moderns weren't so squeamish & they really do want to get at the truth, & of course have the tremendous advantage of so much more information acquired from dug up letters over the years.*

*. . . Isn't it splendid the way the letters keep turning up all the time to satisfy my bursting curiosity to get at the truth, the whole truth, & nothing but the truth, over the lives of the humans long gone but of perpetual interest . . .* [77]

Mary especially remembered the books she read aloud to Norman, and other books she later discovered for herself. She paid generous tribute to the inspired librarian of the local Creswick lending library which was the source of much of the Lindsay children's early reading.

> . . . (don't forget that Lionel was the leader) . . . We were dependent on the books in that big book case of Dad's in the consulting room. The Dickens, Thackerays. Levers etc & the local library. I don't know who started that library but it must have been someone with an appetite for the classics, because there was quite a lot of excellently chosen literature.[78]

And then there is the sting. Norman Lindsay had a continuing distrust of those with formal tertiary education. Mary knew she was on safe ground when she went on to write of her extensive reading, comparing it favourably to that of 'ignorant university educated women'.[79]

From reading these later letters it is possible to get some idea of the range of books passing through that atypical Victorian country home. There was the strong influence of Protestant tracts:

> . . . the Fairchild family's moral tales.
>
> I remember one moral tale in which Pa Fairchild took his offspring to some spot where a rotting corpse hung fluttering from a gibbet. The while he pointed out the shocking fate of these sad enfants who did not heed to admonishments of Father.
>
> All the same. I wish I had those books — much more entertaining than half the sickly whymsical Barryish tosh fed to the modern enfant.[80]

Shortly before she entered a nursing home to die, Mary wrote to Norman about her recent reading. She remained interested in both popular literature and in the writers of her girlhood. She was especially pleased to discover Collette:

> Very interesting to hear that at last someone has created a real young girl. So all the good women writers forget? Or do they refuse to remember their own youth?[81]

Into this quiet life of her later years, filled with mischievous letters, altered facts, books and visits from young relatives and humble collectors, there came, in the late 1950s, a chance to influence the by then very potent legend of her brother Norman and to place her own perspective on record. Mary Lindsay's self image as the pivotal figure in the family could now be endorsed by history. For Mary, Norman's appointment of John Hetherington as official biographer represented a respite from loneliness and another chance to continue her position as a handmaid to the arts.

After she ceased to have contact with Hetherington, Mary appears to have depended on Daryl. Despite their long antipathy, he was the person who

# MARY

consistently looked after her interests. He arranged for furnishings from the original drawing room to be placed in a reconstructed Lindsay room in the Ballarat Fine Art Gallery, and he made sure that she was well cared for in hospital. And the only writing by Mary Lindsay to be published in her lifetime was a dialogue of family life which Daryl included in *The Leafy Tree*. Mary's response to this book of family memoirs, which was the first publication to mention her as someone of importance, was to condemn it and its author.[82]

At the very end of her life Mary asked for no more letters to be sent to her, as she could not read them and did not want the humiliation of asking for help.[83] Despite promises made at various times to leave her property to Norman and other relatives, Mary was the first Lindsay to leave her estate away from the family. The Creswick Hospital where Robert had worked was left $1000, the Creswick Brass Band $600, the Creswick Fire Brigade $400, but her residual heir was the Ballarat Fine Art Gallery.

It was a final Mary twist. Daryl, from his position on the Ballarat Fine Art Gallery Board, could hardly object to the gift but, as he wrote to Bingo, he was less than happy with the way Pearl and her children had been disinherited.

*I was disgusted with her altering her will in particular leaving out Pearl — Its not so much a matter of money as the indecency of it. Both she and Robert were tarred with the same brush.*[84]

Mary died in early 1968. When he heard that she was dead, Norman in Springwood wrote to Rose in Hunters Hill: 'I've had a letter from Pearl's daughter Felicity saying that Mary pegged out in hospital, which was good news'.[85]

# 10

# The ghosts of Creswick

Mary's letters were so intermingled with the stories of Robert and Isabel that an examination of their lives had to be the next logical step in my search. Looking at their photographs, I kept thinking of them as diametrically opposed ghosts, haunting that old termite-ridden house at Creswick, watching it decay around them. I imagined Robert, of the dapper appearance, impeccable manners and air of superiority that was not substantiated by any actual achievement and frowsy Isabel in her own half-world, both haunting Mary as she constructed her family histories.

The house doesn't exist any more. Instead, the visitor to modern Creswick will find a plaque recording the existence of the home of the famous family.

The idea of ghosts at Creswick is not mine, but comes from a letter that Robert wrote to Lionel in September 1931, shortly after he returned to nurse his mother.

. . . the shock of everything was a lot more than I had anticipated. God and Gosh — Gods teeth. and the virgins wound. I hadn't any idea of the horribleness of this Ibsen house — it makes one smile kinder sarcastic like when one reads of this 'delightful old house'! the aftermath of the horrors of ones youth are everywhere — and the ghosts keep one from sleeping at night.[1]

The Ibsen referred to was his play, *Ghosts*, and the reference was also taken up by Mary in a letter written shortly after Robert's death in 1951.

> *... but up here, never having left the home, one unavoidably can never escape from the Ghosts of our youth.*[2]

After I read their letters with their accusations counter accusations and unfulfilled dreams, I started to think that Chekhov, not Ibsen, was the appropriate author, but Ibsen is perhaps an easier name to call upon when making accusations of evil.

Robert made it clear that the sexual relationship between his parents was the evil, and the evidence of it was his youngest sister, Jane Isabel Lindsay.[3] His repugnance at her birth when his mother was nearing menopause, and his revulsion at her existence coloured his judgment of his mother and led him to write and behave in a way which appalled most of his relatives. To a certain extent Isabel remains an enigma, as the main sources of information about her are the hostile letters of Robert and Mary, both of whom were happy to label her a moron. But their attitude is in part caused by the frustrations of their own lives.

Robert Elliot Alexander Lindsay was born on 27 August 1872; he was therefore half way between the amiable, irresponsible Percy and the strong-willed charmer, Lionel. The first record of Robert's impact on the family comes in a letter from his grandfather, Thomas Williams, to his mother, written when the small boy was staying with him, presumably while Jane Lindsay prepared for the birth of Lionel.

> *We could not have a better boy in the house than dear Bertie. The only fault is a little cry when he is being bathed. Yesterday he corrected Grandma for saying 'horrible' and told her she should use right words . . . The day before Aunt Polly was singing 'Give me a penny', and when singing 'I am so hungry and cold' she heard a little voice, 'Are you so cold Auntie?' and looking behind her she saw Bertie in tears . . .*[4]

The younger generation was less approving. Norman gently mocked his brother for his fastidiousness and called him by his family nickname 'Bert', although he knew that he loathed it:

> *Bert was slim, pale, fair-haired, and even as a lad of ten, given to a perverted passion for stylism of appearance. His clothes were always neat, his collars clean, and his bowties daintily adjusted. And if a shocking scandal must be disclosed about him, he was in the habit of washing his face and hands in oatmeal and water to preserve his complexion.*[5]

Separation from a beloved mother and the arrival of a noisy usurper was one trigger for the childhood antipathy between Robert and Lionel. But these two had little in common. Lionel was dark with intense colouring; Robert was fair, coloured in neutral tones. Lionel was robust, always adventuring — climbing trees and exploring old mine shafts — while Robert preferred to stay indoors, assisting his mother with sewing. Lionel was a boy of great and passionate enthusiasms; Robert fastidious with an acute sense of irony. Lionel was often full of self-doubt and foreboding; Robert was better at criticising others. When domestic pragmatism led these two to share a bed, there was natural antagonism.

According to Norman:

*A repulsion as violent as this between the two brothers must have secreted its content of attraction, and that was manifested by the way Bert could not resist stinging Lionel into infuriated assaults on the person, which evoked from Bert screams for succour by Ma.*

*. . . A major theme for warfare was the claim to exclusive ownership of half the bed. Lionel, always first to denounce any intrusion on his rights to property, would draw an imaginary line down the centre of the bed and say 'You blinkin' well stick a toe over my side of the bed and you get a hiding . . .'* [6]

In time Lionel learnt to ignore his elder brother's needling and disdain. In adult life he responded to Robert with courtesy, but a private note indicates how much he loathed his childhood tormentor.[7] Robert ignored the absence of feeling and in the latter part of his life wrote begging letters to his brother. As he grew to maturity, Robert appears to have had an especially complex relationship with his family. For many years he was close to his mother, but loathed his father for his earthy humour and his robust lifestyle. He did, however, appreciate Robert Charles' knowledge of fine furniture and, in his adolescence, when the old Creswick mansion 'The Ferns' was sold, he visited it with his father, noting every detail of the interior:

R.C. [Robert Charles Lindsay] *and I went over to the house when the sale was on . . . It was a rude awakening to find the faded wall papers, the only fitting left in the drawing room, and an old gold harp, which I begged RC to buy for its beauty. . . The dining room had a big table in it on which were some ordinary bits of dinner service, and some cheap wine glasses. The carpet was bright green, with a pattern of red Kentish cherries sprawling over it, and which RC bought. he loved sales and it was owing to him that what good furniture we possessed was bought by him. Jane Elizabeth had no taste above Indian matting for the bedrooms and Nottingham lace curtains. the only ones I liked were a red damask pair, we bought for the old dining room, afterward a bedroom, which were caught back with a white china arum lily with two brass leaves, it was a terrible period. I remember the drawing room chimney, had a water face of strips of glazed paper, gushing out to the fender caught up high in the chimney to give it effects of falling over.*[8]

Lionel and Norman then had not been the only Lindsay children to be enticed by 'The Ferns' once a hotel, later a brothel, and in their childhood, 'a gentleman's mansion'.[9] Its high fence concealed gardens with exotic birds, including peacocks and macaws, which led Lionel and Norman to create a fantasy from the world of the Arabian Nights.

Despite the frequent letters to Norman, Robert was always closest to Mary.[10] There are no hostile references to Mary in his letters, and he always writes of her need to be protected. In their old age they became 'the Creswick Lindsays', a genteel couple living out a fantasy of their own intellectual erudition and aristocratic associations, dependent on their famous brothers.

Norman would always help Mary; Lionel and Daryl saw Isabel as their primary responsibility. None of the successful brothers ever expressed a sense of financial obligation towards Robert. Mary and Robert also shared a special bond in their hostility to Isabel. Robert was twenty-two and working in the local bank at the time of his sister's birth. The 1890s Depression meant that there was no chance of a university education for this generation of Lindsays — for those who could exist within the constraints of their time, art would be the passport to money and fame.

Australia in the nineteenth and twentieth centuries embraced the European conventions applicable to artists. These were typified by a wild bohemian youth spent providing some kind of interest for socially well-connected power brokers, followed by a relatively affluent middle age, and the respect of governments when old. But Robert, who always felt obliged to be a 'gentleman', could not be a bohemian.

By the mid–1890s, Percy pursued the graceful career of a landscape painter and the social obligations of a man about town. He was easily persuaded to join Lionel in his dream of living *la vie bohème* in the big city, where they were soon joined by Norman. The younger children were still at school, but Mary was helping her mother to run the house. Under these circumstances, with a new baby in the house, Robert and Mary saw themselves as the principal victims of their parents' continuing sex life.

From letters it is clear that Robert especially was shocked at the thought that his parents, who were by this time often in dispute over day to day concerns, could have an intimate physical relationship. Isabel, whose very existence was proof that her mother's often expressed disapproval of Dr Lindsay was not absolute, was called by Robert 'that Damnable last result of got between waking and sleeping', an insult which also covered his interpretation of her conception.[11] And she was born when Robert was beginning to question his own sexual identity.

In a letter to Mary written some years after Robert's death, Norman remembered a time when Robert as a young man underwent a conversion to evangelical Christianity, 'a queer quirk in one of our family, and especially in one so fastidious over emotionalism, and with such a hard skeptical streak in him as Bert. I think he got over it very quickly'.[12] Presumably this was while Robert was being the dutiful son, supplementing the family income with his wages from the bank. In one letter Norman recounts an occasion when the wife of a bank manager tried to seduce Robert and he fled to Norman's protection in Melbourne.[13] But this incident has a curious parallel in a letter that Robert himself wrote to Norman, not about himself, but about a man who worked in the bank at Creswick. The story may therefore be a Lindsay embroidery:

*. . . he wore a diamond ring on his small finger — and his hands were stumpy and coarse. he parted his fair hair in the middle and then combed it to stand up on each side , and wore a fair moustache. he had pale blue eyes and the voice of a eunuch — his trousers were very wide., almost entirely covered his very small feet when he stood up — and the heels of his boots were high. Which also helped the deformity of feet too small —*

*he wore a black bell-topper in which he deposited a pair of pale grey (unworn) kid gloves, when picking his hat on the chair by the door, and carried a green malacca cane, with an ivory top. I can remember Mother taking me to the Bank and he showed me the money in little pieces. Masses of sovereigns, and gave me 6 — which I thought particularly mean when he had so much . . . years later when he returned and was in a panic about his house-keeper forcing him into marriage — I remember him, when I was in bed, in deep conversation with Robert Charles in the consulting room, the latter reassuring him that he would be able to perform the marriage act, the voice and the vanity rather suggest the homo–sexuality , and his constant visits to Mother imploring her to get him out of the entanglement help this too. After his housekeeper had been there a week she appeared at the table with him, and he came hopping to Mother for advice, which was to get rid of her at once, and not allow such familiarity, but he hadn't the guts and charged when she threw things at him. Eventually she married him, and he took badly to drink — which was the end of him. He was recalled to the Melbourne Office — when she used to ask for him and have a nice row — twice she called. They said he was out.*[14]

From his disparaging comment on the man's homosexuality it seems that Robert never discussed his sexuality with his brothers, although his siblings were aware of it and discussed him amongst themselves. Perhaps because he was an especially passive child, Robert placed undue emphasis on the importance of social position, unlike his more active siblings who came to revere personal achievement. He knew that his father, by virtue of being the doctor, was one of the most important people in Creswick and that his mother had great social significance. In later life, after the prolonged stay in England where he learnt that Methodists had no status and that doctors were merely respectable in comparison to the aristocracy, he gave this description of the female social hierarchy in his childhood town.

*The Ancienne noblesse of those days were the Tremearnes, Mrs Lewers, Mr Dowling, Mrs Saby, and Aunt Say [Selina Williams, Jane Lindsay's youngest sister]. Mrs Fiddian and Frasers in the distance. Then the middle class. Trades people — the Jebbs, Miss Soloway, the Gardners and the dissenting clergy — these latter were never intimate with the nobility, although occasionally Maggie Jebb, through having been to England, and journeys to Mt Lavina when in Ceylon, would gate crash with Pollie Soloway. When leaving the sacred edifice next door on Sunday morning — and would discuss the lower orders — and the local preacher. Pollie Soloway being a wit had always something caustic about Mactons — giving themselves 'airs'. Maggie Jebb to try to live up to her superiors always quoted her trip to England . . . On her way back she met Mrs Russell-Jones, whom she spoke of with bated breath, who mixed in the rarest society — Maggie must have strayed from the truth considerably, when informing them of their family mansion, little thinking she would see it, much later through a constant change of letters, the noble Russell-Jones suggested a visit to the house of Jebb — and on the first morning was so horrified by having to pass dunnicans, costumes and heads of sewing women to get out of the back gate*

*— she fled early the next morning. Mama after deciding with a shut mouth to leave the beau monde — gave up calling on the Dowlings and Sabys, and only occasionally exchanged the courtesies and dash of tea with the Tremearnes and Lewers. But never with the Jebbs, till much later. Maggie was occasionally tolerated. There were three old maids called Wally one served in Waltons shop, the others attended to cows, but were not on bowing acquaintance with Mama.* [15]

The time he spent attending his mother, going to church, and making polite conversation to 'the gentry' of Creswick gave Robert Lindsay many occasions to note visual effects and social attitudes in the small town. Because Maggie Jebb was the draper's daughter and his mother loved beautiful clothes, he also became caught up in the details of fashion and was aware that even clothes made in Creswick had their origins on the other side of the world.

*One day a shipment of draper's goods arrived (said to be from England) and Maggie arrived at the gate with the fashionable news that two Paris bonnets were formed — small light fitting scull caps covered with flattened white everlasting daisies. — and were what Queen Alexandra was known to be wearing — and in a moment of mental aberration Mama was persuaded to buy one, Maggie the other, and the following Sunday in church caused a sensation, and was much discussed as the village bonnet there was much overtrimming. The following Sunday morning as Mama was devoutly holding her nose over the pews in front of her, she caught sight of the three peasants sitting in front of her with the same exclusive bonnets on, giving the lie to a good story of being the exclusive wear of Royalty. Mama could hardly get out of the church quickly enough, puffing like a war horse and tore the offensive bonnet off her head and then to ribbons, fulminating at the impudence of the peasants daring to copy her, I don't know how she squared the Golden Rule, with her autocratic manner in keeping the vulgar at a distance.* [16]

He was so precise in the way he noticed the hypocrisy of others, especially his mother as she cared for both social position and the all embracing love of God. He was less aware of his own failings.

As Robert came to maturity the family was poor, but with a collective memory of affluence. While their siblings became passionate about art, Robert and Mary started to weave a bitter tale of regret at lost opportunities. For most of his life Robert lived in a world which was to him hideously imperfect. He was called Bert by his family, but he loathed the name as 'common'. His signature in letters to his siblings was a carefully styled ambiguity, but even this was problematic as 'Robert' was a name he shared with his father. His disgust at 'Bert' is recorded in a letter responding to Norman's appreciation of some of his short poetry:

> Thanks too for your kind remarks about the Chinese pieces . . . I did them a long while ago, when I was knocked down in London by a motor vehicle, and was lying in bed with a broken leg and my face plastered and bandaged, with only half an eye to look upon a dreary world, and not quite enough to read with. A friend sent me Arthur Waley's 170 Chinese poems — which sent me on the downward path. Do you know him? . . . Lionel came to town a little time after I came back, and urging me to write, I showed what I had done. He took them to Sydney. A few weeks later he left for England leaving his affairs in the hands of Bingo — I wrote to her — about a year afterwards — but did not get a reply, and some time later, I received a cheque for a couple of £1.0 — to 'Bert Lindsay for Chinoisities' — his address. I can't remember who signed the cheques as our unlamented Mama was making life for M and me, very active to put it mildly. I took it that someone had used one and sent me a cheque for it — otherwise I would have returned it — if I had thought it was for the lot.(the typed ones I sent you) then a fellow I knew in my salad days called and said he had seen a bit of verse in a magazine by Bert Lindsay, and wanted to know if I was the unfortunate suffering under such a name. [17]

In Robert, the family tradition of bawdy storytelling took a prurient turn and many of his anecdotes concern the consequences of sexual relations, for both animals and humans.

> Nothing of news to relate — Strachan's cow is about to calve — so we don't get a jug of skim milk daily — and the milkman's wife has had a miscarriage. A victorious virgin lady at Streatham called in the local Dr. to pronounce and gaze upon her swollen legs, which he did upon her equally swollen stomach — predicting the birth of someone's chick at any moment; she indignantly dismissed the charge, and when asked if she had any dealings with any one, hotly denied she hadn't and the only one who had been near her for months, had never been familiar, merely 'hover around the brush' — enough — [18]

The actual dynamics of the Lindsay children were probably no more intense than in any other large family. Over decades of correspondence there are clamourings for fairness, justice, and the right to freedom as the siblings continually manipulate each other for their own advantage.

In about 1895, when Robert was twenty-three, Norman wrote a long pleading letter to Lionel and Percy in Melbourne. Norman hated school, but was enjoying editing the *Boomerang*, the school paper which had previously been edited by his brothers. He desperately wanted to join them in their life of bohemian adventure, especially as Percy was now being recognised as a promising young artist. In the midst of remarks about screaming children and thumping pianos, there is a throwaway line: 'Bert has one of his slapping fits on, and is slapping me all the time. I've spoken to him severely and I'll kick him when he comes around again.'[19]

Norman wrote at length in *My Mask* of the different ways Robert would instantly drive Lionel to a rage, and he knew that Lionel regarded Robert as corrupted and corrupting. Norman would have known that any hint of harassment by Robert would lead the self-consciously chivalrous Lionel to come to his rescue. It is not surprising that within months of receiving this letter, Lionel had arranged for Norman to leave home. Their mother could not be told of any problems involving Robert, and their father's authority was encapsulated by Norman's comment that 'The Pater has gone into Ballarat to buy a new horse — on the razzle — stayed all night, and isent home yet'.[20] But Norman left Creswick on good terms with Robert. In *The Embattled Olympian*, Norman remembered that it was Bert who came to Creswick station to farewell him when he left town. He led Hetherington to believe that it was the first time he realised that this very inhibited brother actually cared for him. There were other contacts over the years as Robert was transferred to different bank branches in country towns in Victoria. As he removed himself from the vulgar squabbling of children, the elegant but distant persona of Robert Lindsay emerged from that of the sensitive little Bertie.[21]

At the end of 1909, Norman, Ruby and Will Dyson travelled together to London to seek fame at the centre of their world. Robert followed soon after. His departure for London, which effectively left Lionel in Sydney as the sole support for the Creswick family, appears to have irritated Lionel who wrote, 'what's Bert doing, as his family interests him more than they do me'.[22] While there are slightly contradictory accounts of exactly what he did in London and later America, there is general agreement on his choice of career. According to Norman, Robert went to London to be a dress designer. This was expanded by Harry Chaplin in notes he made based on conversations with Robert.

*After banking experience in Creswick, and other Victorian towns, he left for London, where he was employed for some years in a British Government department. Later he established his own business in Belgravia. He had a talent for designing, and whilst living in America was commissioned to design the dresses for the Mardi Gras Carnival in New Orleans. He was joined for a while by his sister Mary.* [23]

Daryl, writing in The Leafy Tree, does not describe the career in quite such glowing terms.
*Apparently he found no market for his costume designs and, to earn a living, got some kind of secretarial post with the Foreign Office. A year or two later he was posted to the British consulate in New York. From there he went to the Consulate in New Orleans and sent to Mary to keep house for him.*[24]

The truth is probably a combination of these stories. For the purpose of his own narrative Norman had to see Robert as mobile enough to always be there to assist him, while Daryl had a long-term perception of Robert as a failure. In London, in 1910, Robert put himself at Norman's service, doing all he could to promote the career of his talented younger brother. Because he could read the implications of the slightest nuances of behaviour, Robert understood the English class system, and later both he and Mary were to claim that the Creswick Lindsays were antipodean relations to an English earl, and that their grandmother, Mary Cottingham, was likewise from an aristocratic family.[25]

In letters written after Robert's death in 1951, Norman recalled how his attempt to break into the English publishing industry was facilitated by Robert:
*He came to London on my first visit there, and when I had to entertain a guest or two to lunch at my studio, usually in the way of business, I always left the event to him, and he always turned out a very effective meal, having a high sense of doing the right thing at such social functions.*[26]

For Norman, Robert's presence in London meant the services of a superior butler, who was even able to smooth over the social awkwardness of having Rose as his unmarried companion. Robert, however, saw matters differently. To him, Norman was both the beloved younger brother and the passport to the world he knew he ought to claim for himself. Years later, exiled in Creswick, he would dwell on that brief period when he would visit the Chelsea Arts Club with Norman and on occasions witness the conversations of those literary figures he most admired:

*I saw a little article on Max Beerbohm in a paper with a portrait. Such a different face from when we met him on our advent in London. Do you remember he asked you to lunch at the Chelsea Arts club on Xmas Day. Very few members were present: and when Lambert took his place, (they all had their own places) in front of Lambert's was a neat little box tied up with a piece of holly at the top. 'Ah' he said 'I am the one especially remembered member', drawing the others attention, as he opened the box, which contained a box of domes of silence — Max had done this as Lambert never stopped talking. I believe he did not speak for over a week — I know his pictures are excellent, but to me he was the most horrible vain bore, I ever met.* [27]

Norman claimed he sent Robert ahead of him to New York, to find accommodation and arrange matters when he planned to move there to work for *Harper's Magazine*. But instead Norman returned to Australia, leaving Robert alone in a strange city. He partly justified his act by claiming that Robert had 'a profession that could just as easily be practised in New York as London', when Norman was only too aware from his own career that people in the arts rely on personal contacts for success.[28] This account also makes Robert appear even more to be Norman's agent, arranging all his affairs for him, tidying up his life.

It is here that Daryl's narrative appears more logical. If Robert, working as a clerk in the British Foreign Office managed to arrange a transfer to the consulate in New York where Norman had some career openings, this would explain his early departure. Norman saw Robert purely as a designer, so in his narrative mentions a partnership Robert formed with a young American he met on the voyage to the States, with whom he established a 'fabrics and dress styles' business in New Orleans. Daryl's account, however, has Robert working at the British Consulate in New Orleans, which was where Mary joined him.

It was some time after working at the consulate that Robert resigned and went into partnership with 'an American called Hollis in a smart millinery establishment'. There are no records of the details of Robert's life or his friendships to guide in reconstruction of these years. What is known is that some time after Mary left New Orleans, Robert returned to New York and then England.[29]

Daryl's account of Robert in the 1920s has him employed in 'some kind of job in the Fisheries Department. What he did there Heaven only knows, as I cannot think of a more unlikely person to be associated with the fish trade!'.[30]

ABOVE: *Robert and Jane Lindsay's wedding photograph 18 May, 1869.*

LEFT: *Mary as a small child.*

ABOVE: *Three 'pirates', Norman, Lionel, and Ray Parkinson c.1896. (Probably photographed in the Fitzroy Gardens.)*

BELOW: *Idyll. Norman and Jacques Casteau at Heidelberg, Victoria, late 1890s.*

ABOVE: *Creswick tableau c.1900. Ruby, Norman, Pearl, Percy (partly concealed), Reg, Will Dyson, and Mary in foreground.*

LEFT: *Rose c.1903, photographed by Norman.*

BELOW: *Norman and Rose, c.1903.*

*Norman and Jack, c.1903.*

ABOVE: *Rose as classic nude, c.1905.*

BELOW: *Rose at Bondi Beach in 1910. Photograph by Montague Grover. A note on the back in Rose's writing reads, 'Dave Smith the Boxer hauls in the fish net.'*

*Rose posing for Norman.*

LEFT: *The inscription on this photo is: 'Rose photographed beside Cave in Lane Cove, childhood days. The cave was used as a hideout by kids …' Print by Keith Wingrove, from a photograph by Norman. Some attempt has been made to mutilate the negative to protect the privacy of the crouching model.*

BELOW: *The Lindsay family at Creswick, c. August 1912. Left to right: Jessie, Jane Lindsay, Mary, Percy, Pearl (holding baby), Colin McPhee. Seated: Norman (holding toddler), Isabel. Note the turn in Isabel's foot. This has to be shortly after the birth of Felicity on 31 July 1912.*

LEFT: *Rose with Jane and Honey, 1920s.*

BELOW: *Rose posing for Norman, 1920s.*

*Rose in Egyptian costume, 1920s.*

RIGHT: *Rose at Springwood.
Photograph by Harold Cazneaux, 1920s.*

BELOW: *Norman in his old age. The inscription on verso by Rose,
'The best black mood photo ever taken of NL By Monte Luke'.*

Above: *John and Mollie Hetherington with Norman, 1960s.*

Left: *Mary at Creswick, 1960s.*

RIGHT AND BELOW: *Ruby and Norman Lindsay, at Creswick, c.1901. Photograph by Lionel Lindsay.*

ABOVE: *Lindsay tableau at Creswick, Isabel on pony, c.1900.*
*Photograph by Lionel Lindsay.*

BELOW: *Lionel and Norman at Springwood, about the time of the start of their great quarrel, c.1916.*
*Photograph by Rose Lindsay.*

RIGHT: *Ruby Lindsay and Bingo at Lindfield, 1909.*
*Photograph by Lionel Lindsay.*

BELOW: *Isabel Lindsay. Aust. c. 1900-1973.*
*Jane Elizabeth Lindsay pen and ink, pencil*
*Mary Lindsay Bequest, 1975*
*Collection: Ballarat Fine Art Gallery*

*Norman Lindsay, Have Faith, early 1930s. Etching, stipple, engraving and drypoint, 27.9 x 25.2. (The reclining figure under the sexually potent bull — note the penis-horn — is readily recognisable as Margaret. The clothed woman whose hand is being kissed by Norman could be Rose. As Rose printed all Norman's etchings the possible messages in this one are boundless.) Courtesy of Lin Bloomfield.*

He probably did have a clerical job as a regular source of income, but in London Robert also had another life. At the end of 1919 he wrote to Mary, who passed his news to Rose and Norman:

> . . . I had a letter from Bert last week. He is doing some occasional designing of hats for a woman he knows who has started a hat shop. He would like if he can to get more work of the sort, & drop his dull permanent job later.
>
> But he won't take any risks unless he's certain of enough other work to keep him going. He had just finished painting 3 leghorn hats with fruit and flowers, for 3 dames. Sounds rather villainous form of decoration, doesn't it?[31]

When Lloyd Rees visited London in 1923, fellow artists Elioth Gruner and Harold Herbert introduced him to 'George' Lindsay, the brother of Norman and Lionel, and it is as George Lindsay that Robert appears in Rees' memoirs.

> The two men joined us and Lindsay seemed very quiet and wore a sort of Australian felt hat, hanging down over his face. Later . . . I found myself . . . in company with the very silent George. Aware of the silence I ventured the question. 'Do you ever think of coming back to Australia?' He very deliberately looked at me and said, 'No, I can't go back there'. I was completely mystified and Gruner never gave me any further details but I found out from Daryl later that George had a little fashion shop in London.[32]

It was a telling pseudonym for someone who could never be a 'Joe', the name Norman, Daryl, Lionel and their Dyson friends called themselves. 'Joe' was a term for mateship, camaraderie, and art. 'George' was Rose Soady's *nom de guerre* when her real identity had to be concealed at all costs. To the outside world it sounded respectable and staid, but to the Lindsays it was a name associated with illicit romance and a double life.

Robert appears to have maintained links with artistic and creative circles during his London years, living life on such an exquisite small scale that he was described by his friend Martin Boyd as someone 'in whom the family artistry was confined to appreciation and discriminating taste'.[33]

The Boyds and the Lindsays are the two eminent families of artists in Australia, so it was intriguing to discover links between them. I knew that Joan Lindsay, born Joan Weigall, was a Boyd relative, but the connection between Robert and Martin was unexpected.

In October 1993 I interviewed Arthur Boyd for the *Bulletin* and he told me that he had painted a portrait of Robert Lindsay in the 1940s when Robert was staying with Martin. A year later Elizabeth Webby showed me James Dalley's catalogue, *Australian Literature of the Nineteen Twenties*, which listed a copy of Martin Boyd's *Retrospect* of 1922, once owned by Robert Lindsay and inscribed by him with a love poem to Boyd. But this remained such a discreet relationship that it is not mentioned in Brenda Niall's biography of Martin Boyd.

'Robert was very kind to me when I first went to London. But he had an accident of some kind and went back to Australia pretty soon,' said Peter when I asked him about his uncle. 'He was a friend of Martin Boyd, the writer. And they were so alike that they could have stepped out of the same chorus line.'

Peter was eighty-five when he said that. His unselfconscious turn of phrase made me realise how quickly attitudes have changed.

For Robert, London represented sexual freedom as well as the adventure of the big wide world. There was a homosexual community in which he could be himself without shaming his family or being ridiculed.

Peter arrived in London in about 1929, so he must have seen Robert just before his departure for Creswick. Robert placed so much emphasis on family that I could see him helping out the young tearaway Peter, off to find adventure and make his fortune far from family. Peter was less interested in visiting uncles in bijou apartments than meeting up with his larrikin cousin Phil Lindsay who had come to London to be a writer, so even without the traffic accident that precipitated Robert's return to Australia, contact would probably soon have been lost.

Robert appears to have come home to Creswick for a variety of reasons. He had heard, perhaps from Daryl, that Mary was not coping with the family situation (Mary always claimed she had pleaded with him to stay in London).

Then there were his own circumstances. The Depression meant that there were no longer duchesses, or even elegant women, wishing to have their hats designed or rooms arranged with style. Wages in clerical jobs were cut, and London was cold and damp. The traffic accident had left Robert with a broken leg; in addition he was ill with a heavy cold. It was the correct thing to return home to nurse one's mother, so there was no disgrace in retreat. And surely a man with his London experience and sophistication could hope to design hats, dresses and interiors in Melbourne. His superior manners had been polished by close contact with the 'best' society, and this too would help him gain business.

An annuity of 25/- per week was purchased from his accumulated savings and Robert returned home to Creswick. On his arrival he wrote to Lionel:
> I didn't see Peter before I left London. Everything was so hurried. I only made up my mind to come out ten days before I sailed. And I got up from my bed of death voiceless . . . thinking if one was to have one's head off, the least time one had to consider to happening the better.[34]

The effects of the Great Depression were even more savage in Australia than Europe, and very bad in rural Victoria. The mines had closed in Creswick years before and now there was no work even for farmhands. Robert's belief that the magic name of 'Lindsay' would enable him to design costumes for the squattocracy was hollow. No one wanted hats, and references, even from duchesses, were valueless. Home was worse than Robert had imagined. Nothing was well organised, Mary was frequently ill with symptoms that ranged from hysteria to migraines, and his elegant, competent, socially aware mother was a senile old lady who still insisted that she was in charge. He wrote to Lionel of the change:
> . . . she's remarkably strong and that strong fighting instinct of the Dissenter gives her amazing energy . . .
>    . . . I thought I'd tell you all this . . . in case Mother writes to you, as she does to Mary, explaining that she's thankful God has given her strength to do all she can, now that Mary is ill, implying she is doing everything, when as a matter of fact all she does is muddle horribly in the kitchen and burn everything from drying clothes to food, while I do everything in the house from bringing up the wood I've chopped, a difficult pastime in which I take no pleasure . . . If I don't do this Mother sends for some old retainers and pays them — for doing nothing.[35]

And then there was Isabel.
> Mother and Isabel are both impossible and hopeless. I paid all the bills when I came out, and said loudly, we wouldn't have any more. We pay cash for everything — and directly my back is turned they are both running up small unnecessary a/cs. It's maddening. This morning a woman arrived with a huge bunch of flowers for which I paid 3/- and then another 2/- to post the blasted things to those old women the Aunts Selina and Polly. These stupid little things are continually happening. If she had sent these crapulous old

*beldames poison I wouldn't have minded, but it's maddening when Mary has for years been going without the bare necessities to keep down expenses.*

*. . . Jane Isabel is about as useful as a headache — God Joe, she's a problem. She has been so hopelessly spoilt by Mother, that she can't do anything and sulks if I ask her to go on a message . . . I've spoken till I'm tired to Mother about her, but Mother is like a wounded tigress, defending her young fiercely.*[36]

This image of Isabel, while hardly friendly, does not quite fit with Robert's later rages against the 'moron'. In her own old age, after Isabel was admitted to hospital with a stroke, Mary wrote that her youngest sister was 'a deplorable victim of Fate, in the form of some retarding to start with, added to the worst possible environment and treatment'.[37] In Mary's eyes it was the over-nurturing by her mother that ultimately disabled Isabel.

*I find it hard to forgive Mother over Isabel. She had a conscience over Isabel. It took the form of destroying her further, deliberately keeping her young, keeping her dependent, helpless and useless, in her muddled attempt at compensating.*

*If there is any human being I hold in contempt its the so called good self sacrificing mother. — The truly good mother can be hard if its to save her child.*[38]

I looked again at Isabel's letter which had accompanied Bingo's wedding present when she went to Columbo to be married away from her family:

Darling Bingo,

Just a Tiny gift from me with all my love and every best wish for you always.

Oh Bing dear we are all so sorry and too disappointed for words that we can't see you. but; we will all be thinking of you. We have Perc, and Pete [Peter Hammond Lindsay, Percy's son] *with us at present. And last night Dan and Joan arrived for a short visit to us. And Joan doesn't seem too well I hope she will be better soon.*

Once more all my love and the Best of Luck darling Bingo
Yours lovingly
Isabel

It wasn't profound, but it was hardly the writing of an idiot. The letters were carefully formed in copperplate, she knew what she wanted to say, and said it well.

Isabel was the last baby, the tenth child born to a 45-year-old woman who loved babies. Her childhood coincided with the others leaving home, the family financial crisis, and the scandal of Norman's marriage. It is not surprising that her mother was in no hurry for her to grow up. When she was not irritated by her, Mary could admit that her youngest sister had some talent. When she wrote of her family to Harry Chaplin, Mary claimed:

*Then my youngest sister Isabel, who at the developing stage in life showed greater promise than her elder sister Ruby — now at middle age her weak little drawings are worthless. She is a hypochondriac who has never done anything that required any effort. I regard her as the victim of a mother's dominance that kept her youngest child always dependent. For twenty years I tried to save my unfortunate little sister, but it wasn't any use. Now, of course it's far too late. What you see there was a natural impulse to art even in this failure.*[39]

There are two pen drawings by Isabel in the Ballarat Fine Art Gallery which confirm her talent. The subjects, a niece practising the violin and her mother in extreme old age, indicate they were made in the late 1920s. Because the circumstances of Creswick at that time appear to have altered her irrevocably, it is extremely difficult to ascertain what kind of person Jane Isabel Lindsay originally was. It is also extremely difficult to understand how her limited life impacted on the family before her mother's final illness.

She was a noisy baby, known for years as 'Goo'. There is a drawing of her by the sixteen-year-old Norman — 'Goo who is at present shrieking herself into a blue fit'.[40] Family photographs show her looking alert, staring straight at the camera, and she appears in some of the photographs of Creswick pageants sitting on a pony.[41] In one photograph, which must have been taken in about 1912, her leg appears at an odd angle, as though it were twisted. The other odd thing about this image is that though she must then have been aged about eighteen, her hair is still down as though she was a child.

Veronica Rowan, Dr Strachan's daughter, who knew Isabel very slightly in the 1920s and 1930s, remembers her as someone who was seen as fey, with less than normal mental ability, but recalls there was a general belief that her eccentric behaviour was a deliberate tactic to avoid difficult situations. Even though she was only in her thirties, the Strachan children thought of her as 'old', and certainly older than Mary. Mrs Rowan's assessment of Isabel is that 'she was canny, and by being "shy" she got out of many unpleasant jobs and could draw away by herself'.[42]

Ron Radford, who knew many Lindsay family friends when he was Director of the Ballarat Fine Art Gallery, claims that there was a general belief that she was autistic.[43] However, there is no record of Isabel having any of the standard characteristics of autism. She may have stood in the main street of Creswick for hours, as still as a tree, but she was warm and affectionate, happy to cuddle her old mother or go on church outings. The most reasoned assessment of Isabel in her old age comes from Dr Earle J. Williams, who befriended Mary and visited the Lindsay home on several occasions in the 1950s. He observed that 'in my experience Isabel Lindsay was simply slow and this in itself rendered her dependent on Mary'.[44]

Isabel remains a background figure in family dramas for many years. She is mentioned in a letter written by her mother to Norman in 1925 as being pleased with the expensive clothes that Rose had sent them: 'Isabel will be writing to you herself. She loves the silk dress and it fits well. She will be sending you a snap taken in it soon.'[45]

Isabel was always protected by her mother when attacked by disapproving siblings, and she appears to have returned the devotion without reservation. But as Jane declined there was no protection, and after Robert's return there was instead a growing and unrelenting hostility as though she was the cause of his troubles.

After the refinement of Belgravia and his pretensions to aristocracy, Robert found the dinner-time scramble at Creswick appalling.

*Everyone tried to lift hot plates, drain vegetables, make sauces and gravies and dish the food. This causes everyone to get in each other's way splendidly, and generally a plate is broken and a finger or two is burnt in the scuffle — Finally when we are all seated, except Isobel — (who taking after her unlamented father, goes down the street, or eats alone.) The vegetables are discovered to still be in the pot, everyone rushes out, to bring them in and again confusion. They are burnt from sitting too long on the overhot stove. Mama carves, She cannot give up one of her habits of a life time, spattering the cloth, the wall, herself in her attack upon the unfortunate joint. by the time Mary and I are served, no one is in much heart for anything. and then to be offered some baked custard or other wholesome dish as an aftermath, accompanied by a cup of doubtful tea, inclines the gentlest to sigh for a juniper tree under which to die. Cursing God, after the manner of Jobs comforters. I have said loudly. I do not like puddings, and seldom does anyone eat them . . .* [46]

# THE GHOSTS OF CRESWICK

After such a long absence Robert saw he had a mission to create an outpost of 'civilisation' in the Antipodes. Mary needed nurturing, but his London values soon came into conflict with his mother's traditions.

*When I arrived several of the people had asked me to dinner and I suggested returning the civility, which was treated with scant approval by Mother. And she wouldn't countenance anything but later in the way of a beverage as it was the depth of winter. I said this could be done so decided I wouldn't have dinner, and asked them to come after dinner, and provided cocktails, whisky and gin. (These are the fashionable drinks here) I also suggested that as Mother was tired, it would be advisable, as she did not know any of the people who were coming — she go to bed. This was treated as an injury, and inferred she was not wanted. So she and Isobel kept up a murmuring conversation in her bedroom, while the guests sensitive to the depressing atmosphere, spoke in subdued whispers, and drank sparingly, and little, giving the impression that they were to be invited later to view the corpse, which was being prepared in the next room. God. I've never put in such an evening. The guests left early, with a guilty air of having discovered unintentionally a hidden secret, and Mary and I were treated the next day as if we were keeping a disorderly house. It was too ridiculous. I explained to Mother, that I was nearly sixty, that I had all my life been in the habit of offering the stranger within my gates whatever I had in the way of wine. And that civilised people were in the habit of passing an evening pleasantly without getting drunk — but of course if she was going to take the matter so seriously I wouldn't ask anyone to come again, which meant both Mary and me having to refuse the small hospitalities, Difficult to get out of — it has come to this, and now when the day has been over long, I take Mary a drink when she is in bed, and we drink silently with closed doors.*[47]

Jane Lindsay appears to have been a traditional Methodist with attitudes towards alcohol that dated back to the eighteenth century. Beer, wine and punch were permitted at parties. And Jane provided wines to mellow her well-organised dinner parties. Mary remembered that:

*. . . Mother provided a limited amount of booze at dinner parties at which she presided. Also I remember always two wine glasses before each guest, one for claret and one small one for port wine, but there was no further drinking for gentlemen left to their port . . .* [48]

John and Charles Wesley had preached against the evils of spirits and these were anathema to Jane. It was many decades since Robert had been in contact with Methodism and he could not understand his mother's attitude. And rather than empathising with Isabel in her retreat from the chaotic household, Robert soon came to regard her as one of the main causes of discord and wrote bitterly to Norman:

*That Damnable last result of got between waking and sleeping, is really the cause as she's the most damnably malicious bitch ever come across, taking it out on Mary directly my back is turned, and Mary too tired to kick her in the behind and tell her to go to Hell. A thing she should have done years ago. I try to keep the peace, hating rows, as they affect my cheap stomach. She has got so bad that one can't ask the bitch to do anything without her flying into a barbarian rage, and rushing to Mother, who then roars at Mary as an inhuman monster. Its just as bloody as when we suffered from the bitulous Robert Charles.*[49]

Although Lionel destroyed many of Robert's letters to him from this period, and some of Norman's appear to have been censored by Rose, enough have survived in various collections to give some sort of picture of the last days of Jane Lindsay, and of the lives of Robert, Isabel and Mary, together in the house at Creswick. Norman's response to Robert's diatribes was to empathise with his plight and to offer him support. The letters were typed, so that Jane would not realise that her much loved younger son was in opposition to her. Although most of these were destroyed, someone, presumably Daryl, placed one in the La Trobe Library so that Norman's attitude to his family could be placed on public record.

*Rose and I enjoyed your highly explosive letter, by which it is clear that you temporarily distract your own attention from an intention of blowing a hole in the old home town and sinking it in the bottomless abyss. You'll do it yet, I suspect.*

*It must be a rather terrifying experience to come back alive to a petrified image of a past existence. I sympathise with you, but at the same time I confess to a sneaking relief that you are back in Creswick. In this mean way I stultify a species of bad conscience for not going there myself. My excuses are so genuine, too. I can't go to Sydney for the day without getting knocked up. I catch colds at the slightest provocation. Sometimes without any provocation. I haven't been in a train for ten years . . .*

*. . . I endorse reflections of yours on the poisonous assumption that family relationships maintain because of themselves a special virtue . . . You*

*and Mary are the only two members of the Lindsay label who are still my friends . . .* [50]

Robert's vision of his mother as long suffering but beautiful was soon tempered by his self-righteous hostility. In his letters to Norman, he sometimes interposed remarks about her with comments on Isabel, so it is hard for the reader to know whether it is his mother or his sister who stands condemned, especially as Robert often called Isabel by her baptismal name of 'Jane'. In a curious way this is appropriate, as Isabel appears to have identified completely with her mother's interests and her mother's needs.

*The moron hadn't returned more than a quarter of an hour before she had Mother storming and raging at Mary and me. (She hadn't been able to move for days) and when I went in to see what was the matter, she raged at me, like a maniac, and ordered me out of the room, grabbed up a candle saying she was going into Mother's room, and she would stay with her. I just saved her setting herself on fire — as there's nothing so inflammable as flannelette. It was all damnably funny. She stood up there like a tragic actress — wild haired and eyed —and dramatically ordered me out of the room — 'How dare you speak to me, open that door at once. I shall be obeyed.' God! The ruling passion! I pushed the moron out and said if she came near, I'd have her locked up — and Mary and I lifted Mama back to bed. She fighting like a cat in a bag, and lay glowering at us like a wounded panther and full of delightful fulminations — that all I wanted was to get her in her coffin so as I could get possession of the house. — I said are you quite in your senses Mother a conscious — 'Yes I am. And never was saner' said the angry parent — so I said I'm glad you are. because I'm going to tell you a few home truths — to begin with you have been a dominating woman all your life. always in the right, hardly a day passed but you shouted and raged at us or Father, and none of us have had a comfortable hour in the dear old home as you call it, it's the most desolate place I've ever been in, and you have stormed your way through — tramping on everyone — because you haven't the capacity of enjoying yourself — you wouldn't allow anyone else the smallest pleasure . . . and although you know perfectly well that Mary has sacrificed her life for you and the others — and just because she has more brains than you have, you have hated her and fought her, in every way — and you can let Isabel go on telling what you know to be lies, and siding with her, and taking it out of Mary, who does everything for you. You haven't the slightest particle of feeling for anyone except yourself — and then Isabel — you think I want this*

> *accursed old house. If it weren't that Mary is still alive, I'd walk out this minute and leave you to the tender mercies of Isabel. You would have nothing, as you are eating my bread and butter at the moment —the shrunken dividends just pay the rates and insurance, and your pension of £1 a week all goes down Isabel's throat . . . like her filthy old father hadn't the guts to say she was sorry — your Christian will never do that. I then went out and had a theatrical scene with the moron, and told her if she showed herself inside Mother's room, I'd lock her up, and told her to pack a bag, and I'd pay for her to go to a boarding house in Ballarat for a fortnight, as I couldn't go on with her anywhere near — fireworks and absurd backtalk, and so. now I've got to have the bitch for three more days as she refuses to go till next Tuesday — I've brought up all the food that's necessary to my room, and am going to leave her the back part of the house, to fend for herself.*[51]

In a letter to Lionel, Robert wrote a second, more moderate account of this incident:

> *I had sent Isobel to Pearl for a week. She was driving Mary mad. I thought she was only simple, but like many childish people, horribly cunning, and she sets Mother against Mary and me, by making out she's not wanted, and being ill treated. God. I could choke her. We had a peaceful week with her out of the house, and the moment she came back yesterday, Mother began to get difficult — ordered Mary and me out of the room. Got out of bed. She hadn't been able to move for weeks . . . and stormed about like she used to when Robert Charles was getting it in the neck, and said she would sleep with Isabel in her room. Grabbed a candle nearly set her nightgown on fire. I pushed Isabel out of the room. I've never seen anyone so easily influenced as she is by Isabel. It's almost uncanny. Mother said 'I command you to open that door.' Me — and 'I command you to get into bed . . . She 'How dare you speak like that to me!' Me How dare you say the things you are saying to Mary and me! And so on. She simply chattered with rage, saying all Mary and I wanted was to get her in her coffin, and other such pleasantries. I almost had to drag her back to bed, screaming hysterically, that I was hurting her. I went for [Dr] Sleeman to get him to give her a hypodermic to quieten her, telling the evil Jane [Isabel] I'd lock her up if she attempted to go to Mother again.*[52]

Robert could not see that he may have contributed to the conflict, or that Isabel and Jane Lindsay might reasonably object to the way he ruled their lives.

# THE GHOSTS OF CRESWICK

He nursed Mary as well as his mother, seeing her as the real patient, and refused to accept that Jane was in any pain. When Isabel retreated into a private world and found salvation in a religious crusade, Norman was told of the comedy of the moron and her faith.

*At the moment an evangelical mission is in progress, in stagnation next door, according to Jane [Isabel] who, not knowing the nature of the news rushed in expecting some such unhealthy excitement, and came back red in the face, having been flicked on the back about her backslidings. After three unsuccessful evenings they roped in the village drunk and kept the show going till seven of the clock till he was saved and sober . . .* [53]

Part of the repugnance Robert felt for Isabel was caused by her physical closeness to her mother. While Robert objected to the incontinent old lady, whose refusal to use a bedpan led to excrement laden sheets each day, Isabel warmed her with her own body, sharing her bed in the cold nights of her last winter. In Robert's mind this act was combined with his mother's last rambling conversations about snatched memories of past romances, and their sexual implications. As he told Norman:

*She's like Sir Galahad, thankful to God that her heart is pure, but is still full of lascivious thoughts — she's always imagining a man in bed with her — a tall handsome man is in the room, or enquiring who the two men are who are in the drawing room — never any mention of a woman — and yesterday she said it was the anniversary of her wedding day. (for curiosity I looked it up to see if she was right and found her months out) — 'I never forget that day' — so a cake had to be made, to celebrate the horrific event — and the way she paws me if I sit near her. almost makes me vomit, and until lately she has had Isabel sleeping with her, liking physical contact. She rambles on about the various men who wanted to marry her — feeling her physical attractions, of the different servants we have had who got married and how many children they had, and then to the children of her old friends, who have grandchildren — continual fornication — and ramblings of the villagers . . . — with the marriage bed in the background — just now having exhausted everyone she could think of, she confided to me that Mary had secretly married the head of police — but didn't want it known.*[54]

Jane Lindsay died on 14 November 1932 and Robert wrote two letters to Norman about the death and funeral:

*It was a fairly gruesome ending. Sleeman kept her under opiates for the last 24 hours, but up till then she screamed incessantly for three days and nights. I nearly went mad — and when it was all over, Mary utterly collapsed, and is in bed now. I made Pearl take the moron back with her. Its strange how peaceful and quiet the house is after being such a house of unrest last week. And amazing how one dissenting human can so dominate the whole place. I thought it would take months to get rid of the feeling, but curiously enough I don't miss her, and it seems something in the past. for the first couple of nights one kept thinking one heard her screaming and calling — but now that's over and Mary, who was horribly jumpy is quieter. Thanks immensely old chap for your kind invitation [\*asterisked on margin] — and your generous gesture, so unlike our splendid brother Dan, poor chap. he's got to go to England for a trip this year. Much against his inclination. I feel quite distressed. I had much pleasure in writing to his female wife a fortnight ago, when she wrote saying that possibly we, living such a sheltered life — might not be aware of such an event as the Melbourne Cup was happening, which necessitated much going backwards and forwards and for she and her lord and master, and the necessity of drinking strong liquors with their friends, and the bore of having to do this same with strangers. I said it wrang my withers to the bones to read of the trials she was enduring from having married an impecunious artist, who had to daily visit the race courses, so as to get the latest information and points about horses, to enable to paint them later — and the boredom of drinking their friends' wines. having met some of them — but I couldn't agree that it was boresome to meet strangers, usually they put their best foot forward, and if one saw them not again one has a pleasanter memory of them, than should they curse ones path a second or third time, and discovered the thinness of their varnish. And think to deny one with discernment, meaning myself, it was much wiser, never to risk a second meeting. I believe this has given much offence, as they love their rich friends who have nothing else to recommend them — than their wealth.* [55]

The second letter, written at Norman's request, gives a detailed description of the final hours. It is a curiously dispassionate piece, written with an eye to detail, reminiscent of Flaubert in the later chapters of *Madame Bovary*.
*Re the observations you ask for the last days. She was unconscious off and on for the last three weeks, and when one went into her room she would either look vacantly at one — or else follow one with a piercing look. — She never stopped talking. day and night she was discusting — she never got*

*further than* — 'No. No, no that is wrong. No Annie. that is naughty'. *She continually spoke of Annie — and confused her with Mary. I think she must have had a lot to do with Annie when they were children — A. must have been a meek soul kept in her place by her elder sister, for it was a continual saga of 'No Annie, you must not do that No No' always 'No' — Then at odd times demanding that Mary take care of her . . . — always herself She quite forgot her tigrish defence of Isobel but never gave one any clue to what she was thinking of. For the last three days and nights she screamed continuously. It was horrible to listen to — in a vigorous voice. Sleeman gave her morphia for the last 24 hours and that quietened her. I would have collapsed if I'd kept up the roarings for ten minutes. She fought with unnatural strength when ever M or I moved her to make her comfortable — calling Mary 'cruel witch' she would let her do things for her, but would keep M waiting interminably — up till the last she fought and struggled for breath, and two or three times, she stopped breathing, and I thought it was all over — and then she began again — a grim determination not to give in.*

*When it was all over, (forgive me if I have written this before, but we had such a hectic time and were both so tired I can't remember, what I wrote, or to whom.) M and I laid her out as I couldn't get any one to come — a gruesome job — it seemed unnatural for her not to be roaring objections — or fulminations — as she was quite warm and remained so for hours afterwards. About an hour after she died, her face became small and her nose pink — it had grown grose — and she looked more like the better photographs of her about the time of her marriage — but I have never seen such determination, and inflexibility. I always have heard that after death all traces of emotion go, and the face becomes peaceful and calm, it did become the latter, but the mouth down — as it was in life. The curious thing to me is that she has left no impression.* [56]

Jane had been the eldest of nine children. I assumed Annie was one of her younger sisters, and as she died a past family crisis had come to haunt her.

The day of his mother's funeral, Robert began painting and redecorating the house to eliminate any trace of Jane's presence. He wrote to Norman of his new happiness.

*When I got back from the cemetery, directly after the funeral was over . . . She died early on Monday morning and was buried at 9 of the clock on Tuesday) I took everything out of the room, except the big wardrobe — distempered the walls and ceiling to bright buttercup yellow, put the old drawing room carpet down in it, had a bed made, with wooden head and top, all of which I covered with a cheerful cretonne — the bedspread to match — and the curtains and chairs 'are of the same aire' — and now I'm just waiting for a mirror I'm having made to fit an old frame. in which a fulsome address to old Tho's once looked out of — to put over the mantle piece — and with a couple of your pictures have made quite a pleasant cheerful room. I distempered the passages jade green, and now the ancient dining room is the only one in the house that remains in its original horror.*[57]

Without his mother's pension to support him, Robert had to look for work. He hoped to become a designer for the pageant celebrating the centenary of European settlement, but was unsuccessful. He did make Norman a series of period costumes in miniature which were used to create accurate evocations of the past, but this was for pleasure and service to the brother who continued to subsidise him and Mary.[58] For a while he became the secretary of the Creswick Hospital for £2 a week, and the dignity of his name on the letterhead. This was supplemented by a £12 annual stipend for playing the organ at the local church. But the hospital job did not last long, as despite his aristocratic air Robert lacked book-keeping skills.

After the war there was a steady stream of guests making pilgrimages to 'the home of the Lindsays'. Many were sent by Norman, partly as company for his brother and sister, but also to enhance the ever-growing myth of the genius artist from the country town.

By the time Keith Wingrove, that avid collector of 'Lindsayana', first visited Creswick in the late 1940s, the house bore little resemblance to the family home of Norman's boyhood. There was a move by Wingrove and others to turn the house into a Lindsay Museum, and Robert started a campaign to have his brothers finance further renovations and build a small cottage on one side of the property. He took malicious pleasure in indicating his distaste for the way Wingrove and others revered a history he would prefer to forget.

*What will enthusiastic visitors to the celebrated home think when they journey thousands of miles in search of history! 'I will tell you Keith and listen attentively, as I am a seer and can predict the future. When Mary and I are translated. (for my part I do not mind if I am thrown down a shaft)... You must listen, after our departure, the one or two things of any interest will go to the Gallery. The house then sold, then pulled down, and the land divided into four small lots, on which will be erected four awful small houses with a winding cement path to the front door. They will have spotted red and green tiles on the roof, the weight of which will later crush and kill the inmates — that will be the end and the house will die anyway — even now the small children do not know us, and the barman at the American [hotel] asked me what my name was when I called for you this morning.*[59]

For the most part Robert spent his days quietly, but talking with regret of the supposedly successful years in London. His Anglophilia became almost comic as he tried to create in his home a small corner of his memories of England, and when Norman suggested to him that there were Australians worth knowing he denied it vehemently:

*I have for years been convinced that the Australian has a low cash mind, and the few I was unfortunate in having any dealings with on the other side, showed up horribly in all their glaring crudity. When I mention this I am told. 'Oh you are too English'. A stupid remark. The truth is that, most Australians, like most Americans, at the back of their hand are secretly envious for not having been born in Europe, especially in England. They are like the Scotch, Stevenson tells of who are wondering what the English are thinking about them, when the English are not thinking about them at all. Here I've not met any mental aristocracy that you speak of. I didn't know it existed.*[60]

He created for the Lindsay family an imaginary aristocratic background and linked the yeoman farmers who were his grandmother Mary Cottingham's ancestors to 'one Robert de Cotyingham, came over with William the Conqueror, and for helping William with his carpet bags on landing William gave him a grant of land in Lincolnshire, where they have always lived.'[61]

The letters he wrote to Norman were full of details of costume and conduct, some of which surface in *The Cousin from Fiji*, *Half Way to Anywhere* and *My Mask*.

*I came across a page of a letter of yours to Mary asking about old Mrs Roycroft. She must have written about it as this moment is the first I knew of its existence . . .*

*Old Mrs Roycroft was a small wizened like woman, with epileptic grey eyes and eye lids like a parrots, which shuttered and when up looked like a venetian blind. she wore a high lace cap always and had a malicious bad tempered mouth. Old Lena Fridenberg says so . . . she told me of her early days when she worked for the old Roycroft beldame, at the age of 12 years. She had to be there by 6.30 am, lay the fires, and milk the cow, and get breakfast by 8.30, then wash up and atttend Florence when she did the marketing, walking behind her to keep her from any familiarity. she got home about 7 pm. (a long walk over the diggings at the back of the station, for which she received 2/6 a week — after standing this treatment for a week she told her mother, she wasn't going there any more but was forced to by her old German Mother. She bought a plaid skirt for 6/- with her first earnings, and when she turned up in it, was attacked by old Elizabeth (Mrs R) for dressing beyond her station and means, and was sent home to change it. The menage consisted of Mrs and Florence and R. Burgoyne. Mrs R was widow Burgoyne — till she married old Roycroft — who had three sons and two daughters, state school teachers who left the house because of the hostility of the step-mother. The three sons lived in a shed at the back of the kitchen which was a large room about 30 yards from the house where they had their meals . . . Roycroft was a paper agent, and the sons delivered them, per foot. Bill the eldest was wardsman at the hospital. Tom Roycroft came out or was sent out from Ireland, He must have been nearing 40 when he arrived. He had a good hand on a horse and an amazing capacity for beer. He was to stay with the Roycrofts for a week or so til he landed a job. then Old Roycroft died, and Tom stayed on and on and on. — Mrs R daily attacking him about getting employment, which he waved aside 'all in good time'. He must have been there for years. He was there when Wilson came to the hospital, he and Lionel being to tours bosom friends. he was always invited to the parties given by the noblesse — which took the nature of Progressive euchre, and when the supper (coffee and cakes) was being set out, Florence would be asked to sing and produced a rather tortured song 'The Garden of Sleep' from her ulster in the hall — or until the awful scandal of being discovered by the old mother one morning, playing with Florences shins in a little summer house in the fruit garden. he was ordered from the house — whereupon Tom asked for the hand of Florence — wether from a long concealed passion or for a further desire to continue under the same roof I don't know — the petition of asking to marry a first cousin was looked upon as incest, and hastened the lover's departure. Whereupon he fled to the American Hotel and became barman and billiard marker — the position perfect. this made things very awkward. Florence continued to be invited to the houses of the ancienne noblesse, while Tom was ostracised — This state existed for several years, til the old woman died, leaving the will I have already told you of. Tom having seen her safely and truly laid in the cemetery hastened back where the prospective bride was already waiting at the gate. So that there could be no finger pointed at her, which would have happened if he had gone inside the house, and they hurried to the church. There had not so far as I know been any rumour of anything illicit behaviour, there must have been a hiatus of six or seven years between the expulsion and the marriage as far as I know. The public never saw them meet . . . I wasn't home when the marriage took place but from hearsay it seemed to turn out all right. Tom had so long been under the despotism that she still kept it up. He would have been used to it.*[62]

It was not surprising that when *The Cousin from Fiji* was first published in 1945, it was dedicated to Robert, as the description of Mrs Domkin is easily linked to his letters about his mother, and the dapper Hilary Shadlet could well be a heterosexual version of his image of himself.

Norman's novels placed a great emphasis on details of costume and the importance of fashion, and in *The Cousin from Fiji* the gallant Hilary arranges to give his love a liqueur in the garden. Hilary is bullied by his sister Elvira, whose dominant voice reads remarkably like Mary's, while there is a strangely muted sister, Salina, who could be based on half-remembered images of Isabel. There is a 'victorious virgin' impregnated by a curate and comic sexual scandals based on money and class. Norman appreciated the letters from Creswick.

Despite the appearance of gracious rural life maintained for visitors, who now included Professor Joseph Burke from the Department of Fine Arts at the University of Melbourne, it was not a happy household.[63] Robert's ambitions greatly exceeded his income and in retirement he wrote to Norman begging for money:

*I have sold nearly all the antiques I brought out with me. In moments of stress, which reminds me of a drawing of yours a long while ago. The wife and husband considering the hopelessness of their finances, the wife saying. 'Well there is nothing to do. Except take boarders.' Please can you lone me. Do not mention this letter to anyone. Mary would never forgive me if she thought I had told you.*[64]

Robert also tried to turn his hand to painting decorative pieces for the house. Mary may have used these to describe him to Chaplin as 'the artistic member of the family', but there is no evidence that this opinion was shared by others, although he did send samples of his work to Norman.[65]

*Its awfully good of you bothering about those wretched so called pictures I had cold feet on my way to the station, and the mental strain I suffered must have been equal to yours when you unpacked them, Its all Percy's fault and Mary's insistence. Please Good Sir. Don't bother, I only did them in the first place to make some colour in the old dining room, which I had calcimined cream, and now sleep in . . . The reason for the crack in the coloured picture is that I couldn't get any canvas, and gummed an old piece of oil cloth on a piece of card board, and as it — the oil cloth — had been folded so long, couldn't get the crease out, and the other on three ply. I was for destroying, but for Mary staying my hand, and having promised to send you something, and not having the courage (after three previous attempts) or stomach to do another its monstrous kind of you offering to send me instructions, as to how to glaze or varnish others if ever I do them, I've got three or four frames and thought of doing one to match the snap I sent you, that I painted on glass. Thanks too, suggesting paints. I have enough, the brushes are the difficulty, as they are all too soft, and I can't get a clean line. I grieve with you when the monotony of living gets you down, and if it weren't for Mary I'd go mad dog and take an axe to the moron.* [66]

Living in close quarters with two people who despised her, and dependent on their scant goodwill, could not have improved Isabel's life after Jane's death. As neither Robert nor Mary mourned Jane, they did not accept that Isabel had any legitimate grief, and Robert especially refused to believe that she had any feelings at all. Isabel was simply another problem. In a letter to Rose, written just after her mother's death, Mary noted in passing:

*We packed Jane Isabel off for a fortnight with Pearl. Very nice indeed — for us. But really she doesn't behave so badly in there. After the manner of most humans, her habit is to take it out of the ones at home.* [67]

Pearl appears to have been relatively close to Isabel, relaying to her brothers the problems this sister was having at Creswick, and when Isabel was with Pearl she could write of her discontent to Daryl and Joan. In 1944, in a rare letter to Daryl, Robert felt obliged to defend himself against Isabel's accusations, and complained of 'Isabel, reading letters and spilling the beans as usual'. [68] There were complaints of Isabel's taste in music and a jealousy of Robert that led to her deliberately kicking over paint tins when he painstakingly painted carpet patterns on the old wooden floor. Always there were complaints of her hypochondria, and a belief by her siblings that they were the only ones to experience pain. So strongly did they believe this article of faith that, in 1950, when Isabel was diagnosed with arthritis, Mary and Robert saw it as her own fault and Mary wrote to Rose:

*The hypochondriac who a succession of medicos have agreed had nothing in the world wrong with her but her own imaginings to which I might add a villanous temper, has now developed something really serious [In margin 'Bert says its a clear case of retribution'] . . . arthritis of the spine. progressive. She will get more & more helpless, & end in a chair.*[69]

As Robert was dying of prostate cancer, Mary tried to create a portrait of a kindly brother, only too pleased to help all around him. She wrote to Harry Chaplin: 'Isabel will have to manage the best she can till I get back. Of course Robert is kindness itself and will do anything he can for her, but he is looking old and tired himself.'[70]

Others in the family felt that Isabel's disturbed behaviour was simply the result of the way she had been treated by Mary and Robert.[71] But her life was not totally bleak. While Robert and Mary openly pretended intellectual distinction and complained of the financial constraints of their existence, Isabel found quiet pleasures around her. Mary wrote:

*. . . In the winter here we spend our time in a sort of dull stupor — at least Robert & I do. Isabel manages a little social respite in the way of church junketings, Mothers meetings, or something of the kind, & gossipings with all sort of odd birds she picks up about the village.*[72]

Joan Lindsay also showed Isabel sympathy, and to a certain extent entered her world, which further alienated Joan from Mary. When Isabel left Creswick on holidays, it was usually to stay with Pearl in Ballarat, where she was secure in the knowledge that there would be no adverse reports sent back to Creswick. Even this was the subject of a complaint by Mary:

*Pearl took Isabel while she was with me, or rather Isabel insisted on going to Pearl's poor beggar! She's too morbidly sensitive — also utterly selfish, and sulks like Hell whenever we have visitors — Jealous because they talk more to me than to her.*[73]

Robert kept up his unrelenting hatred of Isabel until his death. When Mary had a mild stroke in about 1950 he seized on the excuse to send Isabel away to a boarding house, and wrote to Norman asking him to pay the bill.

*Mary has had a stroke. Fortunately she doesn't know anything — and after five days I can just understand her. she thinks it's tiredness not being able to* *walk. The Dr wanted to send her to a private hospital in Ballarat which is out of the question — I wouldn't let her go. Even if it were possible as she is frightened and wants me near all the time. I've sent Jane away and can manage all right. Except that I've got to pay her room 25/- a week which the incomes wont run to. Please send me a tenner — and if I want . . . — I can't ask the others — as they do their bit — Please don't mention anything of this to anyone & <u>burn the letter</u> as one never knows where a letter may go, and I'm not letting anyone know.*

Norman's response to this letter was to pass it on to Rose.
*I enclose a note from Bert. Those poor Creswick Lindsays. I've sent him £12. Best I can do at present. I've told Bert that I've only told you of Mary's trouble. Appearances of that sort mean a lot to him, poor fellow.*[74]

Shortly before his death, Robert sent Lionel sketch plans for the cottage to be built on the subdivided family land. It was built to scale, showing the relationship to the old home, which Robert wished to sell. It was, as always, accompanied by a request for money (£50) and the claim that this would be refunded within two years. The cottage had only two bedrooms; there was no room for Isabel.

After Robert's death in 1952 Rose noted sardonically that 'it appears that she [Mary] is now happier that Bert had gone (I'd be too) she had not rest or peace with him.'[75] In later years Mary expanded on her fiction of Robert's kindness. 'Robert, so witty, infinitely kind but a most indiscreet letter writer, later to his distress upset Lionel', she wrote to Bingo.[76]

By 1956 Isabel's arthritis was making it hard for her to move around, but still there was no sympathy from Mary.
*. . . Kathleen and I are watching poor Jane Isabel steadily it seems getting more and more helpless. Tho' she doesn't seem to have any more pain. If she did we'd know.*[77]

There were attempts to equip Isabel with a wheelchair, but she found it too difficult to move and preferred to crawl through the house on her hands and knees.

In about 1961 Isabel had a stroke, which Mary treated with her usual lack of sympathy:
*She did have a slight stroke, but it seems these slight strokes don't do much damage. However! The two Doctors said it was essential that she should go*

to the Hospital and Kathleen and I couldn't possibly deal with her condition. So she has been there for two months . . . For a long time now her only method of getting around has been crawling on the ground, or by clutching at anything handy.

Always fighting reasonable help, it would take her 10 minutes to get from one room to another.

This huge Hospital, run like a luxurious first class Hotel, has a medical staff so important that their power is 'absolute' I mean that private medicos are ignored. They have done, I know, marvellous things with therapy treatment, if the patient is co operative. However I can't imagine Jane Isabel making the faintest effort even on her own behalf. She hasn't ability enough to blow her nose properly. So a cold lasts a long time with her.

She will hate it, & be utterly wretched as she has been all these years in her own home . . . They put her in a private ward, with wood fire all day, good cooking & every possible comfort. When I thanked the matron — she said 'Well! Miss Lindsay! if anyone wouldn't try to help you it would be a funny thing.' The village apparently knows more than it will say to me about life in Lisnacrieve Towers.

Don't imagine that this Hospital will cost me anything. A pensioner goes in with her pension, out of which they allow the pensioner £1–15–0 a week for clothes etc. also ambulances are provided free of charge . . .

. . . You never heard anything like the lady and the way she rings & rings & rings her bell, & orders everyone about from the Doctors down to the little housemaids.

'Come back at once, I heard her saying to her Doctor, this morning 'Can't you hear me' I hope the staff has a sense of humour.[78]

Mary appears not to have known that Isabel's private room was paid for by Daryl. Isabel was happy at the Queen Elizabeth home, where she was visited frequently by Pearl, much to Mary's irritation which she expressed to Norman:

. . . Only I wish someone would take a battle axe and do for Pearl. My guess is that a very uncomfortable conscience is the cause of her violent behaviour whenever we are up against difficulty here. For a week she's come out every day apparently for nothing but to give me a headache — yesterday in despair I said get out & don't come near the place for a week at least.

. . . the whole thing is a plot to get poor Jane out of the house so that Kath [Howitt, who shared the Lindsay house] & I can have a riotous existence — & so on & so on. Every day a fresh accusation of shameless conduct.[79]

The last four years of Isabel's life appear to have been happy as she was visited by those relatives who cared for her and found the other patients did not treat her with contempt. Mary commented on the way she 'wont wear her reading glasses. She can't sew. She can't do anything except gossip when she can get hold of any bitter old crony cursed like herself,' but Isabel was happy. Her crippled legs were placed in irons and she was taught to walk again; she was fed and washed and treated with affection. The allowance she was paid out of her pension was more money than she had ever handled, and she used it to give presents to nieces, grand-nieces, and grand-nephews. In her last years there was a sense of normality. On Lionel's death in 1961 she was left £100, a bequest which acknowledged her as an individual rather than as a 'problem'.[80]

In December 1964 Isabel wrote her last letter to Bingo, expressing pleasure at the birth of Bingo's first grandson. The writing is slightly awkward but clear:

*You will be surprised to see me writing again to you so soon but; I sent a small box just a little gift to Baby Benjamin I've sent the parcel to you and would be so grateful to you Bingo if you could just wrap the parcel again and send it to Helen's address you see I don't know Helen's address. I have a great friend here, who has been so kind to me, she wrapped up the box and she thinks like me it would be better if you could send it. I don't know much about registering articles over England way and we thought it would go quicker.*

*Helen's baby must be lovely. It gave me a thrill. Fliss had told me your Helen was going to have one, but I didn't know it had and we'd been so long none.*

*You know Bingo you were the loveliest baby always I think, when, your Mother brought you up to Creswick to see us. She used to dress you in little white dresses and your long pointed bonnets with the rosettes on each side, and always a blue sash. You looked the sweetest thing.*

*I've just had a bit of a fall this morning and the nurse was sitting me on a chair at the table as I thought, but instead of that — I found myself on the floor I must have slipped away from evidently trying or thinking I was either on the chair but I've hurt my back down at the bottom. Sister gave me something, its a little easier but its still hurting. No more news. Lots of love*

*Isabel*[81]

Jane Isabel Lindsay died on 24 January 1965. After her funeral Mary wrote to Norman: '~~Pearl~~ Isabel has gone and was cremated today. God! What a relief! For her, poor beggar! As well as for me.'[82]

The name Mary crossed out was that of the other sister she despised, a curious slip. In a slightly more compassionate letter to Bingo Mary wrote about the funeral, not forgetting an attack on Joan.

*Dan & Lady Lindsay came out for the event.— Lots of people were awfully kind to Isabel & her chief pleasure was sending gifts to anyone she liked. You were always awfully kind to her. I did appreciate that too.*

*Lady Lindsay put a special death notice in the Age on the death of her loved sister-in-law. I didn't know that was done in the best circles. In our local paper the villagers don't mind what they spend in long eulogies & advertisements, to do with undying love & devotion over relations. Anyway Joan really did see Isabel 3 times going up by car to Ballarat with Dan during those last 4 years.*[83]

In the same letter she wrote of herself living in her 'self appointed jail', growing ever weaker, feeling alone. She failed to understand that the hostility of her letters helped keep visitors away.

# 11

# The other Jane Lindsay

'I feel as though I've been walking through a sewer,' I said to Helen Glad, Norman's granddaughter. We were talking about her family and the letters Robert had written when old Jane Lindsay was dying. 'I can see why Rose kept them, though. There'd be no way she could let Mary get away with that nonsense of the benign Robert.'

'Rose had a really strong sense of family,' said Helen. 'She could never have treated any relative of hers like that, and she must have been outraged at how Great Grandma wasn't being looked after when she was so ill. And because she had arthritis she understood what Isabel was going through. Mind you,' she added, 'Rose also assumed that *she* would be looked after by family when she needed it. That's why she came to live with us, and I spent my childhood emptying Grandma's potty.'

'What about Norman?' I asked.

'Him? He wasn't interested in looking after her, or anyone else for that matter,' came the swift reply. 'Haven't you read Mum's book? It's just been reprinted so you should get hold of it. I think you'll like it.'

~

A week later in I came across a copy of Jane Lindsay's *Portrait of Pa*. After the mean-spirited, vicious and plain hypocritical letters of Robert and Mary, it cleared the mind and in part restored my faith in the complex nature of family love.

Jane writes with an awareness of the seductive power of the mind of Norman Lindsay, but *Portrait of Pa* manages the difficult trick of being loyal to two quarrelling parents. It is as though the Lindsay passion has been tempered by the pragmatic sensibility of a child of Rose. She writes of the contradictory personas of the father who could make fairies dance on the lawn for her and her sister Honey, but who, as a selfish old man, spent his last years punishing anyone but the most sycophantic admirers.[1]

*In his Olympian hideout for years Pa had been a god amongst his gods, albeit he had to keep one foot well on the ground while he struggled with the realities of paint and pen techniques and posed models for his great fantasy pictures.*

*Now with an old-man obsession for immortality, he had floated off into a world of fantasy. He confused his work with himself, and its possible immortality with his own. In insisting he was more than human, he was only proving he was as human as the name-carvers, the foundation stone layers and monument erectors whom he despised. It was pathetic. And sad. He would have done better to have left his gods to look after his immortality.*[2]

Jane, like her half-brother Jack, writes of the problems of loving difficult parents.[3] Norman was frequently called a genius by his many admirers, 'but genius is hard to recognise at close quarters'.[4] Instead, she noticed the intense, loving and then loathing, relationship between Norman and Rose. Unlike Jack who spent a childhood with a growing sense of abandon, the small Jane was given the idea that as a Lindsay girl she was special, above *hoi polloi*, and even after she was left by her father, when he moved out of the Springwood home to his studio in the city, the abandonment was intermittent as he would frequently return to see Rose. The little Lindsay girls, Jane and Honey, were allowed to pretend that the flower petals they gathered were worth money and swapped them for coins at neighbourhood shops.

*Graciously smiling and bowing these gentlemen accepted the goods, winking at Ma as they handed over twopence or threepence and of course, added two or three shillings to the bill. Ma never lowered herself to check the account. Apart from the fact that she couldn't count, she didn't know the price of anything and simply bought the dearest brand available. Ma liked playing the Countess and richly ordering on the grand scale.*[5]

It was only later that Jane realised the assumption of superiority was not in her own best interests.

In the Springwood of Jane's childhood there was affluence of the most easily displayed kind. The many servants, cars, and expensive clothes were all paid for from her father's success. But for all Norman's passion for art, he had no understanding of the need for formal education and the girls were taught spasmodically by a succession of governesses, interspersed with terms at the local private school, one short stay at the 'vulgar' state school and the erratic tuition of their father.

*Pa taught us geography from his own rules. There were two maps of Europe in Miss Hughes' abandoned atlas, showing the Continent before and after World War I. He told us not to bother about the second map with all those nasty little countries in the centre. It was easier and more sensible before they cut it up . . .*

*Pa pointed out a very bad omission on the north part of the Atlantic Ocean. In fact, there was another continent called Atlantis. To prove this he drew it into the map and showed us where there was a land bridge between the eastern and western continents. He told us that people could walk from Europe to America. The ones who stayed in Atlantis were a wonderful race who built magnificent cities. . . It was not until my teens that my belief in the Atlantis story was shaken.*

*. . . Our lessons included, too, simple sums of adding and taking away, but grammar was ignored. Pa had never bothered much with that himself. The mystery of it has remained with me.*[6]

When Jane wished to attend a serious academic high school in order to realise her ambition of becoming a doctor, her parents paid for her fees as a boarder at Abbotsleigh on the leafy upper north shore of Sydney, but gave her no other encouragement. The passion for a formal education was beyond their comprehension. Jane completed her enrolment herself, the chauffeur drove her to school and her mother sent forbidden cigarettes to cheer her up in this self-imposed incarceration.

*Pa would obligingly meet me on those occasions* [when allowed out with an adult] *and turn me footloose when required. He always gave me some money, asked if I had been writing at all and how I was fixed for reading matter. I told him vaguely of my suspicion that I was not going to do any good at school. He said it was not important anyway. 'You don't learn anything at school,' he insisted . . .*

*Ma said if I was finding life at school so miserable I should give the whole idea away and come home.*[7]

Later, when I met Jane, she told me how she still regretted her lack of formal education and wished her parents had encouraged her.

For Norman the only skills that mattered were creative ones. As his much loved daughter showed no aptitude for painting, he pictured her as a writer. However, his intolerance of formal education meant that she would have to be a self-educated one.[8] When Jane was not writing, Norman lost interest in her, just as in his extreme old age he lost interest in Rose when she was ill and arthritic and could no longer care for him.

*He had retired deliberately into a small orbit of his own. A few friends and sycophants were welcome within it. I was a lost cause — absorbed with babies and never writing a word. Ma had outlived her usefulness. As far as he was concerned, she could live or die as she chose so long as her choice did not disturb him.*[9]

Jane's portrait of Rose likewise shows her as manipulative and difficult, regarding all Norman's work as her property, hiding it from him in case he decided to exercise ownership.

*They were very good at hiding things from each other; but Ma was more ingenious. Sometimes she hid watercolours and pen drawings behind the three-ply backing to the mirror on her wardrobe. She had keys to various cupboards about the house, but such locks did not worry Pa. He was quite good at picking them with a piece of wire if he really wanted to get in. If the lock happened to defeat him, he took the back off any cupboard and chest of drawers. When she discovered he had made off with some small picture to give away or sell in secret, Ma was furious. She was convinced he should have nothing to do with the pictures once he had finished painting.*[10]

Jane's narrative goes back and forth in time, swinging from the death of her father to the return of Norman to Springwood after an absence of six years, to her early childhood, and then to a key event in that childhood. The separation of Norman and Rose was preceded by their sudden trip to England and America. The writing remains vivid and memorable, but also elusive: secrets are kept. The only mention in Jane's book of Margaret Coen is at the very end; she is described as someone who looked after Norman in his fragility.

Jane's image of Norman Lindsay is of a charismatic man who was always aware of the impact he made on others.[11] Norman was always in control of his life, avoiding visitors by greeting everyone at the studio door with a palette in his hand and telling unwelcome callers that he had a model posing. He was aware of exploiting people, but always felt his needs were supreme.

> Making use of people was one of the games Pa played. He never hesitated to ask if he thought someone could do something useful for him, or run a message or do some boring chore. 'If you want to use people, gently inflate them with self-esteem' he would say. He was quite shameless about requests for books and materials to be brought for him. 'Just put it on my account.'[12]

From Jane's story, it was hard to decide which is the more difficult parent. Always there was a struggle between them for control, and almost always it was Norman who triumphed, as Rose would not act against his best interests, while he did not consider her needs except where they coincided with his own. Jane, the witness, records that Rose Lindsay was devastated when Norman left Springwood in 1934:

> One afternoon I came home from school and Ma announced, 'Your father has left home.'
>
> I did not realise that this was a major disturbance in her life. He was always going away for weeks in town and when at home lurked in his studio all the time.
>
> I hardly missed him but Ma was very distressed and bitter.
>
> Sometimes she railed furiously about his perfidious behaviour in abandoning her. Sometimes she was tearful. One day she put her arms round me and burst into tears. 'Your father is so cruel to me,' she cried.
>
> Embarrassed, I mumbled something and detached myself. I was not used to such exchanges between us and completely unable to give her whatever comfort she sought from me.[13]

Throughout the separation Norman continued to visit Springwood and Rose remained his efficient marketing director. However, when there were other visitors present she inevitably constructed a public scene.

> One of Ma's unnerving tricks was to wait till she had an assemblage of guests at the table and Pa was present, passing himself off as a sociable chap, and then make some terrible utterance. It was invariably slanderous, and usually related to his non-existent sex-life with her and what he might be doing about it elsewhere.[14]

Jane describes her mother as constantly sexually aware; placing a sexual interpretation on every one of her daughters' girlhood friendships, assuming all meetings between boy and girl, man and woman, would end up in bed.[15] Jane's young life was a continuing drama of a mother creating conspiracy theories about her daughters' sex lives, a husband plotting against his wife, and a wife, in turn, creating two-edged plots in self-preservation.

At the outbreak of World War II, when Rose decided to flee to America with Norman's best work, ostensibly to keep it out of the hands of possible invaders, it was clear to Jane that her mother had another agenda, was hatching another plot.

*Pa and I were astounded to discover the size of the haul Ma had taken to America. We imagined she would have taken some etchings and pen drawings and a selection of watercolours. But this looked like the sack of Peking.*

*. . . nothing was stored; all had been packed into special crates for shipping. There had been an enormous specially made metal cylinder for the rolled-up oil paintings. This, alone, seemed to indicate that secret preparations for the exodus had been under way for quite a time before we were told.*[16]

With Rose in America, Norman joined Jane at Springwood. He claimed his return was arranged by 'the Gods', and never really left again. Trips away became a rarity, and those who wished to see the great artist had to make their pilgrimage up the mountain. Norman's hospitality, however, did not extend to serving alcoholic beverages. The drunkenness of youth, followed by the mild drinking of wine in middle age, turned to total abstinence in his old age. He damned all alcohol as 'booze' in terms that would do one of his wowser caricatures proud.[17]

After the fire in America which destroyed so much of Norman's early art, Rose returned to Springwood where she lived in quarters separate from Norman's studio. And Rose did not stay by her husband's side for the rest of his life.

By 1956, Norman's neglect of Rose as she became progressively crippled by arthritis led Jane to invite her to live with her family in Hunters Hill. For many years Rose was a frequent visitor to Norman in his Springwood isolation, but as her health made travel harder, it was Jane who made the pilgrimages to attend her father. The Springwood house was gradually reduced to chaos as Norman moved the studio into the old living quarters and furniture was cannibalised for whatever project Norman had on hand.[18] Jane did not tell Rose of the damage Norman wreaked as he stripped the old house to suit his ever urgent purposes.

The most poignant part of *Portrait of Pa* is Jane's description of the obsession of Norman's last years — the desire to turn Springwood into a Norman Lindsay museum. For the last decade of his life it was clear that Norman Lindsay was planning to effectively disinherit his family in order to create a public memorial to himself. In the 1930s, after Norman had some unfortunate dealings with publishers, Rose had acquired all his literary copyrights with an understanding that she would give him half the income for his own use. These royalties, as well as money from selling etchings, were her only means of support.

> By this time, arthritis had so crippled her that living at Springwood was an impossibility. The arthritis of her hip was the result of printing etchings on the big press. She had had to throw her weight heavily on one leg as she pulled the plate through the rollers and eventually this affected the bone and arthritis set in. Now in old age she needed constant attention. Pa had the idea he had no financial or other obligations to his wife. She did not deign to remind him of them.[19]

Jane records her unenviable position as messenger, trying to shield her mother from the acts of her father and to bring her father to an understanding of his responsibility. Norman wished to give the house to the National Trust which was the only body prepared to turn it into a museum to honour him. Rose, however, owned the house and insisted it be sold so that she could be supported. Norman's plan to disinherit his immediate family was a curious echoing of the behaviour of Rose's father when she was a girl. He had deserted his wife and children and sold the family home, leaving them penniless.

In his senility, Norman Lindsay was not an attractive figure. He spent a great deal of time with fans and their letters, writing long rambling replies to collectors like Keith Wingrove who came to rummage around the Springwood tip, collecting detritus from the household.

> The older he got the more letters were poured out of his typewriter, directed at people who would be sure to keep them. Quite a bit of trafficking went on with them. Some enthusiastic collectors made a habit of buying up any on the market. Pa approved of this. It encouraged him to write even more letters and make them longer and longer.[20]

These letters occasionally surface in the rare book market, containing novel facts and repeated opinions, and they clutter the library collections. They are verbose, with very little substance, but because they carry the magic signature, 'Norman Lindsay', they are bought and sold as though they had real value.

Jane was eliminated as executor of her father's will when she failed once to deliver some books he wanted instantly to Springwood. Despite the pain of rejection she continued to see the irritable old man and tend to his needs. But the bond this daughter feels to her father is expressed in her reaction to Norman when he praised her driving on his last journey to the hospital where he died. Grateful for any small crumb of appreciation, she wrote: 'It was music to my ears'.

# 12

## *Interlude 1994*

'I've just been reading *Portrait of Pa*,' Peter said to me one day. 'It's a remarkable book.'

It was a blowing autumn day; the sky was all grey in the view from Peter's window and the harbour was ruffled. Peter wasn't looking at all well. He'd just come out of hospital after a prostate operation, and somehow he wasn't getting better.

'I've had all these injections,' he told me. 'They're supposed to make me stronger, but it doesn't work. Nothing works. And it's so hard to read these days. I can't seem to get glasses strong enough.' He was by then legally blind, and needed his stick to guide him outside the flat.

But *Portrait of Pa* held him entranced. He'd had it for years, had even read it when it was first published. But it hadn't moved him then as it did now. Of all the published accounts of the famous Norman Lindsay, Jane's was the one that rang most true for him, the one that tallied with his experiences and also with the letters we had both been reading

'Helen Glad's a nice girl,' he said. 'She came to visit me with someone from the New South Wales Art Gallery. They're doing an exhibition on the family.'

'Yes, the show's happening next year and I think they're calling it *The Legendary Lindsays*, so it's everyone including Percy and Ruby.'

'It's about time they showed some Lindsay works at the gallery. They're always locked away.'

'Peter, they don't have much choice a lot of the time. The best ones are on paper,' I replied. 'Imagine if they let those poor watercolours fade. They really do have to spend most of their lives in the dark.'

'I hope they show some of Dad's watercolours and not just the prints,' he said. 'Those Spanish paintings are perfect in the way they capture that clear

# INTERLUDE 1994

Spanish light, and look at the way he colours the shadows. I don't know many painters who could do that.' Then he paused and asked, almost shyly: 'Do you think I should talk to Jane about the book?'

Because I knew both sides of the Lindsay family I kept forgetting that they did not know each other. Helen's position as a picture researcher and active guardian of Norman's copyright meant that she had come to know Peter, but he had never met Jane. He had cooperated with her on the publication of Norman's letters, but because this was all done through publishers there had been no personal contact. Now Jane's book had spoken to Peter, probably more eloquently than her own voice. He wanted to befriend this cousin he had never met, even though she lived in the same city, on the same side of the harbour.

I gave him Jane's phone number, and within a week I had an excited call. 'I've just spoken to Jane. We talked for ages; I wish I'd known her before now.'

Peter has no children. He has a few good friends and nephews in Sydney, but the relative he is closest to is his niece, the actor Helen Lindsay, who lives in London. In the last few years all the friends who had known him as a young man have died, many of them slowly from either Alzheimer's disease or cancer. His sister Bingo is now in a hostel in Turramurra, and while she speaks to Peter on the phone there are few visits. Peter is in his late eighties, Bingo is ninety. He has survived asthma and cancer and all sorts of painful diseases, holding onto life because it is still interesting.

In the months following the new friendship with Jane, Peter was quite ill. His body didn't have enough flesh to keep him warm in winter and for a while he was in hospital. But his friends and new-found relatives helped him through the cold and he survived for summer.

# 13

# John and Mary

*I* found myself spending the winter break of 1992 in Melbourne where I studied the papers deposited in the La Trobe Library by John Hetherington's estate. This was when I found the answers to some of the questions that had been nagging me and by the time I returned to Sydney I thought I knew the reason why Hetherington's biography of Norman was so unsatisfactory. I had also confirmed my suspicions of why *Redheap* was banned.

The week before I travelled to Melbourne for the Hetherington papers I reread the letters that John Hetherington had written to Rose, the ones she had placed in the Mitchell Library. I knew that after Hetherington's initially friendly correspondence with Mary, Rose had convinced him that Mary was malign, and that one of the ways she had done this was to show him some of the letters Robert had sent Norman at the time of Jane Lindsay's death. Some time after this his friendliness with Rose also ceased. I did not know why this had happened, or indeed if there had been any communication between Hetherington and Rose after the early 1960s, because the cut-off time for the Mitchell papers was 1962.

There are sixteen boxes of Hetherington papers in the La Trobe Library, and most of them deal with the Norman Lindsay biography. While the letters from Norman to Hetherington are numbered in the recipient's hand, and the date on which they were received was noted (Norman never dated his letters), many of the other letters, including those from Jack, were cut up as part of a scissors-and-paste manuscript. It made it very hard for an outside reader to get any sense of continuity from the jumbled folders.

## JOHN AND MARY

Hetherington had a little notebook in which he jotted down references to Norman's letters and on one occasion a narrative that Norman had given him. Although they were placed in archival boxes, the papers had never been fully catalogued by the library. 'I think you must be the first person to ask for these,' said one of the librarians. 'They don't look as though they've been out before.'

As I sat at the table and read through the notes and letters, looking at the press cuttings and photographs, I realised that I was not the first to ask puzzling questions about the Lindsay family. John Hetherington had been there before, and had made some substantial discoveries. While he had not revealed most of these in the biography, Hetherington had ensured that his notes were retained to indicate both what he had uncovered and how he had been thinking.

The papers soon demonstrated what I knew to be the central problem in Hetherington's book: the way the subject had dominated the author.

Just after Norman encouraged Hetherington to take on the project of recording his life for posterity, he wrote and gave suggestions on how to structure the book:

> I think you'll find your material will split up into four periods; The Creswick prelude, up to the time of leaving home about the age of seventeen. Student days in Melb. terminating in my first marriage at the age of twenty, and about a year later (I'm no good at dates) an offer from Archibald to join the Bulletin staff, which brought me to Sydney. Active period of journalism plus getting along with my own work up to 1909, when I went to London with Bill Dyson and my sister Ruby, who had recently married. A year in London in which I produced the illustrated edition of the Satyricon of Petronius, made contacts with the publishing world, met most of the writers and artists of that era, and returned to Aus, in a lousy state of health, which sent me into hospital for three months. Came to the mountains to convalesce, and have been here ever since, save when I worked myself to a standstill about 1930, and being very fed up with this country over the constant attacks on my works and on myself and a Police prosecution on them which we managed to get squashed before coming to court, my wife and I went off to America for a year . . . [1]

This letter became the basis for the plan of Hetherington's book. Hetherington annotated it by underlining key phrases: 'Creswick prelude', 'Student days in Melb.', 'Active period of journalism', 'Came to the mountains', all of which were significant elements of the completed book. The emphasis, however, was slightly changed so that the less than impressive London years were condensed.

Even the most ardent Norman Lindsay fan could not accept his exaggerated claims about success in London.

At the same time as he wrote to Hetherington, Norman wrote to Mary telling her of the project, requesting her cooperation.

*I think I told you about a writer named Hetherington who has been sending me a series of biographical studies for my opinion of them, and they really are excellent. Writing to him about one, I chanced to put a casual P.S. to the effect that if it ever came to having a biography perpetrated on me, my choice would fall on him. I've just had a letter from him saying that he had often wished to have that very job, and did I mean that P.S. and if so, would I confirm it.*

*. . . The point of the foregoing as applied to you, is this. I've told him that you are the only extant authority on my early days; that you and I have maintained over the years the intimacy of a mutual understanding, and that if anybody knows my general makeup it is you, and that, with your consent, I'd give him a note of introduction to you, if he felt like making the journey to Creswick to interview you. I hope this will not be an infliction on you, but it would mean a good deal to the work if you would so far collaborate on it. Hetherington, by his letters convinces me that he is a fine fellow, personally and intellectually and, since it is more or less inevitable that some one will write a biography of my life, when I'm out of it, I would much prefer a writer of Hetherington's quality of mind. Our dear old Ruff [Tremearne] thought a great deal about him — they were together on the Herald for years. Finally, I would like you to have a place in the biography —* [2]

I hadn't realised the way the book had started. The enthusiastic writer, the god-like condescension of the famous author, graciously permitting praise. Norman's ability to manipulate those around him was truly awe-inspiring. And here he was at it again, this time with Mary. Tremearne had been a childhood friend, someone whose judgment she respected. Mary was now eighty years old and, with all of her close friends dead, she was lonely. There was also the appeal to her sense of history, and the chance to be immortalised as handmaid to the artist. Hetherington appears to have made personal contact with Mary in about May or early June of 1957. Subsequently Mary wrote to Norman, and Rose placed this letter with her papers:

*I met John Hetherington twice when in town, and feel so happy that the NL life will be in his hands.*

> I'm relieved too, because I've been worried so much by all the wrong people about this business and like yourself, began to regard it as our worst bogey.
>
> I never for a moment considered Jo Burke. He found out in half an hour that I couldn't, or wouldn't talk.
>
> I like John Hetherington unreservedly. I like his clear mind and feel his integrity. Yes we must help him in every way we can. [letter censored, presumably by Rose] [3]

Mary wrote regularly to Hetherington, offering him assistance and easing fears he held about the cooperation of those two devout collectors of Lindsay material, Keith Wingrove and Harry Chaplin. With Chaplin in particular, Mary was convinced she would be able to secure compliance:

> Is Harry Chaplin back. If so if you have his address, let me have it. The last letter I had from him from abroad was just before deciding to set off for Australia again. I don't know whether he has arrived.
>
> Under pressure I sent him stuff about our childhood and to my astonishment found he'd kept and put a collection of my letters in a specially bound book. I laughed at the time, but am not sorry now, as if Hetherington gets hold of those letters they will save me the bother of rewriting and thinking up what I'd told Chaplin. They are probably as letters not very wonderful, but they would be accurate and like yourself, when it comes to a biography or autobiography, I agree with you, the truth at any cost... [4]

Chaplin did agree to help with the book, although in a letter to Norman he expressed his reservations as to Hetherington's competence:

> I am sure that he [Hetherington] *does not really appreciate the magnitude of his task, for in writing your life, he is really going to run the whole gamut of the artistic effort of this country from its first real stirrings. For I think it might be safely said, that nothing very much of creative value sprang into being before the nineties. Then when things came to life so many personalities came into the picture, that the book cannot help being a panorama of the literary and artistic effort of the last fifty years, with all the personalities taking their places within its pages ... Taken any way you like, it cannot fail to be an informative commentary upon a phase of Australian cultural endeavour, and even should it fail as a personal biography (in the sense that it fails to depict you as you really are) as a factual record of times and events it should be most valuable.* [5]

Other than indicating that Chaplin shared the belief of his generation that there was no tradition of Australian art until the impressionists, this letter shows that he had a broader understanding of context than Hetherington. It contrasts with a letter from Mary of about the same time, where she claims that it was her intervention that caused Chaplin and Wingrove to assist with the book.

> *Very glad to get your letter this morning. I'd been waiting to get your story over the reaction of our friends Chaplin and Keith [Wingrove] to John H. biography. Nice time I've had with the pair. Their interfering attitude produced some real Jane Elizabeth plain speaking in reply to both.*
>
> *My attitude is & was exactly like your own, except that I included a sort of 'of course you fellows, after grabbing everything you could lay your hands on in Springwood & this home, will be delighted to use your spoils to help a good practised writer turn out the best possible biography.*
>
> *They were, as you say, both insistent that you should write the life, & I, in effect, told them both not to be asses — that it was practically impossible for any human to present a faithful picture of themselves to the universe, & so on & so on — just what you said & which I heartily agreed with.*
>
> *I arrogantly told them that I was a dashed good judge of a man, & that I thought highly of Hetherington as a man & as a writer, & left it at that. Good enough fellows in a way, but they both at times give me a pain in the neck.*[6]

Within a remarkably short time Mary's letters to Norman read almost as though she was the one who had initiated the project.

> *It's about the N.L. Autobiography. I've promised to help & will to the best of my ability & I've sent you for your amusement over the past a lot of stuff, which of course you've never kept. It would have been useful in keeping to create the atmosphere round your childhood.*
>
> *Did you keep that long letter from me that you said you had put away carefully. If so please let me have it. Also have you kept all the Lindsay family & Cottingham (Grandmother Williams) family stuff? Let me know.*
>
> *. . . You are wrong when you say that chatting with the man who has to write the book is enough. It will help Hetherington enormously when he meets you, but for me I see ahead a lot of repetition, of stories suggested by one or other odd remark in your letters, bits of which I might make up & only half remember.*

> *I now wish that I hadn't simply cleared out the drawing room of all the family photos of interest. . . Year after year I've cleaned up & sent away everything of interest. Now there isn't anything left.*
>
> *. . . I've suggested to H. that he may later wish to do the Lindsay family, as both from you & me he'll be getting a lot of that for the N.L. life*
>
> *. . . My idea is to give him* [Hetherington] *everything unreservedly. Then for the NL life delete what isn't necessary.*
>
> *. . . Try to be especially objective about Lionel but not sentimental. Don't forget how he could write & think (when he wrote that splendid appreciation that you raked up) & Hughie McCrae.*
>
> *Because you & I have an awful lot to rake up about Lionel, & even about Dan we've got to watch ourselves carefully. If I were you I'd leave Dan, also any of the younger half of the family, right out of this NL life. They don't come into it in any way.*
>
> *All my 6 brothers had courage — even Dan. the man we so dislike.*[7]

The reference to 'autobiography' in the opening sentence is an important error. Both Mary and Norman assumed the writer was to tell their story, their personal interpretations of particular selected facts. Because of this assumption Mary took on the role of arbiter and tried to set out what should and should not be told. There was another matter of concern to Norman. Mary was suggesting 'that he [Hetherington] may later wish to do the Lindsay family', another book that would honour the whole family and praise other siblings, including herself as the mainstay of their childhood.

Even though it was Mary's suggestion that Hetherington write the family's story, and Norman's insistence that this was not appropriate, Mary's flexible memory later reversed the situation and by 1958 she was writing to Hetherington that she had 'stonkered N's first suggestion that he and I should appoint you official Lindsay biographer'.[8] In 1961, after he had broken off relations with Mary, John Hetherington happily acquiesced with Norman's suggestion that he not pursue a general book on the Lindsays.[9]

Hetherington soon realised that there was a significant difference between family claims for the freedom of the biographer and the actuality of his situation. In 1960 he prepared a brief biography of Norman for his series of artists' profiles and, because he wished to keep Norman's confidence, sent him a copy of the essay.[10] The response came not from Norman, but from Rose, who wrote that 'I did not think it a fair portrait of him', but disclaimed responsibility for the objections, claiming, 'I am the meat in the sandwich'.

She claimed that Norman intensely disliked Hetherington's description of him as 'spare stringybark', 'half-well forced' and especially 'the implication that some of his writing might not be permanent and that he is not unique, and that he was old'.[11]

Hetherington's reply was to withdraw temporarily from the project. He understood that the real opposition came from Norman. At this stage he claimed that, 'I am not capable of being the kind of biographer who consents to, as it were, temper the wind to the shorn subject'.[12] The profile of Norman Lindsay was dropped, but instead a favourable short biography appeared in 1961.[13] A month later Hetherington agreed to return as authorised biographer, but with the realisation that the apparently open and friendly Lindsay family was sometimes less than frank in its dealings.[14]

Meanwhile, Mary was so confident of John Hetherington's partisanship that in sending him some of Norman's letters she indicated they were his for the keeping. On more than one occasion she added a typically conspiratorial instruction.

*Don't send any of Norman's letters back. Everything I have is now at your disposal. We won't tell Norman that I'm sending any letters that will help the biographer to you. That might stop spontaneity!*[15]

To Norman she wrote of the impact John had on her life.

*I love the fellow: & although I have loved many an heroic adventurer or literary hero: only a very few heroes who have walked the earth in my time, have commanded my sincere affection. Yes! John is one you'll understand when you meet him.*[16]

Norman encouraged her, especially as this closeness to his biographer coincided with his own interests. Mary sent John Hetherington details of the births, marriages and deaths of Lindsay ancestors, as well as details of her brothers and sisters. She spent hours in the Creswick library checking newspaper records and all the information was passed on to the Authorised Biographer. Details of the family servants and of the children's hideouts were unearthed, and she wrote nostalgically of the late 1890s when the boys would return to Creswick and impose on their mother's hospitality. Lionel and his bohemian friends were still fresh in Mary's memory, and her recollections of those years gave Hetherington the first indication of the importance of his big brother to the development of Norman's art.

*They were all crazy about the strong man, the high adventurer. On top of the adulation of the pug [boxer] came a period when the pirate became the god of their ideology. Lionel & Raymond [Elkington] planned to write the finest pirate story in the world, to be illustrated by Norman. Lionel, to get the right local atmosphere, hired for a couple of shillings a night, a small unfurnished dark cubby hole in some small obscure pub (I think at Fitzroy).*

*Here the three enthusiasts met to plan & write about the great work. The three sat round a big barrel which acted as a desk, with red spotted handkerchiefs tied round their heads, & any trappings that could be obtained to suggest the pirate & his life.*

*Hunting through dusty second-hand shops, some outmoded firearms were bought cheaply, altho no cutlasses were obtainable. They drank cheap rum (hot), which makes me shudder when I think of Norman and his weak stomach.*[17]

There is no earlier available written account of the Lindsays' pirate adventure, so it can be safely assumed that Mary's letter led Hetherington to further investigate the escapade which finally appeared in the book:

*In a lane running off the eastern end of Little Bourke Street they found a one roomed brick shanty and rented it for 2s 6d a week. They made a rough table and three chairs out of a packing case, hung a drawing of a Skull and Crossbones over the fireplace, and rolled in two or three old barrels to heighten the pirate atmosphere. They even managed an armoury. While painting the sign for the Aquarium Norman and Lionel had discovered a collection of antique pistols, swords and daggers gathering dust in a lumber room; these pieces had apparently been used in some pageant, then stored and forgotten. The Lindsays carried them off under the noses of the Aquarium people, walking out each evening when they finished work with an item or two hidden in their trouser legs. Now they decorated the walls with these vintage weapons, and stood back to admire. The place looked every inch a pirate's lair.*[18]

Mary reiterated Norman's accounts of Lionel as the fiscally mean older brother, but she refused to concede that Lionel was jealous of Norman's work. It was clear to John Hetherington that he needed the cooperation of Lionel Lindsay to clarify differences between Norman's and Mary's accounts of details of Norman's life. Mary had given much information on Lionel's favourable influence on his younger brother. She also intimated that she was the only family member able to get the supposedly difficult Lionel Lindsay to speak.

On 4 August 1958, John Hetherington wrote to Mary:

*I feel I must approach Lionel sooner or later. Dan — this was before you warned Dan off the course — came in to see me after a visit he paid to Sydney, and he told me that Lionel was being 'cagey' on the subject of helping me with the biographical material about Norman. I do not know precisely what he meant by cagey, but I daresay if I could see Lionel face to face, the mountains — or molehills — standing in the path could be eliminated.*[19]

But Mary's closeness to Lionel was an illusion. Daryl had kept Lionel well informed about the family at Creswick, so other than his financial commitment to support Mary and Isabel there was little contact between them. She hesitated to approach Lionel until, urged on by both Hetherington and Norman, she wrote a letter which was perhaps too effusive and openly manipulative to gain his sympathy.

Aug 15th 58

My dear Lionel,

Its many moons since we had an intimate talk. I had thought that almost inevitably, after all those exhausting years looking after poor Jean & seeing to everything, that it would end for you in an almost total collapse, as in my case. — but I don't want to talk about myself, except to say that I'm better now than I have been since Bert's death . . .

You may not realise that I have always known that you & Dan are the two members of this clan who have a certain family feeling which wouldn't allow either of you to let any member of the family end in the gutter. So I now have no anxiety ahead as to Isabel's future. — &, as for the present. Well! there's always something. That seems to be. When youth has departed, part of the scheme of things.

. . . But what I want chiefly to write you today is a letter that I will ask you to treat as confidential— It is fortunate for all of us that l'enfant terrible of the family has never quarrelled with me. Actually he has personally never given me any occasion for one of the family's first class rows & (believe it or not), he will nowadays listen to the voice of reason (being my voice.)

The Springwood people have some apalling friends & under the influence of an N.L. collector — (not Harry Chaplin, who is a good chap and my friend), he started to write his life. — got thoroughly tangled up in presenting a ridiculous figure of himself & fortunately sent it to me nearly in tears "Can't you help me Mame!" he said I don't know what I'm like"?

## JOHN AND MARY

*I stonkered the lot, Also the bulk of a group of reminiscences, He took it very well, when I pointed out that the word 'factual' was a very important ingredient in any auto-biography, & that he was simply out for one thing, & that was what he called "good entertainment.*

*Well! to cut my story short, he decided (with my hearty approval), to cut 'the story of my life' right out, & let any hardy biographers do what they liked after he was under the sod.*

*That meant three weeks rest for me. Then suddenly he burst a bomb on me, saying "I've appointed John Hetherington my biographer."*

*I was in Melbourne at the time. So at once rang John H. up I wanted to find out what he was like. He bolted out to see me, & I found a gentleman, a good man & true, & one I could completely trust. I thought I'd never make another friend, after Millie Lewers died, but John & I are now not only friends, but very intimate friends.*

*... From the start John has been extremely anxious to meet you Lionel! He is well aware that you have one of the finest minds in Australia. He has heard so much in praise of your personality, quite apart from your reputation as a fine artist. As he said to me "Your brother Lionel is a man I have always longed to meet. Do you think you could induce him to let me have an interview."*

*I said "You wait John til I see" — Then in a recent letter from Norman this. "You are doing out the early childhood & life in the home Mame! I'm now writing up the early student days in Melbourne, & I think that Lionel should be asked if he would give his view of that period, as he was just as much involved in it as I was. I intend to completely ignore that long period of the unfortunate rift between us." End of quote.*

*This business of trying to help is the last job in the world that I wanted, but I felt, for all our sakes, that I must butt in. It wont be easy. the Springwood people have been very good to me, & I'll have to pull my punches when it comes to Rose. I have told Dan, what I now repeat to you, (of course in absolute confidence) that N. is an extremely unhappy, lonely man, long estranged from Rose, who spends nearly all her time with the eldest married daughter & her children ... He's being kept alive by shots of extract of liver, by this Doctor.*

*...*

*Getting back to John H., he has an established reputation as a writer with a number of war books to his credit ... He is a man with a fine sensitive mind ... All the same in a letter I had this morning he says "If I thought there was any hope of your brother Lionel giving me time, I could fly across on a Friday morning & spend most of Friday, & Saturday with him"*

*Let me know what you think of this proposition — my comment is that N. is at present eating out of my hand, & it would be wise of you to meet John. You will be very safe in his hands, & you both would, once met, fall for each other on the spot. I don't just like John. I love the man, & now, after this wordy scrawl, I send my love to you, with a special message of affection for Peter. Is it true that Helen the actress is engaged, & that Bingo has gone over for the wedding . . .*

*Mary*

*P.S. Getting back to the N.L. biography. I'm truly thankful that N. has, by a stroke of good luck settled on John H, because for a long time this collector ass & various Sydney satellites, have been badgering him about writing his own story, or putting it in the hands of a biographer & (in that case) I have it on good authority it would have been a matter of sheer idolatory.*

*. . . He's only met N. once. That was when he flew over after the fires devastated Springwood — Rose was there. I gather that she goes back at intervals & chiefly to print etchings. . . Yes! Life can't at Springwood be very gay. I believe the son-in-law calls it 'the morgue'.*

*. . .*

*Pearl comes out occasionally. Its good to know (after all those long troublesome Creswick years) that her lines have fallen in pleasant places. She is a very fortunate woman with 3 good children, who have all offered her homes & who do everything they possibly can to make her later life comfortable. . .*

*You'd better put this letter, full of incendiary gossip straight into the fire . . . However! once started as you see I go on & on, rather like those way back boundary riders who haven't a soul to speak to all the year but once started, let loose a flood of talk. Poor John H. when we meet, has to stand an avalanche of words, but he's a brave man, & his heavy war experience is a help.*

*Love,*

*Mary*

*P.S. By the way, old man., dont send Isabel money. Pearl told me you'd sent her £1. She's a secret lady, who keeps her private affairs to herself. Dan sends £1 a week for her, of which she gets 10/- per week for pocket money. She really doesn't need any more. Mary*[20]

It would have been strategically better for Mary to have sent a shorter, less revealing letter, and to have deferred the attack on Isabel. The previous January Lionel had written to Daryl about taking preventative measures against Mary's growing mythologising of Robert and Norman.

> It seems that Mary has taken to writing some sort of a lucubration on the Family with Robert as a noble figure: so at Peter's suggestion I have written a short sketch of his character.[21]

Lionel's reply to Mary was brief and to the point, cutting through the verbiage.
Dear Mary,

>    I am very busy with a book I am getting published and not well — a heart upset — so this must be but a short note. I will be having nothing to do with Springwood... I cannot forgive Norman and Robert for their vile, lying, attacks on our mother, who was a woman of great character and probity.
>    I prefer to forget Creswick poisoned by Norman, and in defence of the family honour have written a book of reminiscences that is substantiated by letters (under seal) now in the Melbourne University.
>    Glad to hear that you are well. Helen was married in July, and Bingo returns in September.
>    As I have told you above that I will have nothing to do with Springwood, that makes it quite useless for Mr Hetherington to think of coming to see me, as I would tell him nothing.
>    I have heard that he is a very nice fellow, but I can think of nothing so foolish as to have a biography written during the lifetime of the subject. No one with the least intelligence ever believes such lucubrations.
>    I was glad to see Pearl I'm very fond of her and I admire the way she faced life in misfortune.
>    As ever
>    Lionel [22]

By this time Mary lived a life of almost total social isolation. Most of her letters to Norman refer to the biography or to her reading and little else. There are some passing references to Kathleen, Isabel and the married McPhee children, but it is clear that in her eighty-first year, Mary was lonely for intelligent company. As she started to confide her carefully constructed narratives and family secrets to Norman's biographer, so John Hetherington returned the confidence with some details of his own background. It is clear that John

Hetherington did not understand that by listening to Mary's accounts of her brothers and sisters and telling her his stories, he was being drawn into the Lindsay family narratives. Shortly before Mary wrote to Lionel, she had found out enough about Hetherington to pass on some intimate details to Norman.

> I have met Olive, John's wife twice and definitely like her, & she definitely likes me.
>
> Her first marriage was to a medical man, who spent most of his days drinking at his club & being carried home at night. There was one child — a boy — After the divorce Olive & John married, bringing up the boy in their home. That was 15 years ago. The boy was educated for the medical profession — went to England for some further degree, & died suddenly some months after his return to Australia of a brain attack of some sort.
>
> That was 3 years ago. That was almost as much of a blow to John as to the boy's mother. "It wasn't just that he was brought up like my son, Mary" he said, "He was as well my very best friend."[23]

In return for these small revelations about his private life Hetherington was given the gossip that Rose and Norman believed Daryl to have stolen some etchings, and that Lionel's wife had disliked Rose.[24] Mary also started to reveal something of herself and the way she felt about this very attentive man, her brother's biographer. In particular it became obvious that Mary was becoming possessive in her friendship with Hetherington. He encouraged Mary to meet Olive, who was slowly dying and largely confined to the house. There is no evidence that Mary did other than join in the friendship, further honouring her friend for his loyalty to such a sick wife. She wrote to Norman:

> John's wife has an impeccable good taste which shows in their delightful flat & in her dress. She was pleased when I said that Bert, the asthete would have tremendously appreciated the beautiful arrangement of their flat, added to the quiet comfort of it as a home . . .
>
> . . . Really Norman! It sounds quite incredible that in a comparatively short time I am quite as fond of him as I was of our other John or Ruff T. In addition I find John H. more mentally sympathetic than any other human I have ever met, & altho (handicapped by the Lindsay manner) I automatically find contact with any & every human a simple matter. Actually only one or two creatures in a lifetime I can call friends. Speech I have always found a splendid defence to protect my little ego. There is a little hard core in me, (you've got one too) that very few can care touch. In fact you, the big creative human, & me the small unproductive character, have I

*feel much in common. All my life down here I have lived practically a life of solitude. Two men now gone would have called me their 'very best friend', while I have been aware that they both received from me genuine understanding & sympathy, receiving in return affection, but not the same understanding. That of course was due to my innate reserve. But with John my fences were down from the start. After using the family manner all these years to shut out any intrusions on my small personality, it gives me a curiously light feeling to let loose anything I feel & think without the faintest fear of ever being misunderstood.*[25]

In late August 1958, Norman wrote to Mary concerning Pearl's behaviour and then switched to a discussion of Olive Hetherington and her illness followed by some critical remarks on illness and pain. Norman was always intolerant of illness in others and maintained a quaint belief in the power of the mind over the body. While Hetherington lodged this letter with the rest of his papers, he did cross out one sentence referring to Olive's 'invalidism'.[26] It must have been disconcerting for the journalist to find his life was a subject of interest to those he thought of as his sources. He was disturbed by the notion that roles could be reversed and that his private life, and that of his dying wife, could be the subject of frank discussion among these figures of history.

Mary was aware that Hetherington would eventually travel to Sydney and meet Rose, and would be told about Robert by those who did not share her sympathy. She attempted to compensate by giving Hetherington several, partly conflicting, accounts of Robert and his relationship with his mother.

*. . . Bert started life handicapped by a terrific mother complex. He was the most devoted son, & adored by his mother. He was so generous, and was constantly, out of his hard earned small income, sending her gifts that often meant depriving himself of much that would have contributed to a more comfortable form of living.*

*Then, after having spent the bulk of his adult life in London, he decided to return to Australia . . .*

*. . . & he found to his horror, that the once adored mother had become a wreck of the woman who was. It was two years after his arrival that she died, & during those two years he learned to hate her, & you know how fierce love turned to hatred can be —*

*. . . Bert relieved his outraged feelings by sending N. reams & reams of an analysis of his mother's character, (all hopelessly wrong) which N. mopped up & used.*[27]

In addition to myth-making, Mary divulged for Hetherington the private family history, the stories which the siblings knew but did not discuss, and in doing so indicated to him that there were matters the respectable Lindsays did not wish to have aired. When she wrote about Lionel, it was inevitable that she would raise the way he had rescued the family from penury:

> Lionel it was, on a visit to the old house, who saw how desperate the situation was here. Dad drinking, & unable to hold what was left, of what had once been a flourishing practice.
> 
> I couldn't clear out & leave them to it to get a job & I was at my wits end, altho Reg with his miserable pittance of a wage at the Forestry school (that was long before the day of astronomical wages) gave every farthing he could to pay for the daily bread.
> 
> Yes! Lionel it was who said "Oh! We've got to do something about this. I'll see Norman & we'll fix up an allowance."
> 
> Norman of course said "Rather! Why didn't Mame tell me", & forthwith sufficient cash . . . — & Rose's integrity was entirely responsible for the regular Springwood monthly allowance. N. would give his family or any stray sponger whatever they asked for, but as to tying himself down to the impossible task of remembering to write & post a cheque 12 times a year, no artist could attempt such an impossible task. Presently, very shortly afterward Pearl's husband took an overdose of sleeping draft & left her and 3 young children on the rocks. I took a cab up to Pearl's cottage & brought her down. There was nothing else to be done . . . [28]

Drunkenness, poverty and suicide were not what John Hetherington had envisaged for the family of his Australian hero.

It was in her accounts of the family finances and her parents' relationship that Mary became most contradictory. Shortly after writing the above letter to Hetherington, she sent him a copy of a letter she had written to Norman on the same subject.

> . . . a gutter press paper in which it said Dad was just a lousy old sot! The picture you draw of Dad would not quite dispose of that misconception. He did drink of course. So did Perc, but no one could possibly call either of them drunkard.[29]

Nevertheless, she was sometimes consistently deceptive when discussing particular subjects. On 12 November 1958 she wrote of Norman's fiction that 'except for the central character in "A Cousin From Fiji" and that Girl in "Red

Heap", there's not a live woman in any of his novels', even though she knew this was untrue.[30]

By early 1959, letters from Hetherington to Norman indicate that he was starting to find Mary's care for his welfare somewhat overwhelming. He was, in his social attitudes, a very conservative man, operating in an almost exclusively male milieu. In both his marriages his wives took a background position. There is no discussion of any female colleagues in his letters until he marries one, and Mollie, his second wife, was apparently in a subordinate position at The Age. He was not used to the concept of friendship with women, even older women rendered sexless by their age.

Towards the end of 1959, Hetherington prepared to visit Norman and Rose in Springwood. Although Rose was by then living with Jane at Hunters Hill, the couple did spend considerable time together, and their relationship as this stage appears to have been amicable. Unlike Mary's fictions, Rose's truths as told to Hetherington were pointed lessons learned from the harshness of life and salted with a bawdy humour. She did not believe in sanitised history and her cooperation with her husband's biographer appears to have ended when he started acceding to the demands of those she regarded as her enemies. She knew some good stories, and for the purposes of a biography which would acknowledge Norman's faults as well as his virtues, she was prepared to reveal them.

Rose was not the kind of woman John Hetherington admired. Even though Mary had praised her generosity and integrity regarding the Creswick family, she was clearly not a 'lady'. Hetherington, the son of a gambling shop keeper and his prudent wife, had escaped his background by winning a scholarship to a church choir school and understood respectability to be a virtue.[31] In 1958, he had written to Mary of his expectations of Rose, based on his reading of Mary's letter.[32] Mary, while partly critical of Rose's 'mind [which] is inflamed, distorted, filled with revengeful venom', also praised her 'past integrity'. It is hard to completely reconcile Mary's account with Hetherington's interpretation of it.

> You never told me before, in so many words, that you have never really liked Rose, but of course I knew it. I sometimes wonder — this is something I have no way of knowing — if Norman ever really liked her either. I doubt it; as you know, it is possible for a woman to subjugate a man in the physical sense, but not to make him love her, in any sense of the word, as I understand it.
>
> There are things about Rose that must have jarred painfully on Norman's sensibilities throughout their life together, even throughout the early

*stages of their life together, when his judgment of her was, shall we say, somewhat clouded by other factors. One of the many differences between Norman and Rose — not the most important differences, but superficially one of the salient differences — is that Norman is by nature a model of courtesy, while Rose has all the rudeness of the peasant.*

*I suppose these are harsh words, and perhaps you will not endorse them. However, on what I have seen of Norman and Rose, they are true. I don't know who it was that coined the phrase 'the cling of the clay'. Whoever it was, he must have been someone of perception. Breeding, with human beings, as with horses, is as unmistakable as the difference between moonlight and sunlight, and Norman is a person of breeding, while Rose is a person of no breeding.*[33]

Just before Hetherington left for Springwood, Mary wrote him a long letter, enclosing one from Norman, with the note that 'thought I'd better send it C of the Age!' She told Hetherington that Norman was concerned about his welfare: *You'll see he's a bit apprehensive that you'll get rough treatment when at Springwood, unless Rose is there to supply edible food etc, as she always has done for guests in the past.*[34]

The passage that Hetherington marked in pencil did not concern the trivia of hospitality, but rather a short piece in Norman's letter on how much Hetherington's friendship meant to Mary.

*Yes I fully realise the rare and unexpected pleasure you have had in your friendship with John. That is a reward definitely added to the sum total of life, and one, to my mind which has the substitute of eternal continuity in it.*[35]

This passage, combined with Mary's comment about sending mail to *The Age* (where Olive could not open it) and linked with other comments made in passing, left John Hetherington vulnerable to a new interpretation of his friendship with Mary. The bulk of Mary's letter is concerned with how she felt about the two 'interfering' wives — Rose and Jean Lindsay — and how, in her eyes they had destroyed the friendship between Norman and Lionel.

*Really John! I have always felt that its Rose who Lionel has had his knife in all along.*

*Those two damnable wives! Poor Jean the invalid & admirable wife to Lionel, who started the whole trouble. & Rose, who naturally in self defence carried on the war.*

## JOHN AND MARY

> *You may think that I'm sour about other women. It isn't that John! My dead friend Millicent Lewers was, without a hint of sentimentality, the finest woman I ever knew. Its just that my brothers have been exceptionally unfortunate in their wives. Even Jean, the good wife, should have known that her attitude was as destroying to the husband she was devoted to, as it was to Norman.*
>
> *What a fiendish weapon jealousy can be in a wife, or any woman for that matter. Add to that the intense primitive possessiveness of the wife (which is probably the reason for the institution of marriage) & the average husband has to fight for his life. I have watched time & again the insidious working of wives turning their husbands against fine and loyal men friends, while the husbands remained unaware of what was happening.*
>
> *— but enough of your friend Mary in a vindictive mood.* [36]

After Hetherington's visit to Rose, he terminated his friendship with Mary. Letters in the La Trobe and Mitchell Libraries show that when Mary wrote to Hetherington, he passed the letters to Rose and Norman, and he wrote to them, not her. He never trusted her as a person or as an informant again.

There were several reasons for this abrupt change in behaviour. Rose in a hospitable mood was not the vulgar tart he had imagined, but a gracious hostess with an ironic sense of humour. The Springwood he saw was not the 'morgue' Mary had described, and Norman was clearly at ease with himself. However, Hetherington discovered that Rose had an ongoing joke: the supposedly insatiable sexual passion of the elderly Mary Lindsay for Mr John Hetherington.

The joke was a good one to play on the gullible biographer. Mary's language in her letters tends to be extravagant, so Rose and Norman may well have believed what they claimed. Mary's arguments for the pleasures of friendship could be interpreted as the excuses of a frustrated old maid and her expressions of admiration for Hetherington were only too easy to turn against her. When she told her relatives details of John Hetherington's private life, she had embellished the narrative with her own creative insights in the same way as she embellished the Lindsay story. Her letter complaining of destructive jealous wives now had a greater significance.

It seemed logical for Mary to turn to her closest confidant, her brother Norman, for some understanding of why her friend no longer wanted anything to do with her, and to ask if there were any rational explanation for his sudden hostility.

*This note from John Hetherington, that came this morning, gave me a shock.*

*I had become so fond of John. We had I thought established something that I thought was a friendship that would last till the end of my life...*

*I have done everything in my power to help John over his book, not because I approve of any biography unless it is written after the death of the victim & all his associates. — but John's personality got me, as I think it did Rose & Jane later — Rose, now that she has apparently fallen for him too, will of course be tremendously helpful and informative over data...*

*I think John H. is the most chivalrous gentleman who ever came my way — His devotion to his invalid wife is something that I have only seen equalled in books of fiction. You see I have been at their house, & been entertained by both John & Olive who was very nice indeed to me.*

*... Well, right up until just before leaving for Springwood his letters breathed the same affectionate friendliness. Then after his return to Melb I received one letter — expressed his admiration for Rose & Jane, which I felt he wanted them to send on. I posted it on to Jane to Hunters Hill.*

*After that not another word from John. It was borne in on me that he has for some reason turned me down cold. Any of my letters to him were simply ignored. Finally I wrote asking for an explanation and saying that the warmth of my feeling for him, made me feel entitled to ask the reason for his strange change of front.*

*After keeping me waiting some weeks for a reply, I received this morning this smack on the face.*

*He evidently thinks I have been gossiping at Springwood about his private life — because I don't think he & I have a single friend or even acquaintance in Vic. & in any case, if his name or Olive's had come up, I should (understanding him) have always been mindful not to repeat the smallest item that he would have disapproved of.*

*If Rose is at the moment at Hunters Hill, send this note on to her & to Jane. Can any one of you three give me a clue as to why I have lost a friendship I greatly valued. Sometimes a remark passed on without the context, can cause the greatest mischief.*

*... I have been scrupulously careful not to mention to a soul that those two from the time of their marriage have been followed by scandal. Someone told me she had been married twice before. It may not be true & anyway I'm not in the least interested in that side of their lives. They now have almost completely shut in lives at home only seeing a very few friends.*

## JOHN AND MARY

*Now the defence is this: First you are shocked to think of anyone suspecting Mary of indiscretion or disloyalty. — that Mary said to you that John had an invalid wife who he was devoted to, & it must be terribly hard to watch anyone cared for so deeply looking so ghastly ill.*

*Actually I only said this to him, & he looked at me a bit sadly & said "It is wearing Mary," & then shut up.*

*If by any chance, being human, you have dropped a hint to any intimate friend, & he has heard it, just stick the rest on Sydney gossip.*

*You might add that I had 18 years looking after my mother before her death, & have on that account a special sympathy for anyone watching an invalid who suffers — I want you to put this in such a way that he will feel apologetic to me over the stupid business. He knows (I told him) that I had a hell of a time here with Isabel, & has expressed sympathy over that.*

*Don't say too much, but as you love me, put this right, as soon as you possibly can — so that I can get a nights sleep — You see he has been brooding and sulking over my rottenness for nearly 3 months now.*

*My love,*
*Mame*

*PS You might be a bit hurt that anyone should accuse me of anything but the noblest behaviour. That would relieve my feelings and make me laugh once more. . . .* [37]

The best indication of what was actually said to John about Mary is in a letter from Rose.

Dear John and <u>wife</u> Olive,

Your letter arrived this morning . . .

I did not tell you that Mary had sent your letter to me that you wrote on the 16 of December after your visit to Springwood. There was no reason for her to send it unless to force us to realise that you liked Jane and I — and she did not approve.

We enjoyed it: it is a masterpiece (your letter I mean).

. . . Some time before your visit to Springwood, I received a letter from Pearl in which she said 'I wonder what John Hetherington would think of Mary if he really knew her.' Mary had been to visit Pearl and showed her jealousy about Olive, and also she warned me that Mary hated me. — and loved the Stewarts [Douglas and Margaret]. She has never met the Stewarts what really upsets Pearl is the way that Mary treats Isabel. That she is cruel to her— And also Pearl said that Mary Hates Kathleen now and wishes that she had never had her join forces. That Kathleen bought into the place and pays her share all the time and does most of the work and is kind to Isabel.

I will most likely get a letter from Pearl soon, with full details of Mary's present hatreds.

. . . Mary hates Pearl ever since she married Colin McPhee.

[passage marked by Hetherington] I'm wondering if Norman sent Mary a copy of Redheap, if so it will flare up old wounds as the 2 sisters in that is the story of Mary, Pearl and Colin, and more or less true. Except Pearl did not have any early love affair. Norman added that. Mary had. Not Many. John Tremearne (they always called Ruff John) there was a local Dr — who died a while back and the professor in America.

In a letter that she wrote to me after Ruff died she referred to his wife as 'that vile woman' for what reason I do not know as she was always a welcome guest at this house. I met Ruff's wife and liked her. But this will amuse you both. In a letter to Norman a year back Mary said that you became the 3rd John in her life that meant anything to her. I know that one was Ruff but I can't place the other unless the professor was called John, or the local Dr. I know that they were definitely physical affairs — You are a heavenly mental one. So don't get me wrong. I'm not trying to infer otherwise.

If Mary was not so malicious, I would be inclined to feel sorry for her . . . [After describing her visit to Norman at Springwood] I asked Norman if he had heard from her. He said 'Yes. She only writes about books. No news.'

I couldn't see any of her letters about but will search when I go home.

I thought very hard before I warned you about Mary's jealousy of Olive. I realise the danger mark when she wrote other letters. One that I destroyed was very alarming.

Long ago she wrote to Norman and asked him to write to Olive to tell her How much she liked Olive. she didn't want you to know that she had asked. I remember Norman writing to me he said 'Mary must sense that Olive is not too keen on her.

I am glad that Oswald Burke's remarks on what can happen to a person who has a brain cell going off on the wrong track has alerted you to Mary. Also Pearl's account of her cruelty to Isabel is disquieting.

I can assure you that I'd be highly suspicious of a bit [?] of sweets from that Lady. She has turned against me but still writes care of Jane. of course she doesn't know that I am aware of her dislike. she never fails to urge me for *my own sake to stay away from Springwood. It could become an obsession with her to do something about me. I blame Norman a lot for this. he should not have written Mary things that he did. And that I was forced to correct. I have copies of many of letters but this is another story and all harks back to a row over the Stewarts.*

*Also Mary has made many requests for me to return any of Bert's and her letters that were written to either of us about their mother. I can quite understand her wanting them, if she wants to leave a picture of Bert as a sweet and kindly soul.*

*I told her that I had destroyed them. I know that she doesn't believe me, but I did get rid of some of Berts. I am enclosing some of his which will give you some idea of his sweetness.*[38]

Thanks to Rose, John Hetherington knew the identity of two of the principal characters in *Redheap*. Hetherington had read *Redheap* and it was easy for him to see the frustrated anger of Hetty Piper in Mary, the woman on whom the character was based. He apparently failed to notice that if Pearl was the manipulative Ethel, there was no way Mary would have confided her deepest emotional secrets to that most loathed sister. Likewise, Rose's account of Mary's affairs lacks credibility. Mary's closest 'Doctor friend' in Creswick had been Jim Strachan, the husband of her friend. There is a reference in one of Mary's letters to the death of John Tremearne in 1951, but it is only a passing comment on his funeral which was a Catholic ceremony.[39] In any case, as Rose never visited Creswick all of her information on Mary's 'love life' was second-hand.

But the letters of Robert Lindsay were real. After Hetherington read them he could not believe any of Mary's account of her family's history and was therefore inclined to believe Rose's story of the sexual passions of an 83-year-old woman. Other than puzzlement that her friend no longer cared for her, and the observation that 'my firm conviction is that John is a bad case of nervous frustration', Mary never criticised Hetherington.[40] She was, however, concerned for the fate of Norman's letters and other family papers she had given him, including her copy of Lionel's book, *Addled Art*, the Lindsay family history, and photographs, including her parents' wedding photograph.

Despite pleas from Mary, the letters and photographs stayed with Hetherington, and are now in the La Trobe Library. Although Hetherington wanted to accede to Mary's request, Norman told him to keep everything. The most valuable book, the privately printed Lindsay family history, was collected by Daryl through the intervention of the ever helpful Joseph Burke.[41] After her experience with Hetherington, Mary started to appreciate the sense of family duty which motivated her youngest brother. She came to rely on his good sense and assisted him in his plan to create a facsimile Lindsay family drawing room in the Ballarat Fine Art Gallery.

Norman did not approve of this scheme and, in a letter to Hetherington, damned Mary for 'that ridiculous Lindsay shrine which Ballarat Gallery has set up'. [42] Mary continued to send Norman letters on family history which she must have realised he would forward to Hetherington.

Daryl appreciated the brief sketch she had written for Hetherington's benefit on family life in Creswick and incorporated it into *The Leafy Tree*, which appeared in 1965.[43] Mary's talent for writing dialogue, often displayed in her letters, is there used to evoke the organised chaos of her adolescence and Daryl's childhood.

John Hetherington did not remain on good terms with Rose. On 29 June 1963 he wrote to Norman, ostensibly lamenting his confusion over the conditions concerning Commonwealth Literary Fund grants, but in the final paragraph, making a specific request for information.

> I saw a note in one of the Sydney newspaper gossip columns that Rose had sold your correspondence to the Mitchell Library, with a 25-year embargo on its release. What happens in these circumstances? Does the purchasing library send along a van and cart all the stuff away to its vaults at once or does it trust to providence to get its money's worth after your death? Incidentally, a question occurs to me out of all of this: Which of your correspondents all down the years has written the best letters?[44]

The real motivation behind this piece of flattery was to deduce the circumstances of the sale and determine whether it would preclude further access to the letters. In his reply Norman did not address the question. Instead he listed his favourite letter writers (who included Hugh McCrae, Douglas Stewart, John Tierney and, as flattery, Hetherington himself). Then he wrote:

> That action of Rose's in selling her collection of letters to Mitchell Library has made something of a conscience problem in the preservation of letters. I never gave a thought to mine on that account till George Robertson sold to the Mitchell Bert Steven's collection of letters, mine among them. It gave me a shock, and for some years after I refused to write any other letters save those concerning affairs. It took me some time to restore a sense of humour over the business, and realise that nothing is so futile as to try and cover up one's

*private life from the prying eyes of posterity; that is, assuming that one has figured as a notability in one's period. Now I don't care the convention of a damn what comes out about mine. If the culture of this country is going to take its place in world culture, as I don't doubt it must, then the personalities of those who initiated that culture are going to be of extreme interest.*[45]

The answer, by implication, was that the letters had gone, and that there was no likelihood that Hetherington would see any he had not already been shown. Rose had decided that John Hetherington was not capable of writing the kind of biography she wanted. She therefore removed a significant portion of the primary source material from his scrutiny.

# 14

## What John knew

Mary was the single most important thread in John Hetherington's examination of Norman Lindsay, but she was not his only source, and as I read through his notes I realised the breadth of his research as he tried to understand the complex nature of his hero. Quite early in the piece, probably at about the time Mary was campaigning for an account of the entire family, Hetherington reassured Norman that he, as subject, would remain central to the book:

> Of course, nobody else will loom very large in your biography, as I see that biography now. First, there won't be room for anybody else to loom large; second, I am sure you will endorse my belief that, in a biography, the subject must hold the centre of the stage all the time. Your children are important to this biography only in so far as they are your children; Rose only in so far as she is your wife; Hugh McCrae, Doug Stewart and some others only in so far as they were or are your friends. What I am seeking to say is that the inclusion of anything in the narrative, must depend on its relationship with you as the focus of that narrative; nobody or anything outside of you has any right in the narrative, except on those terms.[1]

As I read this I remembered Harry Chaplin's letter to Norman, pointing out the need for some sort of context for his life.[2] Hetherington was not going to meet that demand, nor was his subject going to encourage anything other than the life of a fully fledged hero. Hetherington's other limitations as an author arose directly from his age and the context of his own life. He once wrote to Norman that:

> Alan Moorehead once said to me, 'There are seven rules for the biographer, and all of them say "Don't show your book, before it is published to any near

*female relative of the subject"'. . . I have always found that women are not at all interested in having the truth about the man they love or have loved go into print; they are concerned only to preserve the image of the loved one as they would have liked him to be, and they expect the biographer to twist and distort his story to that end.*[3]

On several occasions he expressed strong distrust of females in any role other than domestic. In Australian newspapers of the 1940s to the 1960s, women journalists were mostly confined to the social pages and any women who moved out of this sphere were treated with suspicion. By the time Hetherington was completing his book, however, a new generation of feminists was entering the work force, including journalism: times were changing.

But Hetherington belonged to the older generation. Shortly after his second marriage in 1967, he wrote to Norman that if he and his wife were able to visit Springwood, there would be no difficulties as 'Mollie is thoroughly experienced in the domestic department, and she would cheerfully cook our meals, leaving us free to talk and discuss all those things which we want to know of one another's views'[4]. This man could never comprehend the ambitions and freedoms of Rose Lindsay, and he could never understand the nature of Mary Lindsay's frustrations.

As a consequence, he neglected some female sources who could have given him valuable information and downplayed the importance of material supplied by others. He paid less attention to the women than to the men who helped shape Norman Lindsay's life, even though the liberating power of women is a recurring theme in Norman's written and visual material. In a candid letter to Joan Burke, Ray Lindsay's widow, Hetherington wrote:

*I might say that Norman's daughters don't loom as large in the biography as his sons — inevitably it seems to me, although I'm probably inviting the wrath of Woman's Lib! by saying it. But they do have a place, and I have to be right in what I say of them.*[5]

Of course, Hetherington was hardly alone in this attitude. I remember Elizabeth Webby telling me a story of the scholar Leonie Kramer, now the Chancellor of the University of Sydney, travelling up to Springwood with Douglas and Margaret Stewart to meet the famous Norman Lindsay. When they arrived she was most surprised to find that she and Margaret were to prepare food in the kitchen while the great men talked literature. I asked Professor Kramer about the incident.

'Yes, it's true,' she said. 'Alec Hope was there too. After lunch Margaret and I were in the kitchen which was an absolute slum with half-open tins everywhere. We looked at the floor and we looked at each other. Then we got down on our knees and we scrubbed that floor. It was filthy.'

It seemed odd that Norman Lindsay, who in his youth had participated in a genuine sexual revolution, should spend his last years surrounded by men of the most rigidly conservative kind. And that one of these should be chosen to be his biographer.

Hetherington's view of women caused him to discount both Mary and Rose as sources and led him to ignore the close relationship between Norman and his elder daughter Jane. Instead, he concentrated on the father–child relationship between Norman and Jane's half-brother Jack, even though it was over three decades since Jack had met with Norman, and for most of that time they had not been in contact. There are no letters to Jane in the Hetherington papers. She appears as an appropriate background figure, the mother of Norman's grandchildren, and mentioned as such in correspondence with the distrusted Rose. Jane doesn't remember meeting Hetherington, although she realises she must have done so and there are greetings to her included in Hetherington's letters to Rose.

Of course there was another reason Hetherington concentrated on the male sources. Mary and Rose had both made him aware of the dark side of the Lindsay family relationships. The quarrelsome, self-seeking letters are central to understanding how Norman saw women, especially those in his immediate family circle. But an analysis of those relationships could have made an uncomfortable book, and Hetherington was not a writer of uncomfortable books. By minimising the importance of the Lindsay women, he evaded the issue.

Through his long correspondence with Norman and his own entanglement with the more manipulative members of the family, John Hetherington came to know most of the Lindsay family secrets. He even managed one formal meeting with Daryl, who had refused to cooperate with the book, by speaking only of Daryl's own career when interviewing him for a feature article.[6]

Despite the possible repercussions, Hetherington closely examined Norman's attitudes to homosexuality and to racial differences, and his observations are neatly recorded in his notes. He was able to cross-check Norman's attitudes to Jack with Jack himself, and thanks to Peter Lindsay he came to some understanding of Lionel. All the accumulated facts were meticulously filed away. But *The Embattled Olympian* reflects little of the research. Instead, it questions only partly the god-like figure of the Lindsay myth. There are some indications in the book that Norman was not always kind, and on occasions could be selfish. But the lasting impression is that the talent was so overwhelming and the revolt against the wowsers so important, that minor peccadilloes of egoism and delusions of other-worldly conversations should be overlooked.

Because Rose was seen as only an appendage to Norman, her motives and position in society were not examined. Her business acumen was described, but not the reasons why an ambitious and unconventional woman would scandalise respectable Sydney by openly cohabiting with a married man. Nor was there any analysis of how she had managed her elevation into relative respectability within a few short years of marriage. The crisis in the Lindsay marriage in the 1930s was avoided and there is no examination of the final ambiguous relationship between the two old people. Norman's career is all.

Yet when Norman authorised the biography, he had asked the author to research it as widely as possible. It is clear from his writing, both published and unpublished, that Norman was so confident about his world view, he remained convinced that any competent biographer would see him the way he saw himself.

There was no consistency, however, in his opinions of his siblings and children. At first he was inclined to be generous with Lionel. He was aware that he had been less than fair to him in the novels and perhaps partly in an attempt to achieve a sort of accommodation with his once loved older brother, he wrote to Mary :

*I think it only just that Lionel should have his say in the matter, to present any point of view about events, if he cares to do so. I've been pretty free with his personality in my personal records, and I think his view point on mine would at least add a balance in the conflict of our personalities.*[7]

After his father's death in 1961, Peter, with his usual generosity to researchers, told Hetherington all he knew.

The first mention of Jack in the correspondence between John Hetherington and Norman Lindsay comes in 1958, but it is hardly an invitation to seek out the Great Man's eldest son. Norman wrote:

*If you accept the understanding that Jack hates me and I dislike him, you will have a balanced outlook on anything he writes in reference to me. We both know perfectly well that this is the relation in which we stand to each other;*

*he knows that I dislike him and he also knows that I know that he hates me
. . . I take the above to be the normal relation in which most fathers and sons
stand to each other, though very few are ever conscious of it . . .*

*The son needs to get rid of the father's dominance in order to make his
own way in life, and the father does not want to be responsible for the son's
up keep, once he is capable of making his own living. When, as in Jack's
case, he has a father who is an established notability by the time the son
reaches maturity, he feels that he is in for a desperate struggle to compete
with the father and establish his own identity, the more especially when he is
driven by an almost megalomaniacal egotism, effectively concealed behind an
impassive mask. I only once saw the mask lifted as I will record. Whatever
genesis his mind may come from, I am convinced that it is Oriental. His
maternal progenitors were Anglo Indians for several generations. It is hard to
believe that native blood does not percolate into such stock from the feminine
side. Of course it does. That's where he comes from, without a doubt in my
mind. In every way he is the extreme from the earth of my begetting. If I
sought a caption for him it would be The Man who Could Not Laugh.
. . . There is a dark, blank space in the content of a mind that cannot laugh.
That dark space is the oriental in him.*[8]

There were other letters in this vein. Hetherington did not speak or write to Jack until the late 1960s, when, at the end of his life, Norman started to communicate again with his son.

Norman was resentful of his sons and especially of the way Jack had turned to Communism and rejected his father's beliefs. In the hatred he felt for what he saw as Jack's betrayal, he lost all inhibitions, all sense of paternal responsibility. Even more distasteful was the way Norman expressed his hatred towards Katie and her family. Throughout his life Norman tended to accuse those he had once loved of marital infidelity in order to justify his behaviour towards them. He accused Katie of having an affair with Will Dyson and, in the letter just quoted, accused her mother or grandmother of being the product of an extramarital affair in India.

Norman Lindsay's racism far surpassed the normal bigotry of early twentieth-century Australia. In comparison to Norman, Lionel (often damned for his racism) was a bleeding heart liberal. For Norman Lindsay to accuse his own son of being a closet 'oriental' was to condemn him to the status of non-human, someone beyond any reasonable consideration. Yet the guiding hand which encouraged John Hetherington in his need to create a favourable study of a contradictory and often hostile subject was Jack's. Norman's most extreme attitudes on race were mitigated by Jack's considered advocacy on his father's behalf:

> Anti-semitism. In an unthinking way that was rather characteristic of the period in which Norman came up: Hilaire Belloc, Chesterton, etc. In Norman's case, and I have no doubt in Lionel's too, it was not based on any actual experience. Norman knew nothing of the world of finance and industry anyway; and he never mentioned any case in which he came up against a Jew in any way. Certainly much of his attitude came via Nietzsche — though Nietzsche himself wasn't anti-Semitic . . . So Norman and Lionel took the Jew as the symbol of the Enemy Within — all the more easily because they had practically no direct experience of Jews. It was this vague sense of something wrong with society for which the Jew became a caricature-scapegoat that Hitler was able to capitalise — though Jews of course existed much more definitely as a social fact in Germany than in Australia.[9]

In 1968 Hetherington left Australia for a long-planned trip to England. Norman by then had come to some kind of understanding with Jack, largely brought about by Jack's habit of sending his father copies of his new books and also because of the personal representations of Harry Chaplin.[10] On 28 May 1968 Hetherington wrote to Norman describing his first correspondence with Jack, who he described as a 'quality writer'.[11] Two months later they met, and Hetherington reported that Norman's eldest son was 'gentle and tolerant . . [with] a very deep but unostentatious affection for you'.[12] The very old Norman Lindsay was pleased to hear of his son's love.

In the years following Norman's death, Jack freely gave of his time to Hetherington with information and well-reasoned judgment. This cooperation may, in part, have been prompted by the posthumous publication of *My Mask*, the untruths of which Jack was eager to rectify.[13] But in any case the torrid, sometimes fruitful but often destructive relationship between Norman and his three sons had led Jack to think a great deal about his famous father. Norman Lindsay is a background figure in most of Jack's own autobiographical writing and his decision to spend his life on the other side of the world from his father was a conscious one. His analysis of his father was ultimately more compassionate than that of the myth makers who took the artist's own evaluation of himself. As Jack noted to Hetherington:

> Taken on his own terms, he seems incredibly stupid and frivolous — without any real development, a mere puppet of Madam Life. And oddly that was

*what he wanted to seem. The receiving end of divine forces over which he in effect operated no control. As I have no doubt said before, Madam Life's Lovers has to be read quite literally if one wants to know what Norman really thought were his motivations at all: Madam Life pushed him about to ensure that he had the sort of life a dutiful artist ought to have.*[14]

Jack also urged Hetherington towards an understanding of why Norman was so bitter at his lack of British success, a bitterness emphasised by Lionel's popularity with the London printmaking establishment.

*I agree that his sense of failure about England went deep. He really had not reason to feel that way. The period was a bad one and he should have known he couldn't fit into the art world etc. Lionel as a more conventional artist could, BD [Will Dyson] made his place as a consistent rebel. Norman just had no point of contact. But with his way of creating absolutes out of any experience or idea he decided England and the old world in general were dead, evil and all the rest of it.*[15]

Jack is most critical of Norman when he discusses his mother and the reality of his parent's marriage. Norman's account of Katie meant that Jack needed to put the record straight, to show the pain he knew she felt at the public dismemberment of her identity as a respectable married woman.[16]

*Naturally I am too involved in the question of his relations with my mother to be a wholly objective witness. But I have done my best to think that thing out in a detached way, and I feel sure that Norman is not to be trusted in anything he says on the matter. He always had to justify himself in all major matters, and it was inevitable he would try to believe that she had acted in the same sort of way as he did himself.*[17]

Many of the letters between Jack and Hetherington cover the details of the various houses of Jack's early childhood, and especially Jack's recollections of Norman's departure for England and the formal separation in 1913. Jack told his father's biographer of his mother's shock at these events, and her deep depression which followed. Jack did not mention what Hetherington already knew: that Katie Lindsay had died of alcohol related dementia in Sydney's Broughton Hall psychiatric hospital in 1949.

In a crucial letter, Jack indicates that Katie was unaware that when Norman left her to go to England in 1909 her marriage was over:

*. . . my mother was a person who could not hide her emotions or sustain 'a*

*role'. I feel sure that if in 1909 any dramatic break had occurred the effects would have been sharp enough to leave some mark on my memory. On the contrary I can recall that she was very happy in the weeks before we left — no doubt because she was going to see Mary and her mother again . . .*

*My mother must have realised for some years of course that her marriage had broken down; but she was not a very logical person. She must have gradually accommodated herself to being Mrs Norman Lindsay without any reality to it, but have imagined this indeterminate position could go on indefinitely.* [18]

There was of course, a reason for Katie's happiness when Norman left for England: Rose remained in Sydney. There was a real chance that the affair was over. Jack also refuted Norman's racist fiction concerning Katie's ancestry by giving details of her father's family.

*No, Mr Parkinson was wholly English, a civil servant, who was at one time Postmaster General at Allahabad, where my mother was born. I think the family was Devonian, and I recall my grandmother speaking of a French aristocrat refugee at the time of the French revolution marrying into the family — but it is possible that that referred to her side.* [19]

Jack also gave what is perhaps the most insightful analysis of Norman Lindsay's relationships with women other than Katie:

*. . . whatever had happened, I feel sure that he would have fallen as a victim to some managing woman, who would take charge of everything for him and control him (outside his art) like any strongminded mother who knew what was best for him. My mother was a thousand miles from being such a character, so I think it was pretty near a certainty that their marriage would not survive — especially as soon as Norman became a 'success'.* [20]

When Norman wanted to claim that Katie had an affair with Dyson when he was in the early stages of his affair with Rose, he used an incident from Jack's autobiography, *Life Rarely Tells,* to 'prove' it. In Jack's story Katie slept with her children while Will stayed in her bed because there was a storm and he could not get home. When Norman heard about this after his return, he was jealous, but Jack remembered her talking about Norman's reaction rather than the event itself.[21] In a series of letters, Hetherington questioned Jack about the incident and Jack's replies show how he was gradually swayed towards Hetherington's belief that his father was telling the truth.

Initially, Jack wrote:

*Relations with Bill. I cannot say whether there was an affair or not, only that they were very friendly in that last period. It is however quite possible they were lovers. You must remember that Norman had been keeping Rose for some three to four years then (I told you that he certainly began well before Phil's birth in May 1906). He was seldom at home except in token-returns and I doubt if there were any relations between him and my mother. So the affair, if it did exist, was no excuse for NLs Rose affair — as I am sure, with his elastic sense of chronology, he would have liked to make out.*[22]

In a handwritten note on his next letter, Jack noted: 'I agree about Will Dyson: his exact role in relation to Norman, my mother, and Ruby has always puzzled me since I tried to think these things out.'[23] He realised by then that Norman had deliberately confused the timing of the relationship with Rose and that it had started when Katie was 'bringing Ray to birth'.[24]

Finally there was a sort of confused acceptance that there may have been some truth in Norman's allegations.

*I should think there is a basis of fact in Norman's tale about Bill Dyson, but as usual it is quite false in tone . . .*

*First point. He expresses total lack of knowledge of the relationship between Bill and my mother. Yet there are the two details I record in LRT (1) Bill had done a painting of her in a blue costume with a hat that had a single feather — I recall it well; and this picture hung in the drawing-room. Did Norman never see it??? (2) There is the anecdote of my saying that Bill had slept in my mother's bed. Norman was immensely upset and rushed out of the house — the episode occurred at breakfast. (As I say in LRT, I heard my mother tell the story several times, and what I remember is her telling it rather than the episode itself . . .*

*. . . What remains a mystery (in part because of blankness as to the chronology of the events) is how Bill D., was metamorphosed from the betraying best-friend into the happy brother-in-law passionately in love with Ruby and going blithely with Norman to England.*[25]

Hetherington took these letters, combined with Norman's account of a confession as sufficient evidence to write:

*How close their relationship was is a matter of conjecture, but Norman had no doubt that for a time they were lovers. He believed that they first became intimate while he was on a visit to Creswick and Will happened to* be in Sydney. If Katie turned to Will, it is hardly to be wondered at. She had been a neglected wife for a long while, and he was not only a good-looking and vital young man but also a sympathetic one. Long afterwards, Norman told a convincing detailed story of a triangular confrontation on his return from Creswick; this ended he said, in Katie and Will admitting their guilt.[26]

The language here is almost identical to that used by Hetherington to describe Norman's own behaviour in 1934 when he left Rose for Margaret: the difference is that Hetherington had been able to verify that particular affair. This account, however, has some complications.

Katie was a woman from a conventional middle-class background. In Australian culture, at that time, marital infidelity was a serious matter. As well as being a scandal, it was grounds for divorce. Would she have told people the story of Norman's jealousy if there was any truth in the matter? Then there is the puzzle of Norman's continuing friendship with Will Dyson at the same time as the alleged affair.

Another problem concerns timing. Because Rose had placed her papers in the Mitchell Library, Hetherington did not know that Katie had first been told about Rose when Ray was born, and that Will was the most likely informant.[27] He was also unaware of Will Dyson's *ménage à trois* with Rose and Norman at the very start of their affair, although this was hinted at by Rose in *Model Wife*.[28]

Then there is the further complication of family feeling. The Dysons were a very close-knit family. By the time Jean Dyson arrived in Sydney to marry Lionel, Will had already warned her off Rose and Jean refused to have any social contact with her.[29] Ruby, who was close to Will by 1907, likewise refused to know Rose.

Jack's account of Katie Lindsay indicates that she inspired protective instincts in men. The realities of early twentieth-century attitudes to marriage meant that her situation as an abandoned wife was hardly an enviable one. It is reasonable to surmise that Will Dyson gave her friendship and encouragement which she did not receive from any other source.

A thought crossed my mind at this point. What if Will had told Katie he thought that Norman would come back to her if Rose were out of the way? Could this be another reason why Ruby and Will had snubbed Rose when she suddenly turned up in London? Perhaps their attitude was not the prudery they were accused of, but rather the result of acting as friends of Katie.

'Do you remember Ruby?' I asked Bingo one day. She was showing me family photographs and there was little Bingo, dressed in a sheet as a child from classical Greece, trailing behind Ruby, also clad in a sheet, looking as beautiful as a goddess.

'How could I forget? She was so beautiful that I used to follow her everywhere. It must have been quite embarrassing for her and uncle Bill, you know.'

'Why?'

'Well, they'd just come up to Sydney because they were newly engaged and of course they wanted to be alone, but I was always there. And of course just after they were married they left for England and I never saw her again because she died.'

'What was Bill like?'

'He was wonderful, uncle Bill. I don't know why Norman said he was bitter, except that he loved Ruby so much and he mourned her when she died. It was so sad to lose her like that.' Then she added: 'The important thing about him was that he was very protective, and chivalrous. But he hated Rose and everything she stood for.'

Jack has written that after Katie was formally separated from Norman in 1913, she gave away all mementos and drawings by him and sank into an alcoholic depression.[30] This information was included by Hetherington in a typescript of his book, but eliminated in the published version.[31]

In Brisbane, where Katie had a supportive family, there was no indication of any other romance. Nor is there any reference to any sexual 'misbehaviour' on her part by Lionel Lindsay in his letters to Norman.[32] Yet Lionel was frequently critical of Katie whom he regarded as an inadequate wife for his 'genius' brother. The allegations only surfaced after both Dyson and Katie were dead and Norman was sanitising his past for history.

By the time I finished reading Box 3 of the Hetherington papers, I was smiling. At last I knew why, inhibitions aside, John Hetherington had written such a bowdlerised account of Norman's life. The key is a letter, enclosed within another letter, sent by Norman to Hetherington in September 1964. The author is Douglas Stewart, poet, editor, and long-time friend of Norman. The subject is John Hetherington as Norman's biographer:

> . . . I agree that Hetherington is the best of the practicable biographers working in Australia. I think his judgment of your novels is poor — that's why I criticised his Lansdowne booklet — but I don't see that need come very much into a biography. When he has the book written he'd be wise to show it to such people as Slessor, Margaret [Stewart's wife], Inglis Moore, Guy Howarth, or myself — in Ms form — so that we can help him get it right. I'm sure any of us would be glad to look at it for him.[33]

Hetherington acceded to Stewart's suggestion and agreed to show the book to all the people mentioned in the letter with the comment: 'He must have a curious idea of my working methods as a biographer if he imagines I would not wish to show the draft biography to those people he mentions.'[34]

On the surface, this exchange could be read as if the concerned acolyte, Douglas Stewart, was trying to safeguard his hero's reputation. Stewart, with his knowledge and admiration of Lindsay, was a natural authority to turn to. He also screened Howarth and Barker's edited letters of Norman Lindsay and explained his position in that publication in the following terms:

> . . . I shall be reading all the letters myself; and both of us [Barker and Stewart] have had long training in detecting and excising libel. Further, though one doesn't of course want to cut the life out of the book, I don't want to include gratuitous scandals such as often went the rounds in Lindsay gossip, nor do I want to include too many of his intemperate and often unfair attacks on such familiar targets as publishers, editors, his wife and family, etc. Jane, incidentally, will have a right of veto on the MS.[35]

In the case of the biography, all three parties, Norman, Stewart and Hetherington, knew there was a great deal more at stake. In agreeing to allow Douglas and Margaret Stewart to have an editorial say in the account of Norman Lindsay's life, Hetherington was agreeing to censorship of the contents.

When Norman first described Douglas Stewart to Hetherington it was as '. . . the most intimate friend I've ever had, though the differences in our ages make that an intellectual rather than an emotional intimacy'.[36] But there was another link. As Norman's affair with Margaret was ending, and he returned to the mountains, he encouraged her to marry his young protege, Douglas Stewart. At the time of the Stewart–Coen wedding, Stewart was apparently unaware of the intensity of her previous relationship with Norman.

'I really put my foot in it there,' said Peter, talking about Douglas Stewart. 'He once asked me if I knew why Rose hated him and Margaret so much. So without thinking I just said, "It's probably because of that affair Margaret had with Norman". And then I saw by his face that he hadn't known.'

In the first stages of his correspondence with Hetherington, Norman kept to the myth that his only extra-marital liaison was with Rose. 'The only model I ever had a sex affair with was Rose,' he wrote. 'And that developed into a full size love affair.'[37] But after Hetherington visited him in Springwood, and Norman realised Mary had told him about Margaret, there was less concealment.

In one remarkable letter Norman argued both against concealment in biography and in favour of the love of an older man for a young woman. There are direct parallels between Norman's interpretation of Charles Dickens' affair with Ellen Ternan and his relationship with Margaret.

*Dickens' with little Ellen Tenan is another instance of the fatuity of trying to hide a clandestine love affair. In his lifetime, Dickens went to tremendous exertions to block out any possible detection of the affair, even to having the child he had by her taken over by a married couple of working people and registered under their paternity . . . The whole event was recently dug up by an industrious grave digger, who even found the cottage in which Dickens secreted his Ellen, and worked out the circuitous route by which Dickens reached it, getting out at wayside stations and dodging round back streets and lanes to slink in at her back door.*

*But putting all that aside, Dicken's affair with Ellen was one of the wisest and sanest actions he ever performed. He had reached his fifties and come to a dead end as a writer. Inspiration petered out in him . . . That, anyway, was the state of mind he was in when he met Ellen, (she was a young actress) and took a part in a play which Dickens was managing and staging, and the affair was on.*

*And out of it he got three of his best novels Our Mutual Friend, Great Expectations, and Little Dorret. And if we want a picture of Ellen and*

*Dickens together, we only have to look up Bella Wilfer sportively playing about with Pa Wilfer in Our Mutual Friend. We owe these novels to Ellen, bless her.*[38]

By then, Norman had been given the assurance by Hetherington that while he would continue to research the book, his biography of Norman Lindsay would not be written in the subject's lifetime. 'This might mean I shall never write your biography, because it is reasonably conceivable that you will outlive me,' he wrote. 'If so, the book must be left to other hands. In fact, I shall not attempt to out anything on paper, or anything connected at least, while you are living.'[39]

Hetherington's notes contain a detailed checklist for an early synopsis with specific references to Douglas Stewart and Margaret Coen. The wording indicates the information came directly from Norman. This was the sequence of events: 'Antecedents of 12 Bridge St', presumably the first studies he painted of Margaret.[40] Then, 'Rose accused me of having affair with Margaret', followed by 'Thereafter Springwood only for weekends', 'Christmas eruption at Springwood', 'Margaret steers me to 12 Bridge Street', 'Writers at 12 Bridge Street', 'Weekday routine', 'Sunday routine', 'Return to Springwood', 'Handed 12 Bridge Street over to the Stewarts'.

Towards the end of the document there is a note:
*Middle age corruption had bust up relations between Rose and myself — extract from Letter 2 attached.*

*Margaret: having seen me established, she took over Doug Stewart — extract from Letter 2 attached.*[41]

I couldn't find the letters from Norman, but there is a corroborative letter from Peter Lindsay, who cheerfully wrote: 'Mrs Stewart (I forget her name, but you undoubtedly know that she served a term as mistress to Norman) . . .'[42] For Norman, Margaret appears to have been a benevolent goddess, later to be translated into the Good Wife.

The best description of Norman's feelings towards Margaret comes in a watercolour inappropriately titled *Nude (Figure Composition)* in the collection of the Tamworth Art Gallery. In it the gods of Olympus are blessing the connection of a gracious muse (looking just like Margaret) and a small Pierrot-like figure. The date, 1933, precedes Norman's departure from Springwood. The ambiguity of his feelings about the romance is expressed in his etching *Have Faith*, which was made sometime in the 1930s. There are figures based on both Margaret and Rose, with a looming priapic bull. Rose was Norman's print-maker. Was this made by the artist as a way of explaining his feelings to his wife? She had ample opportunity to study the sway of the bodies and the tilt of the heads as she inked each plate and wiped it clean for the press.

Hetherington's notes cover Norman's continuing relationship with Douglas and Margaret. Norman was not invited to their wedding at the 'Catholic Church at Randwick. I don't think we dreamed of asking NL to such a ceremony — he'd have been up in Springwood anyway', wrote Douglas Stewart. But he gave the young couple the property at 12 Bridge Street as their first home.[43]

The closest reference to the relationship and its aftermath in Hetherington's published book is oblique:

*What part if any late love played in restoring Norman's nervous balance and his mastery over himself is conjectural. If he had an affair of the heart at that time he never spoke of it. This proves nothing; he was as reticent in such matters as men like Hugh McCrae were cheerfully unguarded. Some of his close friends supposed that the views he often expounded on the value of a new love in stimulating the creative powers of an aging man reflected personal experience. He was fond of citing Charles Dickens in support of his theory; Dickens, he insisted, could not have given the world <u>Great Expectations</u> and <u>Our Mutual Friend</u> unless he had renewed himself in middle age by leaving the mother of his ten children and taking a young actress, Ellen Ternan, as mistress.*[44]

Box 11 of the Hetherington papers holds a copy of the original typescript of *The Embattled Olympian* with handwritten alterations. These indicate a further editing of the text, as anything which could possibly have caused offence to the living was removed. It is not clear whether these are Hetherington's own second thoughts or the suggestions of the book's editor. References to Norman's unsavoury habit of spying on lovers and other people with his telescope have been neutralised. The original has a reference to 'watching the antics of the human animal', but this was amended so that the final version read 'spying on unsuspecting people, especially children'.[45]

Originally, there was an indication of childhood racism with an account of the Lindsay boys pelting the local Chinese residents of Creswick with stones.[46] In the published version, this went, as did the story which came originally from Mary of Norman's childhood nickname of 'Ikey Bentwick'.[47]

Hetherington knew the full extent of the adult Norman's racism. Norman's claim that 'Hitler did a service by killing so many [Jews]', in a 1960s letter, is but one terrible example.[48] Most racists were cowed into guilty silence after news of the extermination camps was released in the 1940s and the country as a whole was a more tolerant place for racial minorities by the 1960s. Norman remained an exception. Just as he kept an index of Norman's relationship with the Stewarts, so Hetherington kept an index of his subject's racist statements. He noted Norman's comments over a wide range of racial prejudices, especially anti-semitism.[49]

In at least one act of censorship, Hetherington was inhibited by his editor rather than by his own coyness. Wendy Sutherland of Oxford University Press wrote expressing concern that the book would finally put in print what was well known within the arts community: that Elioth Gruner was homosexual. Hetherington replied in an unusually robust letter:

*I consider it most important to present a full picture of the man, because he, with Bill Dyson and Julian Ashton, was the only artist of high standing with whom Norman ever had an intimate friendship. As far as I know, Gruner has no close relative still living. Anyway the basic fact of his sexual aberration is a matter of fairly common knowledge, although it has probably never been so clearly spelt out in print.*[50]

Gruner's homosexual status is retained as:
*Norman was a little mystified by the strength of his liking for Gruner. As a rule he recoiled from any man in whom he sensed a homosexual taint, yet never from Gruner. The reason was that Gruner had not only a fine mind but also a nobility of spirit rare in human beings.*[51]

Hetherington and Norman appear to have shared a prurient interest in homosexuality, and there was an exchange of letters between them on homosexuals in the arts and in the army.[52]

The typescript and the published book differ significantly in describing the relative importance of siblings. At first it was the girls who were eliminated from the narrative. Norman is at one point compared to 'the others', but in the book this is changed to 'his brothers'.[53] In the typescript, Thomas Williams takes 'his wife, his children, his grandchildren and friends' to see Solomon J. Solomon's *Ajax and Cassandra* at the Ballarat Fine Art Gallery,[54] but the book turns this into an experience for Norman and Lionel taken separately.[55]

Although Rose effectively barred Hetherington from the Mitchell papers, he was allowed to study the Melbourne University papers, shortly before they were transferred to the La Trobe Library. His response on reading them was to write to Joseph Burke who had arranged the access: 'I am only astonished that Lionel managed to keep his patience for so long'.[56] So even without reading the Mitchell Library papers he knew that Robert Piper, the hero of *Redheap*, was based on Lionel, and knew therefore that part of Lionel's quarrel with his brother was based on the book. From Rose he also knew that Mrs Piper, Hetty and Ethel were closely based on Norman's vision of his mother, Mary and Pearl.

From Mary, Hetherington discovered that some characters were based on the passing parade of Creswick identities who may have had good reason to object to the publication of their private scandals:

> . . . I haven't the faintest idea how much truth there is in the portrait of his wife and her sister. All I remember is being taken with my Mother with the correct paste boards to call on the wife and the new Curate, and seeing a very good looking fair woman reclining on a sofa, apparently in the role of an invalid.[57]

Some time after Rose first told Hetherington that the character of the spinster Hetty was based on Mary, and the flirtatious Ethel was a study of Pearl, Norman wrote further:

> Family relationships have always been a mainstay of the novel. I dealt with them in Redheap. The two sisters in that novel were based on conflict between two of my sisters. With, of course, a considerable variation in externals, to bring them into a eugenic relation to parents and other family relationships not drawn from my family. One has to throw a pretty wide psychological net to garner essential characteristics in such a grouping. Mary wrote me an extremely bitter rejection of that novel when she read a first edition of it. In Creswick it aroused a furious antagonism to me and all my works. I think Mary had a good deal to put up with on that score. Poltoonery advised me to keep away from Creswick after writing that novel. But one must become a conscienceless scoundril in respect to sentiment about human relations to do anything with the metier of the novel.[58]

The reason Norman gave for the banning of the book was one that would have special interest for Hetherington. He had left the Melbourne *Herald* on bad terms with its proprietor, Keith Murdoch. Now he discovered that

Norman both shared his dislike of Keith Murdoch and blamed him for the media campaign against *Redheap*. In particular, Norman wrote to Hetherington that:

> ... *the novel was reviewed by the* [Melbourne] Herald's *London representative, but to its review Murdoch appended in brackets such captions as 'If the censor permits it to enter the country' or words to that effect.*
>
> *You have credited him* [Murdoch] *with having encouraged plastic art in this country. I do assure you, that with the able assistance of that unutterable runt, my brother Daryl, no man could have done more harm to it.*
>
> ... *He jumped straight from jackarooing into the position of Curator, such was the assiduity with which he courted Murdoch, who gave him the job, and is stark evidence that Murdoch knew nothing and cared nothing about its cultural importance.*[59]

Daryl was blamed by Norman, for using his Murdoch connections to create the media row about *Redheap*. Norman also told Hetherington that Montague Grover, whom he regarded as a Murdoch lackey, had been involved in lobbying for the ban.[60]

For some time I had assumed the Hetty–Mary and Ethel–Pearl link, so while this confirmed that my guess was right and that Hetherington had been told the truth, I still wanted to know why he hadn't published it. All those directly portrayed in *Redheap* were dead when The *Embattled Olympian* was published. There was no one left who could reasonably object to the truth coming out. All I can guess is that some relative, either a Lindsay or of one of the other families involved, asked Hetherington to keep silent and that their correspondence is missing from the papers lodged in the library.

I had started reading Hetherington's papers with a fairly low opinion of their original owner. I knew that in order to be polite, he had eliminated much that was central to Norman Lindsay's life, but politeness is hardly a necessary quality in a biographer. After a week of reading, notetaking and photocopying, I understood more. Even in the 1970s there were still too many sensitivities, too many toes which could be trodden on for Hetherington to tell what he knew. If he had written it all, Norman Lindsay would have ceased to be an anti-wowser, freedom-loving hero, and John Hetherington was writing at a time when such heroes were needed.

So he mimicked Rose's act in lodging her manuscripts in a public library. He kept the notes which indicated the larger story and ensured they were placed where future scholars would be certain to find them. There is no restriction on access to the Hetherington papers; all the reader has to do is ask. It was just luck that I was probably the first person to do so.

# 15

# *Redheap* and the justifiable act of censorship

*I* have always enjoyed reading *Redheap*. I first read it over twenty years ago, for pleasure. In essence it is a romp in a country town, a story of a boy growing up, of youthful exuberance unsullied by experience. It seemed absurd to me that the book had been banned for so long, but then Australia was the kind of country that used to ban everything — from James Joyce's *Ulysses* to Mary McCarthy's *The Group*. From what I now know, I would argue not only that the book should have been banned, but really that there was no alternative. For the fiction that was published to such praise by libertarian critics was so full of half-truths that it damaged the private lives of ordinary people. These people were not famous, they had not sought to be notorious or even to hold public office. In *Comedy of Life* Lionel called *Redheap* a calumny — he wasn't wrong.

*Redheap* was first published in London in April 1930. The Melbourne *Herald* led its announcement with 'Norman Lindsay Writes a Novel. Will Police Permit its Sale in Australia? Reviewer Has His Doubts'.[1] The *Sydney Morning Herald* called it 'Literary Matricide'.[2] And other reports followed.[3] On 22 May 1930, the *Sydney Morning Herald* reported that:

> *The Acting Minister for Customs (Mr Forde) announced in the House of Representatives this afternoon that the entry into Australia of the novel* Redheap . . . *is to be prohibited on the ground that it carried passages which are indecent or obscene.*
>
> *Mr Forde was replying to Mr Keane (V) who claimed that the novel contained serious reflections on the morality of a certain community in Victoria . . .* [4]

From 1929, when *Ulysses* was first banned, to 1957, when censorship started to be eased, approximately one thousand books were refused entry to this country. In 1930, as well as *Redheap*, they included Daniel Defoe's *Moll Flanders*, James Joyce's *The Dubliners* and John Cowper Powys' *Apples Be Ripe*. The only distinction awarded to *Redheap* was that it was an Australian book denied entry to its own culture.[5] Later the censorship was compounded by the Post Master General who, when the *Sydney Guardian* prepared to serialise *Redheap*, wrote to the paper's editor threatening to withdraw registration from the newspaper. This would have removed cheap postal rates, which meant that he was effectively threatening bankruptcy. Publication did not proceed.[6]

Daryl Lindsay was almost certainly instrumental in having the book banned, but his political contacts were hardly confined to the media. In *The Leafy Tree* he mentioned James Peacock, the Creswick draper, whose son later became Premier of Victoria. By 1930 Sir Alexander Peacock was Speaker of the Victorian Legislative Assembly and still living in Creswick. His wife's name was Millie, the same as one of the main protagonists in *Redheap*. Peacock was one of the great operators of Victorian politics, a man with the kind of connections to get a book banned, especially as there was considerable local pressure to do so.

The speed of government action meant that by the time reviews were published, the actions of the Minister for Customs were known. This gave the book a certain notoriety and probably led to a more considered response from overseas critics than such a disjointed novel would have otherwise received. The book might not have sold legally in Australia, but (partly as a consequence of its banning) it was successful overseas. William Soskin wrote of the American edition, published under the name *Every Mother's Son*, that:

> His picture of adolescents in a small Australian town contains much brutality, much that is coarse, much that is full-blooded to a bursting degree. But they are fascinating adolescents who are contriving to escape from the burden of a whole generation's social imbecility loaded upon their shoulders.

# REDHEAP AND THE JUSTIFIABLE ACT OF CENSORSHIP

> ... As a matter of fact, Robert is an average mean and vain boy, with average cowardice and normal appetites.
>
> ... All the rather feverish warmth of these little adventures, of Robert and his sister Ethel, of the little fat girl who gave herself to Robert, of the soiled gallants and hard-boiled belles, the author draws into a texture of reality.[7]

In the *New York Telegram* Burton Rascoe wrote:
— the Australians have banned his novel. On the pretext, possibly, of lese majeste, since one of the characters in the novel refers to the late Queen Victoria in a phrase that is slightly irreverent.[8]

The praise, however, was not universal. A. S. Sesnke noted the disjointed nature of the novel when he wrote that '...half way along he [Robert] suddenly finds he has nothing more to say, and every mother's son is unceremoniously dumped in favour of a couple of daughters.'[9] The critic of the *New York Times Book Review* noted:
> The young people are hard as nails (except Millie, who is merely imbecile. That's the trouble with all this emancipation fiction — the girls merely throw themselves away; there isn't a grand passion in the whole fiction shelf).[10]

Nor was all educated Australia opposed to the censorship. Frederick Howard wrote in *Stead's Review* that 'little harm and much good [was done] by administering avuncular kicks in the pants to the small-boy novelists who come to make rude faces at Australia's front doors'.[11]

When Norman and Rose left Australia in 1931, they blamed their flight on the banning of the book. The *Daily Telegraph* trumpeted:

### NORMAN LINDSAY TELLS US 'MUST FIGHT FOR FREEDOM OF EXPRESSION'
#### Our only trouble: Too Many Wowsers

'GOOD-BYE; best country in the world, if it was not for the wowsers —'

Norman Lindsay in a wireless message to 'The Daily Telegraph' last night.

LEAVING Australia yesterday, probably for ever, and taking with him pen drawings, watercolours, and etchings worth a small fortune, Mr Norman Lindsay had some caustic comment to make before the Aorangi sailed yesterday. His wife was not less caustic.[12]

They returned the next year, but *Redheap* remained unpublished in Australia until 1959. However, because it was freely available in both England and America, copies were smuggled into Australia as a sign of daring. Norman appears to have encouraged the public view that it was simply the wowserism of his prudish mother that kept the book banned for so many years.

'I hope they censor the damned thing,' Norman wrote to the writer Godfrey Blunden just after the book was published. 'Why? Because it will test out your courage, and the courage of any other youth struggling with the novel. That's all this rot is designed for'.[13] Later he told Blunden that:

*here we have the Government deliberately throttling literary expression. In America this sort of thing is a war between the extremists of outlook in the State itself . . . Now we can fight the wowser all right, but we can't fight a by-law backed up by police and State.*[14]

In the same letter Norman claims that Ethel is a composite of 'all the surface disguises of a girl I once knew', but she is also 'a satanic statement of the power to affirm', and has aspects of himself 'in so far as I can claim to have stated my own ego in the face of man's attempt to stamp it flat.'

*Redheap* became the *cause célèbre* of anti-censorship, the proof that Australia was a second-rate wowserish society. Douglas Stewart, writing in 1959, remembered that he had first read it when he was a student in Wellington, New Zealand, and for his generation '. . . it was a banned book and it was our banner of freedom'.[15] This attitude to *Redheap* was still current in 1980 when Keith Thomas wrote that the novel was banned 'because it outraged the country town nobility of penny-pinching clergymen, fulminating town clerks, crooked bank managers and stuck-up tradesmen's daughters who lost both their dignity and cover in its pages'.[16]

The ironies of *Redheap* are many. It is a comedy written at a time when both the writer and those he turned into his subjects were suffering from depression. It is a celebration of the supposed pleasures of adolescence written in such a way that it evoked the remembered miseries of its chief subject in his maturity. The first draft was written in part by Norman as a tribute to that boy, the young Lionel Lindsay, but its writing was a significant factor in the demise of the friendship between the writer and subject. It is clear that Pearl and Mary Lindsay, the originals of the two sisters, Ethel and Hetty, both suffered from the publication of the book and were pleased when it was banned. Yet both remained on good terms with Norman for the rest of their lives, largely because they were financially dependent on him.

# REDHEAP AND THE JUSTIFIABLE ACT OF CENSORSHIP

How did it all start, this book of great controversy, this milestone in the history of censorship? The Mitchell and La Trobe Library letters make it clear that at the outset Norman simply wanted to write a comic realist novel. Like Lionel he admired both Charles Dickens and Samuel Butler, and in the years after he left Creswick, individual characters and events came back to reshape themselves into happy fictions. His first book, *A Curate in Bohemia*, was an outstanding success in the way he gave a twist of comedy to the well-known tradition of stories of life in an artist's garret. Only those most familiar with Norman and his circle recognised the poet Hugh McCrae as the original of the curate.

In late 1915 Norman wrote to Lionel:

*. . . I have been getting my peace of mind back by writing some small studies of character. I have done Grand Pa Williams, Bill Cannon and Uncle Johnson. I think they have some qualities of style, and I would like your opinion of them.*

*. . . I am embarking on another novel with Creswick as the background. I have got the thing pretty clearly mapped out, and the characters arranged, but at present I find myself suddenly devoid of a proper method . . . I have a nervous anxiety to begin this story . . . to get it underweigh and see what will become of it. But I can't get started and I have a fancy I will go across to Creswick after the New Year and see if I can pick up the intimate note by a little local colour.*[17]

There is reference to Norman's source material in a postscript to a letter written by Lionel in August or September 1915.

*When you come to town bring my youthful diary. I wish to put it at last to use, having had an idea or two since seeing Creswick (Don't post it. I want it by a sure hand).*[18]

Lionel's 'youthful diary' and the way Norman used it in *Redheap* was the centre of one of the great quarrels between Norman and Lionel. In 1891 the sixteen-year-old Lionel had returned to Creswick after an aborted career as an assistant in the Melbourne Observatory. He was supposedly studying for matriculation to Melbourne University but instead pursued beer, friends and girls. And he kept a diary. It was his record of discontent: of hopes and dreams, small victories and great defeats. The remaining fragments show drawings in a style based on Charles Keene's *Punch* illustrations — boys shooting, smoking, drinking and playing cards. The written entries show similar preoccupations, but there is an additional interest in girls.

*Saturday 23rd (4 pipes)*

*Drew in morning, went for walk with D.S. and Bert R. in afternoon. Evening paraded street for Prissy, she didn't come, met Rowell about 9. then went off with Sarah Westcott. home at 9.30. Smoked 4 pipes under stair*

*Sunday 24th*

*4 pipes 1cgs*

*Church in morning, Evans preacher, after church went a walk with Hawk round the lake. smoked a pipe; went with Rowell to the lake this afternoon, smoked 1 cigar*[19]

For some years the diary was in Norman's possession, a prized relic of his older brother's boyhood preoccupations. There is no definite account of how Norman came to have it, but over the years there were several letters from Lionel asking for its return. In 1915 Lionel told Norman that he wanted it back because he had decided to write a novel based on the lives of two doctors in a country town. He thought that if written properly, an affectionate account could dispel the rumours that persisted about the last years of their father's medical practice.[20] The diary was by then being used by Norman as he wrote the first draft of a book he intended calling *The Skyline*. Lionel's book was never written. Norman became the novelist; Lionel remained the critic.

The two brothers often met to discuss their various literary projects. In a 1916 letter, Lionel wrote of a planned meeting to discuss the shape of their novels:

*Shall I bring up Madame Bovary and the memorys to discuss them out of the novel — Also Rouchfould's maxim which will make excellent discussion — No book for boys this though I believe we both dabbled in it in youth.*

*I agree with all you very clearly express about Conrad. What I personally like about him is the fine modesty of the man and his beautiful sense of the word.*[21]

Knowledge of the early drafts of Norman's writing on their Creswick boyhood survive through Lionel's comments on them. At first they appear to be parts of what later became *Saturdee*[22] and *Half Way to Anywhere*. In a letter of (probably) 1916 Lionel wrote: 'I think Bill Bryant a much nicer fellow than his original and Viola a pleasant chapter which brings back to me with a strange pleasure the most admirable part of my life'.[23] But at the same time as Norman and Lionel had their quarrel over the existence of an afterlife, Norman was

# REDHEAP AND THE JUSTIFIABLE ACT OF CENSORSHIP

working on *The Skyline*. He referred directly to Lionel's diary, quoted passages from it in the text and, as he was working on it, showed it to several friends as an example of his intellectual brother's juvenilia. When Lionel found what Norman had done, he was devastated at the way Norman had humiliated him. The diary incident had caused him

> . . . *more mental suffering than anything I can remember. Since Dalley's and Bert Stevens' enjoyment of it I have imagined it brought out to increase the pleasure of the moment or to grace the banquet physchologist before the advent of each new guest. This is not a question of lack of humour, but of wounded pride. Examined coldly I think my entrusting you with the book was a generous and uncommon sort of action. But I have suffered I can assure you recurring spasms of pain and mental torment: at the thought it was I who delivered my honour unto your keeping.*[24]

*The Skyline* was probably meant more as a tribute to Lionel than an attack on him. The protagonist, Robert Piper, is an optimistic character, a young man who is about to have some kind of brilliant career. He may get drunk, smoke a pipe with excessive pride, write over-ornate poetry and get a girl pregnant, but in the context of the novel, all these acts are affirmations of the pleasures of life. It is clear that Lionel knew of, and at first consented to, Norman using his diary in some way when he was writing the character of Robert. But when he read the first draft manuscript, and realised the extent of the use of his own life, he was devastated:

> *I write this to ease my mental perturbation — and am sorry that your great book should have revived this old wound. I have a strange sense, when I had finished it that for this I was destined to be born — an untimely birth if ever there was one — for I am out of heart with my destiny: You who sit at ease with the immortals know no such qualms. For the game of life is a sport for amusement and artistic utility — pour nous — les autres — it is merely bread without the circus.*
>
> . . . *I would only suggest one alteration for publication and that is the substitution of some other name for Beecham-McCay. There is no necessity to confirm their opinion that I am Robert . . .*[25]

Beecham-McCay is a composite name based on Lionel's boyhood friends, Harry Beecham and Adam (Dum) McCay. By linking the 'Robert' character to their names, Norman was strengthening the signal that the character was based on his brother. The alteration was made, and Robert Piper was born.

There are no surviving letters asking for other alterations of names, although Lionel later claimed he made such a request.[26] Norman responded that:

> Robert was a composite character, and not an observation of his elder brother. There is nothing of you in Robert save the diary and the style of the letter. I never had a thought more of you in my mind when striving to create only a normally sanguine youth.[27]

In his old age, however, Norman happily admitted the link between Robert and Lionel to Harry Chaplin and others. But he continued to conceal some identities, and denied that *The Skyline/Redheap* was a *roman-à-clef*:

> Yes, Robert was Lionel. He had been two years at the Melbourne Observatory intending to become an astronomer, but to get a position as one, he had to pass an exam in the higher mathematics. Mr Bandparts was a certificated school teacher out of a job and took over as Lionel's tutor. Peter, the small brother is myself. The only other character pirated from my family was Uncle Jobson, a north of Ireland uncle of the old man's. The Piper family was built up from a family . . . and Grandpa Piper is presented in a full length portrait, and the scandal of his elopement with the housemaid is still local history.
>
> All the other characters, Dr Niven, Jerry Arnold, old Bill Cannon were direct from life. The drama of conflict between the sisters — Hetty and Ethel, over Niven, plus Arnold, is conceptional based upon the personalities involved. <u>Redheap</u> was the only title given to the novel.[28]

Along with these furphies — the title, the feuding sisters, and their romance — Norman led Chaplin to believe that the character of Ethel was based on his sister Ruby.[29]

From Lionel's detailed critique to the early manuscript it is possible to get some idea of the contents of that version:

> But to have considered it as a work of art: I enjoyed the reading of it immensely, and the good laughter it gave me I am very grateful for: but you had brought back so realistically that old Creswick life that chewing the cud for bitter reflection upon the failure of my life I always seem to go forward along its broken archways; until I lose out of all patience with that feckless and blundering figure who did so little when he had [next page missing]
>
> Firstly I must commend your clean style, direct and unencumbered with explanation. The courage you have in the face of the real problems of existence enchanted me with the true and utterly unEnglish handling of reality. The fidelity of your memory I have long ceased to wonder at but its

## REDHEAP AND THE JUSTIFIABLE ACT OF CENSORSHIP

*evidences delight — are so personally insured and reconstructed. In the characters I think John Martin and Ethel your best imaginative efforts. You have grounded these with a literary quality that is more convincing than life. Old Kneebone is a splendidly drawn character. And that as to his daughter is to have triumphed over all prejudice. I think the scene between Old Kneebone and Bandparts the best in the book and the drunken mother when she takes up the eternal cause of her daughter is handled with rare delicacy. The picture of the miserable father shut out from that awakened sympathy — the clink of a glass as the cheerful muse [?] of a wood fire is as profound as anything Dickens ever wrote.*

*What astonishes me is the breadth of sympathy . . . here you pardon all with a sense of that larger humour which though it is perforce in judgment, has a merciful comprehension of human frailty.*

*We shall have a go at the book when you come up. You shall read it and, if I can support anything that may strengthen it as a work of art you have whatever critical judgment I can command at your exacting service . . .* [30]

There are some significant omissions in Lionel's list of characters. The central character of Robert Piper is there, as are Mr Bandparts, the parson's daughter (not named), her father, old Kneebone and her mother, the drunk. Ethel is present, but Dr Niven and Jerry Arnold are not mentioned. John Martin is the real identity of the fictional Bandparts, and Lionel's use of the name in the context of the manuscript is an indication of how closely he identified the fictional with the historical.

The central incident in *The Skyline* is partly based on a composite of local memories of a parson with an alcoholic wife, and the letters Adam McCay wrote to Lionel about his time at Castlemaine Grammar School when he fell in love with the daughter of a Methodist minister. A letter from McCay to Lionel about the girl is in the Mitchell papers. Lionel most likely lent it to Norman when he was writing the book:

*. . . the object of my youthful affections has the misfortune to be the daughter of the rather straitlaced parents of one of the straitest sects of the Wesleyans. She is eighteen, small and delicate, tender and — I must not drift into rhapsody. But I am fain to let you know what the 'inexpressive she' is like. It is a curious mixture, in someways a regular youngster, in others a real little woman. Hasn't read much, for in such households promiscuous reading is sternly discouraged . . . 'Mama' has told her half a dozen times that we see each other too frequently . . .* [31]

It may well have been that the possibility of hurting his brother beyond endurance was the reason Norman put the novel to one side. He did show it to friends, including Will Dyson and Mary, all of whom admired it, but no attempt was made to have it published.[32] In the letter in which he made peace with Lionel, Norman wrote:

> *In fact, I would be satisfied to let the book lie unpublished, having secured this best of returns for the labour of writing it. I had suffered a considerable depression about it, to tell you the truth, in reading through the typed M.S.S. It seemed to me a poor sort of thing for the two years of more or less incessant labour I gave it . . . But there were times, when it seemed to me I had written well, or at least, said the thing I set out to write. Now I can no longer tell, and must depend for a vision of it through other eyes.*[33]

The final book, *Redheap*, has another narrative concerning women. Throughout the 1920s, Norman and Rose were given the details of the squabbling at Creswick in all its petty intensity. Mary wrote on her health, her family and her depression. Pearl likewise wrote her side of the story and Daryl continually wrote to Norman to ask him for both financial support and fraternal intervention. Even though he was living hundreds of miles away, Norman was being badgered to become involved in a family dispute which revived all the conflicts of his adolescent years. And he read the letters from his mother who, in giving directives to her adult daughters as though they were still under-age, reminded him of the frustrations of childhood. Perhaps there was the additional thought that if he had to read the reams of correspondence emanating from and about Creswick, then the least he could do would be to turn this sordid domestic tragedy into comedy. So Mrs Piper became a harsh, small-minded snob who disapproved of all her children's adventures. Physically she bears a striking resemblance to the middle-aged Jane:

> *Mrs Piper was still what certain middle-aged gentlemen of that era called a 'superb woman', making at the same time an opulent gesture of the arms to express size. But she carried her weight off very well by a graciousness of manner and a voice that was wilfully amiable.*[34]

There are significant differences between the conduct of the fictional Ethel Piper and the person who was Pearl Lindsay. Ethel is pretty and flirtatious, apparently innocent of any intelligence but aware of the realities of the world. She romances the working-class Arnold, but will flee to the security of a middle-class marriage with a doctor when Arnold threatens to become

## REDHEAP AND THE JUSTIFIABLE ACT OF CENSORSHIP

seriously involved with her. Sexually, Ethel is promiscuous and calculating, combining self-gratification with self-protection and childish spite. She has no inhibitions about her involvement with a married man, nor about taking away her sister's hope of romance. In short, Ethel is written as a male-fantasy sex kitten.

Norman gave several, sometimes contradictory, descriptions of the circumstances of writing, or rather rewriting, the book. He told Harry Chaplin:

*I was so disgusted with the silly uproar of censorship over Redheap that I never wanted to see the book again. I admit that having got it again, I sat down and read it with considerable interest . . .*

*. . . Redheap was a definite experiment in the form of the novel. At that time I was seeing a lot of Lou Stone* [the novelist Louis Stone], *and the metier of the novel was much discussed by us. These days I would not endorse the construction of Redheap. It has two central motive's: Robert's affairs with Millie and the Arnold and Ethel, Hetty-Niven mix up, and neither has any relation to the other. Moreover, I note that I have given myself a great deal of latitude in analysing the mental states of the characters, while today I consider that a novel should present its characters externally, and the reader be left to divine their mental states by their speech, gestures, and actions.*

*. . . You ask why Brian Penton's* [writer and newspaper man] *name is on the novel. He was really instrumental in getting it published. I never intended to publish it. I never intended to or pretended to take myself seriously as a writer. Writing has always been for me a temporary escape from the stress of my own work or picture making, and a means of clarifying my thoughts. Moreover, human personality: its mad diversity in idiosyncratic character, its motives for action, and its psychological make up generally, have always been for me the most fascinating of studies.*

*. . . Redheap was written way back in 1918, during World War I. I put it aside and forgot about it, But during the early twenties the problem of the novel was again much discussed by the first essays in it of my son Phil and Brian Penton. They used to visit me to read them in M.S. One day I happened to remember Redheap, and brought it out, and they took it away to read. I forgot for the moment that Godfrey Blunden was another member of this group who was struggling with prose, and it was through reading Redheap that he discovered; as an amazing revolution, that an up country Australian town could be used as the setting for a novel. Up to that, back block subject matter had been held the only legal literary tender.*

> *Anyway, somewhere in the early twenties Penton decided to visit London, and he proposed to take Redheap with him. I was reluctant to let it go. I did not want to confuse the action of my work as an artist by also figuring as a novelist. I did not want to figure as a novelist at all. At the back of my mind, I knew damned well that I ought not to write novels . . .*
>
> *But Penton spent a week end here nagging at me to let him take the novel, so I let it go. I never thought it would find a publisher, but it did, and as Penton was responsible for forcing it on a publisher's attention, I dedicated it the novel to him. Also, I liked him well in those days.*[35]

This timing does not quite add up. Penton was not in London until 1929,[36] but the book was definitely being rewritten by 1927. In an aside to a letter, Kenneth Slessor wrote to Norman, 'I'm anxious to see how your novel is advancing'.[37]

It may well have been the case that Norman was genuinely reluctant to have *Redheap* published, not because of its possible impact on his reputation as an artist, but because it would inevitably lead to an irrevocable rift among family members. Too many of Norman's letters feature retrospective nobility of emotion for him to be believed in this matter. This account is contradicted, in any case, by Norman's bitter tale of George Robertson's decisive rejection of the manuscript. So hurt was Norman that thirty years later he refused to let Angus & Robertson publish the first Australian edition. When Douglas Stewart asked him for the rights he replied:

> I am reminded there that old George Robertson, at his own request, first read that novel in M.S. His response to it was in these terms 'Here, take the damn thing out of my shop'. He actually threw the wad of M.S. at me. I have always believed in the law of nemesis coming full circle in time, and why should I pursue it at this date by passing Redheap back to A&R's.[38]

So *Redheap* was sent to England and America, to achieve fame and notoriety.

Over the years there were many attempts to lift the ban on *Redheap*. In 1951, a newspaper report claimed:

> The reason the Australian censor ever banned 'Redheap' is a mystery.
>
> It is a moderately frank novel of life in a Victorian small town — said to be recognisable as the author's birthplace, Creswick — and nobody but a puritan could find it offensive.[39]

By the late 1950s the campaign increased in intensity. Oliver Hogue wrote in the *Sun*:

# REDHEAP AND THE JUSTIFIABLE ACT OF CENSORSHIP

*It's time for our censors to read a novel AND LIFT BAN*
*. . . 'Redheap' offended somebody 27 years ago, and so it will remain banned for ever unless some importer or the author or other interested party appeals.*[40]

By the 1950s the young bohemians who had gathered at the feet of Norman Lindsay in the 1920s and 1930s were men of literary eminence and some influence, especially in conservative circles. The Menzies government, for all the criticisms heaped on it in subsequent years, was slowly leading Australia to a more liberal acceptance of difference. In 1957 John Hetherington sent a hurried note from the *Age* office to Norman Lindsay about possible reprieves for the many books banned from entry to Australia:

*I was puzzled to know why our Canberra correspondent could get no kind of Ministerial response to my comments about the continued ban on Redheap; so was our Canberra correspondent. But our Canberra man sent me a wire yesterday telling me that Menzies has now come in to the affair. Menzies himself won't confirm it yet, but the story is that he has 'called for a report'. . . Whether my comments led him to do this, or whether he is suffering a state of unease, as any intelligent man must, about the absurdities of our book censorship system, I don't know or care.*[41]

If Hetherington had been more aware of the broad spectrum of Australian political life he would have understood that the mood was for change. In the post-war years one of the private pleasures of federal members of parliament was the right to read books which were deemed to corrupt the general populace. In September 1957 the parliamentary librarian precipitated a crisis by removing *The Catcher in the Rye* from the parliamentary library. The book had been banned on the first attempt to distribute it in Australia, but as there had been no announcement, many copies were in circulation and it was widely discussed in academic circles. The news that members of parliament were to be denied access to an absurdly banned book was made public on 3 October.[42] Two days later the *Sydney Morning Herald* published the news that the Minister for Customs and Excise had ordered a departmental review into the entire censorship process.[43] It was this review that liberated *Redheap* and started the long, slow process of liberalising Australian censorship laws. A newspaper editorial commending the long overdue reform pays tribute to the Minister, Senator Henty, not Prime Minister Menzies.[44]

Once the ban on *Redheap* was lifted, an Australian edition was published by Ure Smith. This edition carried illustrations, which visually distanced the feuding sisters from their originals. Mary, anxious to ensure that she was not to be identified as the original of Hetty, helped with advice on costume and hairstyles. Both she and Pearl wanted to make sure that libraries would hold documents implying that the book had been based on the Jebb family of drapers (and the Pipers certainly were drapers) and had nothing to do with the Lindsay ladies of Creswick and Ballarat.[45] And in her home in rural Victoria, that most respectable matron, Mrs Felicity Shaw, became anxious in case someone should realise that the scandalous character of Ethel was her uncle's impression of her mother, the young Pearl Lindsay. For these Lindsays, the novel was reality.

# 16

## Trust

Even though I knew Helen Glad quite well, and had read *Portrait of Pa*, I'd never met the younger Jane Lindsay, better known by her married name of Jane Glad. By late July 1994, I needed to confirm details of events and attitudes, and so I drove to Hunters Hill.

Jane lives in an old house with a large garden and bouncy dogs. Over a cup of coffee, I asked questions. 'What was it like growing up with Norman Lindsay as your father?' I started. 'Did you realise how important he was to all the people who came to see him, or did you just accept it as normal?'

Jane paused to think before answering. 'I just assumed that because I loved and admired him, it was reasonable for other people to,' she said. 'I think because I was fond of him I kind of took it for granted that other people might not think he was a bad bloke, in the same way. He was good company, so why shouldn't other people enjoy him? I think it was probably as simple as that. I knew he had a lot of people — when he was in Bridge Street people used to trek up there to see him — but I just assumed these were people on the same plane as he was. It was a companionship thing.'

'Did you and your sister have some restraints placed on you by your parents?' I asked.

'No, never. Ma would police us if she thought we were going to get seduced too young. But when we were old enough we went and made our own arrangements. There was that sort of thing. But it wasn't on moral grounds it was just commonsense.'

Young Jane had not developed her ideas without encouragement. Her mother was a constant example. But Norman, the famous anti-wowser, was now shown to me in the unusual guise of upholder of middle-class morality. 'There was a sort of element of stuffiness with Pa,' Jane said. 'You know, not sleeping with my boyfriend because it might embarrass the cook. He had areas of that kind of stuffiness. It must be a hangover from God knows what.'

'Do you remember your Aunt Mary at all?'

'Very vaguely. I think I would only have been about four or five when she last came. What was the date?'

That had been a long shot. Because most of her contemporaries were dead, few people could be accurate about Mary, but I had vaguely hoped for some communication between the maiden aunt and her literary niece. 'You probably don't remember much about your father's quarrel with your grandmother either,' I said gloomily.

'I think that had more to do with the way he related to mail,' she said. 'You see most of his quarrels happened by mail, and not face to face. He might say to someone in conversation "Oh it won't do, old man", but I don't ever remember him quarrelling. But he used to write.'

'With the letters, the unposted letters that Rose used to hide, what would happen when he met the person again?' I asked.

'Why would he meet them?' came the swift reply. 'They probably wouldn't come near him.'

I remembered then the many letters from Norman telling his correspondents they could not visit, because he was too ill or too preoccupied. The man had social isolation down to a fine art. The interest he had in his children, however, was real if spasmodic.

'Pa had this touching faith in females,' Jane said. 'I think this is one of the things he impressed on me. I don't know if he'd be the same if he'd had a son. But he used to constantly say, "It's in the hands of women" and "Women can do anything." He liked women writers. And I think this could be one of the reasons he impressed on me [that I should write]. He didn't do it to Honey. He didn't tell Honey she had to be a writer. He didn't tell her she had to be anything in particular. But he encouraged me. When I was eleven, when I was two years at the public school, he bought me a gelatin [printing] pad and I did the school magazine, which I wrote, printed and sold myself. And he showed the ink and showed me how to use a gelatin pad, which was not bad for a 12-year-old. And I formed the Society of Young Writers. I was sort of off on this thing without too much pressure from him.'

For me, this was a new Norman, far more interesting than the painter of opulent flesh so admired by strange old men. And it was a contrast to the misogynists who surrounded him in his old age.

There is, of course, a hint of nurturing passion in his letters to Jack in the

*Vision* period of the 1920s. Perhaps the standard interpretation of Norman swamping the younger generation with his own ideas isn't quite fair. Perhaps he really did want his brilliant son to become a great literary figure and did what he could to jump-start his career. After all, I knew that it was Norman who had taught Ray Lindsay to paint pirates.

'He used to say to Ray when he was living in Sydney: "Why don't you come and paint and put the model in?" You know, he said Ray threw his talent away, he could have been a much better painter if he'd worked. Which is probably true. But he said about Phil that all those novels he wrote with both hands.'

'What about Jack?' I asked.

'I don't remember Jack, but I vaguely remember Phil. He used to come there and stay at odd times, dances and things like that. I remember for some strange reason him trying to ride a neighbour's horse.'

We were talking about the way Norman's life ended and the National Trust's interest when I asked for the details of Norman's will. There were too many niggling contradictions in those last years.

'I can't help you there,' said Jane. 'I wasn't even given a copy.'

---

The next weekend I drove to the old Lindsay house at Springwood, now a museum. The mountains were still in drought, and with memories of the recent bushfires still strong I wasn't surprised to see that the hill leading up to the house had been carefully culled of excess foliage.

The garden at the Norman Lindsay Museum is a place for freeing the imagination, with fantasy made reality. Norman made statues out of concrete moulded over wire, and turned them into fountains. There are fauns and satyrs that appear without warning as visitors wander down to the bush. It is a place where magic should happen.

But inside there was no magic. It always struck me as absurd that Norman Lindsay, who made his name as the great libertarian of Australian culture, should have left his home to be administered by the National Trust. The political radicals who have appropriated conservation issues in recent years forget that the preservation of old architecture was first lobbied for by the National Trust, which is itself a relic of archaic social values. There was something comic in seeing people who were dressed as for church on Sunday guarding rooms dominated by lush paintings of big breasted women, proudly displaying their maps of Tasmania for the pleasure of male geographers.

On the walls and in the display cases there were prints and paintings by all members of the family, and rare archival photographs. And then there were Norman's incredibly detailed model ships and the puppets from the Tintookies version of *The Magic Pudding*.

I was shocked however at the way in which most of the art was displayed. The big killer for works on paper is daylight. Ultraviolet light causes more than sunburn; it fades colours, yellows paper, and is generally destructive. The most fragile works of all are watercolours. Their pigment fades at different rates so that after a while in the sun there is no way of telling what they once were. Photographs too are very light sensitive and no responsible arts institution would have them anywhere near daylight.

Yet watercolours were hanging on walls streaming with sunlight; photographs likewise were unprotected. The yellowed mounts on prints were further evidence of neglect and, despite the drought, the interior walls of the old house were damp to touch.

There was very little connection between this museum and the home of the artist and his family, the place described so often by visitors as an Australian Olympus. The general air of physical neglect was only one of the problems. The romance of history had been turned into yet another National Trust shop and, to make it worse, a copy of the latest National Trust Bulletin was promoting *Sirens*.

I knew how hostile the Lindsay family was to John Duigan's film, *Sirens*, which is most charitably described as a vehicle for Elle McPherson's body beautiful. After I saw it I could only sympathise with the Lindsays. The ABC archive has tapes of Norman's voice. He was interviewed for television in the 1960s and for radio on several occasions. His voice sounds remarkably similar to Daryl's and Lionel's — rounded vowels with a Scottish overtone. To the modern ear he sounds a bit like Robert Menzies at high speed. *Sirens* has Norman, played by Sam Neill, speaking in a broad Australian accent, while Norman's models are portrayed as sexually available to the bumbling local yokels, who act like characters out of Steele Rudd.

The state of the Springwood house had to be a story for the *Bulletin*. It was newsworthy, it was art, and Norman was associated with the *Bulletin* for over fifty years. After some hassling I arranged to interview Elsa Atkin, Director of the NSW branch of the National Trust, and some of her staff. Because the story related to the nature of Norman's bequest to the Trust I was given a copy of Norman's final will, the one that defined his relationship with the National Trust.

# TRUST

Atkin, a dark woman of determined vivacity, admitted the building as managed by the National Trust wasn't perfect, but argued that it was improving. 'We're moving to try and address a lot of the issues there,' she said. 'We will do the best we can under the circumstances to showcase Springwood in the best possible way.'

The museum had been open for over twenty-one years. It is the National Trust's single most popular venue. Tens of thousands of people had trooped through and most of them were paying guests. Why was everything so neglected?

'You know, the Trust is a community-based organisation,' said Ian Stephenson, curator of the Trust's collections. 'And if you apply the standard of a community museum rather than a major museum it's really been a model.'

The National Trust was established under an Act of Parliament, and is exempt from many of the legal problems that hound community-based organisations. It has traditionally used its status and expertise to call for the preservation of various pieces of the past. If this was amateur hour they had spent a long time posing as professionals. I asked about the finances. Ever since the 1980s when some entrepreneurial members effectively rearranged the Trust's assets to pay for the restoration of Juniper Hall in Paddington, the NSW National Trust has been in perpetual crisis. But the visitor figures as recorded in the annual reports indicate the profitable nature of the Lindsay property. According to Jaspal Singh Rekhraj, the National Trust's financial controller, 'the whole operation [of Springwood] has been deficit funded'.

Nothing added up. Even the small $35,000 fee for using the venue to shoot *Sirens* (the setting is the best part of the movie) barely covered the costs for the three months it was closed for filming. The advisory committee which was supposed to guide the administration of the Springwood property had opposed the filming and at the same time was lobbying for more funds.

The management problems of Norman Lindsay's house made, to say the least, a very confusing story, and I knew it would take some time to sort it out.

But first I wanted to read the will.

There were two documents, a will of March 1969 and a codicil. The will was drawn up and witnessed by Alan Renshaw, a solicitor who later left much of his own estate to the National Trust. Jane Glad, Douglas Stewart and the Union Fidelity Trust were named as joint executors and trustees.

Stewart is named as the recipient of Norman's copy of the diary of Samuel Pepys and Jane Glad was the residual heir, after a number of small bequests and large bequests to the National Trust and the University of Melbourne. John Hetherington was designated official biographer and the owners of manuscript material were directed to grant 'full rights of access to all such materials in Public Libraries and Galleries'. The University of Melbourne was given the pen drawings that Norman had once given Rose 'with the intent that the same shall be preserved made available and displayed for public instruction study and appreciation in the Art Gallery to be established in association with the School of Architecture and Building'. The National Trust received paintings, pen drawings, ship models, statues, studio fittings, book cases and books on condition that:

> The National Trust shall acquire the ownership of the premises at Springwood wherein I reside so that the various items and works of art the subject of this my bequest may be preserved in the said premises and that the premises and contents be maintained and used by the National Trust in accordance with the objects set forth in section 4 of the National Trust of Australia (New South Wales) Act 1960. . . [1]

A letter to the Trustees attached to the will has a final message to Rose:
> I would inform them that over the years I have made adequate provision for the proper maintenance and advancement of my wife, Rose Lindsay, including the gift of the house and land at Springwood, where I now reside and the proceeds of sale of my art works and the royalties from my literary works with the exception of my own living expenses and the cost of materials for the pursuit of my art and therefore have made no provision for her in my said will.
>
> The gift to my daughter, Jane Glad, of the residue of my estate would include all manuscripts of my original literary works, memoranda, letters and writings to which I am entitled at the date of my death and all copyrights and interests in copyrights not otherwise disposed of.

As I read this I remembered the chapter in *Redheap* in which the Piper family are seated at dinner and the senile Grandfather Piper is pretending to be uninterested in food while taking most of it. Norman may have thought that he had no involvement in money, but his secure financial position was largely thanks to Rose. She had been his business manager, print-maker, and frame maker. The letter seemed to be the result of the influence of Norman's last set of advisers, the people he had come to know in the last few years of his life, who denied both his genuinely libertarian past and any significant female influences on him.

The final document was a codicil to Norman's will, signed on 27 October 1969, only weeks before his death on 21 November. Norman Lindsay's last public act was to withdraw the executorship of Jane Glad and Douglas Stewart and effectively to disinherit his daughter. He gave Margaret Coen all his watercolour paper, paint and portfolios, the manuscripts of *My Mask* and *Tabonga Road* and their copyrights, and 'all moneys remaining to the credit of my Bank Account with the Bank of New South Wales Springwood, after payment thereout of my debts funeral and testamentary expenses'.

My edition of *My Mask* is marked 'copyright Rose Lindsay', so Rose must have persuaded someone to give her at least that part of her husband's estate. But it was a sorry end to a grand passion between an artist and his model. I photocopied my copy of the will and gave it to Helen to pass on to Jane.

The next time I saw her, Helen gave me a large bundle of manilla folders. 'Jane said she thought you might find these interesting,' she said. 'The green file's got the correspondence between Norman and Rose on the National Trust and there's a few other things as well.'

Helen is good at understatement. Because of her advice I went straight to the green file and left the rest until after I had finished the *Bulletin* article.

One of the problems with the way Norman's house came to the Trust was that there was no recognition of how the house had changed over more than fifty years of Lindsay occupancy. In its heyday in the 1920s and 1930s, it had been a large and gracious centre for writers and artists. But in the last decade of Norman's life it had been progressively cannibalised by the increasingly eccentric artist, and it was this damaged house that formed the basis of the current museum.

'Norman did a little bit of building on his own shortly before he died. Rose used to say he was the most destructive little builder she ever knew. So there are parts [completely changed] — where the entrance is, that used to be a closed-in verandah. The front door is no longer used as the front door. This is not the house Jane grew up in, or the house I used to visit as a child. It's completely different,' Helen told me.

'I don't think Norman would have been considered one of the world's greatest interior decorators. At the very end of his life he had the house all set up and he blocked in the lead-light windows in what is now the oil room. Where you come into the entrance room where there's the etchings on one side and the pen drawings on the other, that was the middle bedroom. Then there's the verandah and it's quite different to the way Norman left it.'

Bearing in mind how Norman loathed Lionel, Daryl and Ruby, I wondered how he would have felt about the Springwood exhibits where their art is displayed next to his. It was odd that the ego of the dead was not respected when it came to art, but that the house as altered by a senile old man was to be 'preserved' as a fictional reality.

When I opened the green folder Helen had given me, I learned that Rose first found out about Norman's plan to give Springwood to the National Trust on 24 November 1966. By that time she was so crippled with arthritis that she could scarcely walk, but she still kept a lively interest in the place that had been her home for many years. Norman's letter to her is a wonderful piece of soft soap, massaging the ego of the recipient in a vain attempt to win her over to a project he knew she would not like.

*I have been reading your reminiscences published in the Bulletin, and I consider them the best personal record I've ever read, written in this or any other country.*

*They are gay, witty and humorous, and they are full of brilliant little character portraits. —*

*Clarry Stratten dropped dead the other day, and I had been talking to him the day before. A simple image of death, which brought me up sharp, for it also imaged the death of Springwood — sold to be pulled down and in given over to horrible little hovels for horrible little people to dwell in.*

*Why not immortalise your memoirs of it, by making a bequest of it to the National Trust. People will come from far and wide to view the actual scene in which they were lived in the days of your youth and beauty . . .* [2]

Norman was most likely referring to the page proofs of *Model Wife* which was published in 1967. The *Bulletin* memoirs of 1953 were hardly recent, but the prudent Sam Ure Smith was likely to have sent Rose's book to Norman for verification.

Norman's letter was not successful. Rose's strong sense of family duty would not let her see her children's and grandchildren's interests pushed aside. Norman was convinced that if Rose understood his urgent purpose she would agree with him. So in further letters he persisted, perhaps thinking that Rose shared his concern for immortality.

*If we do legally make it over to the Trust, I want your name to be joined with mine in making the bequest. That will dispose of all death duties for either of us. I have arranged to turn the whole house into a picture gallery, and to have the ship models on view in the glassed in verandah room. The fact is, I have more than enough big pictures, and old paintings to do the job, and leave a lot of pictures over. But I must, of course, now keep the best watercolours I can paint for it. I wish I could have some of your collection for it, but I suppose you want to leave those to Jane. But one thing I must ask you to let me have, and that is some examples of my best pen drawings.*[3]

By the end of his life, Norman realised that the new generation of art historians and critics did not believe him to be a genius. Although he continued to be regarded as a major writer of fiction, the accepted view of his later art is expressed in Bernard Smith's damning assessment:

*. . . the paintings, like the pen-drawings before them, were dominated by deep-bosomed, heavily-hipped nudes luxuriating in exotic and bacchanalian settings. As illustrations they are technically superb but possess little, if any aesthetic merit. . . the conception was greater than the accomplishment: his femme ideale is quite unconvincing beyond the realm of adolescent erotica. . .*[4]

The letters of Norman's last years have many references to his planned revenge on those galleries and art institutions which scorned him.

*One thing that gives me more pleasure than anything else in creating my own Gallery is the kick in the pants it gives to the Trustees of all the National Galleries, who have put any works of mine they possessed into their cellars, and have done their best to suppress me and my works over the years. Now, since word has got out of my first proposal of making bequests of work to the Small Town Galleries, the National Galleries are all in a swither to get bequests too. They have sent me their catalogues and Lists of recent purchases, and two of the curators have sent me smarmy letters.*[5]

I knew from other sources that Norman had already tried to leave a large collection of his work to the Art Gallery of New South Wales, on condition that it be permanently displayed, and was angered when his offer was rejected. The National Trust was really his only option.

But Rose remained unmoved. She felt no loyalty to the National Trust and was understandably wary of Norman's new friends who were advocating the merits of that particular beneficiary.

The chief negotiator for the Trust was the solicitor, Alan Renshaw, who also drew up Norman's last will, the one which disinherited Rose. Norman had come to rely on him for most kinds of advice, and first wrote to Rose praising his judgment and taste about a year before the National Trust bequest was first openly discussed.

*Art is a passion with him, therefore I trust him in all his relations with it. And with me.*

*You would never take him for a Lawyer, for he has rather a reticent, nervous way of speaking. In spite of his profession, he is a gentleman.*[6]

One of Renshaw's most important services to Norman was the way he helped solve his problems with the tax office:

*Alan Renshaw has been seeing the Taxation people about a reduction on my tax. He goes to unending trouble over our affairs, and wont let me pay him a penny. I've had to get even by giving him a water colour.*[7]

By mid–1968 Norman was becoming increasingly agitated about the final disposal of his property. On 5 May Rose received two almost identical letters from Norman on the same subject.

*While the whole property remains registered in your name I can do nothing about making a bequest of any part of it without your consent.*

*I do want to have this business settled, for I wont have any ease of mind till it is. At our age, you and I can't expect to have much time left to play about with. And neither of us want it. The bequest should be a joint one with us. I give my pictures and you give all the rest of it.*

*The whole thing will have to be put in the correct Legal form, and Renshaw will do that.*[8]

The second letter was similar in content. The writer gave no indication that he had written before on the same subject.

*Since the whole property is registered in your name, the Trust assumed that they would have to buy your ground to get my bequest of the house and pictures.*

*Renshaw pointed out that I can't make the bequest unless you are joined with me in making it. And I think you should be so joined, for my whole working life is bound up with yours.*[9]

It must have been after she received these two letters from her pitifully senile husband that Rose agreed to negotiate the sale of the house and land to the National Trust so that the works of art could be preserved at Springwood. Norman would still give some art to Melbourne University, a gift he had decided upon after Professor Brian Lewis of the Faculty of Architecture had persuaded him that he was appreciated in the university, if not at the gallery.

Norman wrote in gratitude to Rose:

*I'm sorry I bothered you with all those efforts to grapple with the Trust business; but no one knows better than you how woolly headed I can get when I try to tackle such matters.*

*But now, by finally handling the whole affair over to you and Jane, I feel a vast sense of relief for having got rid of it.*

*Now it depends purely on your decision whether Springwood — the place here, is to be preserved, and handed down to posterity as the place we built, and lived for the major portion of our lives.*

*. . . But I will still have enough pictures left over [after gifts to Melbourne University] to make an exhibit here. Those, being my property, I am prepared to hand over to you, on two simple conditions, which are that if the property is finally made over to the Trust they can only take possession of it on my death and that Harry McPhee be appointed the job of keeping the grounds in order.*

*. . . If you are engaging Renshaw to put the agreement with the Trust in Legal form, will you instruct him to include the above conditions.*

*Bless you for taking the whole blasted business over.*[10]

Less than a month later there was a letter which showed that Norman had misunderstood Rose's offer. He again repeated that the central problem was Rose's ownership of the house and land and asked her to give all to the Trust.

*But the pictures and ship models are my property and I propose to make them over to you if our conditions are endorsed by the Trust. They'll have to endorse them, or they wont get the bequest.*

*I will catalogue all the pictures which will go to the Trust. All the rest will be taken by June before the Trust takes over.*

*The Trust is to have no copyright in the pictures.*

*. . . All this I will explain to Renshaw when he is making up the legal agreement over the bequest.*

> *The bequest will not operate till my death, and the Trust will not take over the place till Jane and Bruce have removed all works which are their property.*
>
> *That last condition makes me grin, for I wont be here to see that it is carried out.*[11]

Rose's reply indicates that she was fast losing patience with the old man's greed for immortality at her expense.

> *I told you from the first that I could not afford to give my asset away — and asked you to make a proposition to me. I said the same to the Trust reps I heard no more from them, and was relieved. The next thing was the letter that you sent down where Mr Renshaw listed all the things that they would want. I thought that was enough for you. Apparently not as you had Mr Renshaw up to straighten the muddle out.*[12]

It was hard to reason with Norman at the end. When he quarrelled with Rose, he wrote to Jane.

> *Renshaw will be up today, Tuesday, so I'll know what he and Rose are doing about the Trust. I intend to have nothing more to do with the bastards. They go on as if they were doing me a good turn taking over the place, and that I now have no rights over my own property. I'll make over the pictures and ship models to Rose, and she can do what she pleases with them — leave them to the Trust, or sell them.*
>
> *I've done what I said I would do — turn the house into a picture Gallery. All I've done in respect to the Melbourne bequest is to select 5 oils and six watercolours to send them. And I would sooner have my work there than anywhere else. Here, only the curiosity mongers and Sunday picnic groups will come, while in Melbourne, the World at large will see them. And in a fine gallery especially created to house them.*[13]

Reading these pathetic pleas, with the knowledge of what later happened to the Melbourne pictures and the Springwood property, was rather depressing.

By October 1968, Norman expanded the nature of his proposed bequests to Melbourne University and the National Trust and asked Rose to send him some of her most prized possessions: pen drawings from early in the century, the few works which had not been destroyed in the American fire.

> *These I must have, divided between the two bequests, if Posterity is to see what I could do with the pen. The recent pen drawings I did, under pressure,*

> *to fill blank spaces in the book, I care little for. My fingers no longer have the flexibility of my younger days.*
>
> *I have just signed my will, made out by Alan Renshaw, and in it I have itemised those works which go to the National Trust, and those which go to the Melb. University. The pen drawings listed here are referred to as being in your possession. When I signed my will they became the property of the two bequests, and a demand will be made for them on my death . . . I would very much like to have the pen and ink drawings to go with them. Please let Jane have them to bring up here. Why wait until the undertaker has done his job on my carcass.*
>
> *It means more to me than anything else that those listed pen drawings should be preserved in a place where they are safe, and will be seen by the public . . .*
>
> *. . . I hope you are not suffering too much with your crippled body.*[14]

The letter bears Rose's sarcastic annotation on Norman's good wishes for her health: 'What a nice old bastard'. Her other response was to send a message through Jane that he would have to take legal action to gain possession of the drawings. Norman's next letter was more conciliatory.

> *Alright, I'll cross that list of pen drawings out of my will. To Hell with the Trust. All I'm concerned for is leaving some of my best work in permanent exhibitions. Cant you realise how important that is to the future art of this country. Would you prefer that we left this place to be swamped by death duties and bought by some monied Tycoon, — or else cut up for building lots. What are the few quid you'll get for selling those pen and inks worth at this time of your life. I feel helpless to try and impress on you the need to stabilise culture values in the world today. They're at the turn of the tide. If they are not established, there will be another world war —*
>
> *Oh to hell with trying to convince you of the above. To you its just the sort of gabble that always bored you. Let it go and do as you please with the pen drawings.*[15]

But Norman still wanted the drawings in Melbourne. His next letter asks Rose to hand them to Douglas Stewart, as 'it means a great deal to me that examples of the best of my pen drawings should be on view in a safe and dignified setting'. Rose finally agreed, but annotated his letter with comments of her own.

*Well well if it had not been for my interest and saving up some best work or at least some of it — you would not have this collection to give away now*
   *P.S*
   *After a fight I gave in and let NL have the drawings for his bequest to the architects gallery where they are still only shown to people who asked to see them —*
   *They should have been kept in Sydney, which was my original scheme. I sold the property to the Trust because I wanted them [the garden sculptures] to be kept in the grounds and not smashed up by vandals.*
   *. . . I could not live in this place on crutches and guard the things and so many things were just taken by droppers in.*[16]

The collector, Harry Chaplin, took a rather different perspective on the dispute between Rose and Norman. In his published catalogue of Lindsay family letters he wrote:
*It was by relinquishing his fifty per cent interest* [in his royalties] *that Norman obtained the pen drawings. Some of the relevant correspondence was given to me by Norman to preserve because he wanted matters of fact to be recorded.*[17]

In the letters Jane lent me, the saddest one of all was the last communication from Norman to Rose:
*R.L. My last word to you here or anywhere else is — Goodbye. N.L.*[18]

This was the context of the will I had read and of the National Trust's interest in the Norman Lindsay estate. It all became so vivid: the urgent courtesy of Renshaw, the flattery of the collectors, the distrust of the still sexually powerful Rose by the elegant men of the National Trust, and the confused and self-centred old Norman who listened to these persuaders rather than to the distant, but strident, voice of Rose.
   It was clear from reading these letters that Norman's intention above all was that his art should be preserved, cared for and properly displayed.
   I wrote my piece.[19] There was a bit of a fuss. The letters column in the *Bulletin* ran claim and counter claim for the next month. The National Trust claimed the works were well conserved and that 'had it not been for the National Trust and the generosity of its supporters, this great national landmark would have been lost to the public'. A visitor to Springwood, a Mr

John Blount, wrote verifying my observations of neglect. Sue Milliken, the producer of *Sirens*, claimed that Norman Lindsay was 'all but forgotten' until the film. This was refuted by the art dealer Lin Bloomfield.

A good time was had by all.

# 17

# *Last secrets?*

As various members of the National Trust were phoning their friends and colleagues asking them to write indignant letters to the *Bulletin*, I was hunched over the rest of the letters that Jane had passed on to Helen.

The second folder contained letters from Robert to Norman. I wondered why Rose hadn't included these in the Mitchell papers. Was it an accident? Had Norman kept them and Rose had simply scooped them up one day? Perhaps they show Robert in a more amiable light, as someone with the self-deprecating sense of humour and amiable personality that Mary always claimed for him.

When Robert received his copy of *The Cousin From Fiji*, he wrote in appreciation to Norman with this anecdote:

> Do you remember a circus in the state school grounds. I don't know if you were of too tender an age to go, but Lionel and I were given 1/6 each, the prices being 6d, 1/-, 1/6 and 4/-. The company not expecting any one to sit to the four shillings, put up that part of the scaffolding very insecurely. I had made a remark or two to Robert Charles on the indignity of so cheap a seat when given 1/-, which I was told was quite good enough, and the attraction was that if it wasn't good enough I needn't go, a filthy retort. However, when the crowd was seated in the cheaper seats, the Dowling family made a stately progress to the 4/- seats and had hardly seated themselves before the whole set of seats collapsed, which R.C., when he heard of the happening, pointed the moral of vanity and exclusiveness.[1]

This voice fitted with a photograph I had seen of the sprightly, dapper Robert, standing next to Mary, dressed in tweeds. I think the photographer was Harry Chaplin and the photograph would have been taken towards the end of

# LAST SECRETS?

Robert's life. This is the Robert who was painted by Arthur Boyd and who played gracious host to Martin Boyd on his Creswick visits.[2]

There is another glimpse of this kinder Robert in a fragment of a letter from Mary to Norman. Because it mentions that Rose is in America, it has to be dated about 1940.

*Bertie is out, round about the estate, redding up the place for Xmas, when we expect Mrs McPhee [Pearl] & daughters out for a day or so.*

*For a gentleman close on 70, with a rotten inside, he commands my admiration. Up on the roof cleaning the spouts, sweeping paths, digging beds, catching each leaf as it falls! Really! The fellow has guts. I'm not too bad myself, considering . . .*[3]

In some of the letters Mary provides details of domestic life with the precise Robert and the eccentric Isabel.

*Bertie will be better when the warm weather stays put for a week or so . . . Anyway! I'm glad he had to give up the old Hospital job. He'd got past it, & it was getting him down badly.*

*At first I had a nice time with that lad insisting on helping in the kitchen. This meant rinsing out the jugs & milk billies with cold water, washing greasy plates & pans with 2 cups of luke warm water (This intense meanness with hot water dates from the time in London when bath water & washing up meant using gas on the stove) & hiding my cooking utensils so well, it meant a prolonged treasure hunt every day. What with these kindly intentions & Isabels objection to the presence of the cook when she was in the kitchen I was nearly demented. Then one day when they were both out of the house I screwed two latches on the two kitchen doors. Then I explained confidentially to Isabel that I had to do it till the dinner was cooked & things washed up on account of Bert, & reversing the story for his ears, said it had to be done to keep Isabel out. Jolly good brain wave I've got them both locked out at the moment, & am cooking in peace & able to get a line off to you at the same time.*

*. . . Our old garden is looking nice just now. Thats our main pleasure. The first thing every morning (we get up early in summer) you'd find Bertie & me poking round to see what has come up in the night. I have to be careful not to show too much interest in Berts pursuits as it makes Isabel so jealous. Of course she is, poor soul! Jealous of everything & everybody, but naturally the ones in the house cause most offence. I wish she'd turn into a Christian Scientist. —a splendid religion for disgruntled persons.*[4]

These letters also give a more rounded image of Isabel, and the first indication that there was a physical as well as a mental problem.

*I mean I'm sure there isn't any pain to speak of but if she stoops or goes down on her knees, there is difficulty in getting put right & on her feet again.*

*Its those legs that are both curved in the wrong way that are we think the chief trouble. She's always tumbling about, & having to be pulled up by the arms.*

*. . . Its a miserable existence not reading or sewing, never doing a thing for any herself or for anyone else; just lying in bed till 11 or 12 oclock in the morning, getting up like a man with a devastating hangover, & putting in the rest of the day brooding over her wrongs, & exploding every now & again into violent bursts of temper.*[5]

For most of 1951, Mary wrote of plans to leave the old house and build a small cottage suitable for herself and Robert. I had already read Robert's letters on the same theme in the La Trobe Library, and it was instructive to compare the two sets of correspondence. While Robert planned only two bedrooms (for himself and Mary), she included three (with Isabel's smaller room away from the rest). While Robert asked Daryl for money in order to finance the scheme, Mary sold her diamond ring to buy a refrigerator.

The idea of selling the family home for £5000 came from Keith Wingrove, who was a devoted collector of Norman's work and memorabilia. His vision of a Lindsay museum predates the Springwood project by some fifteen years but it was only ever a pipe dream. By 1951 the old house was termite-ridden and dilapidated. Its jumble of rooms, built on whenever more space was needed for children, was hardly suitable for a museum promoting the life of a family of artists and writers. But Mary and Robert found retreat into fantasy enticing.

*But wont Jane Isabel perform when she finds a kitchen without a fireplace to mess about in the entire day . . . I promised to turn Mothers bedroom back into pretty much what it was in the old days, tester bed with white muslin curtains, white muslin flowered dressing table with pink bows & all that kind of thing.*[6]

The house was not sold and the cottage not built, for at the end of 1951 Robert died. Original letters say so much more than typescripts. Mary's writing straggles over the page, her words look frail, so that even without reading their content it is clear how deeply she mourned this brother.

## LAST SECRETS?

*. . . it has just occurred to me that Lionel or some other chatty person has got my funeral announcements all over the place. If so, its not true, unfortunately.*

*I was damned tired & the dirty-dogs dragged me back with some infernal new wonder drug.*

*Anyway I got out of the Hospital last week & told to rest for a couple of months,*

*Kathleen Jones Howitt (Cousin) is here, awfully decent, cooking & everything while I live the life of a parasite.*

*I believe Dan became very active boarding Isabel out with some old dame — paying her expenditures . . .*

*Don't think I'm behaving like a fool over Bert going. He's the lucky bloke.*[7]

It was not just Robert's death that Mary mourned. She knew she was the only member of the immediate family to grieve his loss and it is also clear that she knew that some of Robert's damaging letters had survived.

In the years following Robert's death Mary wrote several letters to Norman, trying to change the way history would see her most-loved brother. Presumably these were written in the hope that they would end up in library collections, but Rose kept their noble sentiments to herself.

*The spirit moves me to scribble a page about Robert, called Bert in his youth. My reason is to let off steam over suffering from 12 years (since his death) of violent attacks over his character. To begin with, its surprising that a healthy pair like Mother & Dad should have produced a type that we none of us like. He had two outstanding good qualities, Extraordinarily kind, & extraordinarily generous. The two outstanding generous members of our family were Bert & you. Money never meant a thing to you — To him it meant a lot, because his one interest in life was to help anyone handy who needed help — His strong mother & sister complex made him concentrate most on his mother & on me. On his miserable bank clerk's salary he'd save & save, to give one or other of us something he thought we needed. I never had an evening dress or any decent clothes (at a time when these things mean so much to a young girl) that he didn't (till he left for England) pay for. He somehow managed to pay for the tram fares, pocket money etc on my annual holidays to town. Robert paid for my white satin coming-out frock. He'd save up to give mother silk for a new gown. That would cost I remember £5 — & meant constant sacrifice — staying in beastly cheap boarding houses etc etc when a Bank clerk. Then, all those years away in America & England. Gifts of clothing to Mother & me. Then he financed my trip to England & afterward to America. He tried to get some cash out of Ruby, but without success — & all the time he was helping this or that lame dog — & he didn't want to come out here to Australia. He wanted me to go, after Mother's death, to him.*[8]

I had read similar high-minded sentiments about Robert before. Harry Chaplin, that ardent collector of Lindsay material, owned some of Mary's letters of praise, along with a few of Robert's more intemperate pieces and they are bound together in a fairly favourable view of Robert and catalogued as *A Lindsay Miscellany*.

I asked Helen how she and her family had coped with those pedantic old men, the collectors Chaplin and Wingrove, who came around sniffing at their personal history. From reading Chaplin's published bibliographies and the writings of Wingrove it is clear that these two collectors felt they had a greater interest in the Lindsay family than Helen, Jane, or even Rose.

'I've come to resent people like Chaplin and to a lesser extent Wingrove,' she said. 'People who wanted to get into the intimate details of anybody else's life, I find voyeuristic. It's none of their bloody business. We all have areas where we feel are private. And that's what happened with Norman — he became public property for some of these people. In fact he was reinvented from what they chose to keep. You wonder who does the reinvention. Now I think in lots of cases, for people like his acolytes and his disciples, and it wouldn't have mattered what he said, they would have taken it as gospel. But he did have a particular dynamic personality. Anybody would be seduced by his ability to talk. And to be of interest.'

The problem was that in owning some documents of family history, and therefore feeling he owned the family, Chaplin was able to effectively deny the younger Lindsays access to their own past.

'When Chaplin actually did die it was a relief, because you wouldn't have to ask him to see letters written by your own relatives,' Helen continued. 'He hoarded everything. But I don't think he had a capacity for serious scholarly research. Basically all of his collections were built up by ferreting things away.'

When Chaplin became old and ill, his collection was acquired *en masse* by Pat Corrigan, a Sydney businessman. Corrigan was fascinated by the way

## LAST SECRETS?

the Lindsays had quarrelled, and he also exhibited an interest in the plate glass negatives of the photographs Norman had made of his models, posing nude.

'Pat wanted to do a book, get them printed into a book,' Helen said. 'And we denied copyright, and he was most surprised that Jane said "No". And I said, "Because Pat, you don't know the names of the models who posed for him, and it is not fair for them, without seeking their permission, to have those photographs reproduced. They're all probably all grandmothers now, they may not want people to know. You cannot do it.' It's very interesting when the law is on your side to make people act in a moral way.'

Corrigan later gave all his Chaplin material to the Queensland State Library. From the way Chaplin carefully recorded his hoard and arranged for Walter Stone to compile scholarly bibliographies with the name 'Harry Chaplin' given due prominence, it is clear that he wished to celebrate a link between himself and the Lindsays. In one of life's little ironies, the former Chaplin collection has now been subsumed into the 'Lindsay Collection of Pat Corrigan'. The whole notion of grabbing bibliographic immortality by purchase was alien to any of the Lindsay family themselves.

Rose was certainly aware of the confusion of emotions, of loyalties and of behaviour that surrounded the family's affairs in the 1950s and 1960s. While she appears to have kept some papers perhaps almost by accident, there were others that had continuing relevance to her. These included the aftermath of John Hetherington's dealings with Mary, letters which show neither Norman nor Hetherington in an especially flattering light.

At last I read the letter Mary wrote to Olive Hetherington, the letter which so offended John Hetherington. It is reprinted here in its entirety yet still I cannot understand why the man was so outraged by it.

*Creswick*
*Feb 6th 61*

*My dear Olive,*
*A letter from Norman this morning, gives me the welcome assurance that the biography is not to be published till after our deaths, his and mine.*
　　*I'm sorry to be a nuisance, but, will you, on one of your well days, make a bundle of the memoir Lindsay book, & all the letters, both Normans*

& mine, & send to me by registered post — that is if John has taken all the notes he wants from our wordy correspondence.

My reason for this is a check up by my little Doctor last week. I really feel fairly well, & think he is an alarmist. Still I am 83, & wont feel comfortable till I've put a match to all those intimate private letters.

In a recent letter N. said that he thought that I was the only person he knew who could have managed successfully a 'Life of the Lindsays'. To my surprise I believe Lionel said the same thing.

Well! that will never be done, because last year I made a bonfire of an accumulation of 10 years carefully sifted notes on the family. It would have covered a very big canvas.

I had no intention of writing it myself, but after meeting John I thought, when he's finished the N.L. book, I'll give it to him.

Well! thats all over, & perhaps its just as well.

This of course isn't an R.S.V.P. letter, but I want to tell you that I have never felt so hurt in my life as over your John's unexplained behaviour.

After much grave thought I decided not to do or say a thing that might & almost certainly would have ended in smashing the good friendship between little brother & John. In this matter I must confess that my first thought was for Norman.

Well time goes on, &, at my age, I begin to feel that nothing now really much matters.

— but you were very kind to me Olive! I would like to seize this opportunity, before saying goodbye, to thank you sincerely for all your past generous hospitality, & may I risk a salaam to the handsome Sinutji [the Hetherington cat], whose picture stays in my memory.

Sincerely,
Mary Lindsay
PS Of course not a word to Norman about what the Doctor man said, Besides I think he's wrong. M.L[9]

The wording is courteous, and the request is reasonable. Mary has, as always, exaggerated the possibility of illness and she appears to have manufactured the story of Norman's faith in her as a family biographer. But there is nothing dramatic here. Did Hetherington see his wife as so removed from reality that no one could write to her? Could he continue to believe that an 83-year-old woman lusted after him? It's all very bizarre. Yet Hetherington sent the letter to Norman and from there it must have passed to Rose.

# LAST SECRETS?

Mary's next letter to Norman is an admission of defeat, as she realised Norman was putting John Hetherington's interests ahead of her own.

Well! thats all right if you feel that way, and altho he wipes me out as a dirty dog, I'd put my trust in John. Only I would definitely like my letters, after, as I said, he had finished with them. There is a lot of very useful stuff in those letters, as he & I are both well aware . . .

Of course this is the first time in my life that I've been faced with a very unpleasant episode. The reason for which seems mysterious. I think it is hardly sporting to treat someone who once was a friend, with cold insolence, without an explanation.[10]

Although Mary realised she had lost the letters, she did want family photographs and rare books returned, and when she realised Norman would not help her, she wrote a letter in which the writing struggles across the page, as wild and disturbed as the one sent just after Robert's death.

Creswick

March

Don't worry. Nothing in the world I feel now is worth making a fuss about.

My idea was just a casual remark saying 'Have you by the way got Mary's 'Addled art' by L, I'd like it'

. . . Honestly I'm indifferent to almost anything now. Horrible confession — but life in a concentration camp I believe often ends in that.

. . . & dont for Gods sake worry about that nice person John Hetherington. Someone has put the idea into his head that I'm a dirty dog—

Well! he's got no end of affectionate friends. I honestly now dont care a damn about what the good kindly John or anyone else thinks. This is the very last time I'll cause a ripple of visitation to you. My lad! in that direction.

Its curious, a common fate, I think. To have reached the age of 84 or I think 85, and find just one person you and the good Kathleen of interest left.

. . . <u>Please dont worry about anything</u> to do with poor John Hetherington and his family.

I dont care twopence now. <u>I dont care about anything</u>. Keep up your uninterrupted friendship with him. That has nothing in the world to do with me, & I dont care if God Almighty, the louse, objects to me & my dump — I'd be please to cock a snap at him.[11]

The 'good Kathleen', Kathleen Howitt, the cousin who shared the Creswick house with Mary and Isabel, must have had a trying time with her severely depressed relative. Norman was sufficiently perturbed by the letter to send Mary a large cheque, for which she thanked him, but claimed there was no need of money. He managed to retrieve her copy of Lionel's book *Addled Art* from Hetherington. But the photographs stayed with the biographer. Mary's last attempt to recover them is in a short undated letter:

> Victoria St
>> Creswick,
>> I wish to leave to my niece Jane Glad, the family photos lent to John Hetherington, and authorise her to collect them at a time when convenient to them both.
>> Mary Lindsay[12]

There was one question remaining about this strange affair. Why, in about 1960, did Rose so hate Mary that she defamed her to Hetherington? A note from Norman on one of Mary's letters gave the answer. As with much of this complicated tale, it stemmed from sibling rivalry in the house in Creswick, and events of the distant past.

When *Ma and Pa*, Rose's first book, was published in 1963, Mary wrote to Norman, praising it. He sent her letter to Rose with the following annotation:

> *I send this along to you to dispose of any mischief about Mary caused by that nitwit Pearl, or any other poison pen scandal gabbers. It is always a mystery to me that those who listen to their formula of 'so and so said this and that about you' always attribute malice to the 'so and so' and not to the poison pen who transmits the alleged scandal mongering.*[13]

So Pearl had told Rose stories about Mary, claiming that Mary hated Rose. And Rose believed the cheerful, gossiping Pearl. She forgot that Mary was the sister who had smoothed the path for her with old Jane Lindsay. And she also forgot that Pearl was the sister who would not let her children visit Springwood in case they were corrupted by an irregular household.[14]

With the exception of Ruby, Mary showed a singular lack of charity towards her sisters. The same letter that praises *Ma and Pa* contains these comments:

> *Oh, what about poor old Pearl; whose story would be 'The child that wrecked a family' . . . Absurd in the past to blame Pearl for being what she couldn't help being. There is a bitter bad black streak running thro the family*

## LAST SECRETS?

*that came from Ireland. Lionel and Pearl were its chief victims, and give an Irishman a grievance, he'll defend it to the death . . . That last time I spent looking after her, it was simply a matter of screaming in anguish over her wrongs, all due to me, and then dissolving into tears like a little child and saying she didn't mean it.*[15]

The letters that Mary wrote to Norman in the mid–1960s reveal a lonely old woman whose friends were all dead and who was ever more dependent on her brother for friendship, albeit at a distance.

*. . . Its not a bit of use — I've always had a masculine fear of most women, that has probably been the result of the women who came my way. If you knew, you'd understand what a Godsend Mil Lewers was to me. —*

*— a completely normal friendship, without a hint of anything unhealthy. She accepted & liked me, just as I was, altho different in so many ways, in character.*

*The wise ones say, that, to be intimate friends, is due to ones character.*

*So there's a Mary L. indictment, because it seems that now you are the one and only friend I have in the Universe.*

*Of course in the long run one lives and dies alone.*

*All the same I hang on to you, and know you wont let me down . . .*[16]

In this context, 'unhealthy' must be a reference to lesbianism. The denial could have been made because of some passing comment in a letter from Norman. If it were not this, and the comment came spontaneously, it could be an indication of a complex sexual attraction. There are several references in Mary's letters to Mil Lewers, a friend of all the Lindsays since childhood, who, like Mary, had never married. She died in the 1950s after a long degenerative illness. She and Ruff Tremearne were part of the texture of the lives of the Lindsays, but very much background figures in the letters.

I turned to the last two folders. The smaller blue one contained letters written to Jane from Mary. Jane knew how to keep secrets. There had been no lies told when I spoke to her, just an implication that she'd had little contact with Mary as she could not remember what she looked like. Now that Jane trusted me, I was given access to letters Mary had written to her, letters which dated from when Jane was eleven and had continued until well into the 1950s.

They started with Mary Lindsay's plea for contact with her two nieces. Rose and Norman were in America, which means the year was probably 1931. The tone is arch and aunt-like, but the news is hardly cheerful.

*This is going to be a very stupid letter, because I'm in bed ill & not feeling very amusing. Everyone in this house takes turns in being ill — First your Grandmother — then Uncle Bert (who has come out from London to live here), & now old Auntie Mary. The Doctor came this morning & I said "I'm sick of your old medicine I'm going to get out of bed & get dressed." — but he pushed me back into bed, & said "If you move out of that place Miss, till I tell you to, its a good smart smack you'll get" — that's a nice thing to say to a person who is an Aunt, don't you think? I haven't much news except that its been raining & raining & raining for months. To day its fine & the sun came out a little bit for a change. The fowl yard is like a swamp & the fowls are so uncomfortable & damp that they are all as cross as two sticks fighting & cackling at each other all day long. There is a very large tall black rooster called King Charles, & another tall red rooster called Ginger. They hate each other & fight all the time. So we are going to have King Charles for dinner next week to stop the continual rows.*

*Isabel is in a great state because her black cat went down to the Gas works & came back covered with tar. She's fussing all day with it trying to get the tar off, but it just sticks like glue, & Jan the cat is so savage because he can't get clean, that he meiws from morning till night. So you see we are having a nice time with the animals in & outside the house.*[17]

The next letter reads even more like a black comedy.

*Well! old friends. It seems a long time since I sent you both a line, & now I'm so bustled having Grandma in bed ill again, that I've got to send one letter between you. — & I hope there wont be any fights & black eyes over deciding which half belongs to which lady. Auntie Isabel gets quite cross when our friends sometimes send a letter between us — but I tell her that Jane &Honey have very much nicer natures than the people in this house.*

*I'm glad you are having such nice weather. Last week it was quite hot for days & days. — then suddenly there was a violent thunder storm that went on all day & most of the night. The rain came down in floods, & the noise on our zinc roof was so loud, you had to shout to make yourself heard — Grandma, who has been in bed a long time now, has a big old dinner bell on the little table by the side of her bed. Its so large, that its really rather like a small church bell, & when she wants me when I'm out in the yard, or*

## LAST SECRETS?

*cooking in the Kitchen, she rings it, & I come dashing along to see what she wants.*

*Well! right in the middle of the storms, I was just lifting a lemon pie out of the oven, when I heard something that sounded like a very loud water fall in the front passage. I ran along (the pie in my hand) to investigate, & stepped into a river of water streaming down from the walls, soaking the carpets and everything.*

*I looked up at the ceiling just in time to see the rain burst a big hole thro the canvas & paper. Before there was time to jump on one side down came the water on top of me & the lemon pie & gave us both a splendid shower bath — I rushed into my bedroom to pull off my sopping clothes, leaving the lemon pie on the floor to drown, when I heard through the noise, loud ringing from Grandma's room. — So I tore in there & found streams of water pouring down her walls & a pool under the bed like a small lake — Presently Uncle Robert came in looking like a drowned man. He'd been up on the roof clearing the gutters which were choked up with dead leaves & we set to with tubs & all the old cloths we could find to clear up the mess. — the house was filthy for days afterwards & I've still got wet carpet trying to dry over the lines in the yard. — Thats the sort of thing that happens in Creswick if you are careless & forget to keep your roof gutters clean.*

*I haven't very much news, my dears: As I haven't been outside the house for so long. I don't like leaving Grandma, because sometimes she's a very naughty patient & wont stay quietly in bed unless she is watched. On Friday, the Doctor said "Now! Mrs Lindsay, you must not move out of that bed, or you'll be very ill again" — & do you know half an hour afterwards, when I went to collect the eggs, I found the lady poking about in her dressing gown by the fowl houses just seeing how her fowls were getting on.*

*Thats a nice patient for you, isn't it. I'm sure you two don't give Mrs Gosson starts by behaving that way when you are ill.*

*Now its time to stop writing & get Grandma's arrowroot. She says she's sick of arrowroot, & she can't bear it — but I make her take every spoonful. That's the best of being a nurse. You can push a person into bed and then bully them properly.*[18]

These letters blended in my mind with Robert's raging epistles to give a picture of the last days of Jane Lindsay — the sordid physical surroundings, Mary and Robert's vain attempts to have some kind of civilised lifestyle, the old lady incontinent and confused, and Isabel clinging to her mother who was fading into a shadow land. If Mary wrote like this to her nieces, what did she write to her brothers? Was it shame that led to letters being destroyed, and was this the reason Mary continued to be supported by them?

Realistically, the family had little choice in the matter. Daryl and Joan had left their house at Baxter in order to wait out the Depression in cheaper premises. Percy was scarcely making a living with his lyrically beautiful oil paintings and mediocre illustrations. Both Norman and Lionel were travelling on the other side of the world. The three relatively affluent brothers were supporting both the Creswick household and Pearl's family in Ballarat. In the Lindsay family, as in many others, it was the lot of the unmarried poor to care for the old.

Mary's next letters are to Jane alone, and date from the late 1930s and early 1940s. They indicate a renewed correspondence after a considerable gap. The reason for her interest in Jane at this stage was apparently Norman's news that Jane had become a writer. Mary writes almost wistfully that she too may have been a writer, 'but a devastating Mother complex decided that I should stay at home and cook chops'.[19]

They have a self-conscious literary quality, the aunt's letters to her niece, the writer.

*There is a splendid sight thro the window as I write. I wish you could see it. Its my sister Jane Isabel being a gardiner. To-day she sees herself in the pictorial role of the Gardiner's daughter. She has dressed for the part as she sees it. On her head is a large ancient flapping imitation panama hat, under which wisps of grey hair straggle down over her face & the back of her neck. I can't see the tops of her stockings, but know they are both hanging down over her knees. The other parts of the stocking legs hang in wrinkles down to her ancles under which are two disreputable shoes, rucked across the toes, an inch & a half too long. One heel with a few cabled stiches across emerges from the left shoe. Both feet turn in nearly meeting each other. They look weary & dejected.*

*A dirty apron hanging below her skirt in front lends an addled air of informality. Thoroughly absorbed in the character of the Gardiner, it is not easy to concentrate on the actual business of gardening. She is slowly but surely ruining Robert's border of primroses. Weeds or bulbs she pulls out & throws aside just as the fancy takes her. I think her vision of the Garden bed is somewhat obstructed by the longest wisp of grey hair which floats across one eye down to the tops of a pointed drooping nose. Two wrinkles each side follow that nose's downward course. Jane the Gardiner has a worried air — an air of deep abstraction. She is entirely happy, being a gardiner.*

*Have you got any good loons over there to watch? Is your next novel forming? If so, what about putting in a loon? There are so many in the bush — loons or half loons.*[20]

Mary was cruel in her heavy-handed humour. Other letters congratulate Jane on her pregnancy and the birth of Helen, and warn her not to have anything to do with Betty, Will Dyson's daughter, who was planning to return to Australia. And along with the small pieces of malice and embroideries of family history there was a hope that Jane would continue to write. 'I have a hunch that some day my talented niece Mrs Glad, may decide to write the family history,' she wrote. And so she prepared to give Jane the same assistance she later gave John Hetherington.[21]

Even more than the Hetherington letters, the correspondence with Jane shows Mary as the self-conscious handmaid to her family's history, wanting to be the one in the background assisting the creator, never brave enough to write in her own name. It is very much to Jane's credit that when she wrote about her family, it was her own book, in her own words, with her own observations.

I turned to the last folder. It was thicker than the rest, which is why I had left it to the last. I realised then that I should have read it first, for here were the sources of Mary's contradictions, and the final piece in the puzzle of the banning of *Redheap*.

There were three long letters from Mary to Norman, all written more or less about the same time in the early 1920s. They were written in reply to Norman's request for information on Mary's girlhood experiences at Creswick. He was in the process of reworking *The Skyline* and needed her insights. As I read her account of restrictions and fears, of thwarted desires, and of friends, shivers ran up my spine.

*What I'm trying to get at is my complete conviction that woman, left alone, is simpler, more honest, more direct: that instinctively she knows better what she wants from life, is less confused than man with his incomplete logic, and half developed reason, — that the life of subterfuge, in which in self-defence she becomes so adroit, is not natural, but has been forced on her, chiefly by man.*[22]

This was not the start of a new polemic, a call for liberation, but an analysis of despair. For Mary Lindsay realised that she, and every other single woman of her acquaintance was seen as less than human because they had not married.

*Clear-eyed women, speaking in rare moments of confidence, among themselves, will say 'Slaves every one of us, slaves to sex from the moment of birth.'*

*. . . Do you remember Rose Anguin, The parson's daughter next door? A lovely girl she was — now an old maid . . . This is what she said to Gert Fraser last week —*

*'Don't talk to me. I don't count, neither do you, any fool cow of a married woman in the room counts for more than we do.' In that bitterness was the sincere conviction of utter failure. She had failed. She knew it. Everyone else knew it. — Any fool woman annexed to a man did actually count for more. At least she had made some attempt at fulfilment of life.*[23]

Lionel once claimed that reading Freud had changed Norman's ideas in *Redheap* and made it the book he so hated, but when I read the novel Freud was not the writer who sprang to mind. I always wondered which unknown mind had influenced Norman's thinking, who had helped turn the early comedy of *The Skyline* into *Redheap*. Now I knew it to be his sister.

The letters are very confusing. As with most Lindsay letters, Mary's writing roams all over the place, making amazing tangential connections. However, the general thread of her argument is that women need to be sexually fulfilled and that men and matriarchs conspire against young girls to make this impossible. She describes a society which was especially harsh on promiscuous females. There were picnics where girls would desperately hope that a boy would 'accidentally' brush against them. But if a girl appeared to welcome the embrace she would be damned as shameless. And so Mary's letter moves to the fate of Millie Lewers' sister, Gwyn, who was apparently seduced by a man from the city and then started openly admiring the opposite sex.

*Lots of men were attracted by the pretty face for an hour or so, or even for some days, but one by one she frightened them off. Too ~~ardent~~ in the chase, her eagerness was clear to all: even to the men.*[24]

Gwyn died young, and manless, but there are elements of her escapade on a bicycle in the liberated life of Ella Belairs of *The Cousin from Fiji*.

Because I knew that the Lindsay boys were worldly wise for their generation, I assumed that the girls were also aware of the physical nature of the sexual act. Their father was a country doctor, there were ten children, in the 1890s two of their brothers wrote for a magazine, *The Free Lance*, which was financed by an importer of condoms. But Mary writes of a world where neither she nor her friends have any idea of the realities of childbirth or conception.

> *One thing was clear. With all this mouth whispering. It was something monstrous. Too unclean for open talk . . . The horror was enhanced by specially selected verses from the Old Testament being forced before my shrinking eyes. So extraordinarily strong is an early association of ideas, that, to this day, I find it hard to think of those early books in the bible as anything but a catalogue of abominations — .*[25]

Mary writes proudly of her behaviour when Lionel brought his intellectual friends home and started talking about the mechanics of seduction to impress his siblings.

> *Responsive girls were mentioned without disgust or disapproval. Too many words, one felt vaguely, for genuine emotion. Still stimulating, and very interesting. Lionel, swanking on the verandah in the moonlight, confided partial glimpses of his affairs "One did not put one's arm round a girl's waist, according to the accepted tradition of courtships," he said. "On the contrary, a fellow slipped his hand higher under her arm. Thus holding her firmly by the breast". No doubt this feat had been successfully accomplished quite recently. One detected the swank. —* [26]

At the age of eighteen Mary discovered what every primary school child now takes for granted. And she did this by asking.

> *. . . in a moment of courage, one night I tramped Master Dum McCay up the spring hill road in the moonlight, and asked him point blank to explain. — I have now an amused remembrance of a distinctly disconcerted young man, hands in pockets eyes straight ahead, walking jerkily and with extreme rapidity rather apt to veer from one side of the road to the other, a wild flow of words keeping pace with — his embarrassed fleet feet, the while he gravely expounded, in set technical terms, this man and woman business. I am quite sure that none of the other nicely brought up girls of my acquaintance could have done such a thing.*[27]

Mary's first letter was concerned with attitudes to sex, the later letters give examples of the consequences. Now I started to hear more of the Lewers family, the mother and siblings of Mary's friend, Mil. There were older sisters who married, pretty younger sisters who died, and a mother: 'Like Queen Victoria she looked, and not so unlike her in character —. Sitting in her armchair, with plump hands folded on a spreading lap, she sent forth her decrees.'[28]

In this context Mil Lewers was hardly going to have a liberated life. But when Millie was about sixteen or seventeen, the young Lionel Lindsay was in love with her.

*He used to write her name all over his blotting pad, twinned with 'darlings' and 'dearests' galore. Also he wrote poems to a goddess in blue, after seeing Mil in a frock of that colour at the opera in Ballarat one night. The 'darlings' I discovered for myself. The poems he showed me himself.*[29]

So Millie was the girl whose name was written in the diary that Norman used for *Redheap*; she was the model for the heroine who bore her name. And she was the one who was to be protected at all costs by the book being banned. For rather than having a fully fledged affair with the young Lionel (resulting in an abortion as per the book), the affair itself was stillborn. Millie was too respectable to do much more than flirt. Lionel's only conquests in Creswick were shop girls and miners' daughters. Mary contrasted the promise of the glowing young Millie of the 1890s with the reality of the middle-aged spinster of Ballarat.

Mary's account of Millie provides a more substantial reason for banning *Redheap* than the insult to Norman's mother, the defaming of Pearl, or the ridicule of Mary. Millie Lewers was respected in the Creswick district. To portray this lonely middle-aged woman as a footloose teenager was probably a good joke for Norman, especially as it would humiliate Lionel, but it was cruel.

And so I came to understand the smokescreen around the identity of the main characters, the deliberate drawing of attention to the Jebb family, the grudging identification of the Robert, Hetty and Ethel characters were all designed to protect Millie Lewers who died shortly before the ban was lifted. She had to be the reason.

The third letter from Mary contained more Creswick history, but also revealed the meaning of old Jane Lindsay's dying words. Robert had recorded her saying, 'Don't do it Annie', telling Annie that certain feelings were 'bad'. I had assumed he was right in concluding that she was warning her sister Annie against carnal sin. In another one of Jane Glad's letters, Mary had written to Norman of an Annie Stevenson who had once attempted to seduce their father, and how he had tried to resist her charms by praying out loud beside his bed. Now I read fascinated as Mary placed Annie Stevenson, and her sexual feelings, in the context of small town Victoria.

Annie Stevenson had the misfortune of being both sexually attractive and, because of her family circumstances, 'available'. Early in her career she was the governess who taught Mary Lindsay and the Lewers girls, but later she became the town's notorious 'loose woman'.

*I remember the night she and Auntie Lena sneaked down to the studio Percy had in that cottage by the gas-works. They listened at the window. Percy, Lionel, and Hughie Smythe were doing out women, and the special iniquity of those ladies who made a chap feel 'bad'. Annies name was mentioned. She told me about it the same night. The hurt was so bad it was a relief to tell someone, and the little girl who was always sympathetic and who never told, was useful as a vehicle for release. I can see now her face crimson with the shame of it. There was also a look of added knowledge, of sudden shamed illumination. These boys had given her a picture of herself, the picture she perhaps presented to the world, and in fear and shame and still with a sense of fascination, she looked at it and hated it, and looked again, still fascinated.*[30]

Confronted with these male expectations of her morality, it was not surprising that Annie was intrigued by the implications.

*I can remember a conversation on massage. She had heard of men being actually Employed for noxious complaints to massage women. She brought that topic up time and again, saying 'that would make a woman feel bad.' 'How could a woman help feeling bad with a man's hand all over her'. Always the Calvinistic term bad used to express sexual desire. — I've often wondered which man it was she first let herself go with.*[31]

The letters lose their credibility at this point, as Mary decides, on very little evidence, the order in which Annie took her lovers. After her confident assertions about the power of sex, it was sad to read the idle speculations of a small-town old maid, fantasising about another person's love life.

The letters indicate, perhaps, why Mary turned against her mother in the 1920s. In them she blames mothers as much as men for hiding the truths of life from young women. Thanks to her mother, Mary Lindsay was both sexually inexperienced and menopausal at the time she wrote. It would have been impossible for her to write those letters and not resent the keepers of the rules.

The letters also suggest the reason for her rages, and why Dr Strachan sedated her with morphia. In the same house as Mary lived Pearl, the sister who had married the man she wanted and produced three children. And there was Isabel who was evidence that while Mary was trying to understand the mystery of sex, her parents were actively partaking of it. Her anger was entirely logical.

# 18

# *A conclusion of loyalties*

In January 1995 *The Legendary Lindsays* exhibition opened at the Art Gallery of New South Wales, and in March travelled to the Ballarat Fine Art Gallery. It was a joint project of Ursula Prunster and Helen Glad, and was designed to make the art of the whole family understandable to a wider public. It contained the work of all members of the Lindsay family who were exhibiting artists, an achievement which would have been impossible in their lifetimes. Photographs showed the Lindsays and the Dysons posing in tableaux, with Percy ascending like an angel, disembodied from the family concerns to the last, while spectacular 'in your face' nude studies of Rose revealed how dependent Norman was both on her and on photography as a source for his art. There were drawings and watercolours by Ruby, wonderful prints and drawings by Lionel, etchings, drawings and watercolours by Norman.

As I looked around the gallery walls I was struck by the sheer poetic beauty of Percy's small oils and regretted that I had come to know so little of him. His life runs like a cheerful, irresponsible counterpoint through the self-righteous anger of his siblings. Because he was not a compulsive hoarder of petty family details, it is easy to pass him over. By all accounts Percy was the charmer of the Lindsay boys, but most family references to him concern his fiscal irresponsibility. When he died in 1952 his friends gave him three cheers at his funeral. He was that kind of bloke. His gentle, moody landscapes evoked the feeling of the old town of Creswick in a way that photographs never could.

## LETTERS & LIARS

It was a country town in the afternoon of its existence, a place for old people to keep their memories and for young people to leave.

As well as Percy's oil paintings, there was his palette, showing the range of the colours and the mix of tones he preferred. Daryl was right in his assessment of his eldest brother's talent.

Isabel was not included in the exhibition, but 1995 was the year she 'came out' as an artist in Joan Kerr's *Heritage*, a mammoth study of women artists that was published later in the year.

The opening of *The Legendary Lindsays* was crowded with family, friends of Lindsays, and those who wished to be friends of Lindsays. One aggressive couple bailed up Peter, insisting that they knew him well, but they thought they were talking to his cousin Peter Hammond Lindsay, Percy's son.

The speeches, as is the case with most of these events, missed the point and praised Norman as the genius accompanied by his siblings. Despite the evidence on the walls of Percy's paintings, Lionel's prints, Ruby's drawings and Daryl's paintings of Mulberry Hill, the legend was too strong.

In the past the myth of Norman Lindsay as the artistic hero who saved the country from wowsers was an important one. In the first part of this century, Australia needed a god to descend from Olympus and free it from suburban respectability. But now that pubs open on Sunday, sex is no longer linked exclusively to marriage, and art knows no rules, our culture is strong enough to handle some truths.

This is important because the legend ignores those who helped create it. The popular story of Norman Lindsay would not exist if it were not for the machinations of Mary and Rose. And it overlooks the way the lives of the members of the family echoed the changes that were happening in the world around them. In the tightly structured, middle-class society of the Lindsays' early and middle years, marriage was for life and separation and divorce were scandals. But small hypocrisies enabled an elderly doctor to leave his wife and travel for adventure. When women became pregnant outside of marriage they were disgraced, but in many households the first child was born 'prematurely'. Norman and Rose Lindsay were only scandalous because they refused to pretend and openly lived together without being married. Then, after some years of marriage, they openly separated. The only reason for concealing the third party in their triangle was her position in the world of respectable lies. The liars were there for her protection.

# A CONCLUSION OF LOYALTIES

By the time the exhibition opened, I was feeling strangely distant from the Lindsays and their passions and intrigues. My research had become a Ph.D. and it was off with the markers for assessment. But I wrote about *The Legendary Lindsays* for the *Bulletin*; a big double-page spread on the size and variety of the family.

I have come to realise that the onion is never fully peeled, the story can never end. Geoff Fiddian, the son of Sam Fiddian, who was a friend of the Lindsay children, read my article and wrote to me about more of Isabel's letters. These are with the Creswick historic society. He also gave me details of the business dealings behind the Lindsay feud with Dr Strachan. Earlier this year a friend in Ballarat mentioned that Felicity Shaw had died. Presumably this means the letters she wrote to Peter, which included her assessment of the family secrets, can now be accessed in the National Library where he placed them for safekeeping.

Only last month a friend mentioned that, less than a year before he died, Keith Wingrove sold his collection of Lindsay material to the State Library of NSW. This included the papers that scholars and others had been denied access to in his lifetime. I knew that Wingrove had come to Sydney because he had given Peter a notebook that Lionel had kept in the 1890s. It contains all Lionel's early poems and pasted-in copies of his first publications. Lionel had assumed he lost when it he first went to Melbourne, so it probably came from Mary.

'I suppose it makes up for the scrapbook of mine that he stole,' said Peter when he showed it to me. Wingrove's bad habit of stealing memorabilia was a common subject for discussion among the Lindsay family.

~

Add a bit of information and the pattern changes. New stories emerge, old ones appear more interesting. The lives of these members of the Lindsay family are not quite like a kaleidoscope where shapes constantly make pretty designs. Rather, the exercise of reading through the past is like solving an ever-evolving jigsaw puzzle where new pieces are introduced to throw the whole pattern into confusion. There will always be another piece to the puzzle.

# LINDSAY

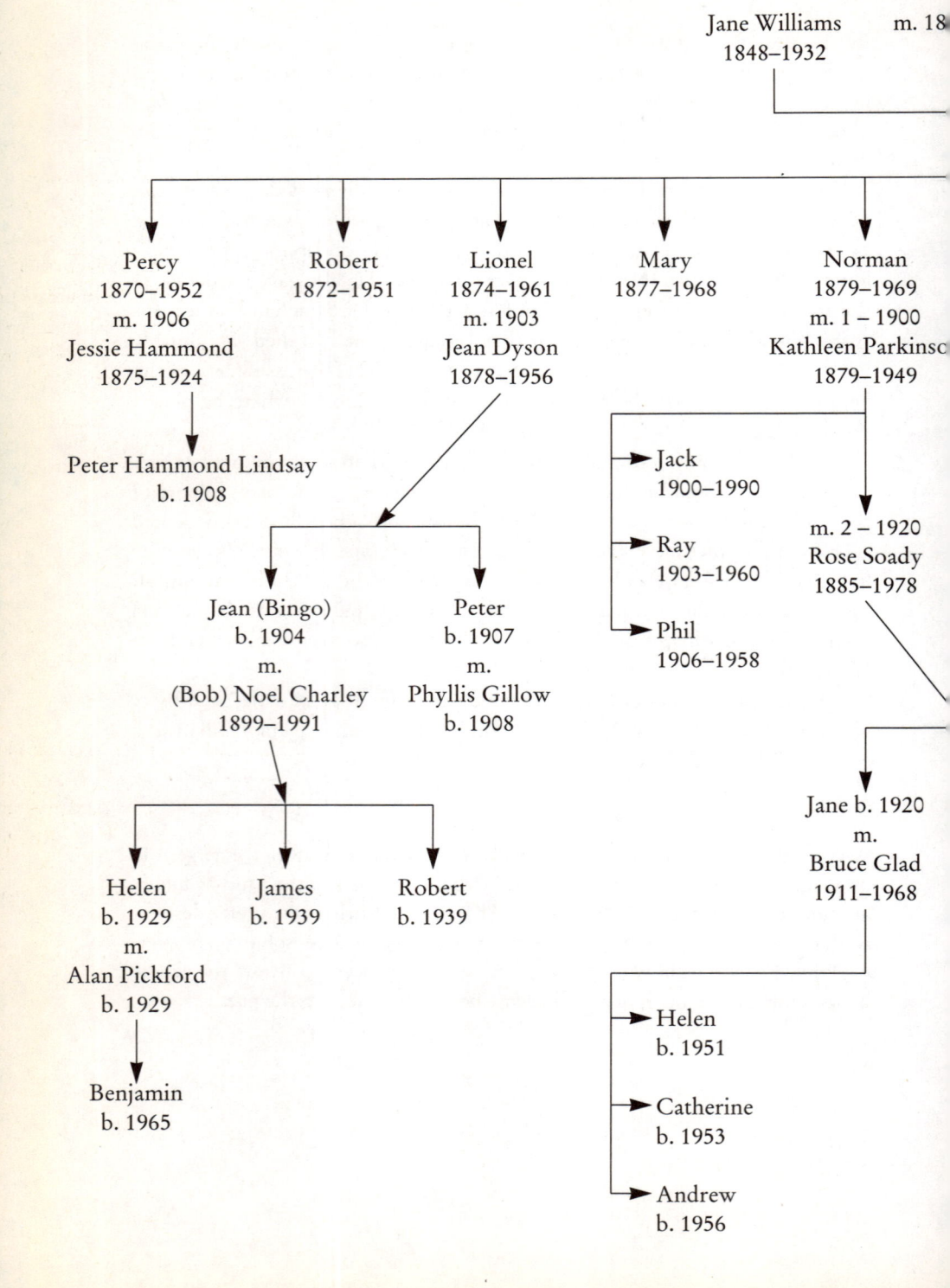

Jane Williams     m. 18
1848–1932

- **Percy**
  1870–1952
  m. 1906
  Jessie Hammond
  1875–1924
  
  → Peter Hammond Lindsay
  b. 1908

- **Robert**
  1872–1951

- **Lionel**
  1874–1961
  m. 1903
  Jean Dyson
  1878–1956
  
  → **Jean (Bingo)**
  b. 1904
  m.
  (Bob) Noel Charley
  1899–1991
  
  → Helen b. 1929 m. Alan Pickford b. 1929 → Benjamin b. 1965
  → James b. 1939
  → Robert b. 1939
  
  → **Peter**
  b. 1907
  m.
  Phyllis Gillow
  b. 1908

- **Mary**
  1877–1968

- **Norman**
  1879–1969
  m. 1 – 1900
  Kathleen Parkinso
  1879–1949
  
  → Jack 1900–1990
  → Ray 1903–1960
  → Phil 1906–1958
  
  m. 2 – 1920
  Rose Soady
  1885–1978
  
  → **Jane b. 1920**
  m.
  Bruce Glad
  1911–1968
  
  → Helen b. 1951
  → Catherine b. 1953
  → Andrew b. 1956

# FAMILY TREE

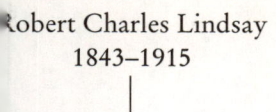

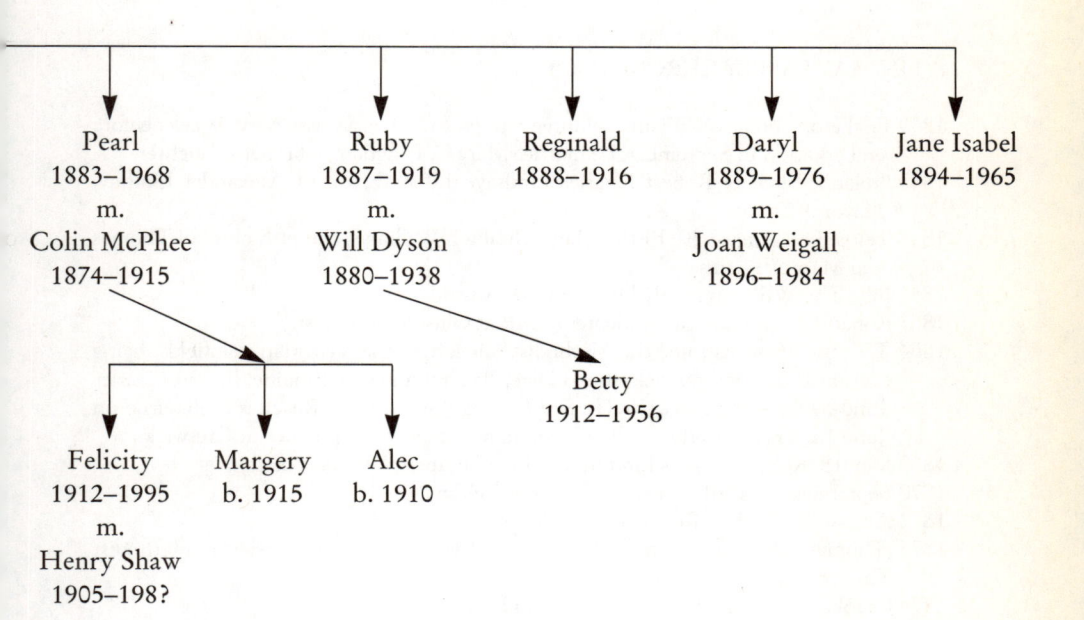

Robert Charles Lindsay
1843–1915

**Pearl**
1883–1968
m.
Colin McPhee
1874–1915

**Ruby**
1887–1919
m.
Will Dyson
1880–1938

**Reginald**
1888–1916

**Daryl**
1889–1976
m.
Joan Weigall
1896–1984

**Jane Isabel**
1894–1965

**Betty**
1912–1956

**Felicity**
1912–1995
m.
Henry Shaw
1905–198?

**Margery**
b. 1915

**Alec**
b. 1910

**Helen (Honey)**
b. 1921
m.
1. Bruce Glad
2. Ritchie Siou
3. Edward Marino

# Chronology

## A LINDSAY FAMILY CHRONOLOGY

1839 England. Thomas Williams volunteers to go to Fiji as a missionary. Weeks before embarkation in September, he marries Mary Cottingham, a farmer's daughter.
1843 Ireland. Birth of Robert Charles Lindsay, the sixth son of Alexander Lindsay, Mayor of Derry.
1848 Teloa, Fiji. August 30. Birth of Jane Elizabeth Williams, the fifth child of Thomas and Mary Williams.
1853 July. The Williams family leaves Fiji for Australia.
1863 Robert Charles Lindsay graduates as MB at Glasgow University.
1864 Thomas Williams joins the Methodist mission to the Victorian goldfields, being stationed first at Creswick, then Colac, Ballarat and Castlemaine. Robert Charles Lindsay takes a passage on *The Red Rose* as ship's doctor. Reaches Melbourne on June 15. Travels to the goldfields where he establishes a practice at Creswick.
1869 May 18. Robert Charles Lindsay and Jane Elizabeth Williams marry.
1870 September 17. Birth of Percival Charles Lindsay.
1872 August 27. Birth of Robert Elliot Alexander Lindsay.
1873 Thomas Williams elected Chairman of the Australasian Wesleyan Methodist Conference.
1874 October 17. Birth of Lionel Arthur Lindsay.
1877 February 26. Birth of Mary Eleanor Beatrice Lindsay. Robert Charles and Jane Lindsay build their new house and call it 'Lisnacrieve', after the Lindsay home in Ireland.
1878 Thomas and Mary Williams retire to Ballarat in order to be close to their eldest daughter and her children.
1879 February 22. Birth of Norman Alfred Williams Lindsay.
1883 Birth of Pearl Irene Leonore Lindsay.
1887 March 20. Birth of Ruby Lindsay.
1888 [Exact date unknown.] Birth of Reginald Graham Lindsay.
1889 Lionel Lindsay leaves home to become pupil assistant at the Melbourne Observatory. He does not study for matriculation. Starts to keep a diary and write poetry. Ernest Daryl Lindsay born December 31.
1893 January. Lionel and Percy study painting with Miller Marshall and Walter Withers in Ballarat.
March. Lionel leaves for Melbourne to work as an artist on the *Hawk*. The depression and its effect on the Lindsay family worsens.
1894 [Date unknown.] March. Jane Isabel Lindsay born.
circa 1895 Percy joins Lionel and paints in Melbourne. Norman starts painting classes with Walter Withers and Miller Marshall.
1896 Norman joins Lionel and Percy in Melbourne in order to ghost for Lionel while he concentrates on the *Free Lance*, short-lived weekly magazine. Norman also publishes cartoons in the *Free Lance*.

# CHRONOLOGY

1897 Norman illustrates for the magazine *Tocsin*.

circa 1898 Lionel, Norman and Ray Parkinson start work on a novel of pirate life, collect pirate-like material, and sign their names in a blood oath.

1900 Kathleen (Katie) Agatha Parkinson, sister of Ray, falls pregnant to Norman Lindsay. She and Norman marry on May 23 and Jack is born on October 20. Jack Elkington takes Norman's 'Boccaccio' drawings to Sydney and shows them to Julian Ashton.

1901 Norman is offered work as cartoonist on the *Bulletin* and moves to Sydney. Three months later he is joined by Katie and Jack.

1902 Rose Soady becomes an artist's model to help support her family after her father deserts them. She is the subject of Sydney Long's *Flamingoes*. Lionel Lindsay travels to Spain, London, then in Italy becomes engaged to Jean Dyson.

1903 On his return to Australia Lionel travels to Sydney and becomes a staff cartoonist for the *Evening News*. Katie travels to Melbourne for support during the birth of her second child, Raymond, born August 26. Norman asks Rose Soady to join himself and Will Dyson as a model for a house-party at his home in Northwood. By November, Norman and Rose are regarded by their friends as a couple. Lionel and Jean Dyson marry in Sydney. Ruby goes to Melbourne to study art, with Mary's connivance, and stays with Percy.

1904 Jean (Bingo) Lindsay, daughter of Lionel, born. Norman exhibits *Pollice Verso* at the Royal Art Society.

1906 April 3. Philip Lindsay, son of Norman and Katie, born.

1907 March 23. Percy marries Jessie Hammond, the daughter of a Creswick shopkeeper. Lionel becomes proofreader for *The Lone Hand* to help support the family in Creswick. Norman also sends regular payments to Creswick. Peter Lindsay, son of Lionel, born. *Pollice Verso* is exhibited in Melbourne and bought by the National Gallery of Victoria for 150 guineas.

1908 Peter Hammond Lindsay, son of Percy, born.

1909 Norman illustrates Hugh McCrae's anthology *Satyrs and Sunlight*. Ruby marries Will Dyson, September 30. In October, Norman joins Ruby and Will on their journey to England via Naples and Pompeii. Robert Charles leaves Creswick, at first becoming a ship's doctor.

circa 1909 Pearl marries Colin McPhee.

1910 Robert travels to England. Rose joins Norman in England. Mary is offered the position of women's editor on the Sydney *Star* but declines it. November 25, Norman and Rose return to Australia. Rose begins to manage Norman's finances.

1911 Norman becomes ill with pleurisy on his return to Sydney and does not resume living with Katie. He and Rose move to the Blue Mountains. Katie and the children move to Brisbane to be with the rest of her family. Mary travels to London to join Robert.

1912 Rose buys a house at Faulconbridge for Norman and herself. Betty Dyson, daughter of Ruby and Will, born in London.

1913 Norman's *A Curate in Bohemia* published. His *Crucified Venus* exhibited at All Australian Exhibition, Melbourne, in September, and is removed by the management committee after many complaints. After Julian Ashton threatens to remove all New South Wales exhibits it is rehung.

1915 Robert Charles becomes ill after rescuing miners at White Cliffs and returns home where he dies on September 19. Reg and Daryl enlist in the AIF and embark for France. Daryl writes to Mary, who is staying with Robert in New Orleans, and asks her to come home to help. Colin McPhee suicides, leaving Pearl a widow with three children. Lionel and Norman talk of writing novels of Creswick and Lionel lends Norman his boyhood diary.

1916 *Art in Australia* commences publication and both Norman and Lionel Lindsay become frequent contributors. Will Dyson is appointed official war artist for the AIF. Daryl is appointed his batman. On December 31 Reg Lindsay is killed at the Somme.

1917 Norman receives Reg's last letter posted days before his death, and his brother's bloodstained notebook. He turns to spiritualism. Lionel reads Norman's draft of *The Skyline*, which later becomes *Redheap*. He is distressed at the use of his diary but regards Norman's novel as so superior to his own that he stops writing fiction. Norman starts etching, tutored by Ure Smith and Lionel. Lionel teaches Rose print-making. On Lionel's suggestion, Percy moves to Sydney.

1918 Norman publishes *The Magic Pudding*. Lionel writes the introduction to *The Pen Drawings of Norman Lindsay*. At about this time, Mary becomes an annual visitor to Norman and Rose.

1919 Ruby and Daryl Lindsay visit their Irish relatives. On March 12, after returning to London, Ruby dies in the influenza pandemic. Daryl returns to Creswick and holds his first exhibition at Decoration Galleries. Jack and Katie visit Sydney to finalise her divorce from Norman. Will Dyson publishes *Poems in memory of a wife*.

1920 Norman and Rose marry on January 14, two days before the birth of their daughter Jane. The divorce from Katie is made absolute on January 28. Jack comes to Sydney and befriends his father. Norman's *Creative Effort* published. Cecil Palmer produces *The drawings of Ruby Lindsay*. Norman visits Creswick for the last time.

1921 Jack settles in Sydney. Daryl returns to London where he studies at the Slade School under Henry Tonks.

1922 Daryl marries Joan à Beckett on February 14. On June 4, Helen (Honey) is born to Rose and Norman. Rose is told she may not safely have any more children. In May, Lionel and Norman quarrel again, and this time their rift is permanent.

1923 The Society of Artists organises an exhibition of Australian art in London. Lionel's work is praised but Norman's is damned for its sexually explicit nature. Travelling with the exhibition, Lloyd Rees is introduced to 'George' Lindsay, Robert's London pseudonym. Robert is working in a milliner's, decorating hats. Norman starts to rework his Creswick novel and asks Mary for background information on her girlhood. Jack, now living in Sydney, starts to co-edit, with Norman and Kenneth Slessor, *Vision*, a literary periodical which promotes Norman Lindsay's ideas as well as writing by Jack, Kenneth Slessor, R. D. FitzGerald and other young writers.

circa 1924 Mary suffers a breakdown and is treated with morphia.

1925 In March, Norman has a notorious but critically unsuccessful exhibition in London. Jack and John Kirtley establish Fanfrolico Press for rare and beautiful editions to promote Norman's ideas.

# CHRONOLOGY

1926 Jack travels to England, feeling he will advance his father's cause there, but later moves away from him. Jack and John Kirtley take Fanfrolico Press to London, publishing deluxe editions of translations by Jack, illustrated by Norman as well as other writers. Harold Wright, from the Bond Street art dealers, P. & D. Colnaghi, writes to Lionel and invites him to exhibit in London. Lionel, Jean and Bingo travel to London and then Spain.

1927 Lionel's exhibition is a critical and financial success in London and he and Jean continue to travel throughout Europe and Africa.

1929 Norman finishes *Redheap* and arranges to publish it in London. The quarrelling between Mary, Pearl and Isabel at Creswick becomes so bad that Daryl moves Pearl and the children to Ballarat. Bingo marries in India. After adventures in Australia and New Guinea, Peter Lindsay travels to England where he stays until the late 1940s. He meets Robert Lindsay in London. A friendship starts between Norman and Margaret Coen, and art student who models for him.

1930 *Redheap* published in London in April, but banned in Australia in May. In the USA it is published as *Every Mother's Son*. Fanfrolico ceases publication. Jane's health deteriorates. Robert prepares to return from London. A special Norman Lindsay number of *Art in Australia* is published in December. Margaret Coen writes a letter to Norman praising *Redheap*.

1931 Robert and Mary nurse the feeble and senile Jane. Isabel is also living in the house. After an attempt is made to prosecute *Art in Australia* for obscenity in 1931, Norman and Rose leave for England and America on July 23. *Art in Australia* June 1931 special issue on Daryl Lindsay. Lionel returns briefly to Australia before resuming his travels in Europe, India and Africa.

1932 Norman and Rose return to Australia in April. Jane dies November 14. Lionel and Jean travelling in Europe.

1933 Norman's *Saturdee* published by the Endeavour Press, a venture of P. R. Stephensen, subsidised by Norman Lindsay.

1934 Norman leaves Springwood for 12 Bridge Street, Sydney, in order to be close to Margaret Coen, with whom he is having an affair. Jane, Norman's daughter, enrols in boarding school so that she may later study medicine at university, but is given little encouragement and soon leaves.

1939 Daryl Lindsay appointed curator of National Gallery of Victoria.

1940 June 19. Rose leaves Springwood to go to America with Norman's best work, trying to escape the war. The works are destroyed in a fire. Norman returns to Springwood in Rose's absence and does not leave until his final stay in hospital. Margaret Coen moves into the studio at 12 Bridge Street. With Norman's encouragement she forms a relationship with the young New Zealand poet, Douglas Stewart.

1941 Lionel Lindsay knighted. Daryl appointed Director of the National Gallery of Victoria. January 21, Rose returns to Springwood after the fire in America.

1940s Rose develops arthritis which gradually cripples her.

1945 Norman's *The Cousin from Fiji* published. Margaret Coen and Douglas Stewart marry.

1946 Peter Lindsay returns home from Europe to nurse both his parents and works on the *Australian Encyclopaedia* and undertakes other freelance writing projects.

1947 Norman's *Halfway to Anywhere* published.

circa 1950 Isabel is diagnosed as having arthritis.

1951 Late in the year, Robert Lindsay dies and Mary becomes acutely ill for some months.

1952 September 21. Percy Lindsay dies.

1956 Jane buys a house at Hunters Hill. Rose moves in with Jane, her husband Bruce Glad and their three children. In December, Daryl Lindsay retires as Director of the National Gallery of Victoria and is knighted. Jean Lindsay, Lionel's wife, dies after struggling for many years with acute asthma.

1957 John Hetherington is appointed Norman's official biographer.

1958 The Lionel Lindsay gallery opens in Toowoomba. Philip Lindsay dies, January 14.

1959 John Hetherington visits Rose, reads some of Robert Lindsay's letters, and declines thereafter to correspond with Mary.

1960 Ray Lindsay dies.

1961 May 22. Lionel Lindsay dies. Later that year, Isabel is admitted to hospital with acute arthritis.

1965 Isabel Lindsay dies. Norman publishes *Bohemians of the Bulletin*. Daryl publishes *The Leafy Tree*.

1966 After assistance from John Hetherington, Norman publishes *Scribblings of an Idle Mind*.

1967 Publication of Lionel's *Comedy of Life*, edited by Peter Lindsay.

circa 1966 onwards Norman tries to leave the Springwood property to the National Trust but Rose refuses to disinherit their children. After some years of negotiations their final communications with each other are hostile. Rose finally agrees to sell the house to the Trust.

1968 Mary Lindsay dies. Her residual heir is the Ballarat Fine Art Gallery. Norman makes a new will, leaving his art to the National Trust as long as the Springwood property is purchased and turned into a Norman Lindsay Gallery. The will names Hetherington as Norman's official biographer.

1969 March. Norman Lindsay makes another will, with Jane Glad and Douglas Stewart as executors, leaving the bulk of his estate to the National Trust (NSW). On October 26, he signs a codicil to his will effectively excluding his family from his estate and replacing Jane as executor with Margaret Stewart. Norman Lindsay dies November 21.

1976 December 25. Daryl Lindsay dies.

1984 December 30. Joan Lindsay dies and the house she shared with Daryl becomes another Lindsay museum.

# Bibliography

PUBLISHED MEMOIRS BY MEMBERS OF THE LINDSAY FAMILY (INCLUDING AUTO-BIOGRAPHICAL FICTION)

Lindsay, Daryl, *The Leafy Tree: My Family*, F.W. Cheshire, Melbourne, 1965.
Lindsay, Jack, *Fanfrolico and After*, The Bodley Head, London, 1962.
Lindsay, Jack, *Life Rarely Tells*, The Bodley Head, London, 1958.
Lindsay, Jack, *The Roaring Twenties*, The Bodley Head, London, 1960.
(These three volumes were re-published as *Life Rarely Tells*, Penguin, Melbourne, 1982.)
Lindsay, Jack 'The Life and Art of Norman Lindsay', 33 (1) *Meanjin* (March 1974), pp. 27–411.
Lindsay, James, *The Lindsay Memoirs — A Record of Lisnacrieve and the Lindsay Family*, private publication, Derry, circa 1870s.
Lindsay, Jane, *Portrait of Pa*, Angus & Robertson, Sydney, 1973; re-issued 1994.
Lindsay, Joan, *Time Without Clocks*, Cheshire, London, 1962.
Lindsay, Lionel, *Comedy of Life*, Angus & Robertson, Sydney, 1965.
Lindsay, Lionel, *Discobolus and Other Verses*, private publication, Sydney, 1959.
Lindsay, Norman, *A Curate in Bohemia*, New South Wales Bookstall Company, Sydney, 1913.
Lindsay, Norman, *Halfway to Anywhere*, Angus & Robertson, Sydney, 1947.
Lindsay, Norman, *My Mask, For What Little I Know of the Man Behind It, An Autobiography*, Angus & Robertson, Sydney, 1970.
Lindsay, Norman, *Redheap*, Faber and Faber, London, 1930; Ure Smith Sydney, 1959.
Lindsay, Norman, *Rooms and Houses, An Autobiographical Novel*, Ure Smith, Sydney, 1968.
Lindsay, Norman, *Saturdee*, Endeavour Press, Sydney, 1934.
Lindsay, Norman, *The Cousin from Fiji*, Angus & Robertson, Sydney, 1945.
Lindsay, Rose, *Ma and Pa: My Childhood Memories*, Ure Smith, Sydney, 1963.
Lindsay, Rose, *Model Wife: My Life with Norman Lindsay*, Ure Smith, Sydney, 1967.
Lindsay, Rose, 'Rose Lindsay's Memoirs: Artists and Models', *Bulletin*, 18 February 1953, pp. 27, 34.
Lindsay, Rose, 'Rose Lindsay's Memoirs: In Paris with Hugh D. McIntosh', *Bulletin*, 18 March 1953, pp. 27, 34.
Lindsay, Rose, 'Rose Lindsay's Memoirs: Into the Machine Age', *Bulletin*, 13 May 1953, pp. 27, 30.
Lindsay, Rose, 'Rose Lindsay's Memoirs: Some Studios in Sydney', *Bulletin*, 4 March 1953, pp. 27, 34.
Lindsay, Rose, 'Rose Lindsay's Memoirs: Visitors to Springwood',*Bulletin*, 15 April 1953, pp. 27, 29.
Williams, Thomas, *Fiji and the Fijians — The Islands and Their Inhabitants*, Alexander Heylin, London 1858; reprinted Fiji Museum, Suva, 1982.

MANUSCRIPTS
*Mitchell Library, Sydney*
Leon Gellert Papers MSS 3456
W. H. Gill Papers MSS 285
Lindsay Papers (deposited by Rose Lindsay) MSS 742
Lionel Lindsay Papers MSS 1969
J.R. McGregor Papers MSS 2615
Sydney Ure Smith Papers MSS 31
Harold Wright Papers MSS 515
Harold Wright Papers uncatalogued MSS Set 478
*Dixson Library, Sydney*
William Dixson outwards correspondence file WD1
*La Trobe Library, Melbourne*
John Hetherington Papers MSS 9740
Lindsay Family Papers MSS 9104, 10375 (deposited by Peter and Daryl Lindsay)
Peter Lindsay Papers MSS 9242
Correspondence between Robert Menzies and Lionel Lindsay MSS 10375
*National Library of Australia, Canberra*
Jack Lindsay papers
*Fisher Library, University of Sydney*
Harry Chaplin papers
*Private Collections*
Jean Charley papers
Peter Lindsay papers
Glad Family papers
Other papers from confidential sources

INTERVIEWS
The following members of the Lindsay family were interviewed:
Peter Lindsay, Jean Charley, Helen Lindsay, Helen Glad, Jane Glad, Felicity Shaw.

CRITICAL COMMENT AND CONTEXT
Boyd, Martin, *Day of My Delight: An Anglo-Australian Memoir*, Lansdowne, Melbourne, 1965.
Buckridge, Pat, *The Scandalous Penton*, University of Queensland Press, Brisbane, 1994.
Chaplin, Harry F., *A Lindsay Miscellany*, Wentworth Books, Sydney, 1978.
Chaplin, Harry F., *Norman Lindsay: His Books, Manuscripts and Autograph Letters in the Collection of and Annotated by Harry F.Chaplin*, The Wentworth Press, Sydney, 1969.
Chaplin, Harry F., *The Fanfrolico Press: A Survey*, Wentworth Press, Sydney 1976.
Coleman, Peter, *Obscenity, Blasphemy, Sedition: Censorship in Australia*, Jacaranda, Brisbane, 1962.
Dutton, Geoffrey, *Kenneth Slessor: A Biography*, Viking, Melbourne, 1991.
Farwell, George, 'Genius at home', (review of John Hetherington's *Norman Lindsay: The Embattled Olympian* and Jane Lindsay's *Portrait of Pa*), *Sydney Morning Herald*, 15 December, 1973, p.15.
Henderson, G.C. (ed), *Journal of Thomas Williams, Missionary in Fiji, 1840–1863*, Angus & Roberston, Sydney, 1931.

# BIBLIOGRAPHY

Hetherington, John, *Australian Painters: Forty Profiles* , F.W. Cheshire, Melbourne, 1963.
Hetherington, John, *Australians: Nine Profiles*, F.W. Cheshire, Melbourne, 1960.
Hetherington, John, *Norman Lindsay: The Embattled Olympian*, Oxford University Press, Melbourne, 1973.
Hetherington, John, *The Morning was Shining*, Faber and Faber, London, 1971.
Hope, A.D., *Siren and Satyr: The Personal Philosophy of Norman Lindsay*, Sun Books, Melbourne, 1976.
Howarth, R. G. and Barker, A.W. (ed), *Letters of Norman Lindsay*, Angus & Robertson, Sydney, 1979.
Hughes, Robert, *The Art of Australia*, Penguin, England, 1970.
Jose, A. W. and Carter, H.J. (ed), *Australian Encyclopaedia*, Angus & Robertson, Sydney, 1925.
Kirkpatrick, Peter, *The Sea Coast of Bohemia: Literary Life in Sydney's Roaring Twenties*, University of Queensland Press, Brisbane, 1992.
McMullan, Ross, *Will Dyson: Cartoonist, Etcher and Australia's Finest War Artist*, Angus & Robertson, Sydney, 1984.
McQueen, Humphrey, 'Lindsay: Genius or Craftsman?' (review of John Hetherington's *Norman Lindsay: The Embattled Olympian*), *Canberra Times*, 4 January 1974, p. 9.
Moore, William, *The Story of Australian Art*, Angus & Robertson, Sydney, 1934.
Pearl, Cyril, 'A noodle-inspired farce from the past' (review of John Hetherington's *Norman Lindsay: The Embattled Olympian*), *Nation Review*, 14–20 December 1973, p. 294
Philip, Franz and Stewart, June (ed), *In Honour of Daryl Lindsay*, Oxford University Press, Melbourne, 1964.
Pollak, Michael, *Sense & Censorship: Commentaries on Censorship Violence in Australia*, Reed, Sydney, 1990.
Prunster, Ursula, (with contributions by Helen Glad and Robert Holden), *The Legendary Lindsays*, Art Gallery of New South Wales, Sydney, 1995.
Rees, Lloyd, *Peaks and Valleys*, Angus & Roberston, Sydney, 1985.
Roe, Jill, review of John Hetherington's *Norman Lindsay: The Embattled Olympian*, XVI *Historical Studies* (1975), pp. 465–66.
Slessor, Kenneth (ed), 'Norman Lindsay Number in honour of the eightieth birthday of Norman Lindsay, born 23rd February, 1879', *Southerly*, No.1, 1959.
Smith, Bernard, *Australian Painting 1788–1969*, Oxford University Press, Melbourne, 1962.
Smith, Bernard, *The Critic as Advocate: Selected essays 1945–1988*, Melbourne, 1989.
Smith, Vivian (ed), *Letters of Vance and Nettie Palmer 1915–1963*, National Library of Australia, Canberra, 1977.
Stephens, A.G., 'Red Page', *Bulletin*, 18 August 1900, inside cover.
Stephens A.G., 'The Rise and Fall of Norman Lindsay', *Pacific*, 18 January 1924.
Stewart, Douglas, *Norman Lindsay: A Personal Memoir*, Nelson, Melbourne, 1975.
Stewart, Meg, *Autobiography of My Mother*, Penguin, Melbourne, 1985.
Thomas, Daniel (ed), *Creating Australia*, ICCA, Adelaide, 1988.
Turnbull, Clive, 'He changed our life current', (review of John Hetherington's *Norman Lindsay: The Embattled Olympian* and Jane Lindsay's *Portrait of Pa*), *The Age*, 27 October 1973, p. 12.

Underhill, Nancy D.H., *Making Australian Art 1916–1949: Sydney Ure Smith Patron and Publisher*, Oxford University Press, Melbourne, 1991.

Newspaper References
'Death of John Hetherington', *Sydney Morning Herald*, 18 September 1974, p. 17.
'Norman Lindsay letters bought by Mitchell Library', *Sydney Morning Herald*, 12 June 1963, p. 14.

# Endnotes

**1. LEGEND**
1. A.D. Hope, *Siren and Satyr: The Personal Philosophy of Norman Lindsay*, Sun Books, Melbourne, 1976, p. 3.
2. Godfrey Blunden, *Norman Lindsay Watercolours*, Ure Smith, Sydney, 1969; describes Lindsay in the Introduction as 'perhaps the only authentic genius Australia has produced'.
3. John Hetherington, *Norman Lindsay: The Embattled Olympian*, Oxford University Press, Melbourne, 1973.
4. Robert Hughes, *The Art of Australia*, Penguin, England, 1970, p. 84.

**3. LIONEL'S STORY**
1. Lionel Lindsay, *Comedy of Life*, Angus & Robertson, Sydney, 1966, p. 11.
2. *ibid.*, p. 13
3. *ibid.*, p. 7
4. *ibid.*, p. 13
5. *ibid.*, p. 3
6. *ibid.*, p. 7. The punctuation is as appears in the published book.
7. *ibid.*, p. 16
8 I have written on Lionel's life in detail in Joanna Mendelssohn, *Lionel Lindsay: An Artist and His Family*, Chatto & Windus, London, 1988. Most of the diary was destroyed by Lionel, but a few pages remain in a private collection.
9. Lionel Lindsay, *op.cit.*, pp. 48–49.
10. *ibid.*, p. 42
11. *ibid.*, pp. 87–88
12 *Comedy of Life* calls this 'Chartersville'.
13. Lionel Lindsay, *op.cit.*, p. 58.
14. *ibid.*, pp. 110–11
15. *ibid.*, p. 133
16. *ibid.*, pp. 133–35
17. Lionel Lindsay to Peter Lindsay, 6 June 1940, La Trobe Manuscripts (hereafter MSS) 9104/362. The eccentric spelling and punctuation are in the original letters.
18. A copy of this document was given to the Mitchell Library by Peter Lindsay.

**4. DARYL LINDSAY AND *THE LEAFY TREE***
1. Daryl Lindsay, *The Leafy Tree: My Family*, F.W. Cheshire, Melbourne, 1965.
2. *ibid.*, p. viii
3. James Lindsay, *The Lindsay Memoirs — A Record of Lisnacrieve and the Lindsay Family*, Derry, circa 1870s. Peter Lindsay has donated his copy of this book to the Mitchell Library.

4. Thomas Williams, *Fiji and the Fijians — The Islands and Their Inhabitants*, Alexander Heylin, London, 1858; reprinted Fiji Museum, Suva, 1982.
5. Daryl Lindsay, *op.cit.*, p. 5.
6. *ibid.*, p. 73
7. This takes the form of a dramatic script; *ibid.*, pp. 77–79.
8. *ibid.*, p. 77
9. *ibid.*, p. 9
10. *ibid.*, p. 11
11. *ibid.*, p. 14
12. *ibid.*, p. 16
13. *ibid.*, pp. 14, 17, 197
14. *ibid.*, p. 18
15. *ibid.*
16. *ibid.*, p. 41
17. *ibid.*, p. 30
18. 'I don't think it had ever occurred to Lionel that art might be a profession.' Norman Lindsay, *My Mask, For What Little I Know of the Man Behind It, An Autobiography*, Angus & Robertson, Sydney, 1970, p. 35.
19. Daryl Lindsay, *op.cit.*, p. 46.
20. *ibid.*, p. 52
21. *ibid.*, p. 54
22. *ibid.*, p. 57
23. *ibid.*, p. 58
24. *ibid.*, p. 61
25. *ibid.*, p. 62
26. *ibid.*, p. 66
27. *ibid.*, p. 67
28. *ibid.*, p. 68
29. *ibid.*, p. 70
30. *ibid.*, p. 122
31. *ibid.*, p. 73
32. *ibid.*, p. 113
33. *ibid.*, p. 128
34. *ibid.*, p. 130
35. See Franz Philipp and June Stewart (eds), *In Honour of Daryl Lindsay*, Oxford University Press, Melbourne, 1964.
36. Daryl Lindsay, *op.cit.*, p. 164.
37. *ibid.*, p. 176
38. R.G. Howarth and A.W. Barker (eds), *Letters of Norman Lindsay*, Angus & Robertson, Sydney, 1979.
39. Daryl Lindsay to Jean Charley, 23 August 1966, p. 5, private collection.

## 5. NORMAN ACCORDING TO NORMAN
1. Norman Lindsay, *op.cit.*
2. John Hetherington's news cuttings of his own writing are MSS 7/16 1329 and 2/16 in his papers at the La Trobe Library. They start on 12/11/1934 with municipal news.

# ENDNOTES

3. Even in the 1950s and 1960s only relatively few journalists were given their own by-lines. Most feature stories were still written by 'A Staff Correspondent'.
4. Hetherington, *op.cit.*, p. 2.
5. *ibid.*, pp. 4–5
6. *ibid.*, p. 4
7. *ibid.*, facing p. 81
8. *ibid.*, p. 12
9. *ibid.*, p. 17
10. *ibid.*, p. 26. The book, *A Consideration of the Art of Ernest Moffitt*, was privately published in Melbourne in 1899.
11. *ibid.*, pp. 31–32
12. *ibid.*, p. 39
13. *ibid.*, p. 46
14. *ibid.*, p. 60
15. *ibid.*, p. 101
16. *ibid.*, p. 105
17. *ibid.*, p. 123
18. *ibid.*, p. 125
19. *ibid.*, p. 204
20. *ibid.*, pp. 214–15
21. Douglas Stewart, 'Norman Lindsay's Novels', *Southerly*, No. 1, 1959, p. 3.
22. Norman Lindsay, *op.cit.*, p.13.
23. *ibid.*, p. 2
24. *ibid.*, p. 33

## 6. MEMOIRS OF A MUSE
1. Daryl Lindsay to Jean Charley, 30 April 1968, private collection.
2. Joan Lindsay to Jean Charley, 10 May (no year), private collection.
3. Rose Lindsay, 'Rose Lindsay's Memoirs: Artists and Models', *Bulletin*, 18 February 1953, pp. 27, 34; Rose Lindsay, 'Rose Lindsay's Memoirs: Some Studios in Sydney', *Bulletin*, 4 March 1953, pp. 27, 34; Rose Lindsay, 'Rose Lindsay's Memoirs: In Paris with Hugh D. McIntosh', *Bulletin*, 18 March 1953, pp. 27, 34; Rose Lindsay, 'Rose Lindsay's Memoirs: Visitors to Springwood', *Bulletin*, 15 April 1953, pp. 27, 29; Rose Lindsay, 'Rose Lindsay's Memoirs: Into the Machine Age', *Bulletin*, 13 May 1953, pp. 27, 30.
4. 'He started to write his autobiography again, and got about as far as with all the previous ones.' Rose Lindsay, *Model Wife: My Life with Norman Lindsay*, Ure Smith, Sydney, 1967, p. 262.
5. *ibid.*, p. 42
6. Interview with Rose Lindsay, *Sydney Morning Herald*, 11 November 1967.
7. Rose Lindsay, *Model Wife*, p. 13.
8. *ibid.*, p. 26. Will Dyson was always called 'Bill' by family and friends.
9. *ibid.*, p. 29
10. *ibid.*, p. 32
11. *ibid.*, p. 34
12. *ibid.*, pp. 56, 64–65

13. *ibid.*, p. 109
14. *ibid.*, p. 120
15. *ibid.*, p. 138
16. *ibid.*, p. 234
17. *ibid.*, p. 197
18. *ibid.*, p. 142
19. *ibid.*, pp. 138–39
20. *ibid.*, p. 123
21. *ibid.*, pp. 182–83
22. *ibid.*, p. 180
23. *ibid.*, p. 218
24. *ibid.*, p. 207
25. *ibid.*, p. 235
26. When these celebrities visited Victoria they were likewise invited to the gracious Mulberry Hill home of Daryl and Joan Lindsay.
27. Rose Lindsay, *Model Wife*, p. 262.
28. *ibid.*, p. 211

## 7. ROSE'S MANUSCRIPT SECRETS

1. Rose Lindsay, *Ma and Pa*, Ure Smith, Sydney, 1963.
2. Wingrove died in 1994. Shortly before his death he sold many of his papers and other ephemera to the Mitchell Library. The Chaplin collection is in the Fisher Library, University of Sydney, and in the Queensland State Library as part of the Corrigan collection.
3. Rose Lindsay to Norman Lindsay, no date but written shortly after Norman's departure in 1909, Mitchell MSS 742/2, pp. 6–7.
4. *ibid.*, p. 15
5. *ibid.*, p. 26
6. The relationship between Norman and Lionel is covered in detail in Joanna Mendelssohn, *Lionel Lindsay: An Artist and his Family*.
7. Lionel Lindsay to Norman Lindsay, fragment, n.d., Mitchell MSS 742/6, p. 261.
8. Lionel Lindsay to Norman Lindsay, 31 January 1910, Mitchell MSS 742/6, pp. 101b–102.
9. Rose Lindsay to Norman Lindsay, dated Thursday 1910, Mitchell MSS 742/2, p. 201.
10. Will Dyson to Norman Lindsay, n.d., Mitchel MSS 742/12, pp. 35–38. Dyson shared the Lindsay disdain for spelling and punctuation.
11. Will Dyson to Norman Lindsay, n.d., Mitchell MSS 742/12, pp. 49–51.
12. Hetherington, *op.cit.*, p. 62.
13. Will Dyson to Norman Lindsay, Mitchell MSS 742/12, p. 11.
14. Hetherington, *op.cit.*, p. 87.
15. Jack Lindsay claims, 'Will Dyson told her all about it.' Jack Lindsay, *Life Rarely Tells*, Penguin, Ringwood, 1982, p. 23.
16. Norman Lindsay to Katie Lindsay, Mitchell MSS 742/13, p. 5.
17. Norman Lindsay to Will Dyson, late 1903, Mitchell MSS 742/15, pp. 69–72.
18. Rose Lindsay, *Model Wife*, p. 33.
19. Jack Lindsay, *op.cit.*, p. 4.
20. *ibid.*, p. 32

# ENDNOTES

21. William MacLeod to Norman Lindsay, 6 July 1918, Mitchell MSS 742/13, pp. 217–19. Although justification for using MacLeod as his agent in this instance could be that *Bulletin* shares were part of the settlement, MacLeod used his personal letterhead, not *Bulletin* stationery. After the divorce, the maintenance payments, which were to continue indefinitely, were made directly by the Bulletin, an arrangement which had been in place since 1910.
22. Two letters from Elkington are cited in Harry Chaplin, *A Lindsay Miscellany*, Wentworth Books, Sydney, 1978, p. 17 and p. 25. The second of these is from the period when Norman was living in London.
23. Lionel Lindsay to Norman Lindsay, December 1915, Mitchell MSS 742/7, p. 71.
24. This letter was reproduced in full as part of Joanna Mendelssohn, 'A last letter from the killing fields of France', *Sydney Morning Herald*, 11 November 1988.
25. Norman Lindsay to Lionel Lindsay, captioned by Peter Lindsay as 'Received when LL had pneumonic flu/Reg was dead/ 1917–18', La Trobe MSS 9242/2906.
26. Mary Lindsay to Norman Lindsay, 20 April 1919, Mitchell MSS 742/10, p. 118c.
27. Lionel Lindsay to Norman Lindsay, 18 October 1918, Mitchell MSS 742/6, p. 209.
28. Lionel Lindsay to Norman Lindsay, May 1917, Mitchell MSS 742/6, pp. 161–63.
29. Howarth and Barker, *op.cit.*, p. 144.
30. Norman Lindsay to Rose Lindsay, dated by Rose as 4 July 1921, Mitchell MSS 742/19, p. 68.
31. Howarth and Barker, *op.cit.*, p. 147.
32. Rose Lindsay to Norman Lindsay, 16 April 1920, Mitchell MSS 742/3, p. 87b.
33. Rose Lindsay to Lionel Lindsay, 26 December 1915, La Trobe MSS 2002/4760.

## 8. MISTRESS AND WIFE

1. Howarth and Barker, *op.cit.*, pp. 168–72.
2. *ibid.*, p. 170
3. Norman Lindsay to Rose Lindsay, n.d., Mitchell MSS 742/19, p. 180.
4. Rose Lindsay to Norman Lindsay, June 1922, Mitchell MSS 742/2, pp. 257–59.
5. Jane Lindsay to Norman Lindsay, 11 June 1918, Mitchell MSS 742/10, p. 1.
6. Jane Lindsay to Norman Lindsay, 4 October 1919, Mitchell MSS 742/10, p. 21c.
7. There is a passing reference to this in Robert Lindsay to Norman Lindsay, n.d., Mitchell MSS 742/13, p. 479.
8. Jane Lindsay to Norman Lindsay, November 1919, Mitchell MSS 742/10, pp. 29–31.
9. Jane Lindsay to Lionel Lindsay, La Trobe MSS 9104/4769.
10. Jane Lindsay to Rose Lindsay, 30 December 1920, Mitchell MSS 742/22, p. 141.
11. Norman Lindsay to Jack Lindsay, Mitchell MSS 742/24, p. 175.
12. Dr? to Rose Lindsay, 19 December 1921, Mitchell MSS 742/22, p. 37c.
13. Howarth and Barker, *op.cit.*, p. 150.
14. Jack Lindsay to Norman Lindsay, 22 October 1919, Mitchell MSS 742/24, p. 1.
15. Norman Lindsay, *op.cit.*, p. 14.
16. Meg Stewart, *Autobiography of My Mother*, Penguin, Melbourne, 1985.
17. Margaret Coen to Norman Lindsay, 1930, Mitchell MSS 742/14, pp. 317c–19.
18. Helen Glad has indicated that a number of watercolours and etchings with Margaret as the model can be clearly dated to 1930–33.
19. I have not sighted these cartoons, but Helen Glad saw them some years ago.
20. Howarth and Barker, *op.cit.*, p. 325.

21. Margaret Coen to Norman Lindsay, probably early 1940, Mitchell MSS 742/14, pp. 327–29.
22. *ibid.*, pp. 335–39
23. Meg Stewart, *op.cit.*, p. 212.
24. Hugh McCrae to Rose Lindsay, 24 October 1941, Mitchell MSS 742/23, pp. 117c–19.
25. Margaret Coen died in 1993. In the early 1970s, when I was researching Sydney Long, I had several meetings with Coen. She was large and maternal, lively but calm, a similar personality to that described by Peter Lindsay to me, and similar to the persona evoked in her daughter's book.
26. Mary Lindsay to Rose Lindsay, 6 December 1933, Mitchell MSS 742/22, pp. 215c–17.
27. Daryl Lindsay to Mary Lindsay, 19 March 1934, Mitchell MSS 742/22, p. 135.
28. Rose Lindsay to Keith Wingrove, 14 June 1953, Mitchell MSS 742/23, pp. 263ff.

## 9. MARY
1. Norman Lindsay, *op.cit.*, p. 35.
2. Mary Lindsay to Daryl Lindsay, 15 December 1956, La Trobe MSS 9242/3294.
3. Mary Lindsay to Daryl Lindsay, 29 August 1898, Mitchell MSS 742/26, p. 1.
4. Daryl Lindsay, *op.cit.*, p. 77.
5. Will Dyson to Norman Lindsay, n.d., Mitchell MSS 742/12, pp. 3–4.
6. Howarth and Barker, *op.cit.*, p. 53.
7. Mary Lindsay to Lionel Lindsay, 16 December 1947, La Trobe MSS 9104/4862.
8. Daryl Lindsay, *op.cit.*, p. 73.
9. *supra*, n. 2.
10. Lionel Lindsay to Norman Lindsay, undated fragment of letter, Mitchell MSS 742/7, p. 319.
11. Mary Lindsay to Norman Lindsay, circa 1958, Mitchell MSS 742/10 p. 135.
12. Lionel Lindsay to Norman Lindsay, circa 1910, Chaplin papers, now in Corrigan collection, State Library of Queensland.
13. Lionel Lindsay to Norman Lindsay, 26 July 1910, Mitchell MSS 742/6, p. 129b.
14. Lionel Lindsay to Norman Lindsay, 22 April 1910, Mitchell MSS 742/7, p. 118.
15. Mary Lindsay to Norman Lindsay, late 1950s, Mitchell MSS 742/10, p. 161.
16. Mary Lindsay to Norman Lindsay, circa 1963, private collection.
17. Norman Lindsay to Lionel Lindsay, n.d., La Trobe MSS 9242/3152.
18. Lionel Lindsay to Norman Lindsay, n.d., Mitchell MSS 742/7, p. 85.
19. Mary Lindsay to Norman Lindsay, n.d., Mitchell MSS 742/10, p. 103.
20. Mary Lindsay to Norman Lindsay, 20 April 1919, Mitchell MSS 742/10, pp. 113–15.
21. Norman Lindsay to Daryl Lindsay, 18 July 1921, La Trobe MSS 2005/3202.
22. Ruby's letter and its resting place are cited in Harry Chaplin, *op.cit.*, p. 108.
23. *supra*, n. 20
24. Leon Gellert, 'Leon Gellert Says', *Sunday Telegraph*, 24 December 1967.
25. Leon Gellert to Rose Lindsay, n.d., Mitchell MSS 742/22, p. 49. Gellert also wrote at least one admiring letter to Mary (Mitchell MSS 742/22, n.d., p. 51).
26. Mary Lindsay to Rose Lindsay, 24 February 1919, Mitchell MSS 742/10, pp. 107–109.
27. Mary Lindsay to Rose Lindsay, 5 January 1920, Mitchell MSS 742/22, p. 195c.
28. Jane Lindsay to Rose Lindsay, n.d., Mitchell MSS 742/22, p. 145.
29. Jane Lindsay to Norman Lindsay, circa 1920, Mitchell MSS 742/10, p. 9c.

# ENDNOTES

30. Ill-health first emerges as a theme in Thomas Williams' journal, and continues with his many descendents. Despite this, the Lindsays are an exceptionally long-lived family.
31. Jean Charley remembers Mary's last Sydney visit as 1925. Jane Lindsay wrote to Norman about the Tasmanian holiday on 6 January 1922, Mitchell MSS 742/10, p. 65.
32. Jane Lindsay to Norman Lindsay, 3 April 1925, Mitchell MSS 742/10, p. 75.
33. Jane Lindsay to Norman Lindsay, circa 1923, Mitchell MSS 742/10, p. 83.
34. Daryl Lindsay to Lionel Lindsay, circa 1923, La Trobe MSS 9242/192–94.
35. Letter from Veronica Rowan to the author, 5 January 1994.
36. *ibid*.
37. Daryl Lindsay to Lionel Lindsay, 5 June 1929, La Trobe MSS 9242/225–7.
38. *ibid*.
39. Daryl Lindsay to Lionel Lindsay, 3 December 1929, La Trobe MSS 9242/237.
40. Norman Lindsay to Daryl Lindsay, circa 1929, La Trobe MSS 9242/3202.
41. Mitchell MSS 742/15, p. 137.
42. Robert Lindsay to Lionel Lindsay, 8 January 1932, La Trobe MSS 9104/4906–7. Peter Lindsay has annotated this letter: 'More domestic drama. It must all be taken with a grain of salt.'
43. Robert Lindsay to Norman Lindsay, 22 July 1932, Mitchell MSS 742/13, p. 113.
44. Mary Lindsay to Lionel Lindsay, n.d., La Trobe MSS 9242/4854.
45. Mary Lindsay to Rose Lindsay, n.d., Mitchell MSS 742/22, p. 209.
46. Rose Lindsay, *Ma and Pa*, pp. 191–211.
47. Mary Lindsay to Rose Lindsay, 28th October 1933, Mitchell MSS 742/22, p. 229.
48. Mary Lindsay to Rose Lindsay, (?) June 1957, Mitchell MSS 742/22, p. 286.
49. *ibid*.
50. Pearl McPhee to Rose Lindsay, 18 July 1961, Mitchell MSS 742/23, p. 5.
51. Mary Lindsay to Norman Lindsay, 1958, Mitchell MSS 742/10, p. 159.
52. Mary Lindsay to Lionel Lindsay, 15 August 1958, La Trobe MSS 9104/4870–1.
53. Mary Lindsay to Jean Charley, 1950s, private collection.
54. Mary Lindsay to Norman Lindsay, 26 January 1960, Mitchell MSS 742/10, p. 2.
55. Daryl Lindsay to Jean Charley, 30 April 1968, private collection.
56. Daryl Lindsay to Mary Lindsay, 19 March 1934, Mitchell MSS 742/22, pp. 133c–37.
57. Mary Lindsay to Rose Lindsay, n.d., Mitchell MSS 742/22, p. 237.
58. Mary Lindsay to Daryl Lindsay, n.d., La Trobe MSS, 9242/3284.
59. Mary Lindsay to Rose Lindsay, n.d., Mitchell MSS 742/22, p. 289.
60. Robert Lindsay to Norman Lindsay, n.d., Mitchell MSS, 742/13, p. 141.
61. Joan Lindsay, *Facts Soft and Hard*, W.F. Cheshire, Melbourne, 1964. Mary Lindsay to Jean Charley, December 1964, private collection.
62. Daryl Lindsay to Jean Charley, 23 August 1966, private collection.
63. Lionel Lindsay to Daryl Lindsay, 13 January 1959, La Trobe MSS 9242/1684.
64. Mary Lindsay to Daryl Lindsay, n.d., La Trobe MSS 9242/3291.
65. Lionel Lindsay to Daryl Lindsay, 31 December 1957, La Trobe MSS 9242/1660.
66. *supra*, n. 64.
67. Mary Lindsay to Norman Lindsay, 28 January 1951, private collection.
68. Mary Lindsay to Lionel Lindsay, 16 December 1947, La Trobe MSS 2002/4862.
69. Daryl Lindsay to Lionel Lindsay, 16 December 1951, La Trobe MSS 2003/589–91.
70. Mary Lindsay to Norman Lindsay, Mitchell MSS 742/10, p. 141.
71. Mary Lindsay to Rose Lindsay, 25 August 1958, Mitchell MSS 742/22, p. 316.

72. Daryl Lindsay to Lionel Lindsay, 3 November 1953, La Trobe MSS 2003/661–3.
73. Pearl McPhee to Lionel Lindsay, n.d., La Trobe MSS 1999/1439–40.
74. Mary Lindsay to Daryl Lindsay, La Trobe MSS 9242/3289.
75. Pearl McPhee to Rose Lindsay, 18 July 1961, Mitchell MSS 742/23, p. 5.
76. Mary Lindsay to Lionel Lindsay, 16 December 1947, La Trobe MSS 9104/4862.
77. Mary Lindsay to Norman Lindsay, n.d., Mitchell MSS 742/10, p. 166.
78. *ibid.*, p. 162
79. *ibid.*
80. *ibid.*, p. 217
81. *ibid.*, p. 231. At this time Mary's reading also included *The Irish RM*, Scott, Conrad and Dickens.
82. Mary Lindsay to Jean Charley, n.d., private collection.
83. Norman Lindsay to Rose Lindsay, n.d., private collection.
84. Daryl Lindsay to Jean Charley, 3 April 1968, private collection.
85. Norman Lindsay to Rose Lindsay, 1968, private collection.

## 10. GHOSTS

1. Robert Lindsay to Lionel Lindsay, 5 September 1931, La Trobe MSS 9104/4894.
2. Mary Lindsay to Daryl Lindsay, circa 1951, La Trobe MSS 9242/3295.
3. Although most reference books and letters by her siblings spell her name as 'Isobel', in her own letters the name is clearly spelt 'Isabel'.
4. Chaplin, *op.cit.*, p. 77.
5. Norman Lindsay, *op.cit.*, pp. 29–30.
6. *ibid.*, pp. 30–32
7. This was written as a part of *Comedy of Life*, but Peter Lindsay discarded it as inappropriate.
8. Robert Lindsay to Norman Lindsay, ? 1948, Mitchell MSS 742/13, pp. 161–62.
9. Lionel Lindsay, *op.cit.*, p. 7.
10. There is no evidence that Robert and Norman actually saw each other after 1910.
11. Robert Lindsay to Norman Lindsay, n.d., Mitchell MSS 742/13, p. 110.
12. Norman Lindsay to Mary Lindsay, n.d., circa 1957, Hetherington papers, La Trobe MSS 1318/1b 14/16.
13. *ibid.*
14. Robert Lindsay to Norman Lindsay, fragment dated 5 March 1940, Mitchell MSS 742/13, p. 129.
15. Robert Lindsay to Norman Lindsay, ? 1940s, Mitchell MSS 742/13, pp. 141–42.
16. Robert Lindsay to Norman Lindsay, n.d., Mitchell MSS 742/13, pp. 142–43.
17. Robert Lindsay to Norman Lindsay, 10 October 1945, Mitchell MSS 742/13, pp. 133–34.
18. Robert Lindsay to Norman Lindsay, n.d., Mitchell MSS 742/13, p. 105.
19. Howarth and Barker, *op.cit.*, p. 16.
20. *ibid.*
21. Daryl Lindsay, *op.cit.*, pp. 66–67.
22. Lionel Lindsay to Norman Lindsay, n.d., Chaplin papers now in the Corrigan collection, State Library of Queensland.
23. Chaplin, *op.cit.*, pp. 81–82.

24. Daryl Lindsay, *op.cit.*, p. 67.
25. There is no evidence for this claim. Peter Lindsay, in his preface to *Comedy of Life*, specifically refutes it.
26. Howarth and Barker, *op.cit.*, p. 419.
27. Robert Lindsay to Norman Lindsay, n.d., Mitchell MSS 742/13, p. 145.
28. Norman Lindsay, *op.cit.*, p. 218.
29. Daryl Lindsay, *op.cit.*, p. 67, claims the year was 1913, but this is not borne out by records of Mary's movements.
30. *ibid*.
31. Mary Lindsay to Rose Lindsay, 5 January 1920, Mitchell MSS 742/22, p. 195.
32. Lloyd Rees, *Peaks and Valley*, Angus & Robertson, Sydney, 1985, p. 128.
33. Martin Boyd, *Day of My Delight*, Lansdowne, Melbourne, 1974, p. 223.
34. Robert Lindsay to Lionel Lindsay, 8 September 1931, La Trobe MSS 9104/4897.
35. *ibid*.
36. Robert Lindsay to Lionel Lindsay, 8 September 1931, La Trobe MSS 9104/4894.
37. Mary Lindsay to Norman Lindsay, late 1950s, private collection.
38. Mary Lindsay to Norman Lindsay, circa 1954, private collection
39. Mary Lindsay to Harry Chaplin, 21 September 1948, in Peter Lindsay's collection of annotated Chaplin letters.
40. Howarth and Barker, *op.cit.*, p. 17.
41. The glass negatives of many of the Creswick and St Kilda photographs taken by Lionel are held in the Mitchell library. Some prints are in the State Library of Queensland and still others are in family hands.
42. Letter from Veronica Rowan to the author, 5 January 1994. The precise term used was 'lame under the hat'. Mrs Rowan left Creswick for boarding school when she was ten and had little contact with the Lindsay family after that time.
43. Conversation with Ron Radford, Adelaide, November 1993.
44. Letter from Dr Earle Williams to the author, 19 September 1994.
45. Jane Lindsay to Norman Lindsay, 3 April 1925, Mitchell MSS 742/10, p. 75.
46. Robert Lindsay to Lionel Lindsay, 21 October 1931, La Trobe MSS 9104/4898–9. The juniper reference is presumably to gin.
47. Robert Lindsay to Lionel Lindsay, 21 October 1931, La Trobe MSS 9104/4900–1.
48. Chaplin, *op.cit.*, p. 101.
49. Robert Lindsay to Norman Lindsay, circa 1932, Mitchell MSS 742/13, p. 107.
50. Norman to Robert, n.d. but 1931, La Trobe MSS 9242/3232.
51. Robert Lindsay to Norman Lindsay, 22 July 1932, Mitchell MSS 742/13, pp. 115–19.
52. Robert Lindsay to Lionel Lindsay, 22 August 1932, La Trobe MSS 9104/4920.
53. Robert Lindsay to Norman Lindsay, 24 June 1932, Mitchell MSS 742/13, p. 107.
54. *supra*, n. 51, pp. 119–21.
55. Robert Lindsay to Norman Lindsay, 19 November 1932, Mitchell MSS 742/13, pp. 123–27.
56. Robert Lindsay to Norman Lindsay, fragment, n.d., Mitchell MSS 742/13, pp. 147–49.
57. Robert Lindsay to Norman Lindsay, late 1932, Mitchell MSS 742/13, pp. 149–51.
58. Norman Lindsay to Robert Lindsay, circa 1933, La Trobe MSS 9242/3251.
59. Robert Lindsay to Norman Lindsay, 10 October 1945, Mitchell MSS 742/13, p. 137.
60. *supra*, n. 57, p. 153.
61. Robert Lindsay to Norman Lindsay, fragment, Mitchell MSS 742/13, p. 166.

62. Robert Lindsay to Norman Lindsay, 1 November 1945, Mitchell MSS 742/13, pp. 139ff.
63. Conversation with the late Sir Joseph Burke, April 1985. He recalled Isabel as subdued and quiet, but certainly not subnormal.
64. Robert Lindsay to Norman Lindsay, n.d., Mitchell MSS 742/13, p. 144.
65. Mary Lindsay to Harry Chaplin, 21 September 1948, Peter Lindsay's annotated Chaplin letters.
66. Robert Lindsay to Norman Lindsay, fragment, n.d., Mitchell MSS 742/13, p. 145.
67. Mary Lindsay to Rose Lindsay, November 1932, Mitchell MSS 742/22, p. 209.
68. Robert Lindsay to Daryl Lindsay, 12 January 1944, La Trobe MSS 2002/4881.
69. Mary Lindsay to Rose Lindsay, 8 November 1950, private collection.
70. Mary Lindsay to Harry Chaplin, 5 March 1951, Peter Lindsay's annotated Chaplin letters.
71. Pearl McPhee to Rose Lindsay, 18 July 1961, Mitchell MSS 742/23, p. 5.
72. Mary Lindsay to Rose Lindsay, 3 August 1934, Mitchell 742/22, p. 257c.
73. Mary Lindsay to Rose Lindsay, 12 March 1934, Mitchell MSS 742/22, p. 243c.
74. Norman Lindsay to Rose Lindsay, n.d., Mitchell MSS 742/21, pp. 27–28.
75. Rose Lindsay to Keith Wingrove, 14 June 1953, Mitchell MSS 742/23, p. 263.
76. Mary Lindsay to Jean Charley, circa 1966, private collection.
77. Mary Lindsay to Rose Lindsay, 5 August 1956, Mitchell MSS 742/22, p. 269.
78. Mary Lindsay to RoseLindsay, 20 June circa 1961, Mitchell MSS 742/22, pp. 341–42.
79. Mary Lindsay to Norman Lindsay, circa 1961, Mitchell MSS 742/10, p. 253.
80. *supra*, n. 71
81. Isabel Lindsay to Jean Charley, December 1964, private collection.
82. Mary Lindsay to Norman Lindsay, n.d., private collection.
83. Mary Lindsay to Jean Charley, 29 January 1965, private collection.

## 11. THE OTHER JANE LINDSAY

1. Jane Lindsay, *Portrait of Pa*, Angus & Robertson, Sydney, 1973, pp. 37–39.
2. *ibid.*, p. 184
3. Jane has no memory of meeting Jack, although he did know her when she was a very small child.
4. Jane Lindsay, *op.cit.*, p. 4.
5. *ibid.*, pp. 40–41
6. *ibid.*, p. 46
7. *ibid.*, pp. 73–78
8. *ibid.*, p. 5
9. *ibid.*, p. 173
10. *ibid.*, p. 64
11. *ibid.*, p. 4
12. *ibid.*, p. 120
13. *ibid.*, p. 73
14. *ibid.*, p. 81
15. *ibid.*, pp. 83, 105–106
16. *ibid.*, pp. 10–11
17. *ibid.*, p. 114
18. *ibid.*, p. 174

# ENDNOTES

19. *ibid.*, p. 176
20. *ibid.*, p. 120

## 13. JOHN AND MARY

1. Norman Lindsay to John Hetherington, April 1957, Hetherington papers, La Trobe Library, 14/16 1318/3(c).
2. Norman Lindsay to Mary Lindsay, n.d., Hetherington papers 14/16, 1318/1(b).
3. Mary Lindsay to Norman Lindsay, n.d., Mitchell MSS 742/10, p. 131.
4. *ibid.*
5. Harry Chaplin to Norman Lindsay, 15 July 1957, Mitchell MSS 742/11, p. 150.
6. Mary Lindsay to Norman Lindsay, n.d., Mitchell MSS 742/10, p. 137.
7. *ibid.*, pp. 149–51
8. Mary Lindsay to John Hetherington, 8 August 1958, Hetherington papers 3/16.
9. John Hetherington to Norman Lindsay, 30 July 1961, Hetherington papers 6/16.
10. John Hetherington, *Australian Painters: Forty Profiles*, F.W. Cheshire, Melbourne, 1963.
11. Rose Lindsay to John Hetherington, 16 August 1960, Hetherington papers 9/16.
12. John Hetherington to Norman Lindsay, 18 August 1960, Hetherington papers 9/16.
13. John Hetherington, *Norman Lindsay*, F.W. Cheshire, Melbourne, 1961.
14. John Hetherington to Rose Lindsay, 8 September 1960, Mitchell MSS 742/22, p. 109.
15. Mary Lindsay to John Hetherington, 16 December 1957, Hetherington papers 9740 9/16.
16. Mary Lindsay to Norman Lindsay, n.d., fragment, Mitchell MSS 742/10, p. 145.
17. Mary Lindsay to John Hetherington, 31 May 1958, Hetherington papers 9740 9/16.
18. Hetherington, *The Embattled Olympian*, p. 31.
19. John Hetherington to Mary Lindsay, 4 August 1958, Hetherington papers 9/16.
20. Mary Lindsay to Lionel Lindsay, 15 August 1958, La Trobe MSS 9104/4870–2.
21. Lionel Lindsay to Daryl Lindsay, 24 January 1958, La Trobe MSS 9242/1661. A copy of the manuscript remains in the possession of Peter Lindsay.
22. Lionel Lindsay to Mary Lindsay, 20 August 1958, Hetherington papers 3/16.
23. Mary Lindsay to Norman Lindsay, probably June 1958, Mitchell MSS 742/10, pp. 185c–88.
24. Mary Lindsay to John Hetherington, 8 August 1958, Hetherington papers 3/16.
25. Mary Lindsay to Norman Lindsay, circa 1958, Mitchell MSS 742/10, pp. 190–91.
26. Norman Lindsay to Mary Lindsay, late August 1958, Hetherington papers 9/16.
27. Mary Lindsay to John Hetherington, 8 July 1958, Hetherington papers 3/16.
28. Mary Lindsay to John Hetherington, n.d., Hetherington papers 3/16.
29. Mary Lindsay to Norman Lindsay, Hetherington papers 15/16. The article mentioned was a feature on Norman Lindsay by Emery Barcs which appeared in the *Daily Telegraph*, 18 June 1949.
30. Mary Lindsay to John Hetherington, 12 November 1958, Hetherington papers 3/16.
31. In his autobiography, *The Morning was Shining*, Faber and Faber, London, 1971, John Hetherington concentrates on his schooldays as the seminal experience of his life.
32. Mary Lindsay to John Hetherington, circa 21 November 1958, Hetherington papers 3/16.
33. John Hetherington to Mary Lindsay, 26 November 1958, Hetherington papers 3/16.
34. Mary Lindsay to John Hetherington, 26 October 1959, Hetherington papers 3/16.
35. Norman Lindsay to Mary Lindsay, November 1959, Hetherington papers 9/16.

36. *supra*, n. 34
37. Mary Lindsay to Norman Lindsay, early 1960, Mitchell MSS 742/10, pp. 207–10.
38. Rose Lindsay to John Hetherington, January 1960, Hetherington papers 9/16.
39. Mary Lindsay to Rose Lindsay, 10 February 1951, Mitchell MSS 742/22, p. 266.
40. Mary Lindsay to Norman Lindsay, n.d., Mitchell MSS 742/10, p. 213.
41. See exchange of letters: John Hetherington to Norman Lindsay (11 March 1961 and 12 March 1961, Hetherington papers 6/16) and Mary Lindsay to Norman Lindsay (Mitchell MSS 742/10, p. 219).
42. Norman Lindsay to John Hetherington, 20 June 1964, Hetherington papers 13/16.
43. Daryl Lindsay, *op.cit.*, pp. 77–79.
44. John Hetherington to Norman Lindsay, Hetherington papers 6/16.
45. Norman Lindsay to John Hetherington, August 1963, Hetherington papers 13/16.

## 14. WHAT JOHN KNEW

1. John Hetherington to Norman Lindsay, 19 September 1958, Hetherington papers 6/16.
2. Harry Chaplin to Norman Lindsay, 15 July 1957, Mitchell MSS 742/11, p. 150.
3. John Hetherington to Norman Lindsay, 3 January 1967, Hetherington papers 6/16.
4. John Hetherington to Norman Lindsay, 8 June 1967, Hetherington papers 6/16.
5. John Hetherington to Joan Burke, 9 September 1972, Hetherington papers 3/16.
6. *The Age Literary Supplement*, 4 August 1962, p. 18. Reprinted in Hetherington, *Australian Painters: Forty Profiles* .
7. Norman Lindsay to Mary Lindsay, early August 1958, Hetherington papers 9/16.
8. Norman Lindsay to John Hetherington, late August 1958, Hetherington papers 9/16.
9. Jack Lindsay to John Hetherington, 1971, Hetherington papers 5/16.
10. Most of Jack Lindsay's letters to his father written at the end of Norman's life were bought by Harry Chaplin, and are now in the collection of the Queensland State Library. They are described in Harry Chaplin, *Jack Lindsay: A Catalogue of First Editions Extensively Annotated by the Author, Together with Letters, Manuscripts and Associated Items*, Wentworth Press, Sydney, 1983.
11. John Hetherington to Norman Lindsay, 28 May 1968, Hetherington papers 6/16.
12. John Hetherington to Norman Lindsay, 28 July 1968, Hetherington papers 6/16.
13. There are numerous references to statements made by Norman in the letters, most of which can be traced to *My Mask*.
14. Jack Lindsay to John Hetherington, 21 March 1972, Hetherington papers 3/16.
15. Jack Lindsay to John Hetherington, fragment, 25 August 1971, Hetherington papers 5/16.
16. I have kept to Hetherington's spelling, 'Katie', but the name is frequently spelt 'Katy' or 'Katey'. Her marriage certificate names her as Kathleen.
17. *supra*, n. 15
18. Jack Lindsay to John Hetherington, 16 February 1972, Hetherington papers 15/16.
19. Jack Lindsay to John Hetherington, December 1971, Hetherington papers 15/16.
20. Jack Lindsay to John Hetherington, 5 July 1971, Hetherington papers 5/16.
21. Jack Lindsay, *op.cit.*, p. 24.
22. Jack Lindsay to John Hetherington, December 1971, Hetherington papers 15/16.
23. Jack Lindsay to John Hetherington, 16 February 1972, Hetherington papers 15/16.
24. *ibid.*
25. Jack Lindsay to John Hetherington, 5 March 1972, Hetherington papers 15/16.

# ENDNOTES

26. Hetherington, *The Embattled Olympian*, p. 77.
27. The letter denying the affair from Norman to Katie was clearly written before Lionel Lindsay's wedding at the end of 1903; Mitchell MSS 742/13, p. 5.
28. Letters from Dyson in Mitchell MSS 742/11.
29. Information from Jean Charley in conversation with the author, July 1992.
30. Jack Lindsay, *op.cit.*, p. 32.
31. Hetherington papers 11/16, p. 242.
32. Letters from this period are found in Mitchell MSS 742/6, pp. 81–155 and in the Chaplin papers.
33. Stewart's letter is dated 7 August 1964. Norman sent it to Hetherington with an enclosing letter, early September, Hetherington papers 3/16.
34. John Hetherington to Norman Lindsay, 13 September 1964, Hetherington papers 6/16.
35. Douglas Stewart to John Hetherington, 19 April 1974, Hetherington papers 3/16.
36. Norman Lindsay to John Hetherington, March 1959, Hetherington papers 9/16 (58).
37. Norman Lindsay to JohnHetherington, n.d., Hetherington papers 10/16.
38. Norman Lindsay to John Hetherington, April 1961, Hetherington papers 13/16.
39. John Hetherington to Norman Lindsay, 25 March 1961, Hetherington papers 6/16, p. 3.
40. According to Peter Lindsay, Rose discovered the affair when she saw a nude watercolour of Margaret, painted by Norman Lindsay.
41. Hetherington papers 5/16.
42. Peter Lindsay to John Hetherington, 27 October 1972, Hetherington papers 3/16.
43. Douglas Stewart to John Hetherington, 14 September 1972, Hetherington papers 3/16.
44. Hetherington, *The Embattled Olympian*, pp. 207–208.
45. Hetherington papers 11/16, p. 124; Hetherington, *The Embattled Olympian*, p. 87.
46. Hetherington papers 11/16, p. 6.
47. *ibid.*, p. 16. Daryl gives the story in *The Leafy Tree* at p. 54 but, because of the differences in age between him and Norman, Mary was his most likely source.
48. Quoted in Hetherington's index to Norman Lindsay's letters, 5/16, 'Racism 2'.
49. Hetherington papers 5/16.
50. John Hetherington to Wendy Sutherland, 16 December 1972, Hetherington papers 3/16.
51. Hetherington, *The Embattled Olympian*, p. 173.
52. Norman Lindsay to John Hetherington, March 1959, Hetherington papers 9/16; April 1959, May 1967 Hetherington papers 13/16; John Hetherington to Norman Lindsay 21 March 1959, 5 July 1959, Hetherington papers 9/16.
53. Hetherington papers 11/16, p. 4. Hetherington, *The Embattled Olympian*, p. 2.
54. Hetherington papers 11/16, p. 14.
55. Hetherington, *The Embattled Olympian*, pp. 7–8.
56. John Hetherington to Joseph Burke, 6 January 1972, Hetherington papers 3/16.
57. Mary Lindsay to John Hetherington, n.d., Hetherington papers 3/16.
58. Norman Lindsay to John Hetherington, April 1962, Hetherington papers 13/16, 9740, 11.
59. Norman Lindsay to John Hetherington, Hetherington papers 1318/1(a) 14/16.
60. *ibid.*

## 15. REDHEAP AND THE JUSTIFIABLE ACT OF CENSORSHIP
1. Melbourne *Herald*, 14 April 1930.
2. *Sydney Morning Herald*, 19 April 1930.
3. See *Sydney Morning Herald*, 18 April 1930 'Novels of the Day'; *Sydney Morning Herald*, 22 May 1930; *Sydney Morning Herald*, 17 April 1930; *Smith's Weekly*, 31 May 1930.
4. *Sydney Morning Herald*, 22 May 1930. Quoted in Hetherington papers 5/16.
5. Peter Coleman, *Obscenity, Blasphemy, Sedition: Censorship in Australia*, Jacaranda, Brisbane, 1962, p. 19.
6. *ibid.*, p. 23
7. *New York Evening Post*, 18 September 1930.
8. *New York Telegram*, 3 October 1930.
9. *New York Sun*, 27 September 1930.
10. *New York Times Book Review*, 28 September 1930.
11. *Stead's Review*, 2 June 1930, p. 15.
12. Undated newspaper cutting of early 1931, in Colin B. Berkelman's copy of *Redheap*, Rare Books Library, Fisher Library, University of Sydney.
13. Howarth and Barker, *op.cit.*, p. 287.
14. *ibid.*, p. 291.
15. Douglas Stewart, 'Norman Lindsay's Novels', *Southerly* No. 1, 1959, p. 3.
16. Keith Thomas, 'Back of Bourke or Bopping in Balmain', *The Australian*, 6 July 1980.
17. Reproduced in 'Unpublished Letters: Norman Lindsay to Lionel Lindsay: Redheap — Creative Effort — The Magic Pudding: From the Collection of Peter Lindsay', *Southerly* No. 4, 1970, pp. 289–90. This letter is dated as 1914, but the way it links to Lionel's letters with their war references and the references to their father's death, indicates 1915 as a more likely date.
18. Lionel Lindsay to Norman Lindsay, circa September 1915, Mitchell MSS 742/7, pp. 85–86.
19. The remaining fragment of the diary is in the possession of Peter Lindsay, Lionel's son. Sarah Westcott could be a relative of Norman's girlfriend Dolly Westcott.
20. Lionel Lindsay to Norman Lindsay, Mitchell MSS 742/7, p. 79.
21. Lionel Lindsay to Norman Lindsay, 1916, Mitchell MSS 742/7, p. 245.
22. The first version of *Saturdee* appeared in *The Lone Hand*, July 1908.
23. Lionel Lindsay to Norman Lindsay, circa 1916, Mitchell MSS 742/7, p. 95. The big brother in *Saturdee* and *Half Way to Anywhere* was Bill Gimble.
24. Lionel Lindsay to Norman Lindsay, fragment, n.d., Mitchell MSS 742/7, p. 283.
25. Lionel Lindsay to Norman Lindsay, fragment, n.d., Mitchell MSS 742/7, pp. 288–90.
26. Lionel Lindsay, *op.cit.*, p. 135.
27. Howarth and Barker, *op.cit.*, p. 90.
28. Norman Lindsay to Harry Chaplin, n.d., Chaplin papers, Fisher Library. An extract from the letter is printed in Harry Chaplin, *Norman Lindsay: His Books, Manuscripts and Autograph Letters in the Collection of and Annotated by Harry F. Chaplin*, The Wentworth Press, Sydney 1969, pp. 28–29.
29. Chaplin, *A Lindsay Miscellany*, p. 104.
30. Lionel Lindsay to Norman Lindsay, 8 September 1918, Mitchell MSS 742/6, pp. 180ff.
31. Adam McCay to Lionel, n.d. but must be about 1897, Mitchell MSS 742/26, p. 29.

# ENDNOTES

32. There is a passing reference to *The Skyline* in a letter from Will Dyson to Norman, 26 July 1918, Mitchell MSS 742/12, p. 7.
33. Howarth and Barker, *op.cit.*, p. 94.
34. Norman Lindsay, *Redheap*, Angus & Robertson, Sydney, 1974, p. 18.
35. Norman Lindsay to Harry Chaplin, 18 May 1950, collection of manuscripts and press cuttings in Chaplin papers, Fisher Library, collected in one volume as '*Redheap*' A *Miscellany*, no pagination.
36. Patrick Buckridge, *The Scandalous Penton*, University of Queensland Press, Brisbane, 1994, pp. 80–81.
37. Kenneth Slessor to Norman Lindsay, 11 June (?) 1927, Mitchell MSS 742/14, p. 83.
38. Draft letter from Norman Lindsay to Douglas Stewart, probably 1957, Mitchell MSS 742/16, p. 119.
39. 'Collins Street Calling', 22 August 1951, in an unidentified Melbourne paper, Harry Chaplin, '*Redheap*' A *Miscellany*, manuscripts.
40. *Sun*, 16 September 1957.
41. John Hetherington to Norman Lindsay, n.d., private collection.
42. *Sydney Morning Herald*, 3 October 1957, p. 4.
43. *Sydney Morning Herald*, 5 October 1957, p. 7.
44. *Sydney Morning Herald*, 10 October 1957, p. 2.
45. Pearl McPhee to Lionel Lindsay, 22 December 1959, La Trobe MSS 9104/1442.

## 16. TRUST
1. Copy of the will of Norman Lindsay lodged with the National Trust of Australia (NSW).
2. Norman Lindsay to Rose Lindsay, November 1966, private collection.
3. Norman Lindsay to Rose Lindsay, undated letter circa 1967, private collection.
4. Bernard Smith, *Australian Painting 1790–1960*, Oxford University Press, Melbourne, 1962, p. 197.
5. Norman Lindsay to Rose Lindsay, circa 1967, private collection.
6. Norman Lindsay to Rose Lindsay, 1965, private collection.
7. Norman Lindsay to Rose Lindsay, circa 1967, private collection.
8. Norman Lindsay to Rose Lindsay, 5 May 1968, private collection.
9. *ibid*.
10. Norman Lindsay to Rose Lindsay, May 1968, private collection.
11. Norman Lindsay to Rose Lindsay, 19 June 1968, private collection.
12. Draft of reply from Rose Lindsay to Norman Lindsay, n.d., private collection.
13. Norman Lindsay to Jane Lindsay, 1968, private collection.
14. Norman Lindsay to Rose Lindsay, October 1968, private collection.
15. Norman Lindsay to Rose Lindsay, October 1968, private collection.
16. Rose Lindsay's comment on late 1968 letter from Norman Lindsay, private collection.
17. Chaplin, *A Lindsay Miscellany*, p. 62.
18. Norman Lindsay to Rose Lindsay, n.d., private collection.
19. Joanna Mendelssohn, 'Downfall of a Legacy', *Bulletin*, 20 September 1994, pp. 93–94.

## 17 LAST SECRETS?
1. Robert Lindsay to Norman Lindsay, 5 October 1945, private collection.
2. Mary Lindsay to Norman Lindsay, 28 January 1951, private collection.

3. Mary Lindsay to Norman Lindsay, 1940, private collection.
4. Mary Lindsay to Norman Lindsay, n.d., private collection.
5. Mary Lindsay to Rose Lindsay, 27 April 1951, private collection.
6. Mary Lindsay to Rose Lindsay, 24 July 1951, private collection.
7. Mary Lindsay to Rose and Norman Lindsay, December 1951, private collection.
8. Mary Lindsay to Norman Lindsay, 1960s, private collection.
9. Mary Lindsay to Olive Hetherington, 6 February 1961, private collection.
10. Mary Lindsay to Norman Lindsay, n.d., private collection.
11. Mary Lindsay to Norman Lindsay, March 1961, private collection.
12. Mary Lindsay, private collection.
13. Norman Lindsay to Rose Lindsay, 1963, private collection.
14. There is a passing reference to this in a letter from Mary Lindsay to Norman Lindsay, circa 1959, private collection.
15. Mary Lindsay to Norman Lindsay, 1963, private collection.
16. Mary Lindsay to Norman Lindsay, n.d., private collection.
17. Mary Lindsay to Jane and Honey Lindsay, circa 1931, private collection.
18. Mary Lindsay to Jane and Honey Lindsay, circa 1931, private collection.
19. Mary Lindsay to Jane Lindsay, 10 December 1940, private collection.
20. Mary Lindsay to Jane Lindsay, 1940s, private collection.
21. Mary Lindsay to Jane Glad, 1 July 1956, private collection.
22. Mary Lindsay to Norman Lindsay, 1920s, private collection.
23. *ibid.*
24. *ibid.*
25. *ibid.*
26. *ibid.*
27. *ibid.*
28. *ibid.*
29. *ibid.*
30. *ibid.*
31. *ibid.*